Shojo Beat

Demon Love Spell

3

STORY AND
ART BY
**MAYU
SHINJO**

Contents

Story Thus Far

Miko Tsubaki is the daughter of the head priest of the Otsubaki Shrine, and she is destined to follow in his footsteps. She works hard day and night to become a great priestess, but it seems she inherited none of her father's powers...

One day Miko seals the powers of the incubus Kagura—the strongest demon—by accident. Now Miko has become a target for other demons to attack, but Mini Kagura protects her in return for her love.

Miko proposes a "Lovey-Dovey day" once a month on which Kagura can make out with her. But on that day, Miko's soul is eaten by a low-ranking demon who orders her to kill Kagura. She stabs Kagura with a sword, but the shock of possibly killing him helps Miko regain her soul, and she heals Kagura with her love. When she thinks he's dying, Kagura is overjoyed to hear Miko say she'll make love with him, but she shrinks him again instead?!

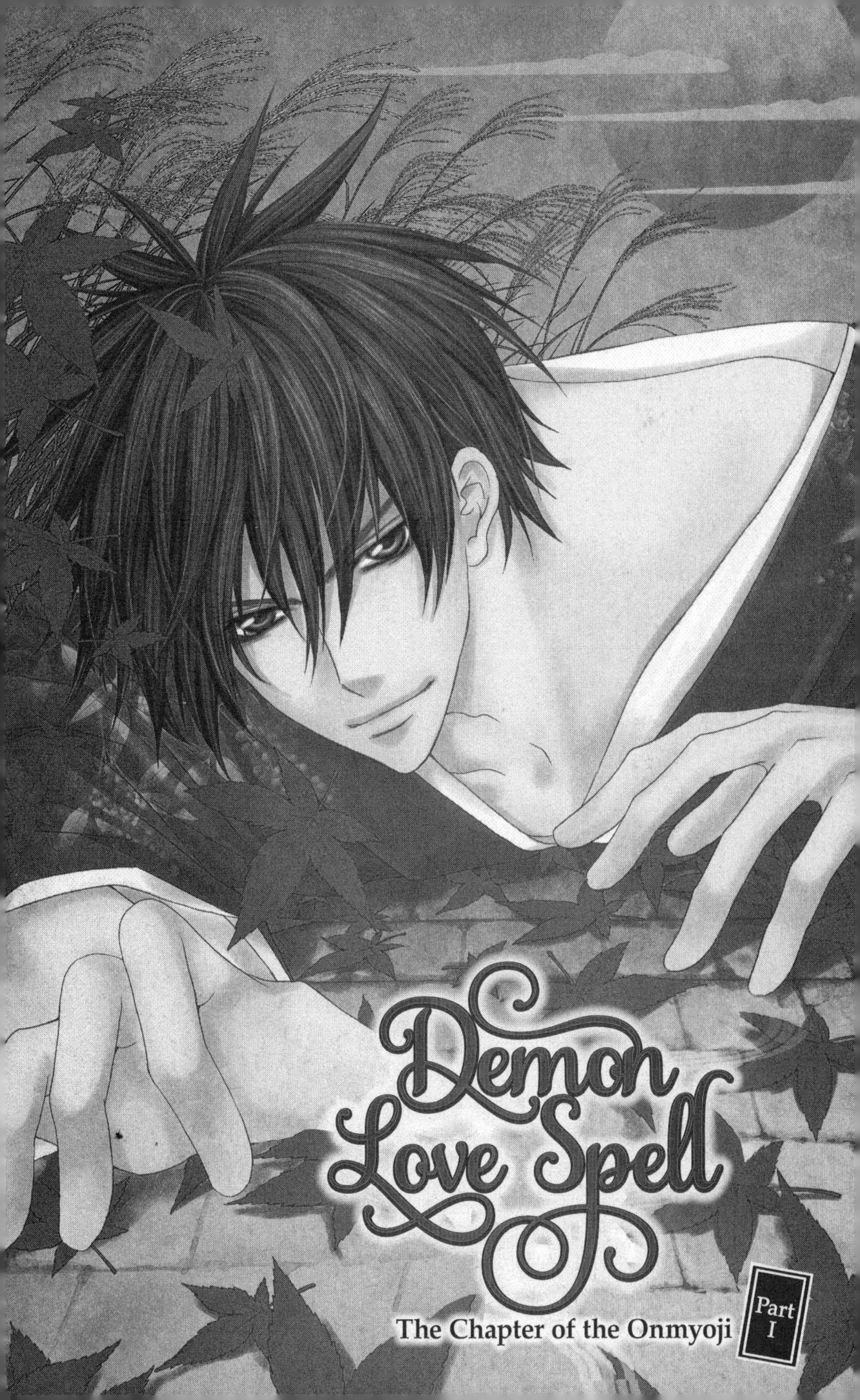
Demon Love Spell
The Chapter of the Onmyoji
Part I

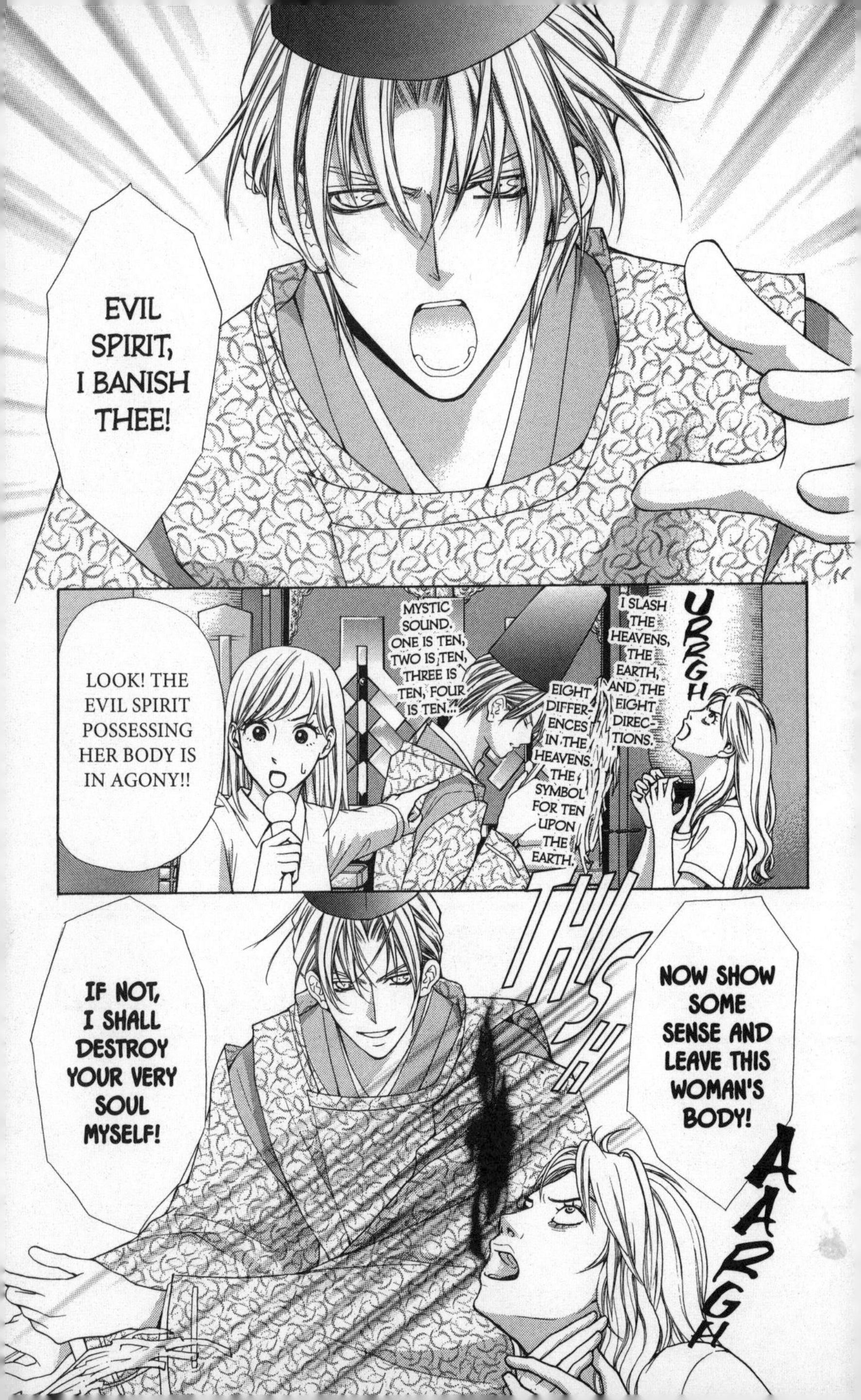
EVIL SPIRIT, I BANISH THEE!
URRGH
I SLASH THE HEAVENS, THE EARTH, AND THE EIGHT DIRECTIONS.
EIGHT DIFFERENCES IN THE HEAVENS. THE SYMBOL FOR TEN UPON THE EARTH.
MYSTIC SOUND. ONE IS TEN, TWO IS TEN, THREE IS TEN, FOUR IS TEN...
LOOK! THE EVIL SPIRIT POSSESSING HER BODY IS IN AGONY!!
THSHH
NOW SHOW SOME SENSE AND LEAVE THIS WOMAN'S BODY!
AARGH
IF NOT, I SHALL DESTROY YOUR VERY SOUL MYSELF!

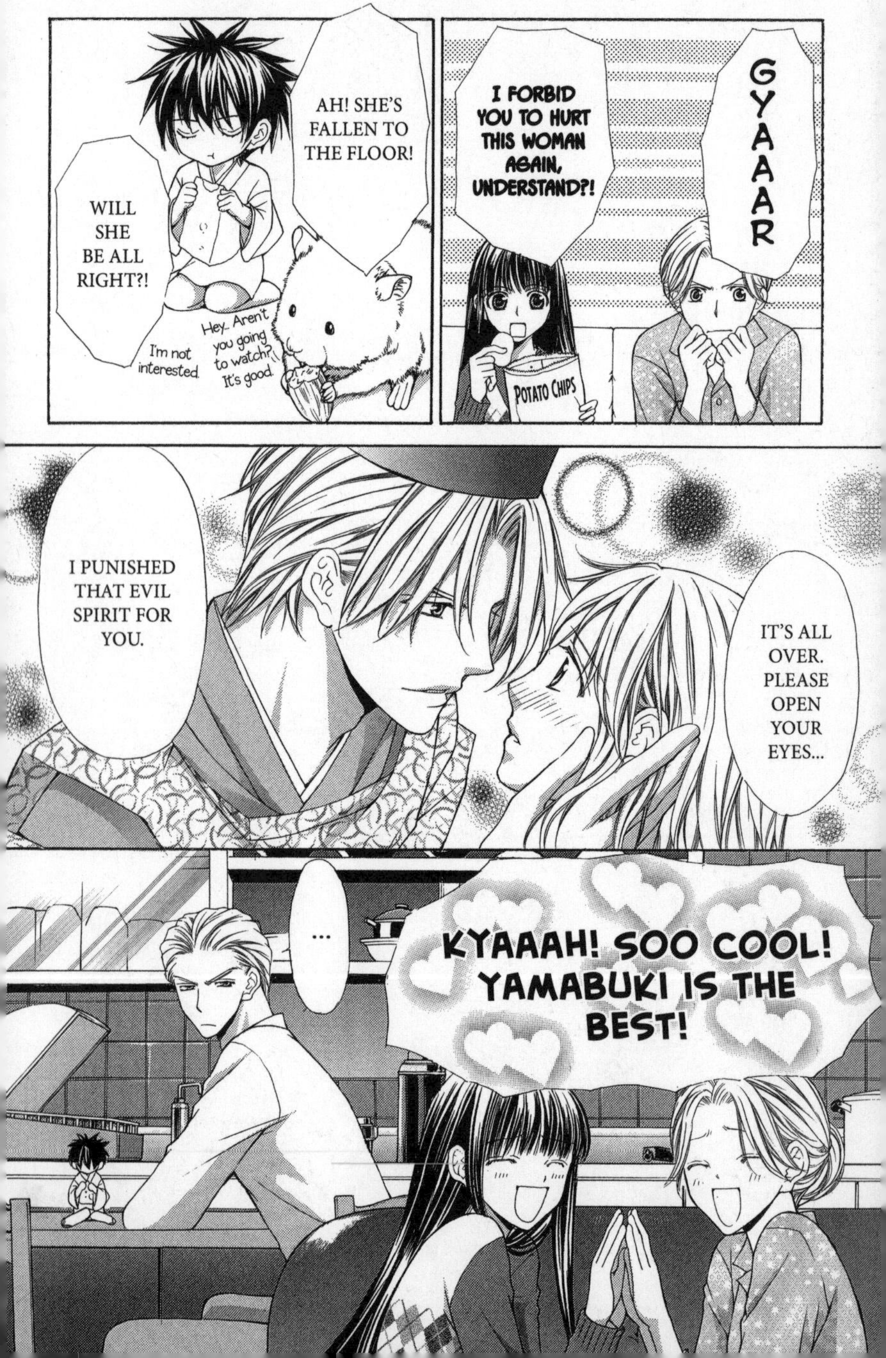
GYAAAAR
I FORBID YOU TO HURT THIS WOMAN AGAIN, UNDERSTAND?!
POTATO CHIPS
AH! SHE'S FALLEN TO THE FLOOR!
WILL SHE BE ALL RIGHT?!
Hey... Aren't you going to watch? It's good.
I'm not interested.
IT'S ALL OVER. PLEASE OPEN YOUR EYES...
I PUNISHED THAT EVIL SPIRIT FOR YOU.
KYAAAH! SOO COOL! YAMABUKI IS THE BEST!
...

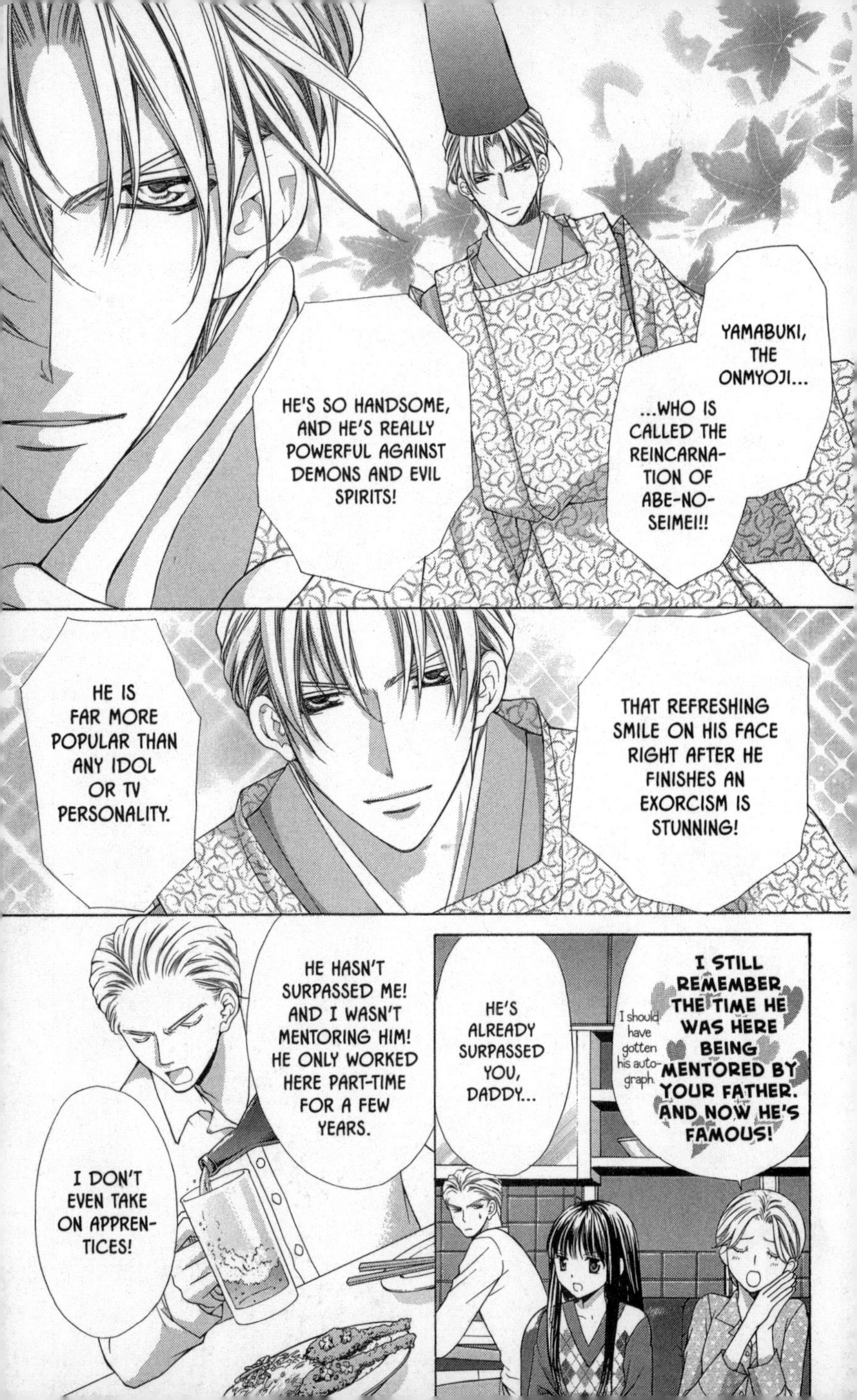
YAMABUKI, THE ONMYOJI...
...WHO IS CALLED THE REINCARNATION OF ABE-NO-SEIMEI!!
HE'S SO HANDSOME, AND HE'S REALLY POWERFUL AGAINST DEMONS AND EVIL SPIRITS!
THAT REFRESHING SMILE ON HIS FACE RIGHT AFTER HE FINISHES AN EXORCISM IS STUNNING!
HE IS FAR MORE POPULAR THAN ANY IDOL OR TV PERSONALITY.
I STILL REMEMBER THE TIME HE WAS HERE BEING MENTORED BY YOUR FATHER. AND NOW HE'S FAMOUS!
I should have gotten his autograph.
HE'S ALREADY SURPASSED YOU, DADDY...
HE HASN'T SURPASSED ME! AND I WASN'T MENTORING HIM! HE ONLY WORKED HERE PART-TIME FOR A FEW YEARS.
I DON'T EVEN TAKE ON APPRENTICES!

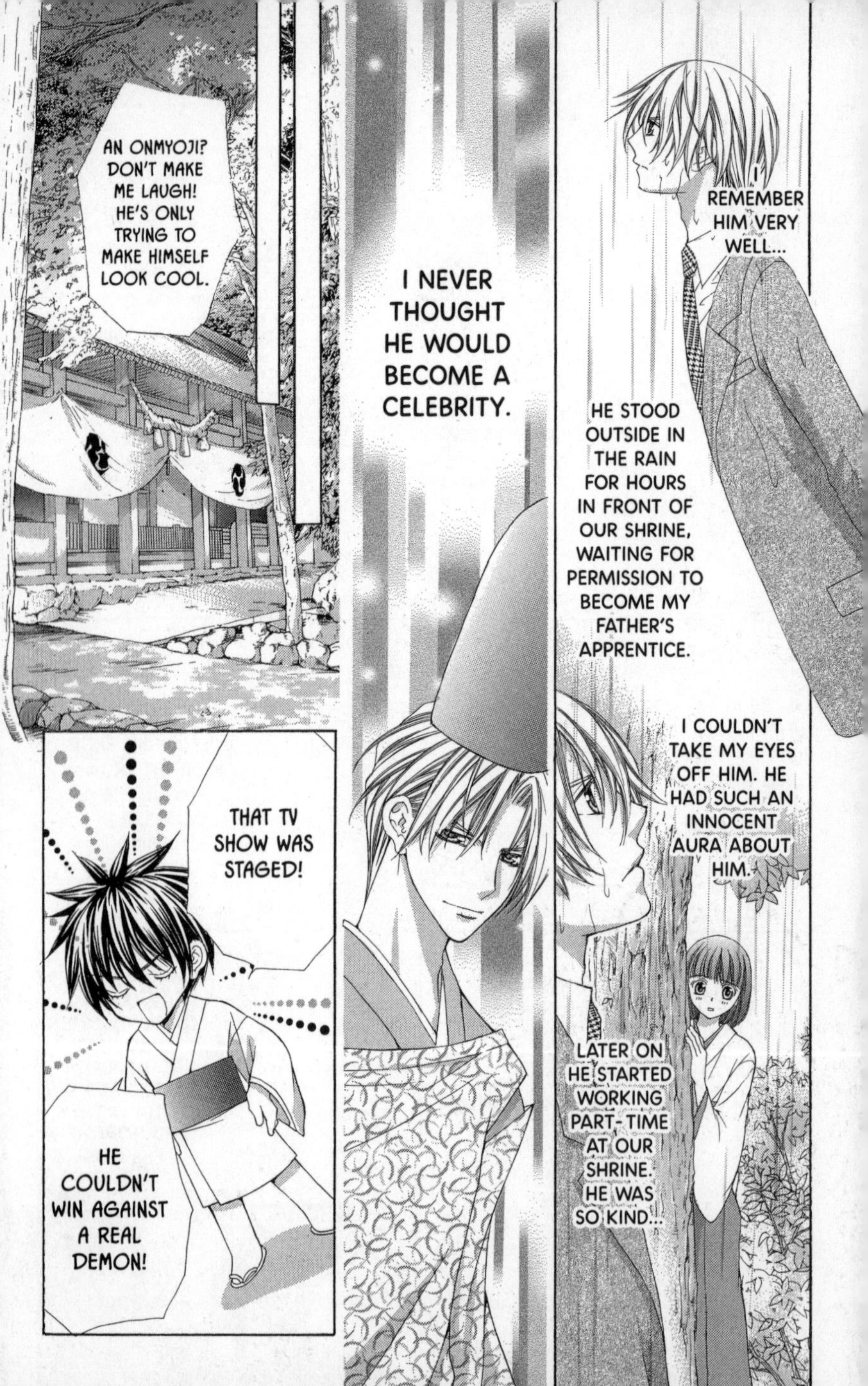
I REMEMBER HIM VERY WELL...
HE STOOD OUTSIDE IN THE RAIN FOR HOURS IN FRONT OF OUR SHRINE, WAITING FOR PERMISSION TO BECOME MY FATHER'S APPRENTICE.
I COULDN'T TAKE MY EYES OFF HIM. HE HAD SUCH AN INNOCENT AURA ABOUT HIM.
LATER ON HE STARTED WORKING PART-TIME AT OUR SHRINE. HE WAS SO KIND...
I NEVER THOUGHT HE WOULD BECOME A CELEBRITY.
AN ONMYOJI? DON'T MAKE ME LAUGH! HE'S ONLY TRYING TO MAKE HIMSELF LOOK COOL.
THAT TV SHOW WAS STAGED!
HE COULDN'T WIN AGAINST A REAL DEMON!

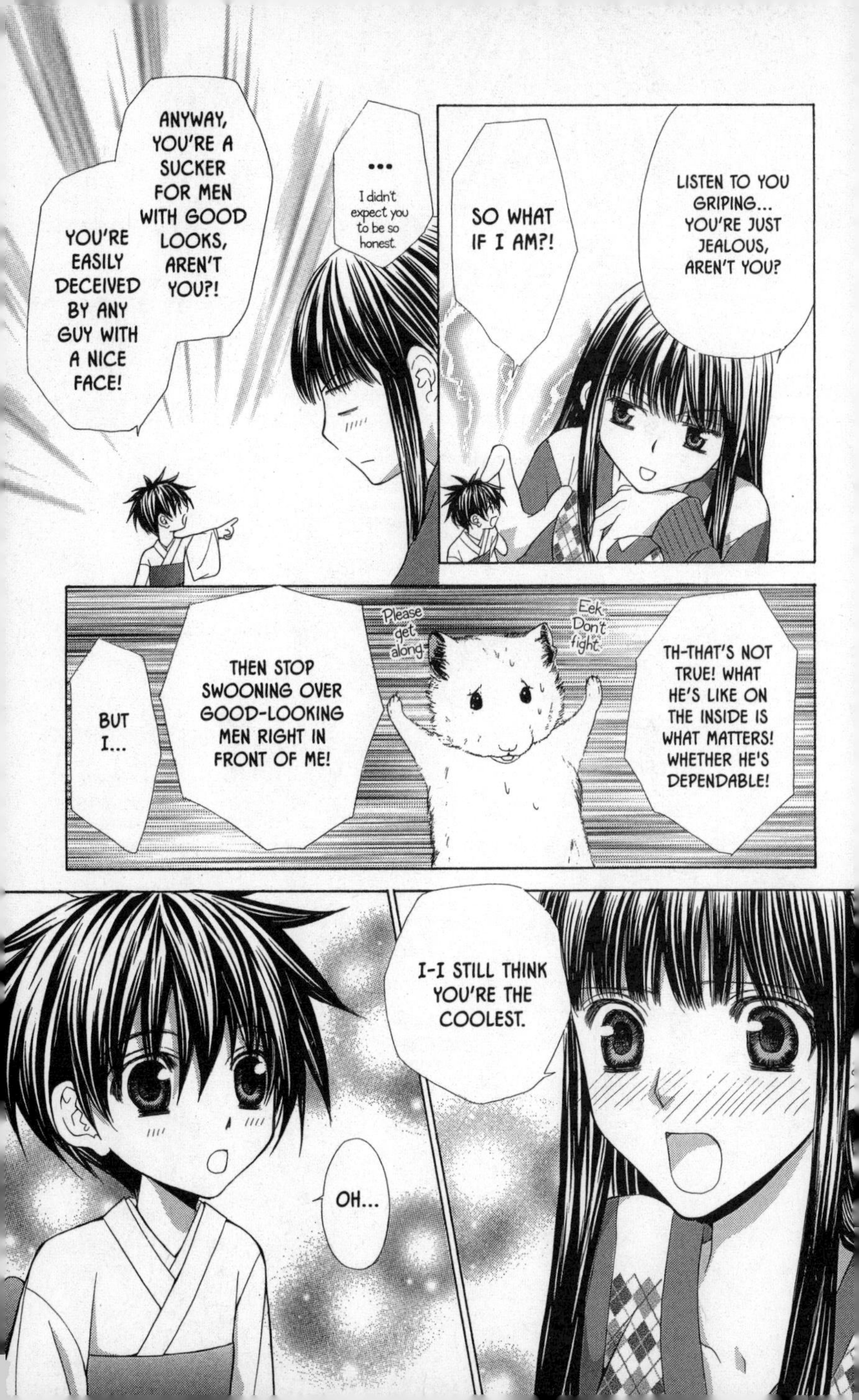
LISTEN TO YOU GRIPING... YOU'RE JUST JEALOUS, AREN'T YOU?
SO WHAT IF I AM?!
...
I didn't expect you to be so honest.
ANYWAY, YOU'RE A SUCKER FOR MEN WITH GOOD LOOKS, AREN'T YOU?!
YOU'RE EASILY DECEIVED BY ANY GUY WITH A NICE FACE!
TH-THAT'S NOT TRUE! WHAT HE'S LIKE ON THE INSIDE IS WHAT MATTERS! WHETHER HE'S DEPENDABLE!
Eek Don't fight
Please get along
THEN STOP SWOONING OVER GOOD-LOOKING MEN RIGHT IN FRONT OF ME!
BUT I...
I-I STILL THINK YOU'RE THE COOLEST.
OH...

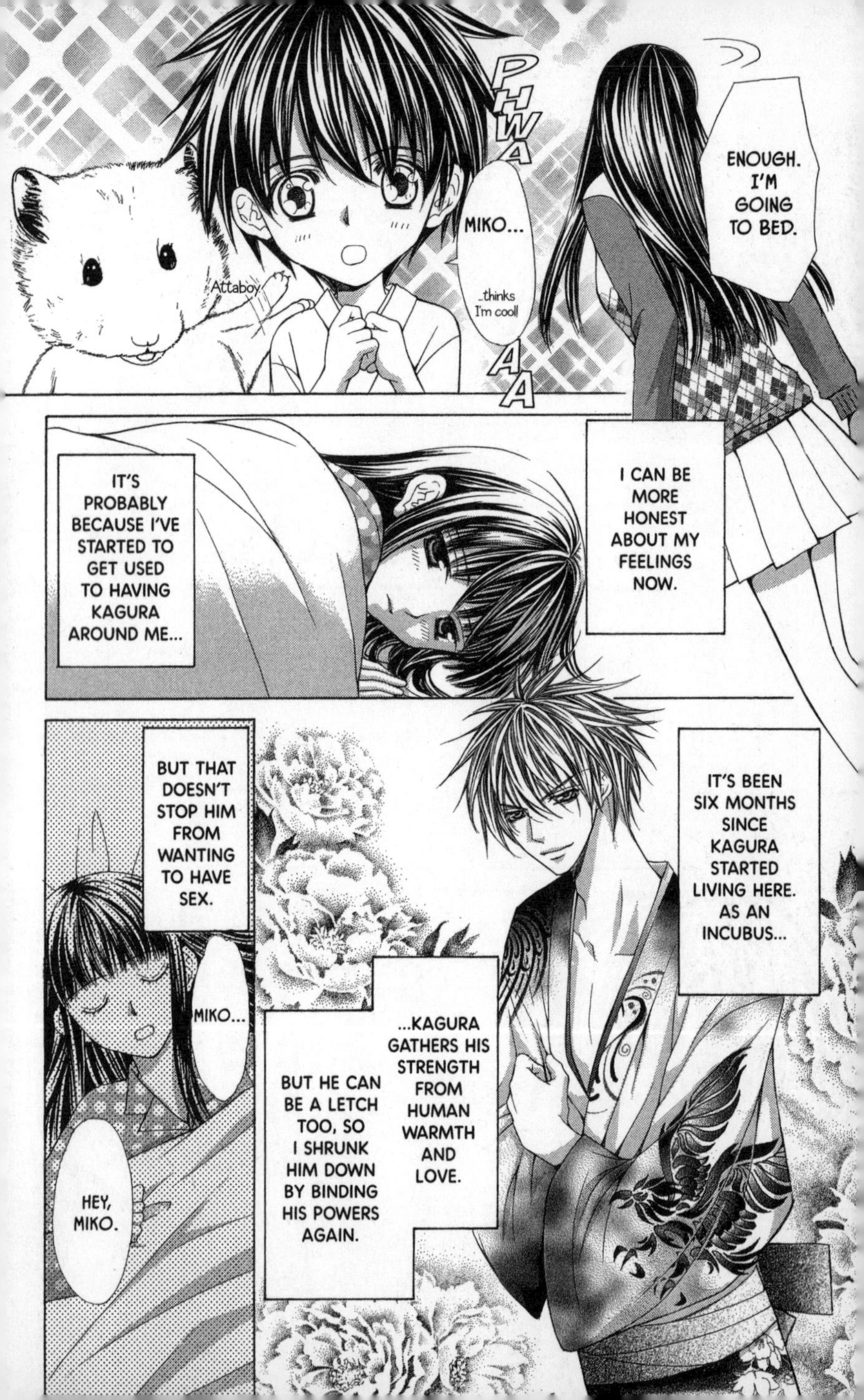

ENOUGH. I'M GOING TO BED.
PHWAAA
MIKO...
...thinks I'm cool!
Attaboy
I CAN BE MORE HONEST ABOUT MY FEELINGS NOW.
IT'S PROBABLY BECAUSE I'VE STARTED TO GET USED TO HAVING KAGURA AROUND ME...
IT'S BEEN SIX MONTHS SINCE KAGURA STARTED LIVING HERE. AS AN INCUBUS...
...KAGURA GATHERS HIS STRENGTH FROM HUMAN WARMTH AND LOVE.
BUT HE CAN BE A LETCH TOO, SO I SHRUNK HIM DOWN BY BINDING HIS POWERS AGAIN.
BUT THAT DOESN'T STOP HIM FROM WANTING TO HAVE SEX.
MIKO...
HEY, MIKO.

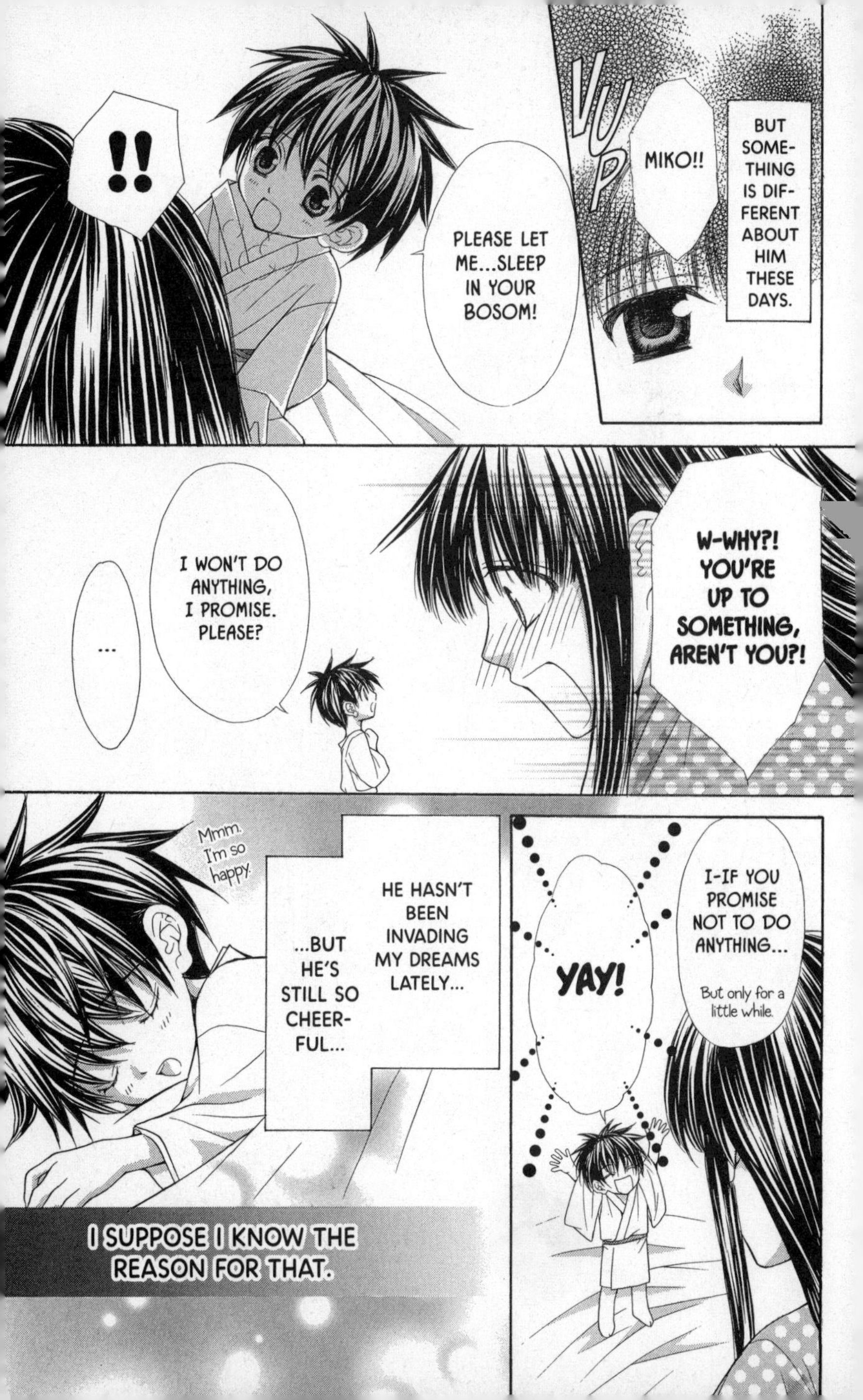
BUT SOMETHING IS DIFFERENT ABOUT HIM THESE DAYS.
VUP
MIKO!!
PLEASE LET ME...SLEEP IN YOUR BOSOM!
!!
W-WHY?! YOU'RE UP TO SOMETHING, AREN'T YOU?!
I WON'T DO ANYTHING, I PROMISE. PLEASE?
...
I-IF YOU PROMISE NOT TO DO ANYTHING...
But only for a little while.
YAY!
HE HASN'T BEEN INVADING MY DREAMS LATELY...
...BUT HE'S STILL SO CHEERFUL...
Mmm. I'm so happy.
I SUPPOSE I KNOW THE REASON FOR THAT.

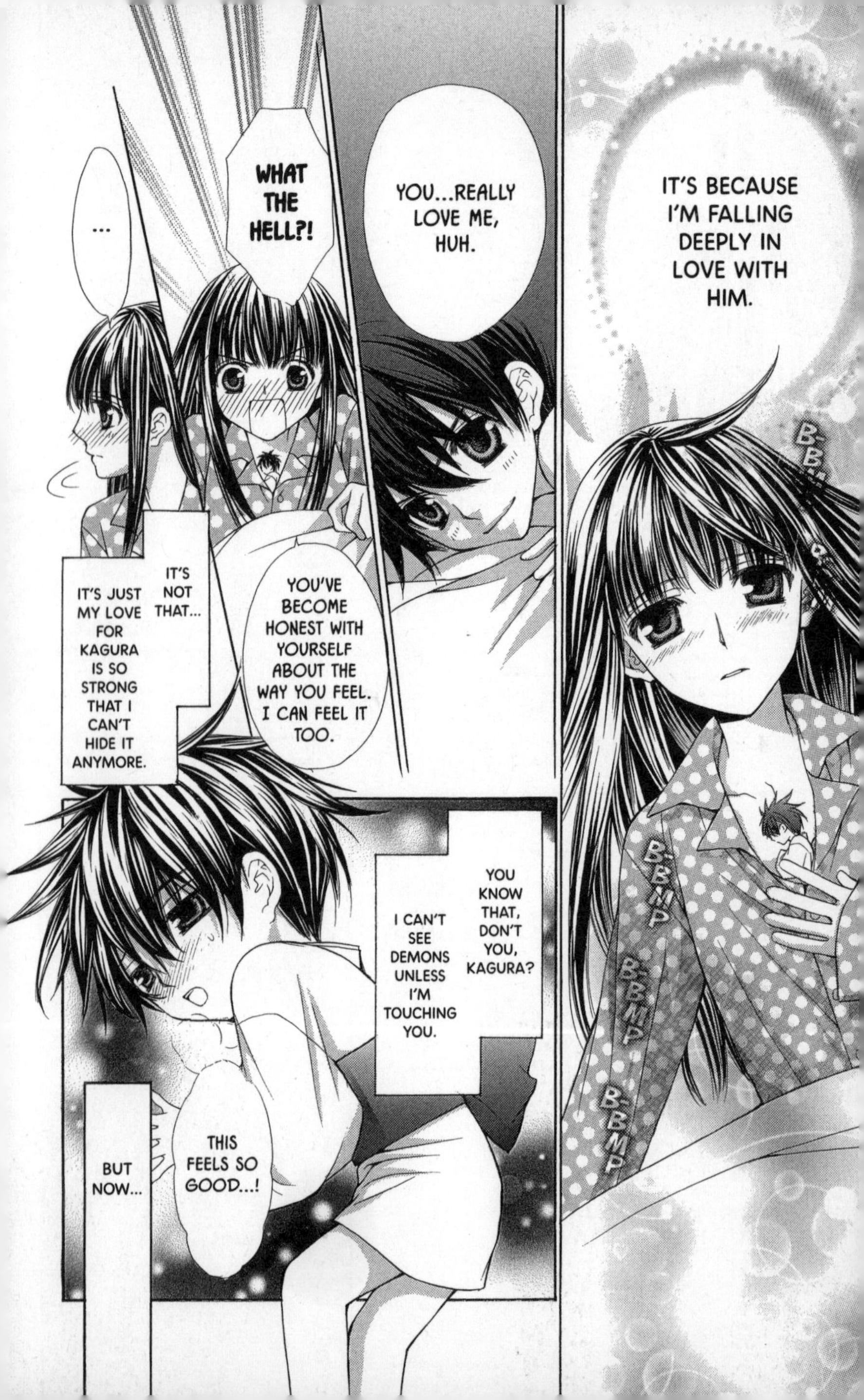
IT'S BECAUSE I'M FALLING DEEPLY IN LOVE WITH HIM.
B-B...
BBMP
BBMP
B-BMP
YOU...REALLY LOVE ME, HUH.
WHAT THE HELL?!
...
YOU'VE BECOME HONEST WITH YOURSELF ABOUT THE WAY YOU FEEL. I CAN FEEL IT TOO.
IT'S NOT THAT...
IT'S JUST MY LOVE FOR KAGURA IS SO STRONG THAT I CAN'T HIDE IT ANYMORE.
YOU KNOW THAT, DON'T YOU, KAGURA?
I CAN'T SEE DEMONS UNLESS I'M TOUCHING YOU.
THIS FEELS SO GOOD...!
BUT NOW...

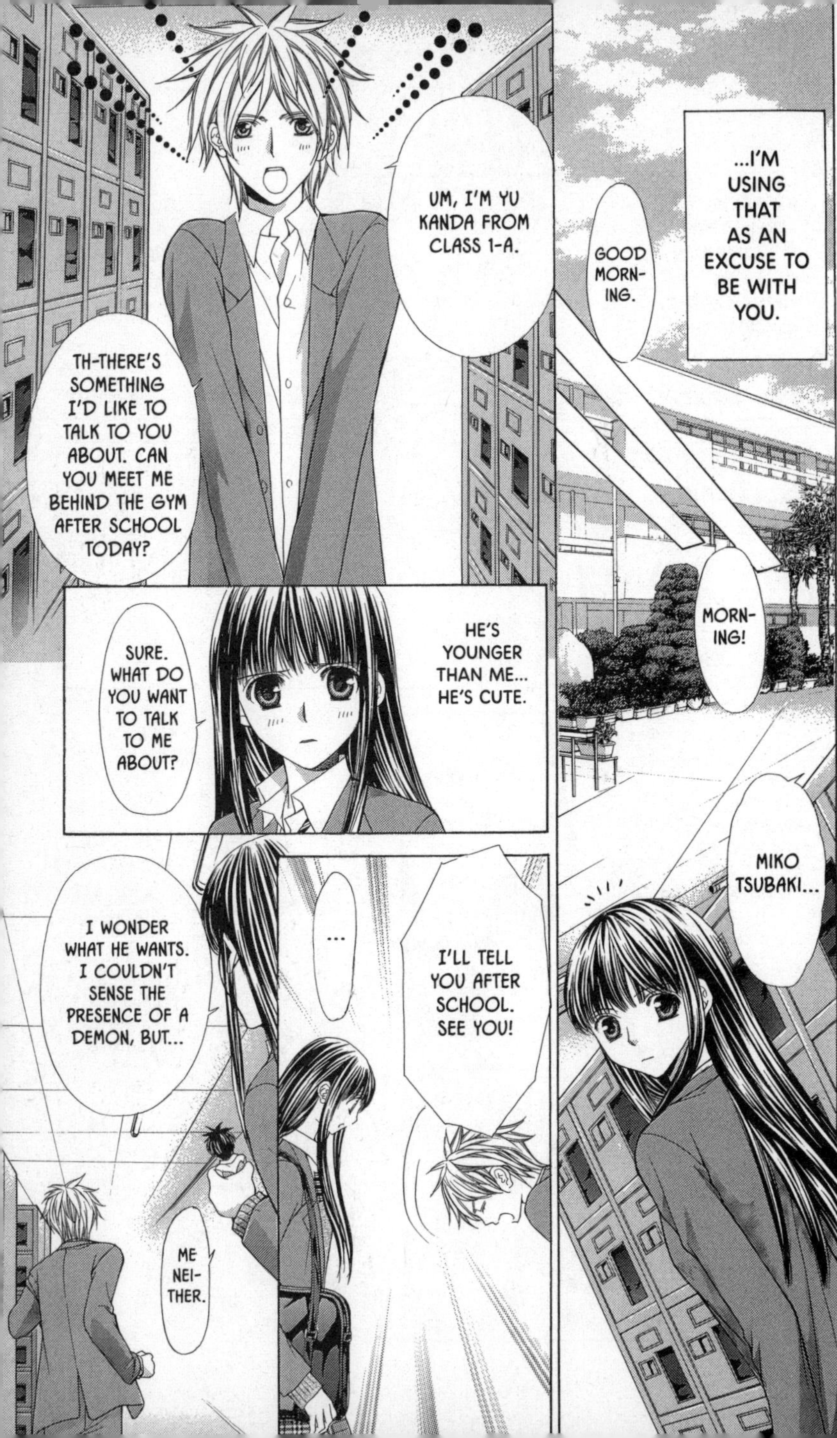
...I'M USING THAT AS AN EXCUSE TO BE WITH YOU.
GOOD MORNING.
MORNING!
MIKO TSUBAKI...
UM, I'M YU KANDA FROM CLASS 1-A.
TH-THERE'S SOMETHING I'D LIKE TO TALK TO YOU ABOUT. CAN YOU MEET ME BEHIND THE GYM AFTER SCHOOL TODAY?
HE'S YOUNGER THAN ME... HE'S CUTE.
SURE. WHAT DO YOU WANT TO TALK TO ME ABOUT?
I'LL TELL YOU AFTER SCHOOL. SEE YOU!
...
I WONDER WHAT HE WANTS. I COULDN'T SENSE THE PRESENCE OF A DEMON, BUT...
ME NEITHER.

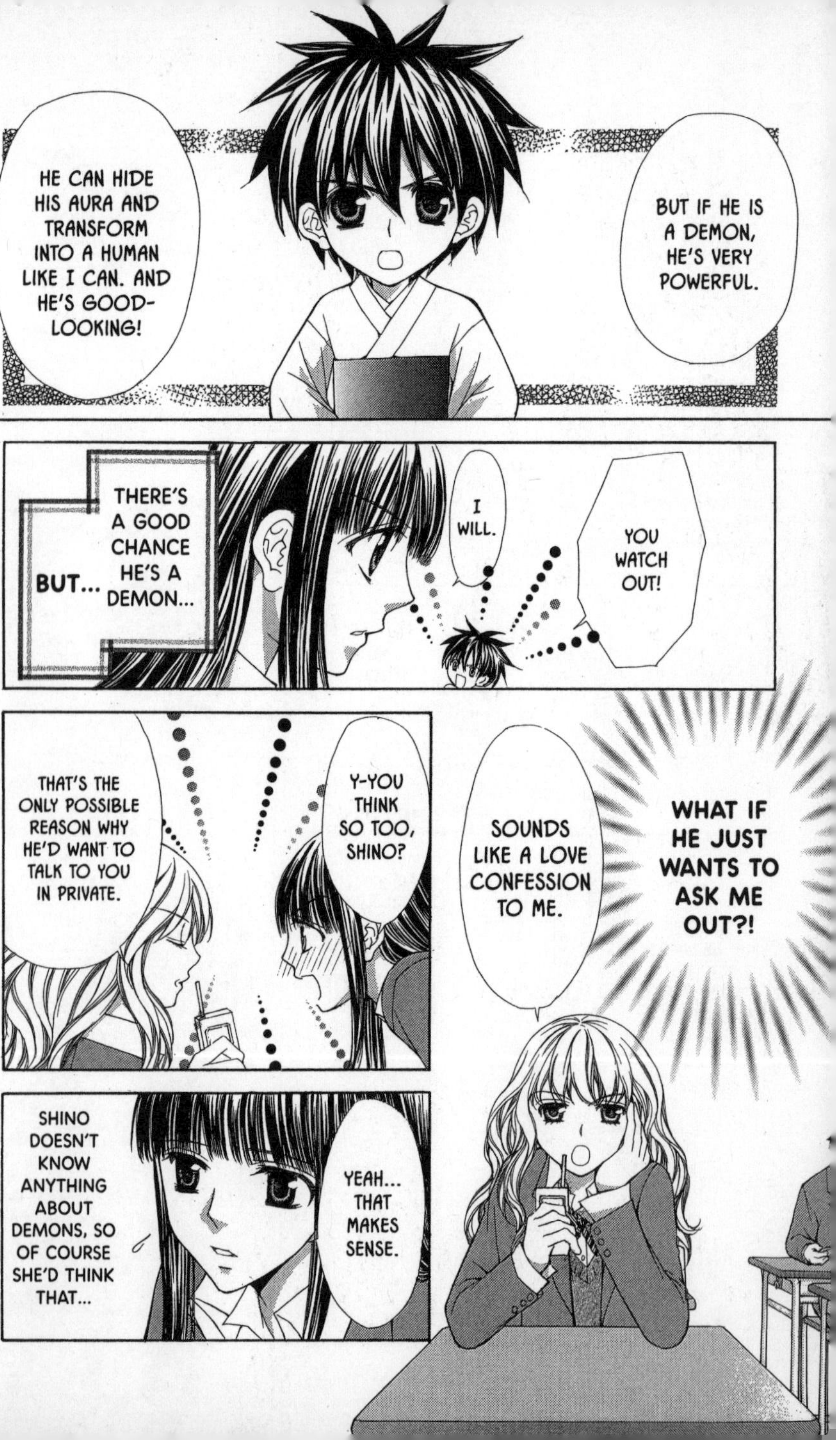

BUT IF HE IS A DEMON, HE'S VERY POWERFUL.
HE CAN HIDE HIS AURA AND TRANSFORM INTO A HUMAN LIKE I CAN. AND HE'S GOOD-LOOKING!
YOU WATCH OUT!
I WILL.
THERE'S A GOOD CHANCE HE'S A DEMON...
BUT...
WHAT IF HE JUST WANTS TO ASK ME OUT?!
SOUNDS LIKE A LOVE CONFESSION TO ME.
Y-YOU THINK SO TOO, SHINO?
THAT'S THE ONLY POSSIBLE REASON WHY HE'D WANT TO TALK TO YOU IN PRIVATE.
YEAH... THAT MAKES SENSE.
SHINO DOESN'T KNOW ANYTHING ABOUT DEMONS, SO OF COURSE SHE'D THINK THAT...

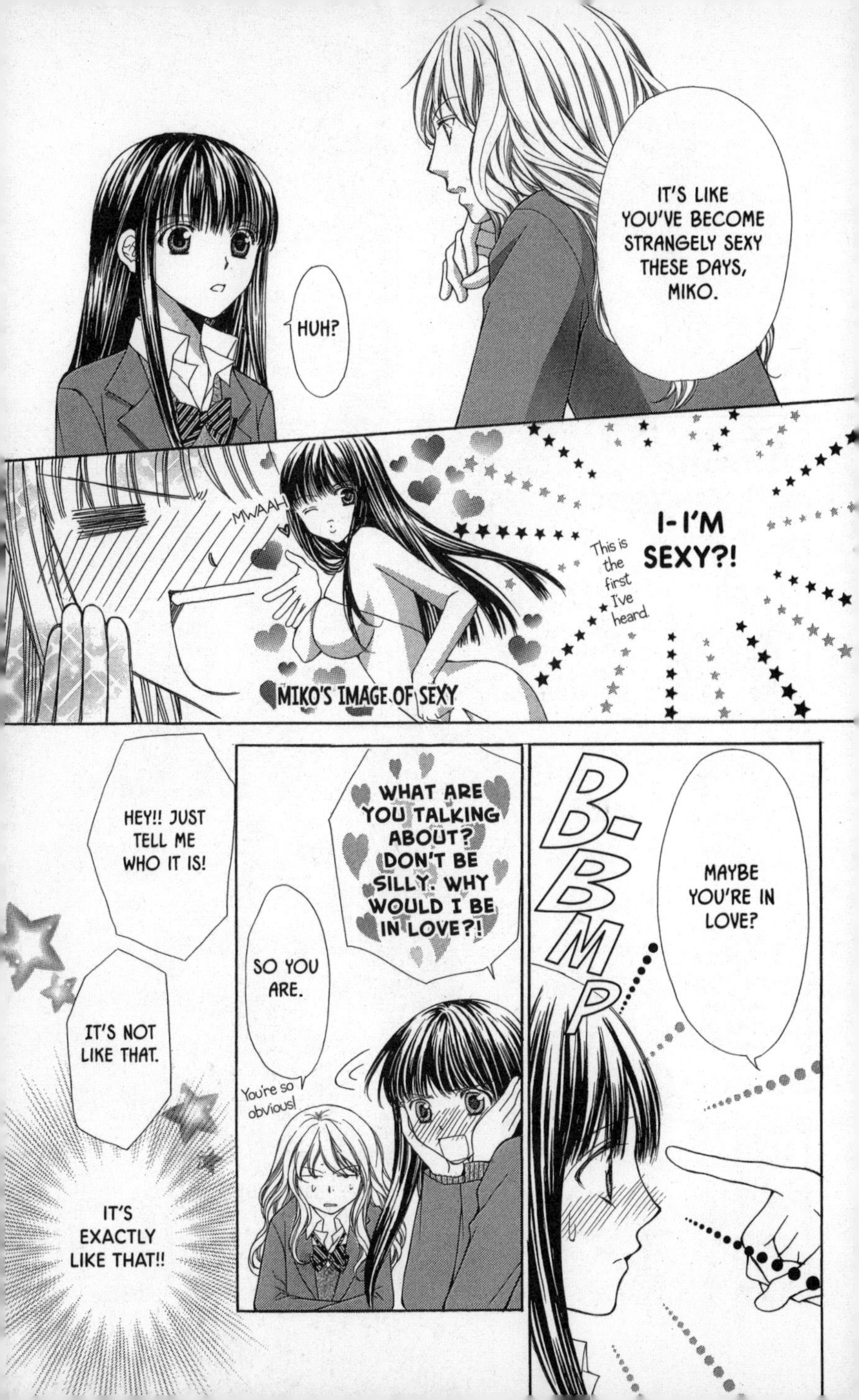
IT'S LIKE YOU'VE BECOME STRANGELY SEXY THESE DAYS, MIKO.
HUH?
I-I'M SEXY?!
This is the first I've heard.
MWAAH
MIKO'S IMAGE OF SEXY
MAYBE YOU'RE IN LOVE?
B-BMP
WHAT ARE YOU TALKING ABOUT? DON'T BE SILLY. WHY WOULD I BE IN LOVE?!
SO YOU ARE.
You're so obvious!
HEY!! JUST TELL ME WHO IT IS!
IT'S NOT LIKE THAT.
IT'S EXACTLY LIKE THAT!!

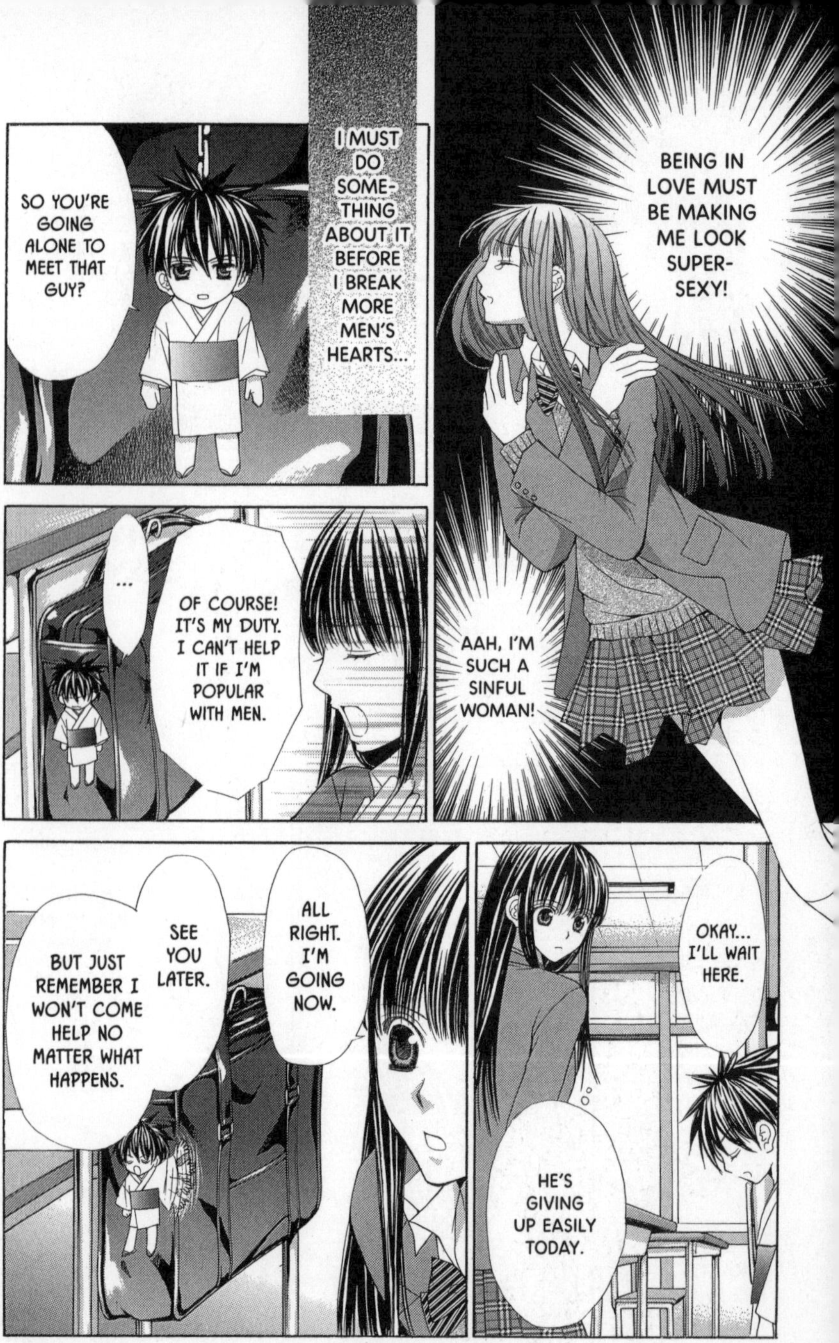
BEING IN LOVE MUST BE MAKING ME LOOK SUPER-SEXY!
AAH, I'M SUCH A SINFUL WOMAN!
I MUST DO SOME-THING ABOUT IT BEFORE I BREAK MORE MEN'S HEARTS...
SO YOU'RE GOING ALONE TO MEET THAT GUY?
OF COURSE! IT'S MY DUTY. I CAN'T HELP IT IF I'M POPULAR WITH MEN.
...
OKAY... I'LL WAIT HERE.
HE'S GIVING UP EASILY TODAY.
ALL RIGHT. I'M GOING NOW.
SEE YOU LATER.
BUT JUST REMEMBER I WON'T COME HELP NO MATTER WHAT HAPPENS.

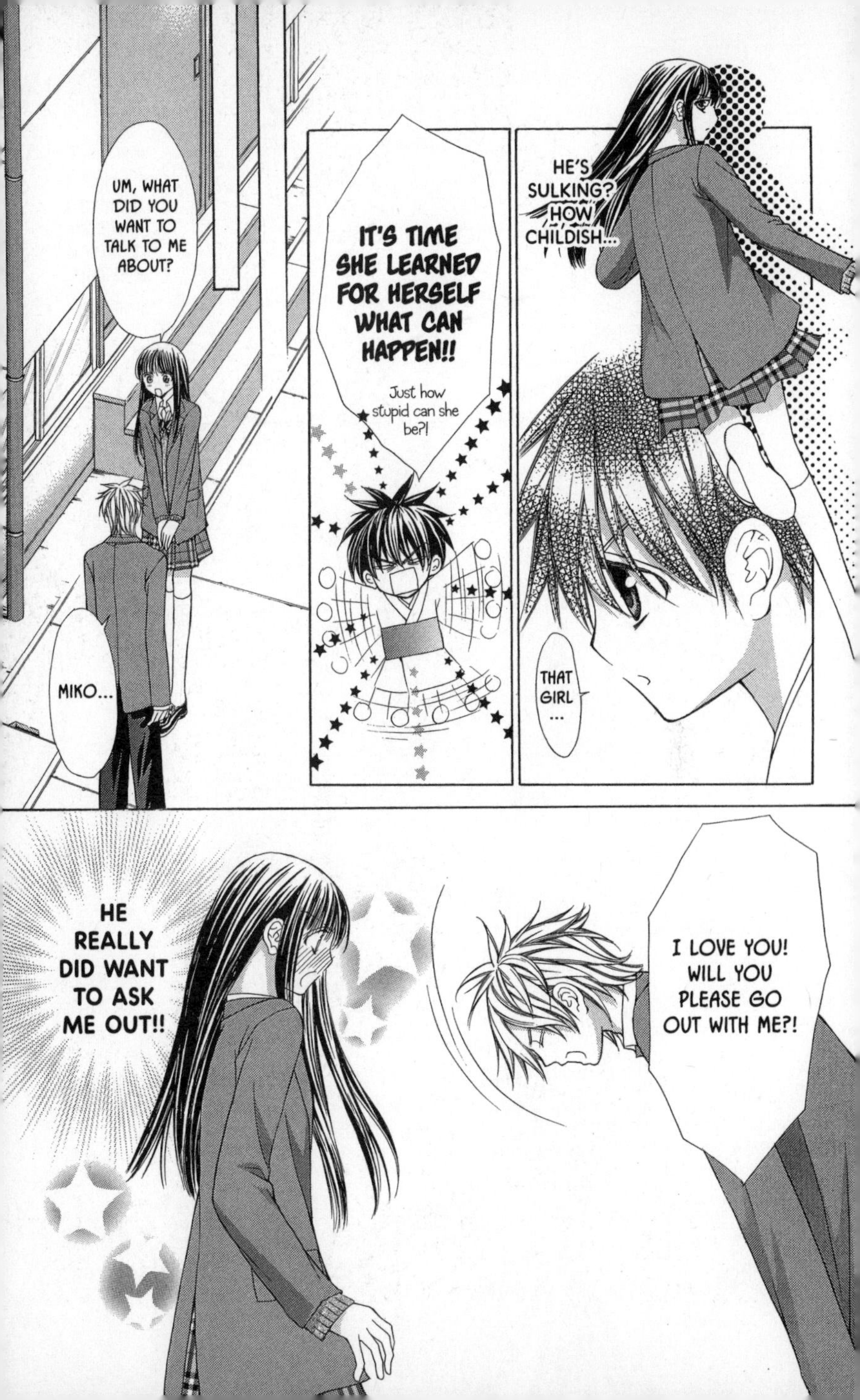
HE'S SULKING? HOW CHILDISH...
THAT GIRL...
IT'S TIME SHE LEARNED FOR HERSELF WHAT CAN HAPPEN!!
Just how stupid can she be?!
UM, WHAT DID YOU WANT TO TALK TO ME ABOUT?
MIKO...
I LOVE YOU! WILL YOU PLEASE GO OUT WITH ME?!
HE REALLY DID WANT TO ASK ME OUT!!

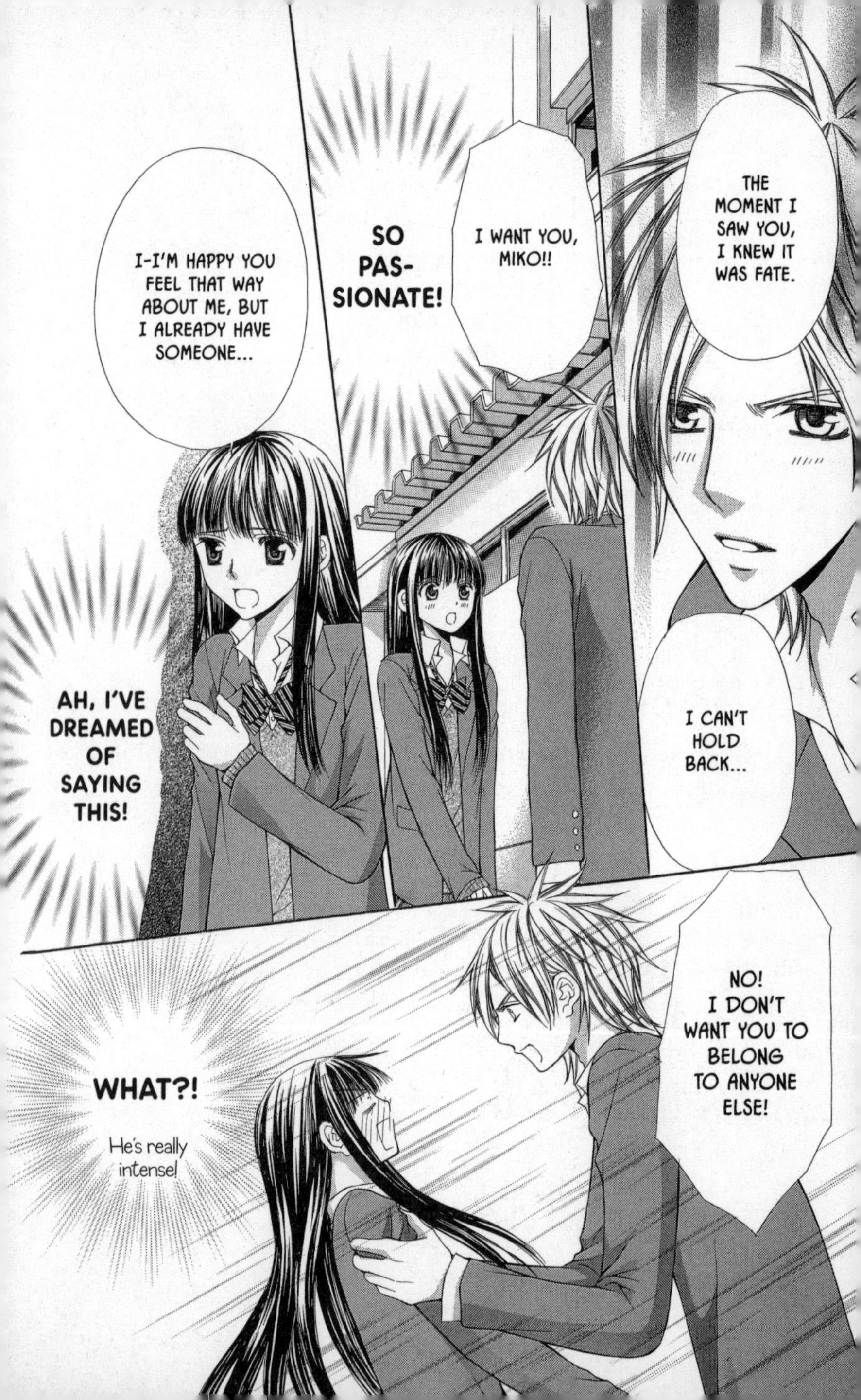
THE MOMENT I SAW YOU, I KNEW IT WAS FATE.
I CAN'T HOLD BACK...
I WANT YOU, MIKO!!
SO PAS-SIONATE!
I-I'M HAPPY YOU FEEL THAT WAY ABOUT ME, BUT I ALREADY HAVE SOMEONE...
AH, I'VE DREAMED OF SAYING THIS!
NO! I DON'T WANT YOU TO BELONG TO ANYONE ELSE!
WHAT?!
He's really intense!

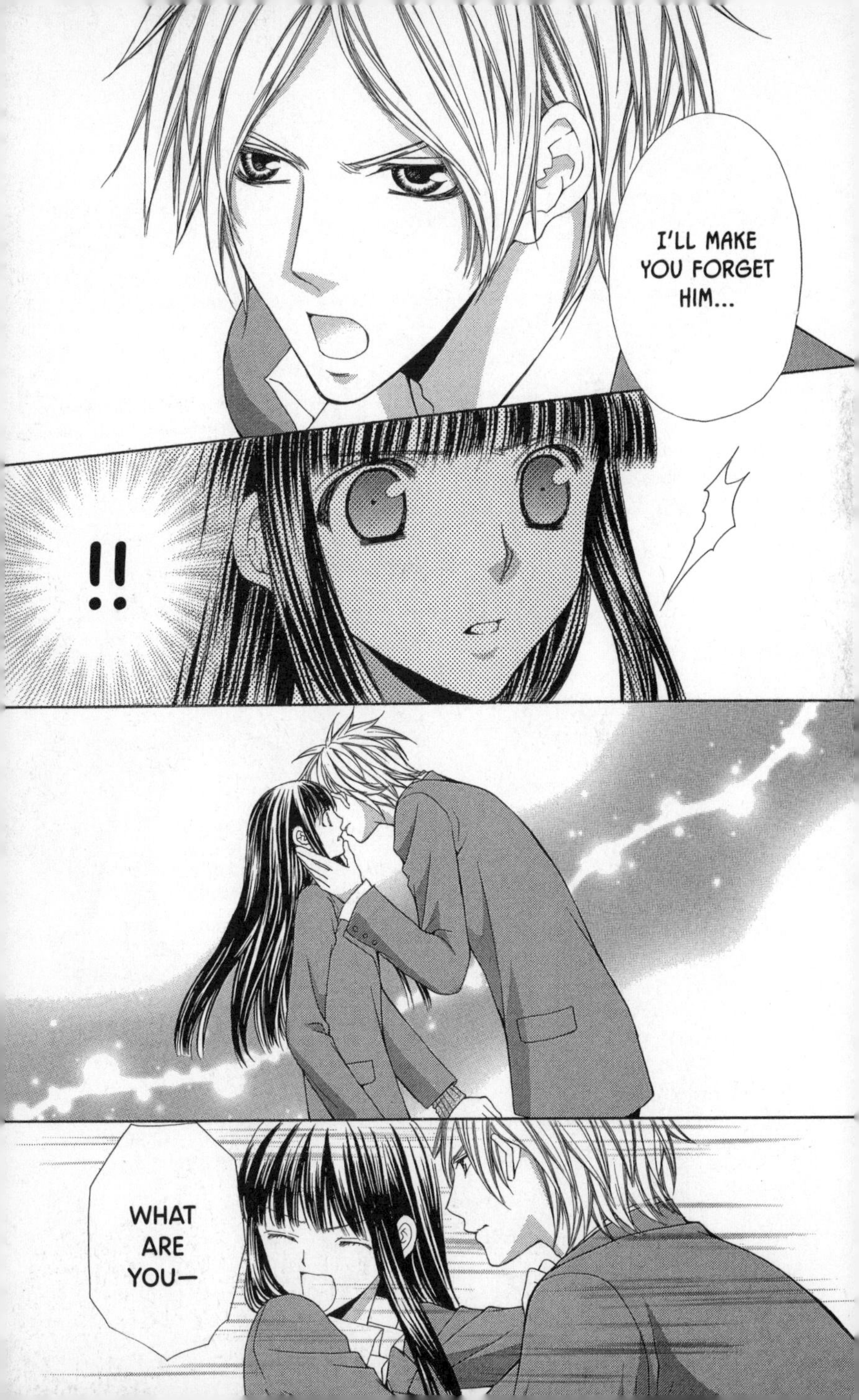
I'LL MAKE YOU FORGET HIM...
!!
WHAT ARE YOU—

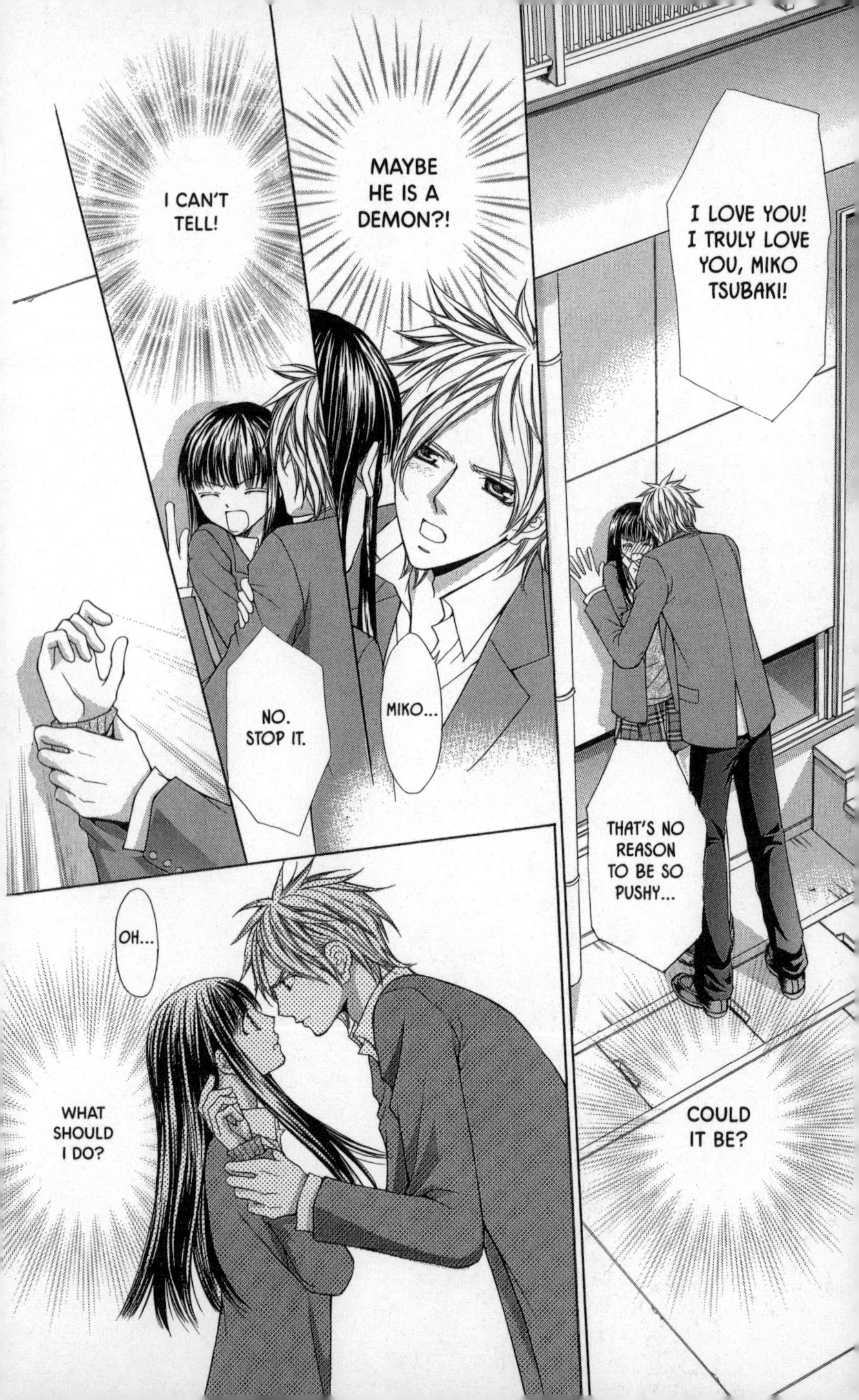
I LOVE YOU! I TRULY LOVE YOU, MIKO TSUBAKI!
THAT'S NO REASON TO BE SO PUSHY...
COULD IT BE?
MAYBE HE IS A DEMON?!
MIKO...
I CAN'T TELL!
NO. STOP IT.
OH...
WHAT SHOULD I DO?

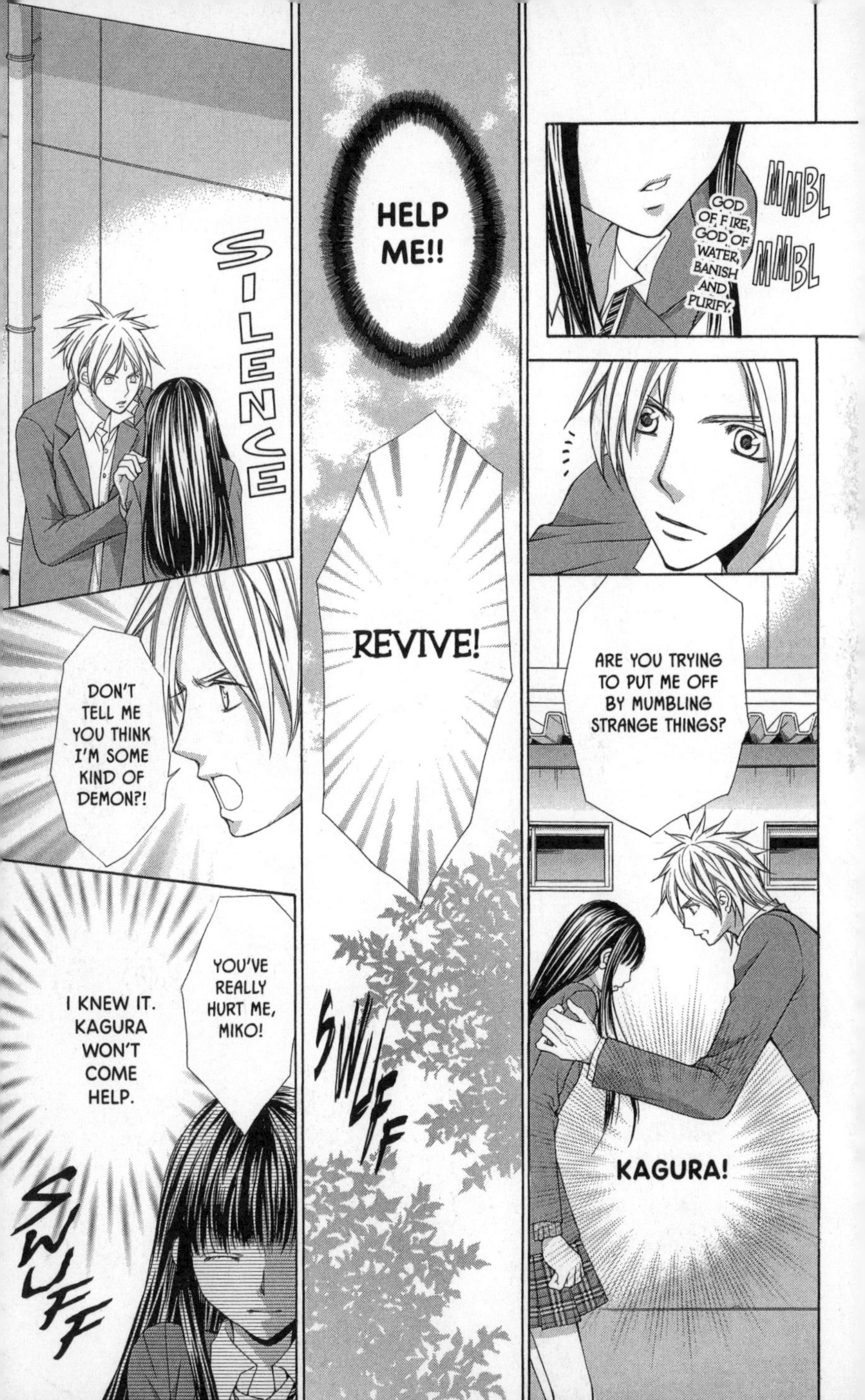
MMBL
MMBL
GOD OF FIRE, GOD OF WATER, BANISH AND PURIFY.
ARE YOU TRYING TO PUT ME OFF BY MUMBLING STRANGE THINGS?
KAGURA!
HELP ME!!
REVIVE!
SWUFF
SILENCE
DON'T TELL ME YOU THINK I'M SOME KIND OF DEMON?!
YOU'VE REALLY HURT ME, MIKO!
I KNEW IT. KAGURA WON'T COME HELP.
SWUFF

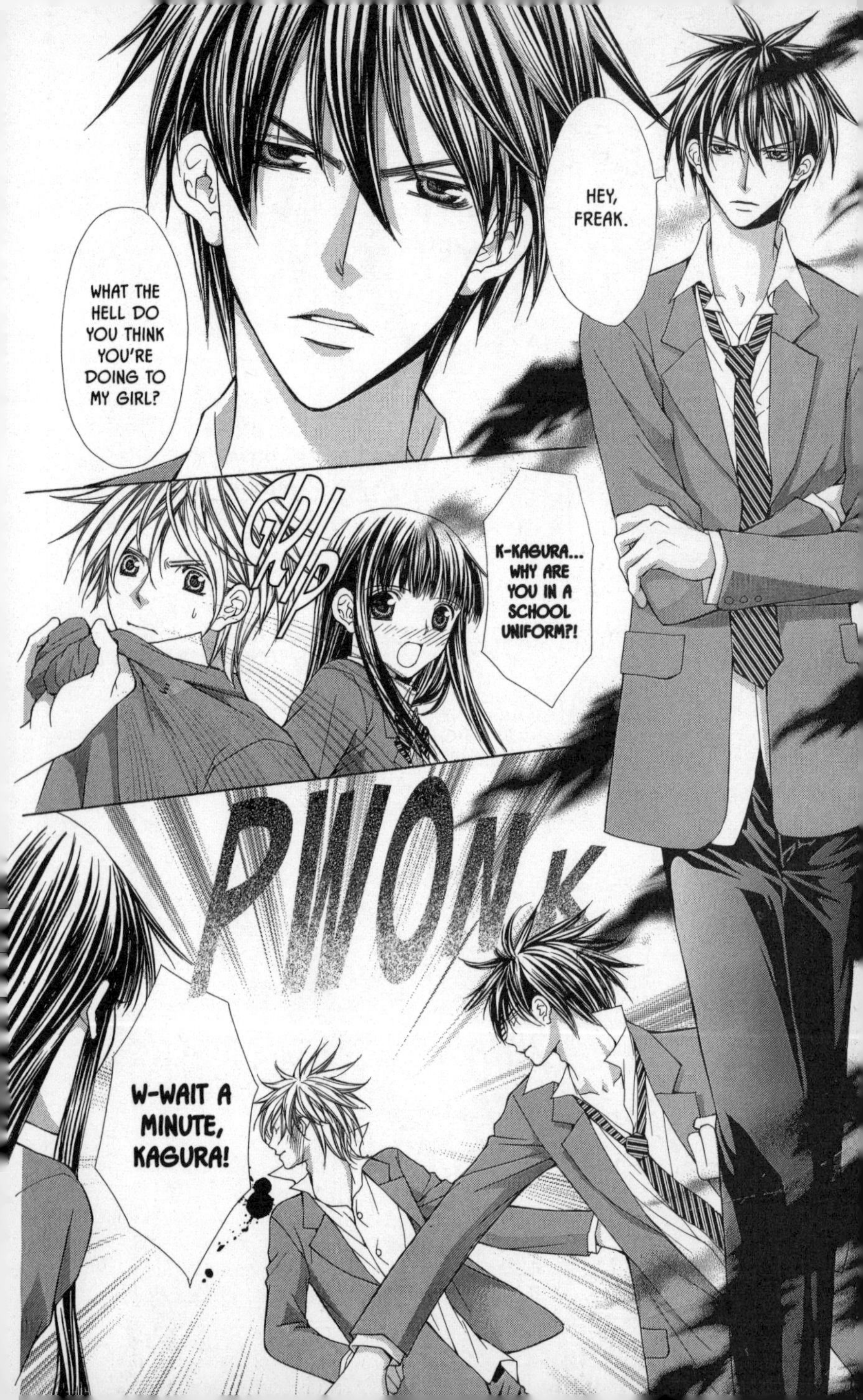
HEY, FREAK.
WHAT THE HELL DO YOU THINK YOU'RE DOING TO MY GIRL?
GRIP
K-KAGURA... WHY ARE YOU IN A SCHOOL UNIFORM?!
PWONK
W-WAIT A MINUTE, KAGURA!

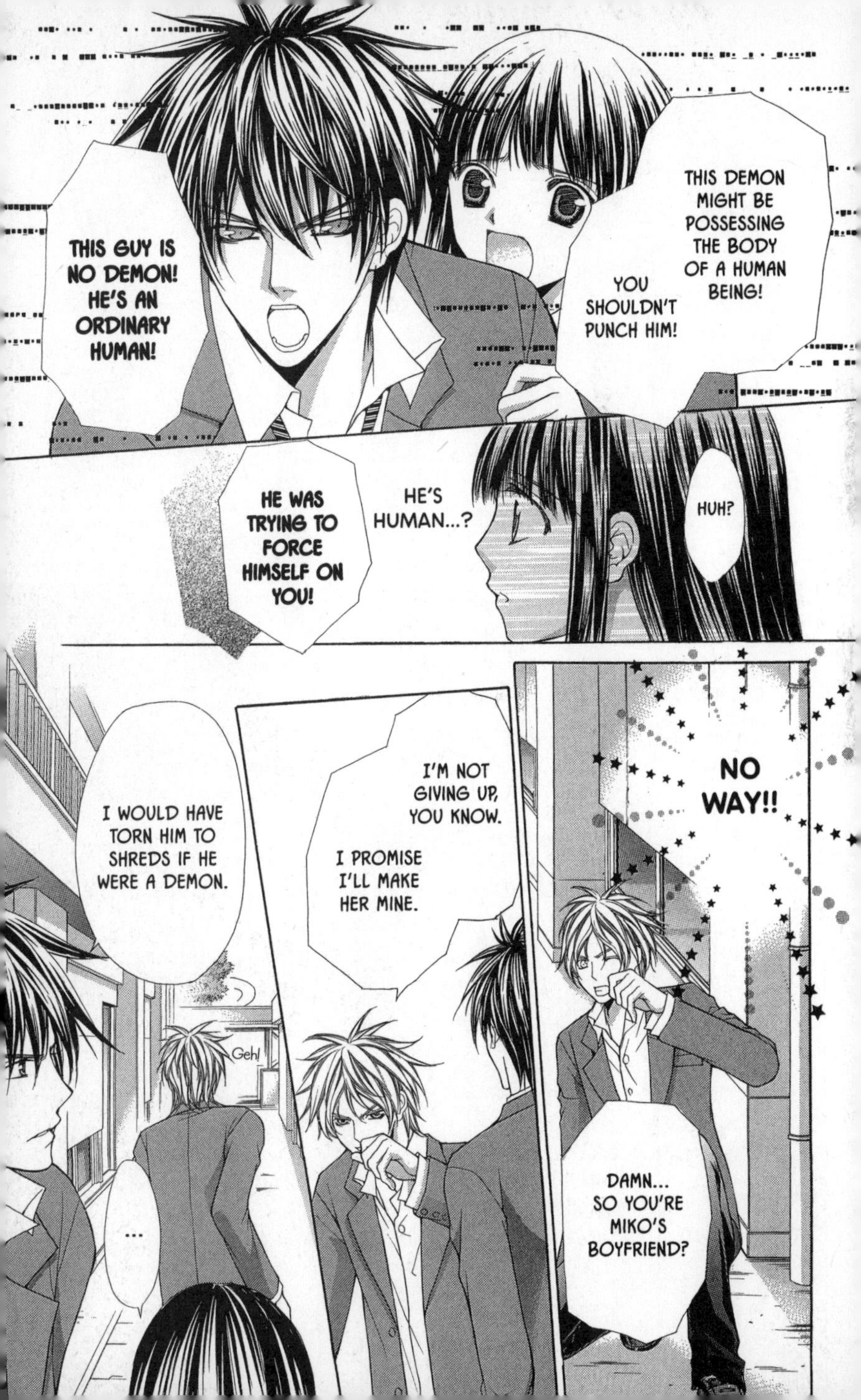
THIS DEMON MIGHT BE POSSESSING THE BODY OF A HUMAN BEING!
YOU SHOULDN'T PUNCH HIM!
THIS GUY IS NO DEMON! HE'S AN ORDINARY HUMAN!
HUH?
HE'S HUMAN...?
HE WAS TRYING TO FORCE HIMSELF ON YOU!
NO WAY!!
DAMN... SO YOU'RE MIKO'S BOYFRIEND?
I'M NOT GIVING UP, YOU KNOW.
I PROMISE I'LL MAKE HER MINE.
Geh!
I WOULD HAVE TORN HIM TO SHREDS IF HE WERE A DEMON.
...

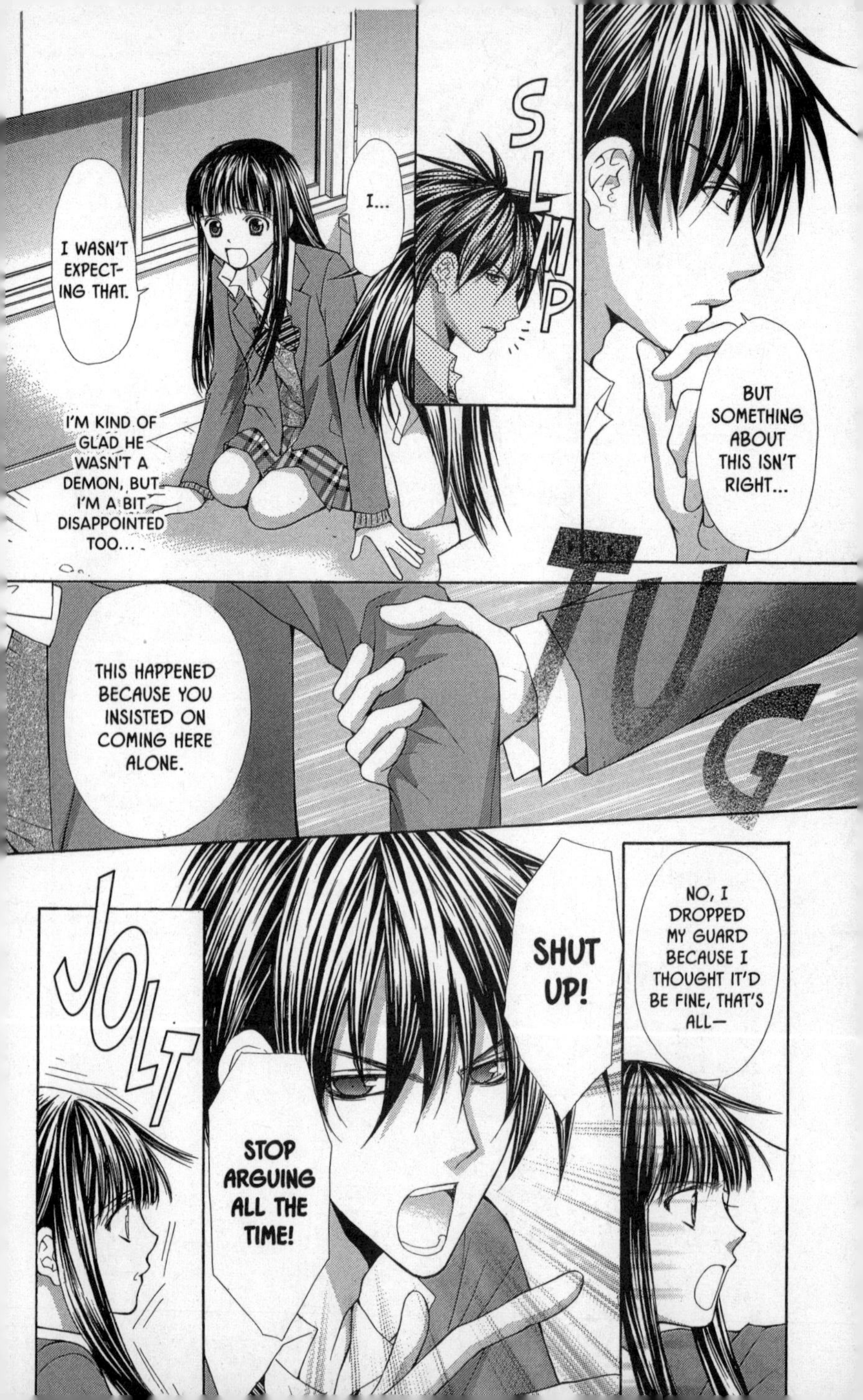

BUT SOMETHING ABOUT THIS ISN'T RIGHT...
SLMP
I...
I WASN'T EXPECTING THAT.
I'M KIND OF GLAD HE WASN'T A DEMON, BUT I'M A BIT DISAPPOINTED TOO...
TUG
THIS HAPPENED BECAUSE YOU INSISTED ON COMING HERE ALONE.
NO, I DROPPED MY GUARD BECAUSE I THOUGHT IT'D BE FINE, THAT'S ALL—
SHUT UP!
JOLT
STOP ARGUING ALL THE TIME!

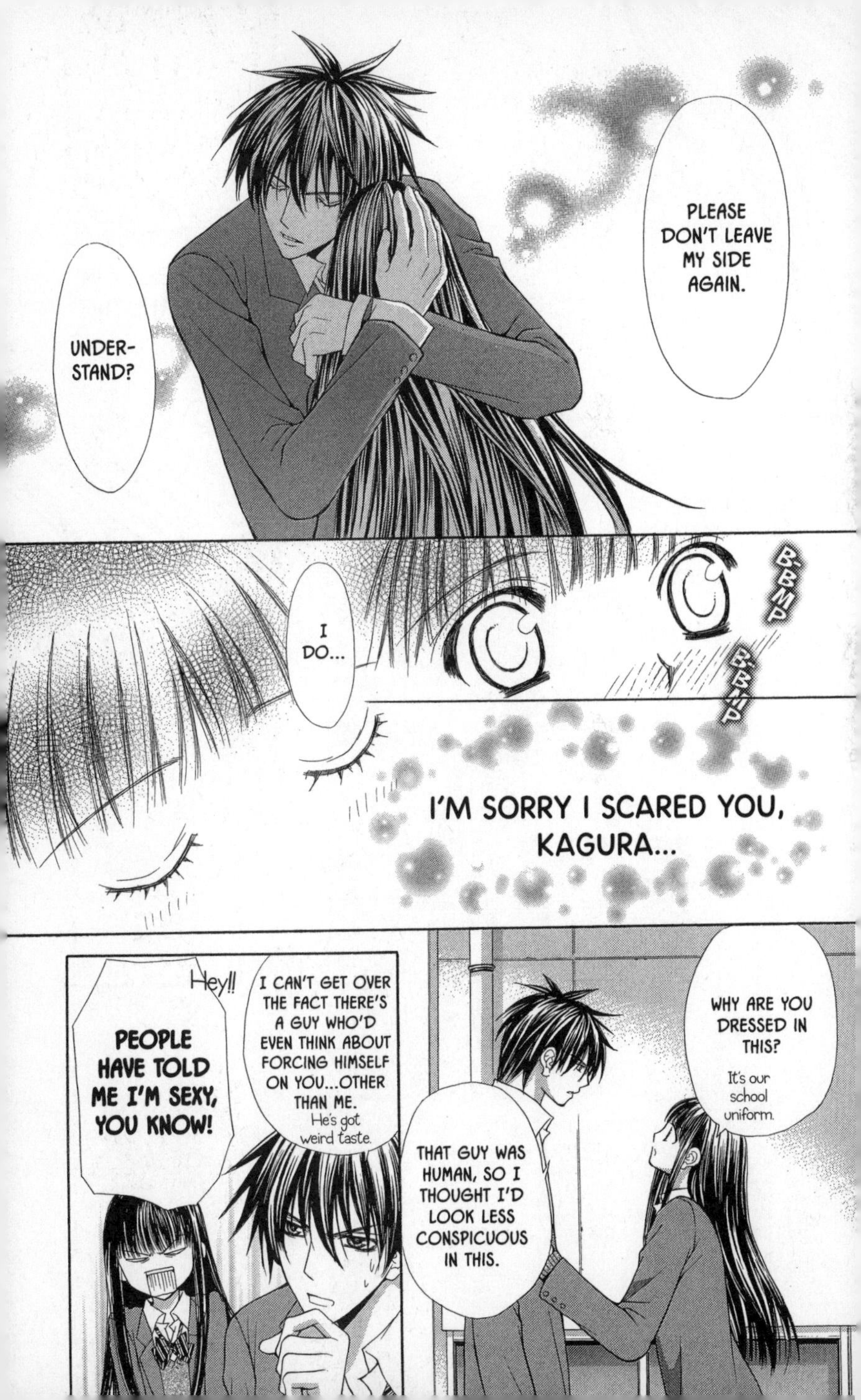
PLEASE DON'T LEAVE MY SIDE AGAIN.
UNDER-STAND?
B-BMP
B-BMP
I DO...
I'M SORRY I SCARED YOU, KAGURA...
WHY ARE YOU DRESSED IN THIS?
It's our school uniform.
THAT GUY WAS HUMAN, SO I THOUGHT I'D LOOK LESS CONSPICUOUS IN THIS.
I CAN'T GET OVER THE FACT THERE'S A GUY WHO'D EVEN THINK ABOUT FORCING HIMSELF ON YOU...OTHER THAN ME.
He's got weird taste.
Hey!!
PEOPLE HAVE TOLD ME I'M SEXY, YOU KNOW!

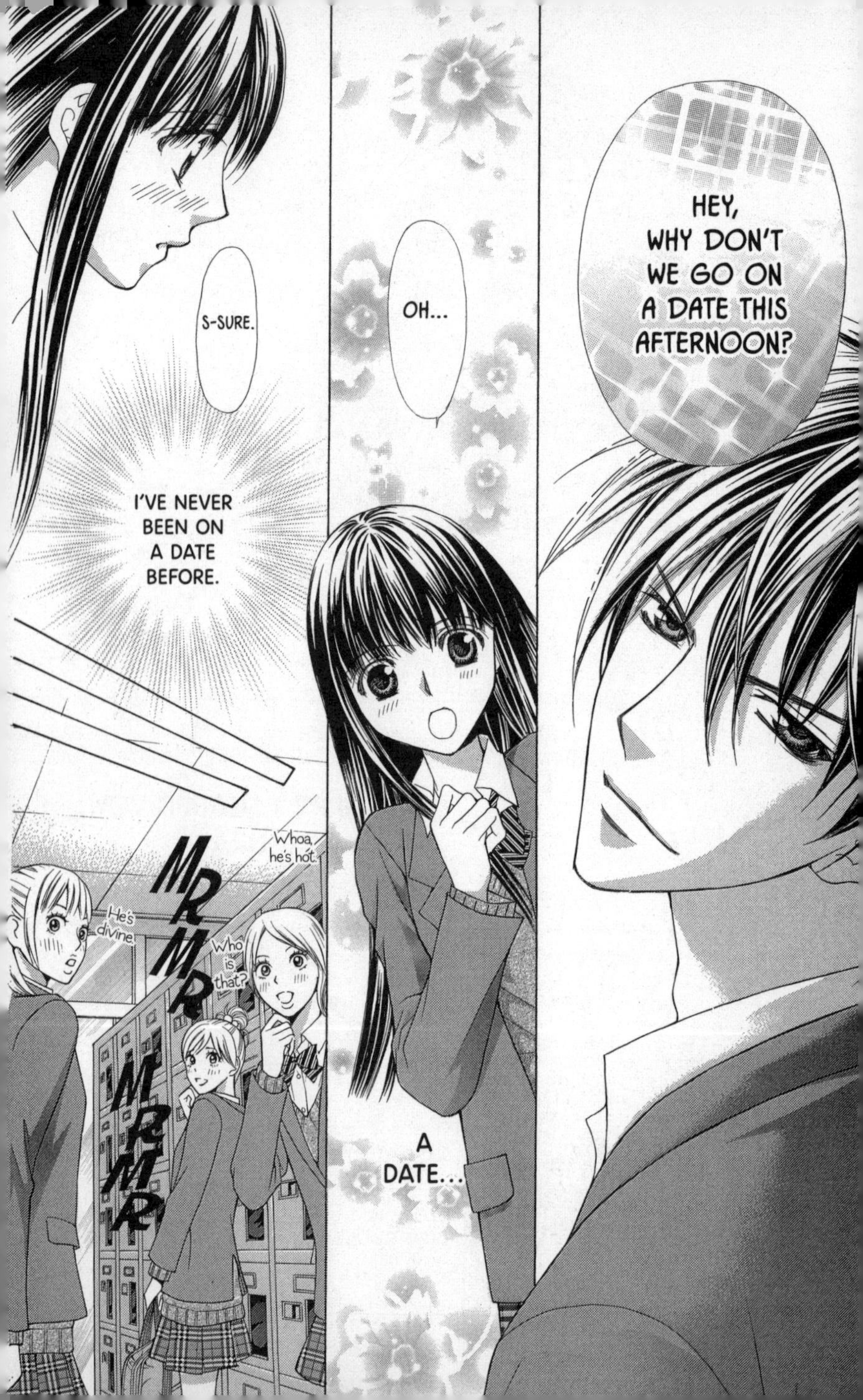
HEY, WHY DON'T WE GO ON A DATE THIS AFTERNOON?
OH...
A DATE...
S-SURE.
I'VE NEVER BEEN ON A DATE BEFORE.
Whoa, he's hot.
MRMR
Who is that?
He's divine.
MRMRMR

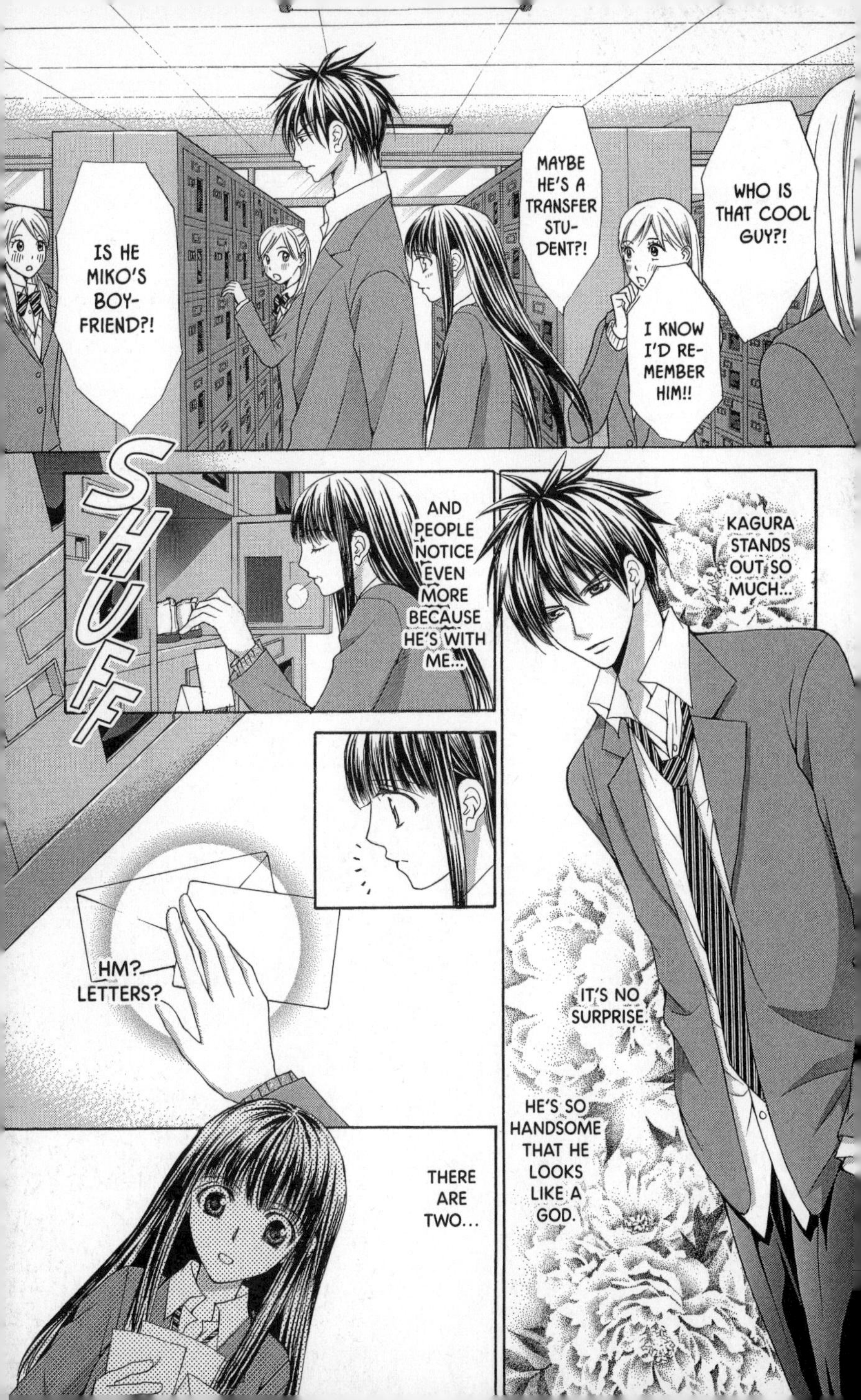
WHO IS THAT COOL GUY?!
I KNOW I'D REMEMBER HIM!!
MAYBE HE'S A TRANSFER STUDENT?!
IS HE MIKO'S BOYFRIEND?!
KAGURA STANDS OUT SO MUCH...
IT'S NO SURPRISE.
HE'S SO HANDSOME THAT HE LOOKS LIKE A GOD.
AND PEOPLE NOTICE EVEN MORE BECAUSE HE'S WITH ME...
SHUFF
HM? LETTERS?
THERE ARE TWO...

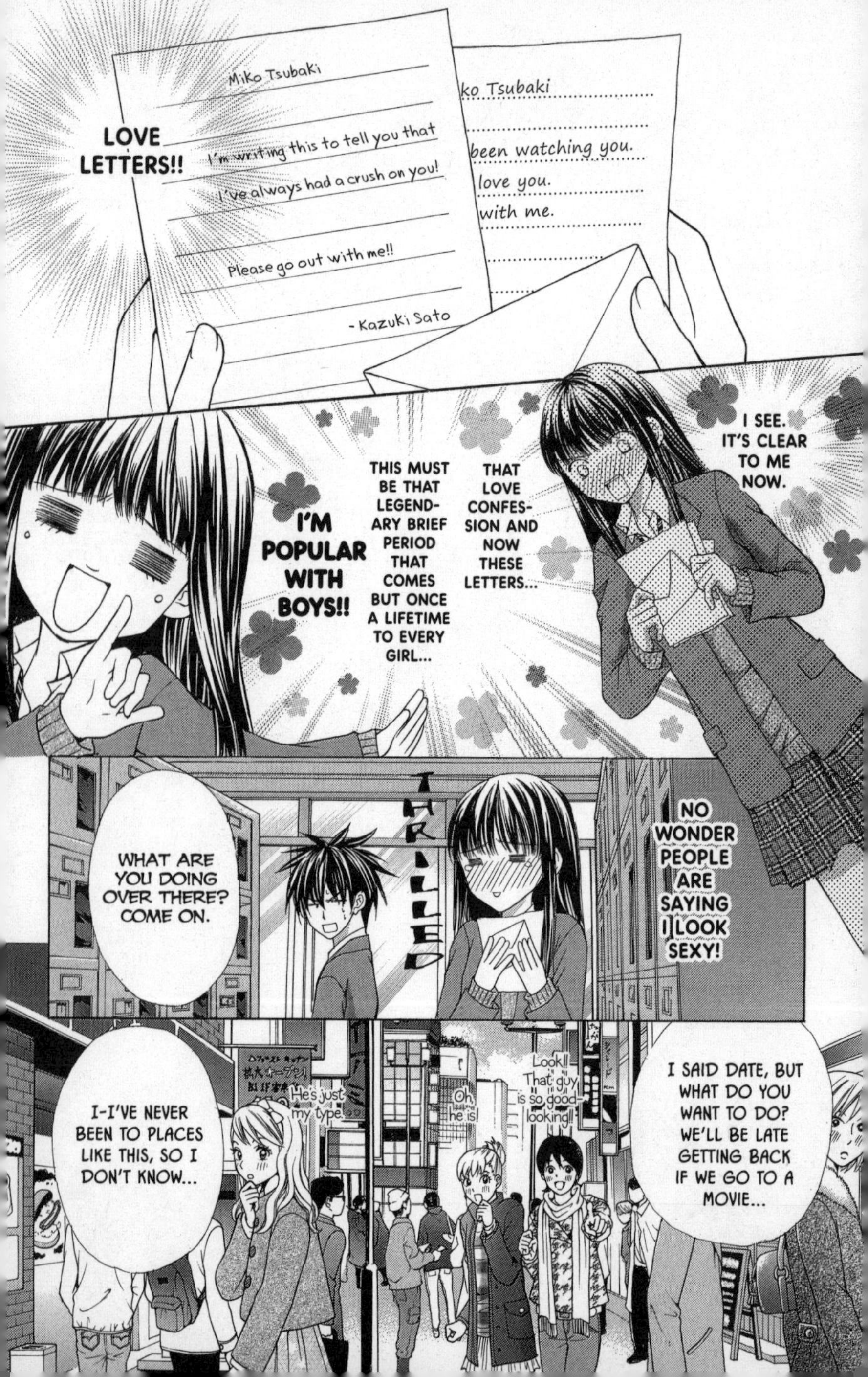
ko Tsubaki
been watching you.
love you.
with me.
Miko Tsubaki
I'm writing this to tell you that
I've always had a crush on you!
Please go out with me!!
- Kazuki Sato
LOVE LETTERS!!
I SEE. IT'S CLEAR TO ME NOW.
THAT LOVE CONFESSION AND NOW THESE LETTERS...
THIS MUST BE THAT LEGENDARY BRIEF PERIOD THAT COMES BUT ONCE A LIFETIME TO EVERY GIRL...
I'M POPULAR WITH BOYS!!
NO WONDER PEOPLE ARE SAYING I LOOK SEXY!
THRILLED
WHAT ARE YOU DOING OVER THERE? COME ON.
I SAID DATE, BUT WHAT DO YOU WANT TO DO? WE'LL BE LATE GETTING BACK IF WE GO TO A MOVIE...
Look!! That guy is so good-looking!!
Oh, he is!
He's just my type.
I-I'VE NEVER BEEN TO PLACES LIKE THIS, SO I DON'T KNOW...

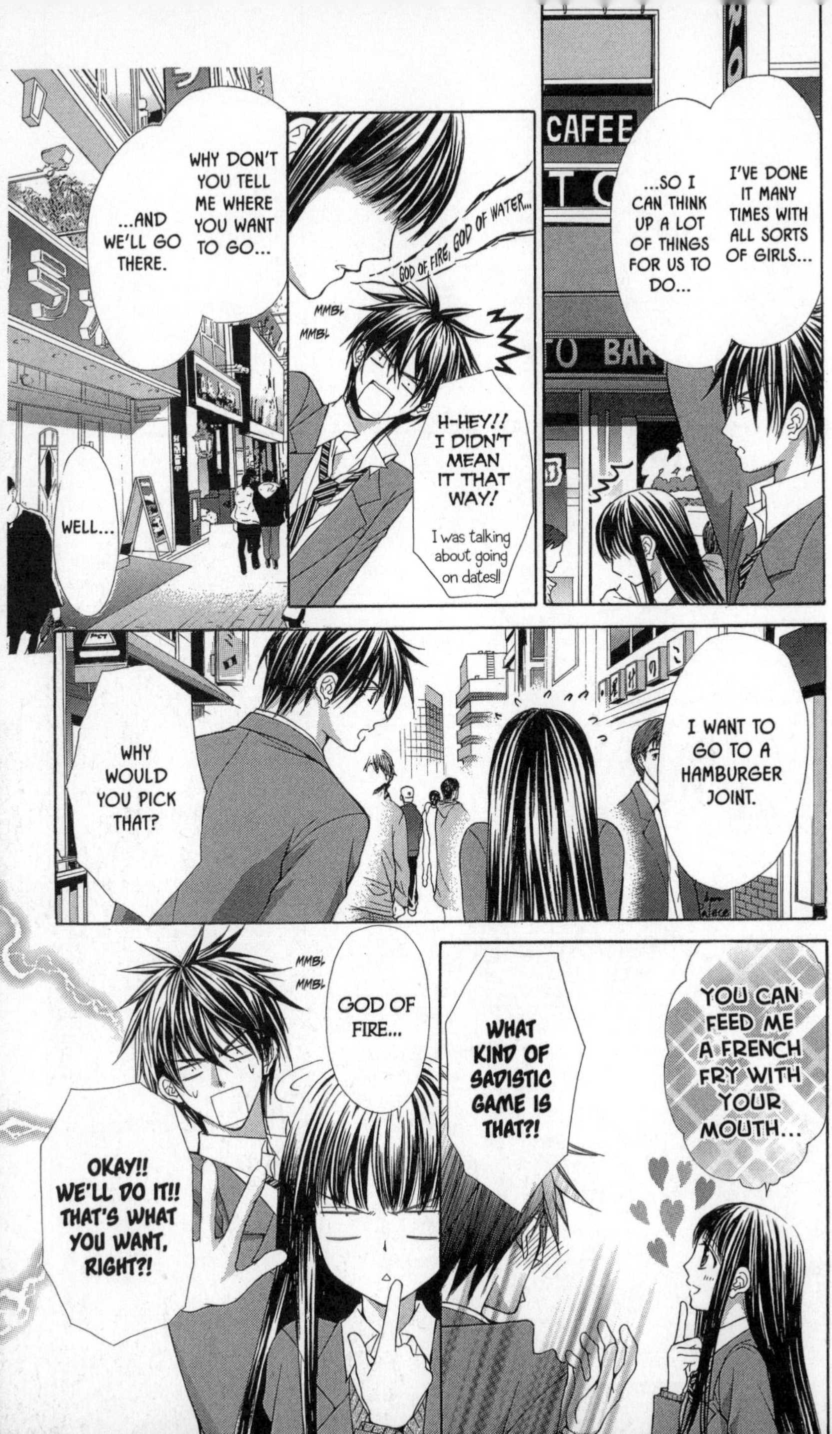
CAFEE
I'VE DONE IT MANY TIMES WITH ALL SORTS OF GIRLS...
...SO I CAN THINK UP A LOT OF THINGS FOR US TO DO...
GOD OF FIRE, GOD OF WATER...
MMBL MMBL
H-HEY!! I DIDN'T MEAN IT THAT WAY!
I was talking about going on dates!!
WHY DON'T YOU TELL ME WHERE YOU WANT TO GO...
...AND WE'LL GO THERE.
WELL...
I WANT TO GO TO A HAMBURGER JOINT.
WHY WOULD YOU PICK THAT?
YOU CAN FEED ME A FRENCH FRY WITH YOUR MOUTH...
WHAT KIND OF SADISTIC GAME IS THAT?!
GOD OF FIRE...
MMBL MMBL
OKAY!! WE'LL DO IT!! THAT'S WHAT YOU WANT, RIGHT?!

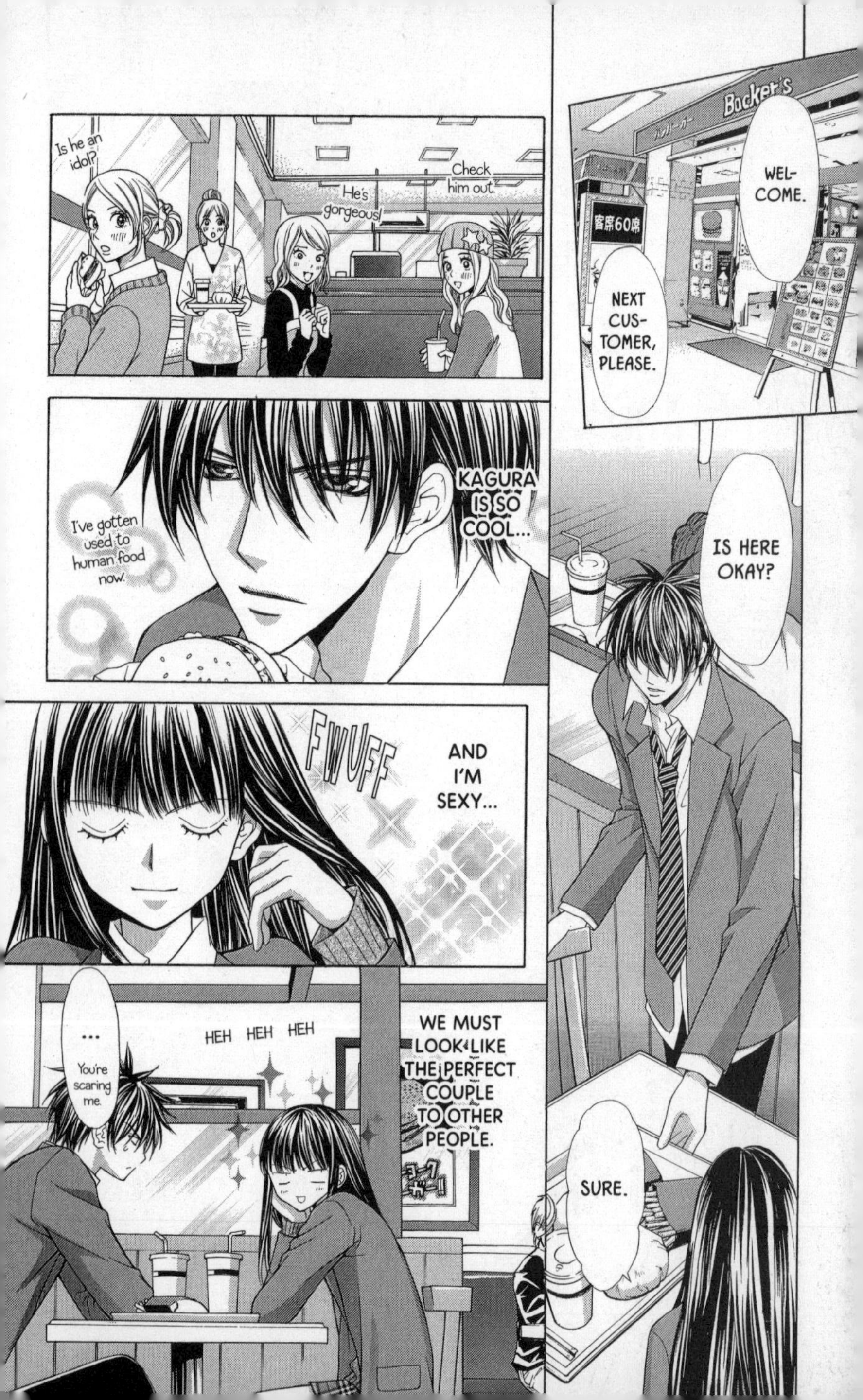

Backer's
客席60席
WEL-COME.
NEXT CUS-TOMER, PLEASE.
IS HERE OKAY?
SURE.
Is he an idol?
Check him out.
He's gorgeous!
KAGURA IS SO COOL...
I've gotten used to human food now.
FWUFF
AND I'M SEXY...
WE MUST LOOK LIKE THE PERFECT COUPLE TO OTHER PEOPLE.
HEH HEH HEH
... You're scaring me.

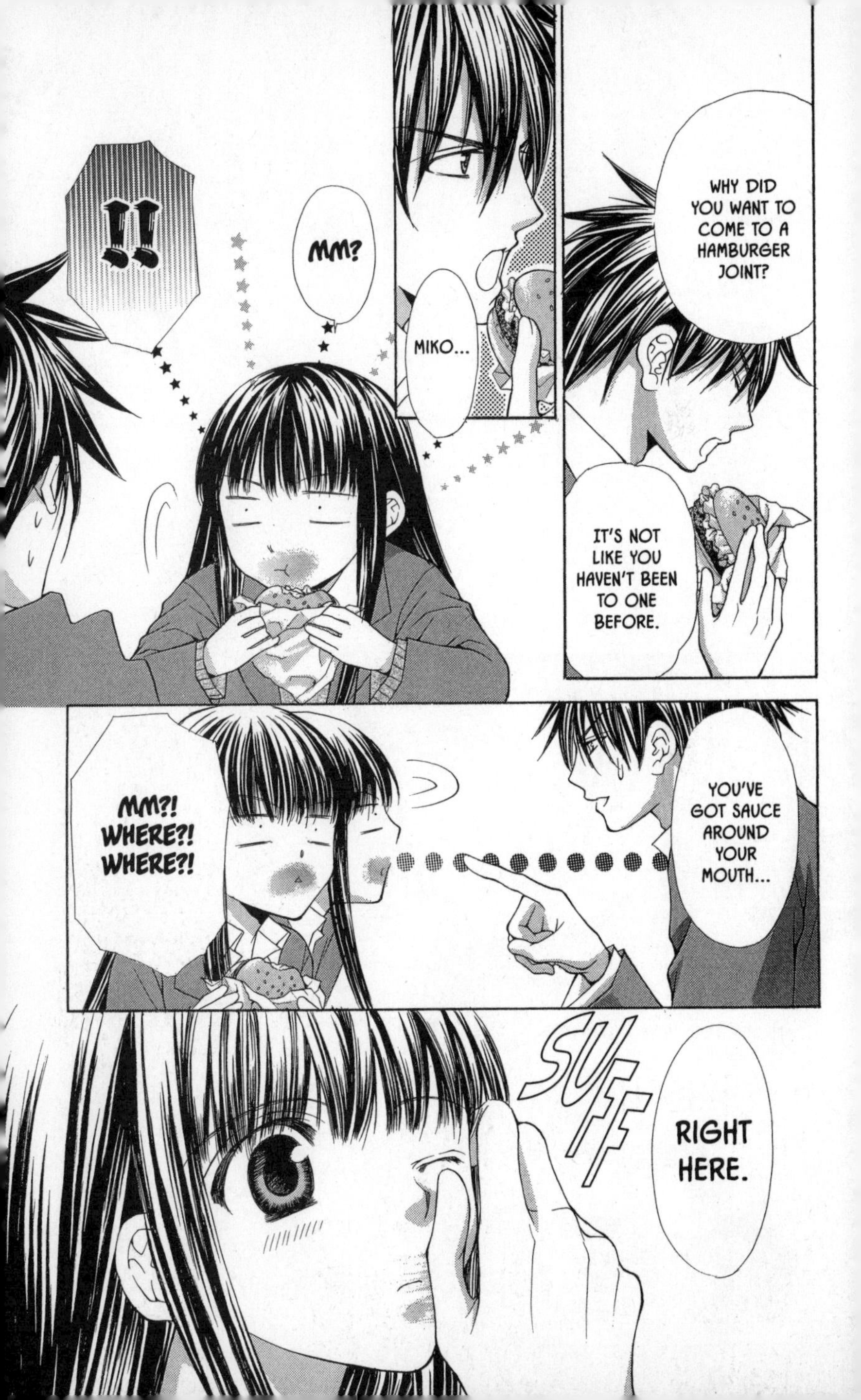
WHY DID YOU WANT TO COME TO A HAMBURGER JOINT?
IT'S NOT LIKE YOU HAVEN'T BEEN TO ONE BEFORE.
MIKO...
MM?
!!
YOU'VE GOT SAUCE AROUND YOUR MOUTH...
MM?! WHERE?! WHERE?!
SUFF
RIGHT HERE.

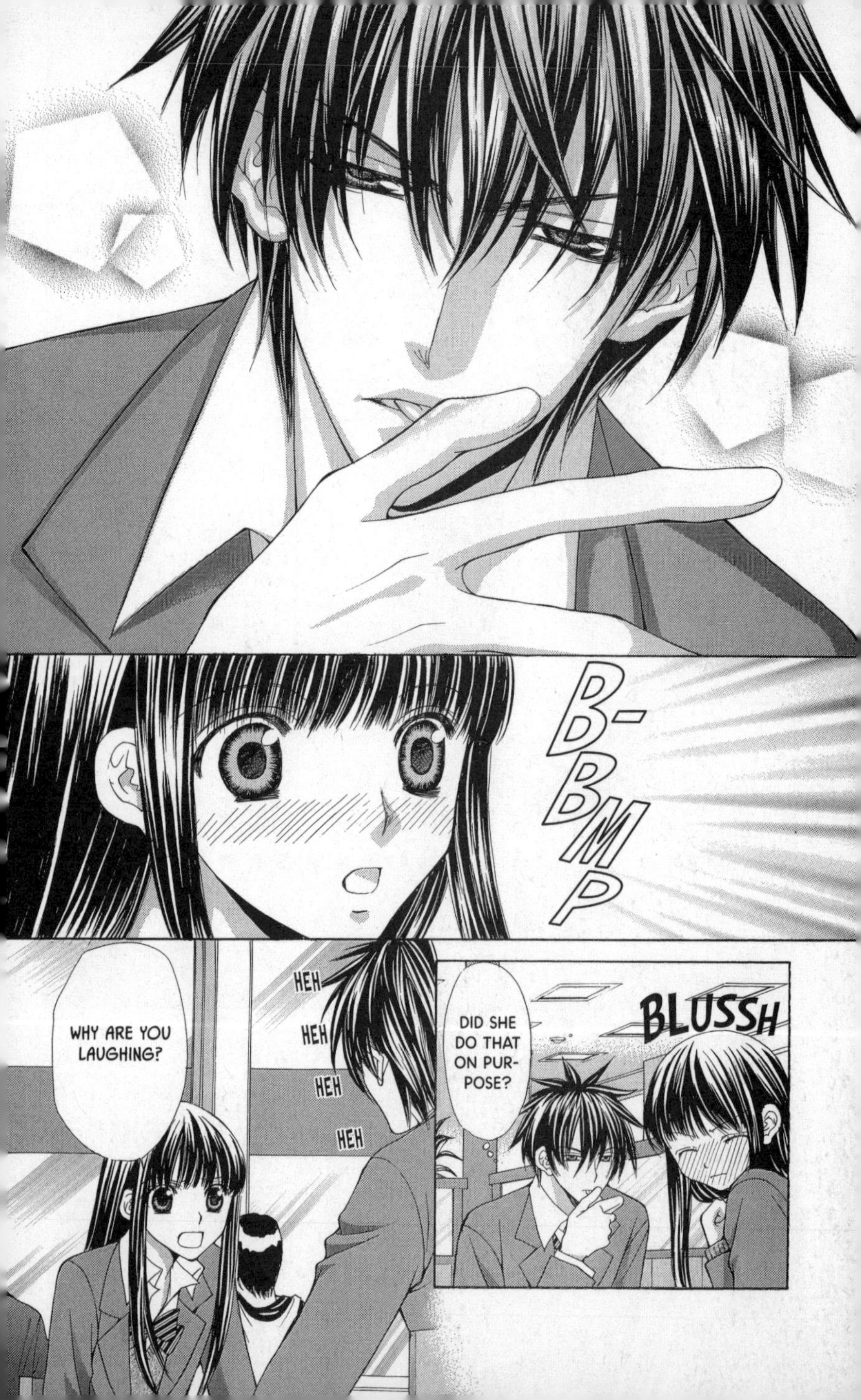
B-BMP
BLUSSH
DID SHE DO THAT ON PUR-POSE?
HEH HEH HEH HEH
WHY ARE YOU LAUGHING?

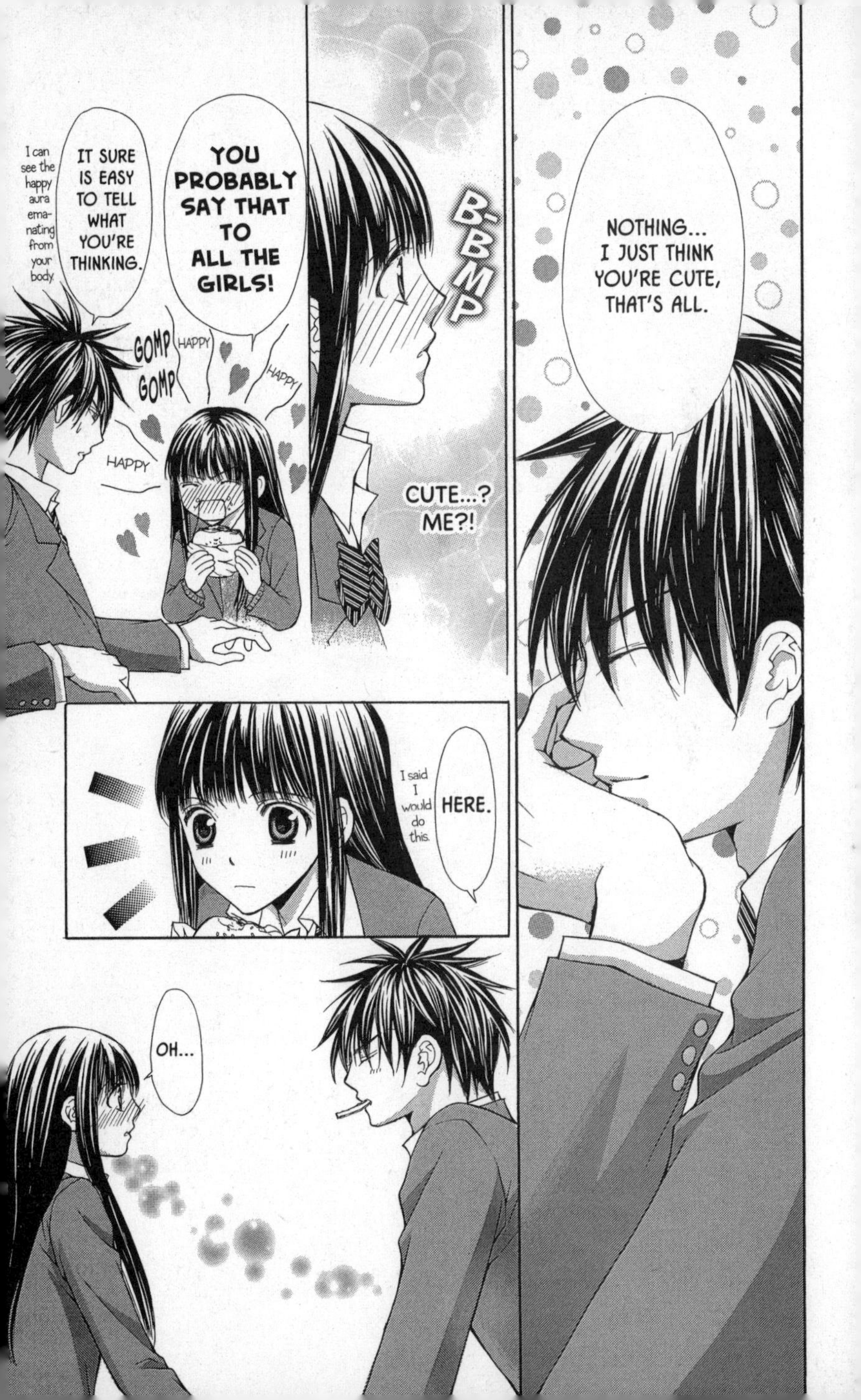
NOTHING... I JUST THINK YOU'RE CUTE, THAT'S ALL.
B-BMP
CUTE...? ME?!
YOU PROBABLY SAY THAT TO ALL THE GIRLS!
HAPPY
HAPPY
HAPPY
GOMP GOMP
IT SURE IS EASY TO TELL WHAT YOU'RE THINKING.
I can see the happy aura ema-nating from your body.
HERE.
I said I would do this.
OH...

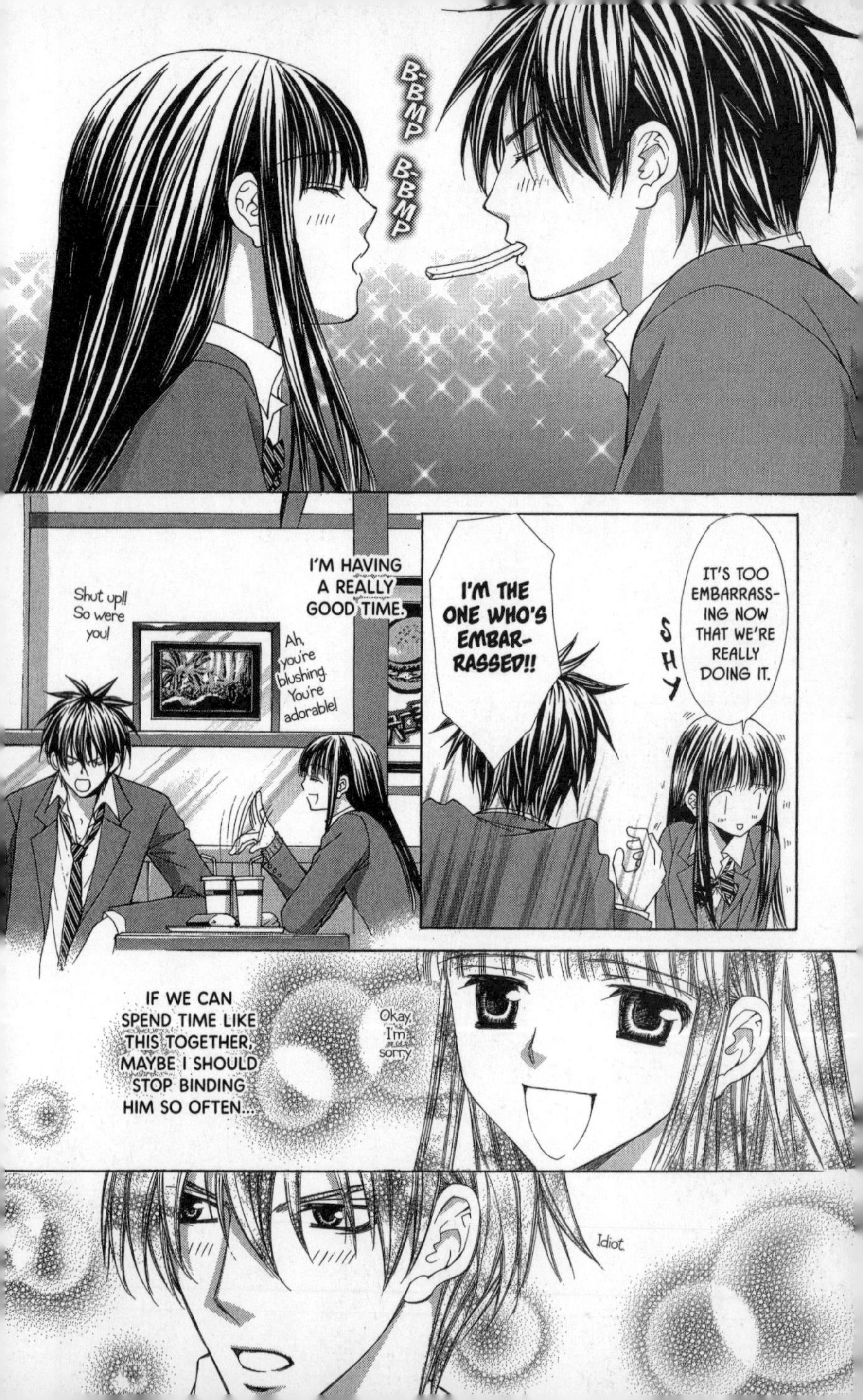
B-BMP B-BMP
IT'S TOO EMBARRASSING NOW THAT WE'RE REALLY DOING IT.
SHY
I'M THE ONE WHO'S EMBARRASSED!!
I'M HAVING A REALLY GOOD TIME.
Ah, you're blushing. You're adorable!
Shut up!! So were you!
Okay. I'm sorry
IF WE CAN SPEND TIME LIKE THIS TOGETHER, MAYBE I SHOULD STOP BINDING HIM SO OFTEN...
Idiot.

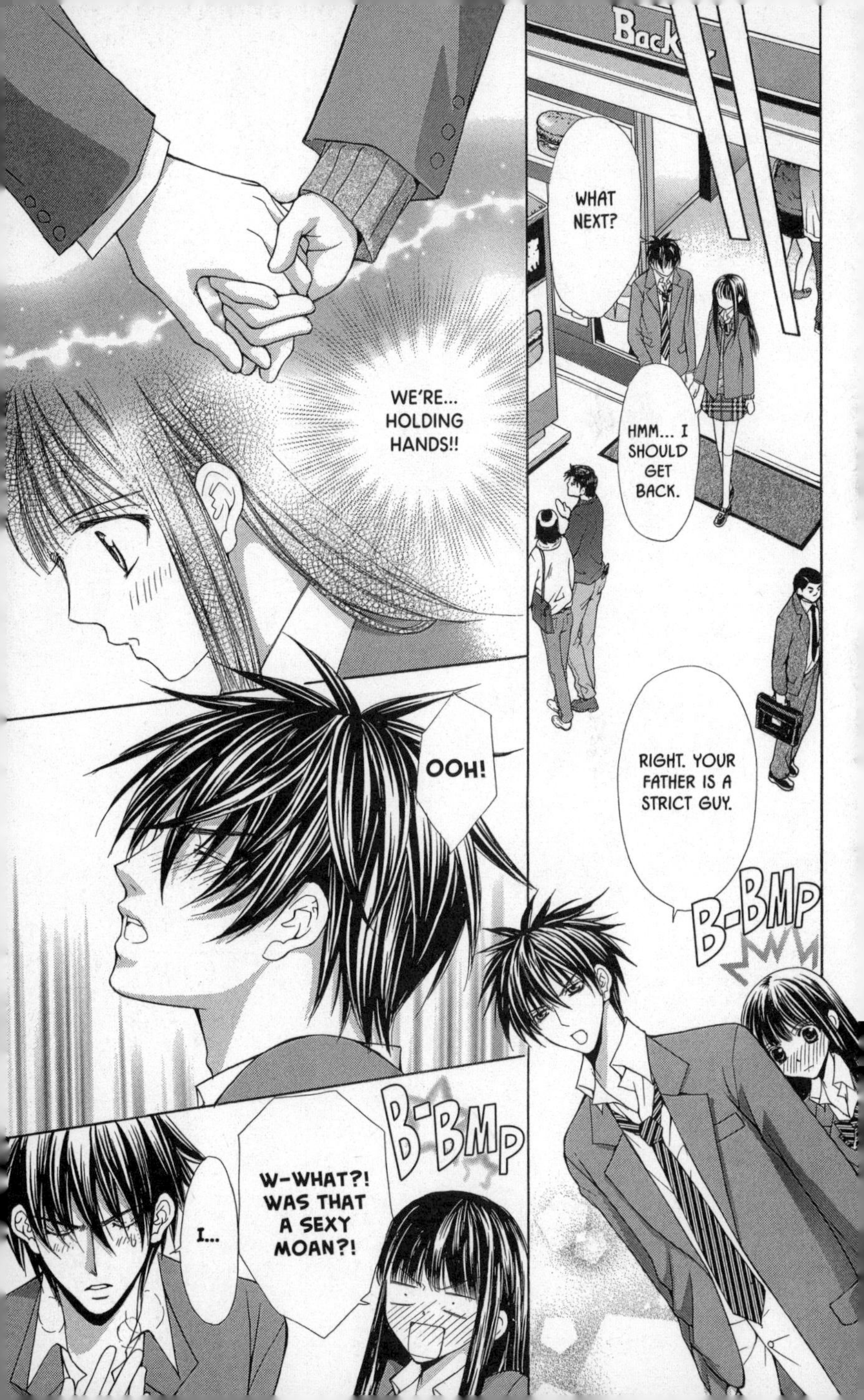
Back
WHAT NEXT?
HMM... I SHOULD GET BACK.
RIGHT. YOUR FATHER IS A STRICT GUY.
B-BMP
WE'RE... HOLDING HANDS!!
OOH!
B-BMP
W-WHAT?! WAS THAT A SEXY MOAN?!
I...

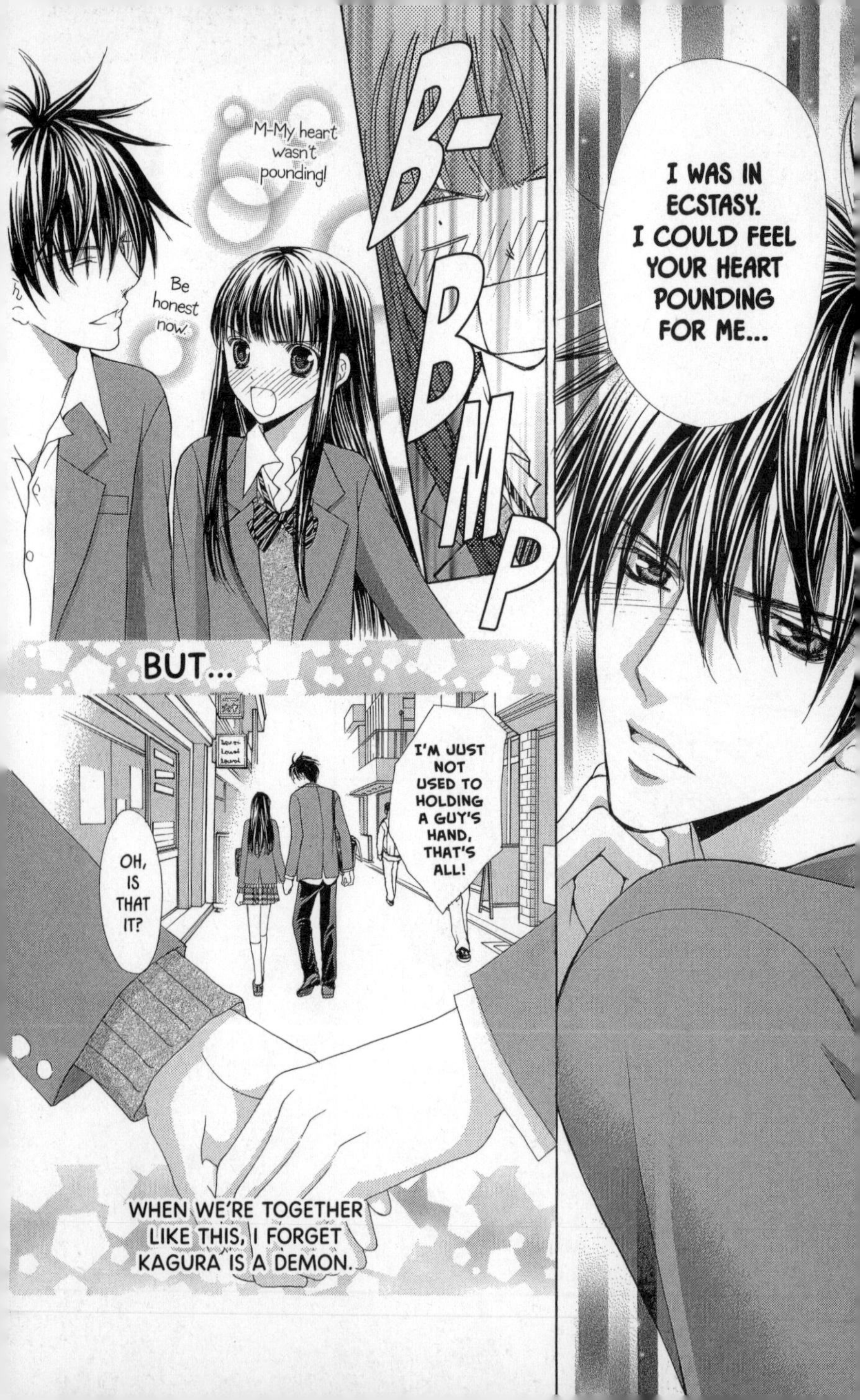
I WAS IN ECSTASY. I COULD FEEL YOUR HEART POUNDING FOR ME...
B-BMP
M-My heart wasn't pounding!
Be honest now.
BUT...
I'M JUST NOT USED TO HOLDING A GUY'S HAND, THAT'S ALL!
OH, IS THAT IT?
WHEN WE'RE TOGETHER LIKE THIS, I FORGET KAGURA IS A DEMON.

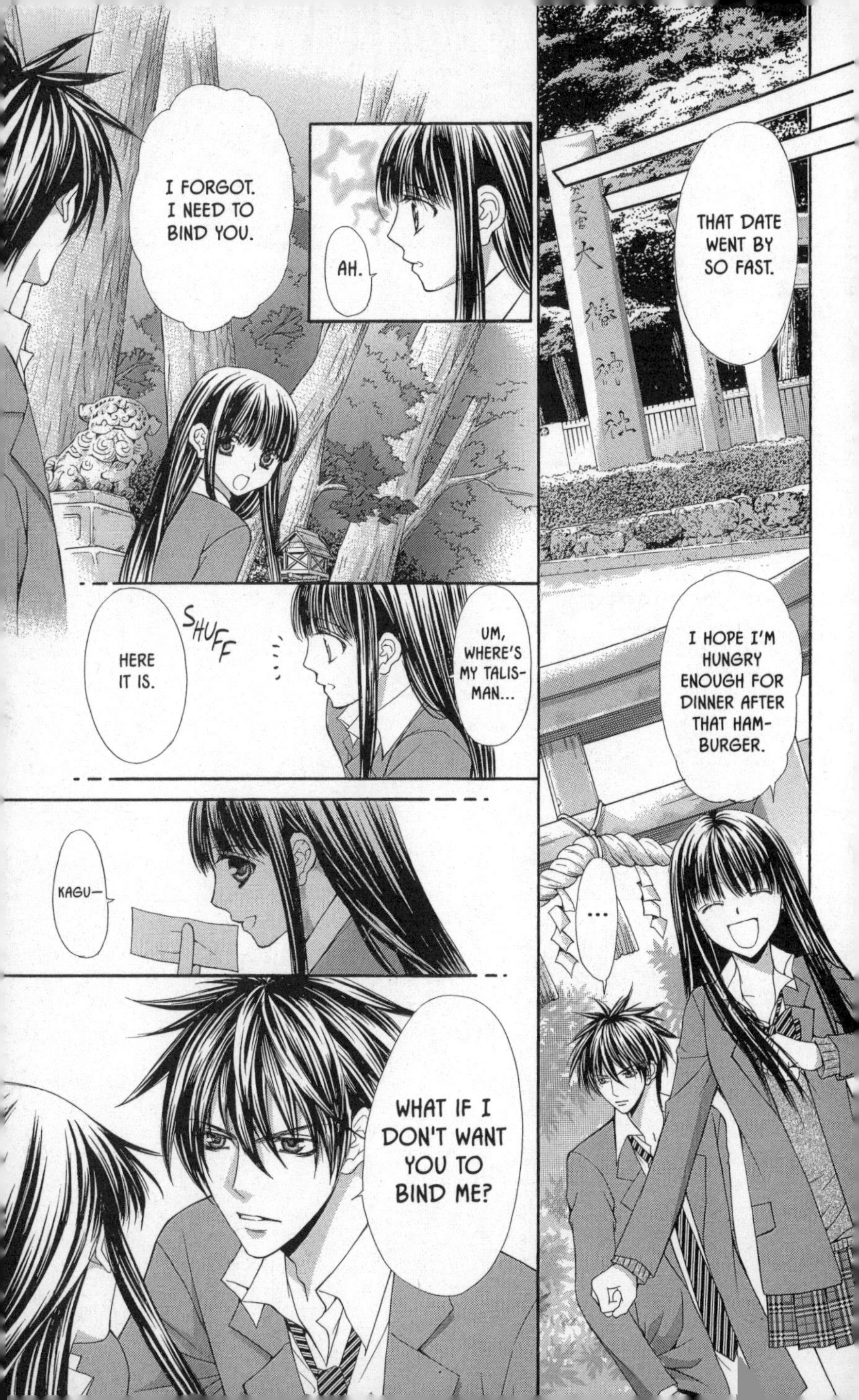
THAT DATE WENT BY SO FAST.
I HOPE I'M HUNGRY ENOUGH FOR DINNER AFTER THAT HAMBURGER.
...
AH.
I FORGOT. I NEED TO BIND YOU.
UM, WHERE'S MY TALISMAN...
SHUFF
HERE IT IS.
KAGU—
WHAT IF I DON'T WANT YOU TO BIND ME?

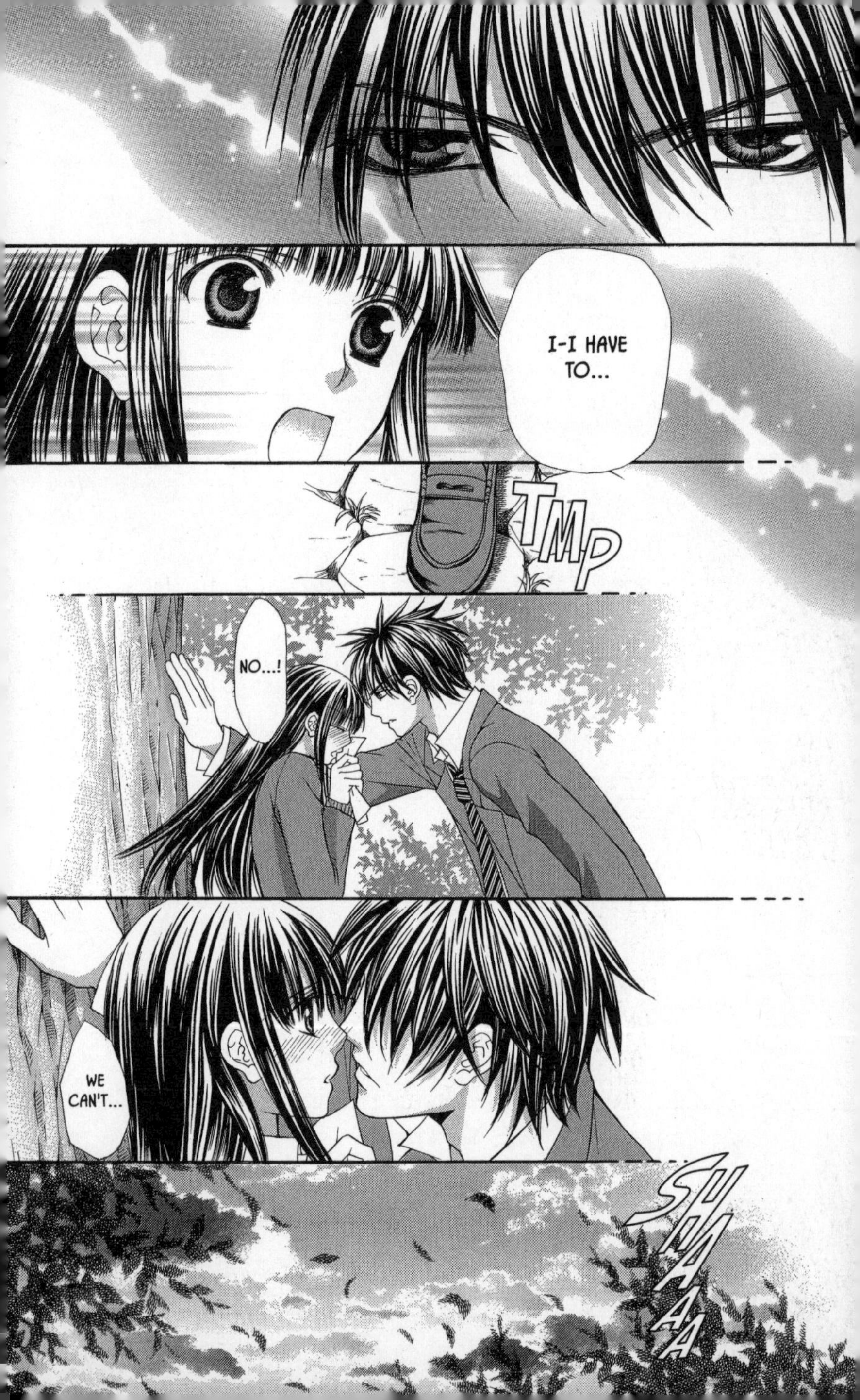
I-I HAVE TO...
TMP
NO...!
WE CAN'T...
SHAAAA

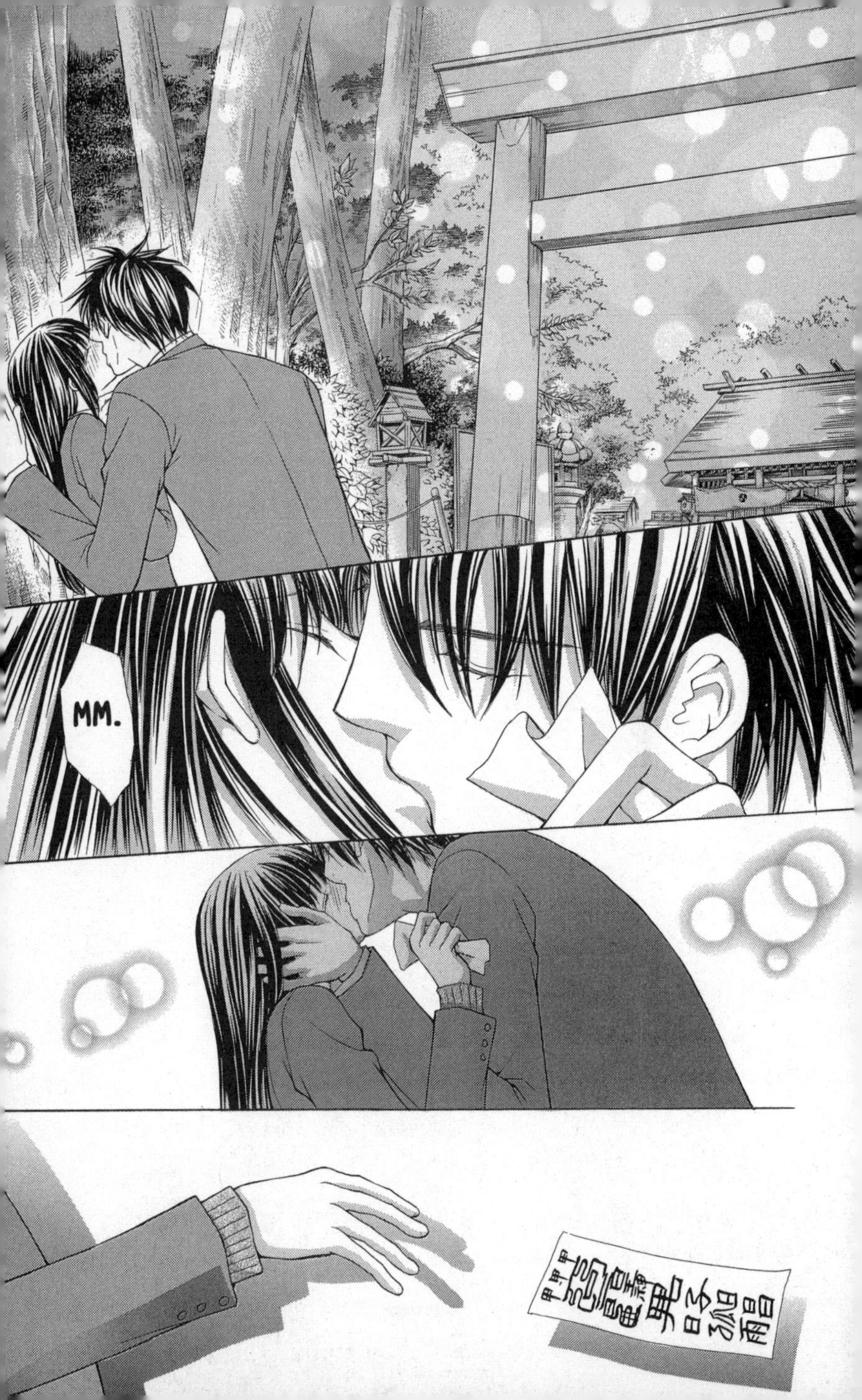
MM.

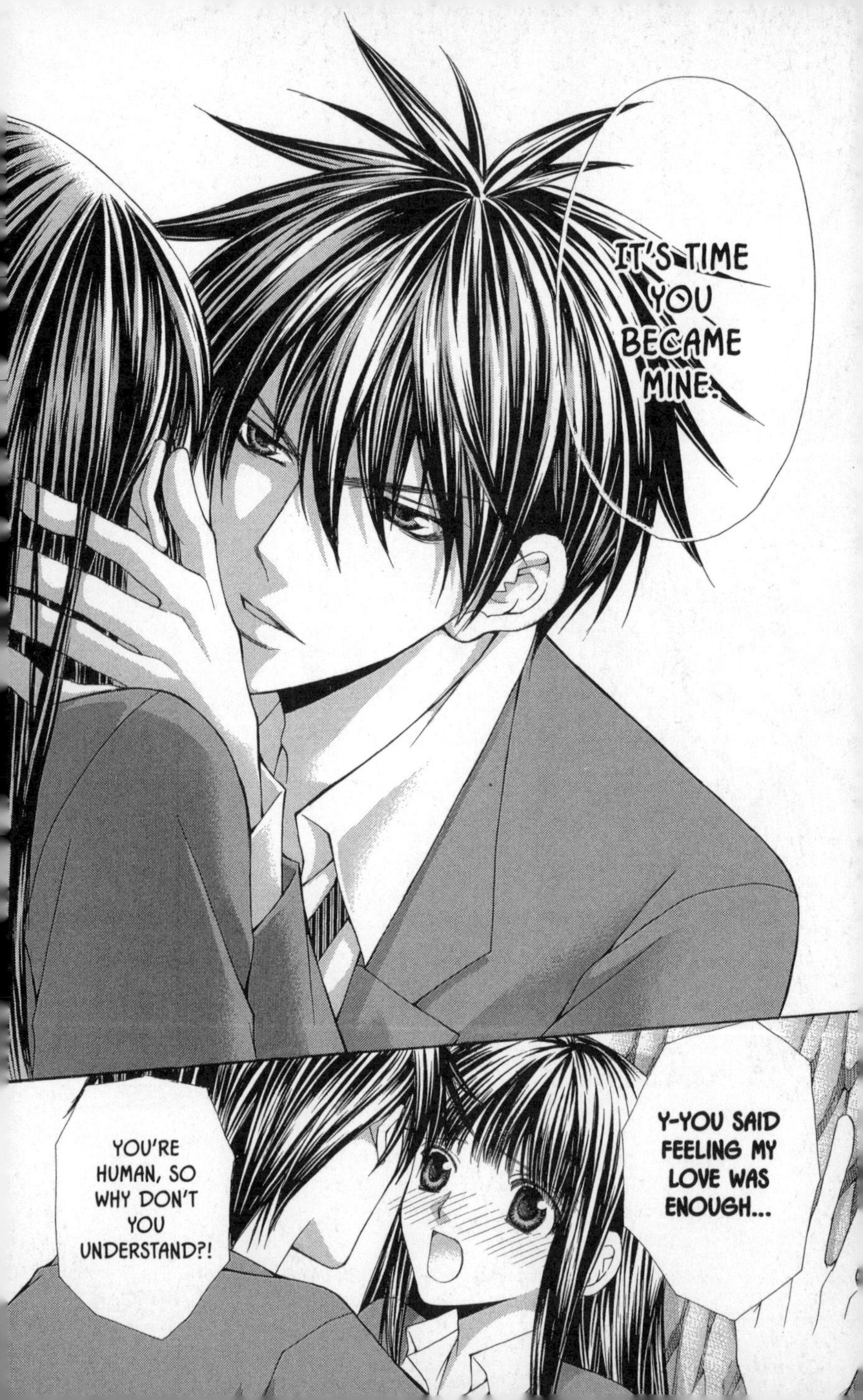
IT'S TIME YOU BECAME MINE.
Y-YOU SAID FEELING MY LOVE WAS ENOUGH...
YOU'RE HUMAN, SO WHY DON'T YOU UNDERSTAND?!

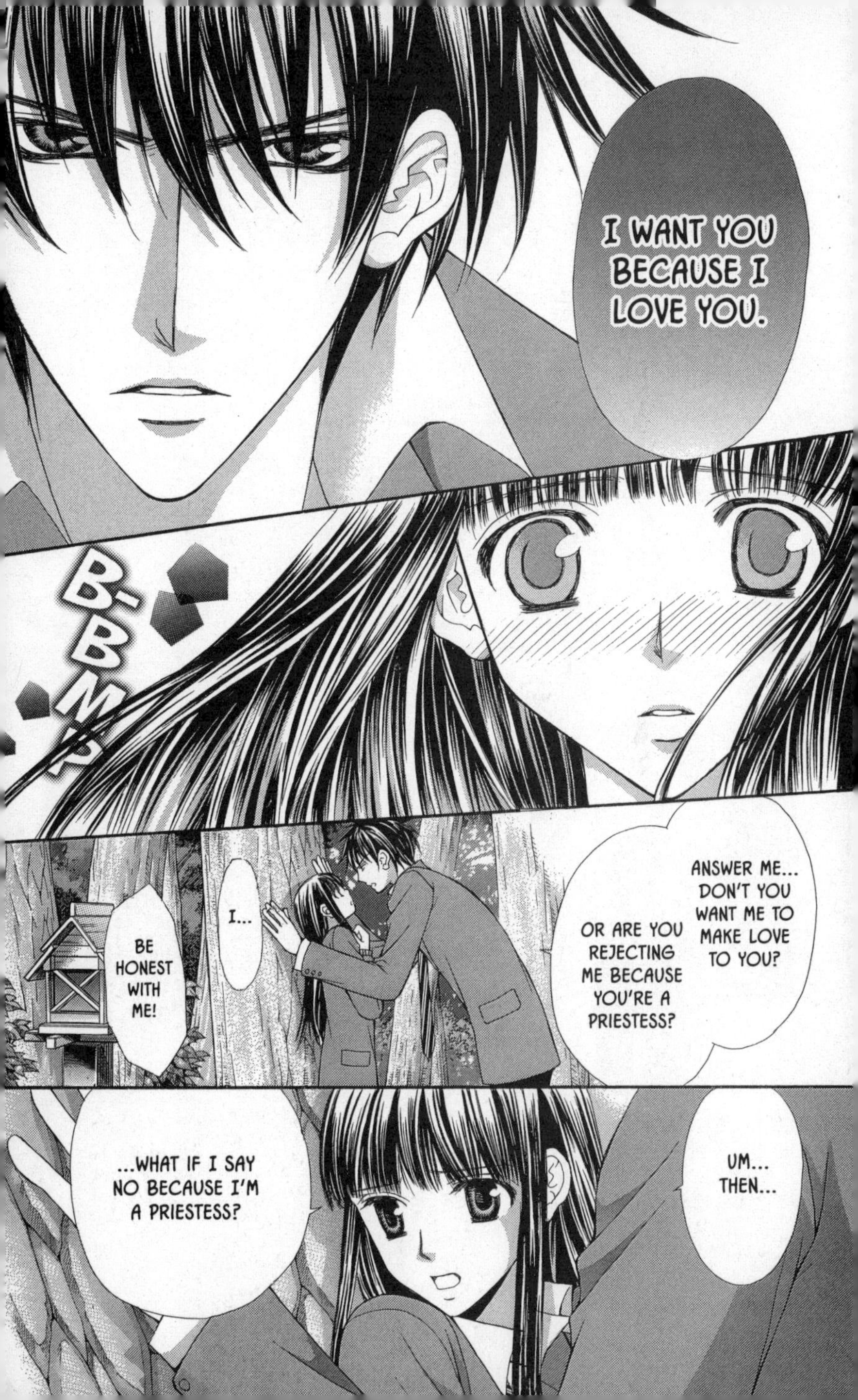
I WANT YOU BECAUSE I LOVE YOU.
B-BMP
ANSWER ME... DON'T YOU WANT ME TO MAKE LOVE TO YOU?
OR ARE YOU REJECTING ME BECAUSE YOU'RE A PRIESTESS?
I...
BE HONEST WITH ME!
UM... THEN...
...WHAT IF I SAY NO BECAUSE I'M A PRIESTESS?

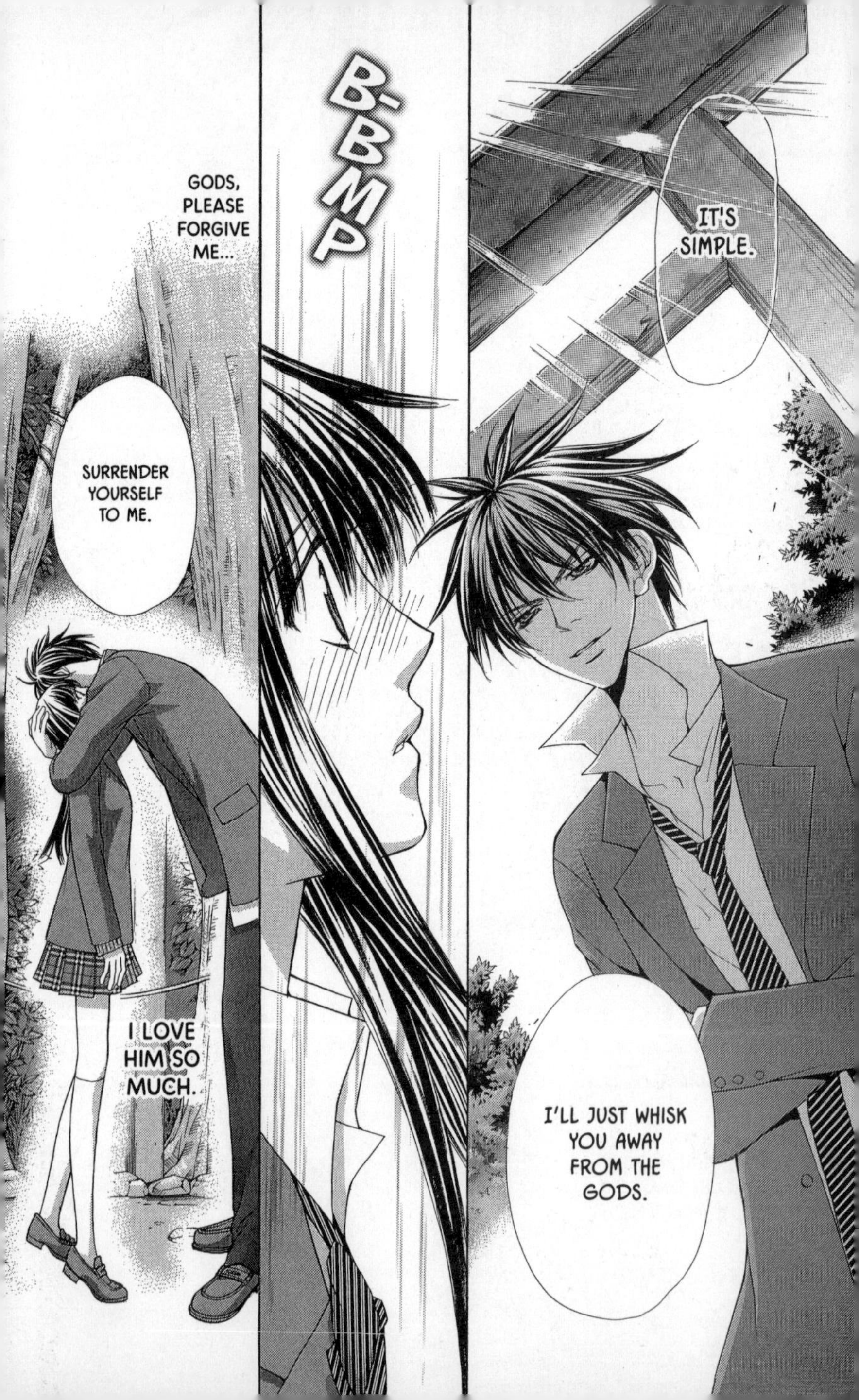
IT'S SIMPLE.
I'LL JUST WHISK YOU AWAY FROM THE GODS.
B-BMP
GODS, PLEASE FORGIVE ME...
SURRENDER YOURSELF TO ME.
I LOVE HIM SO MUCH.

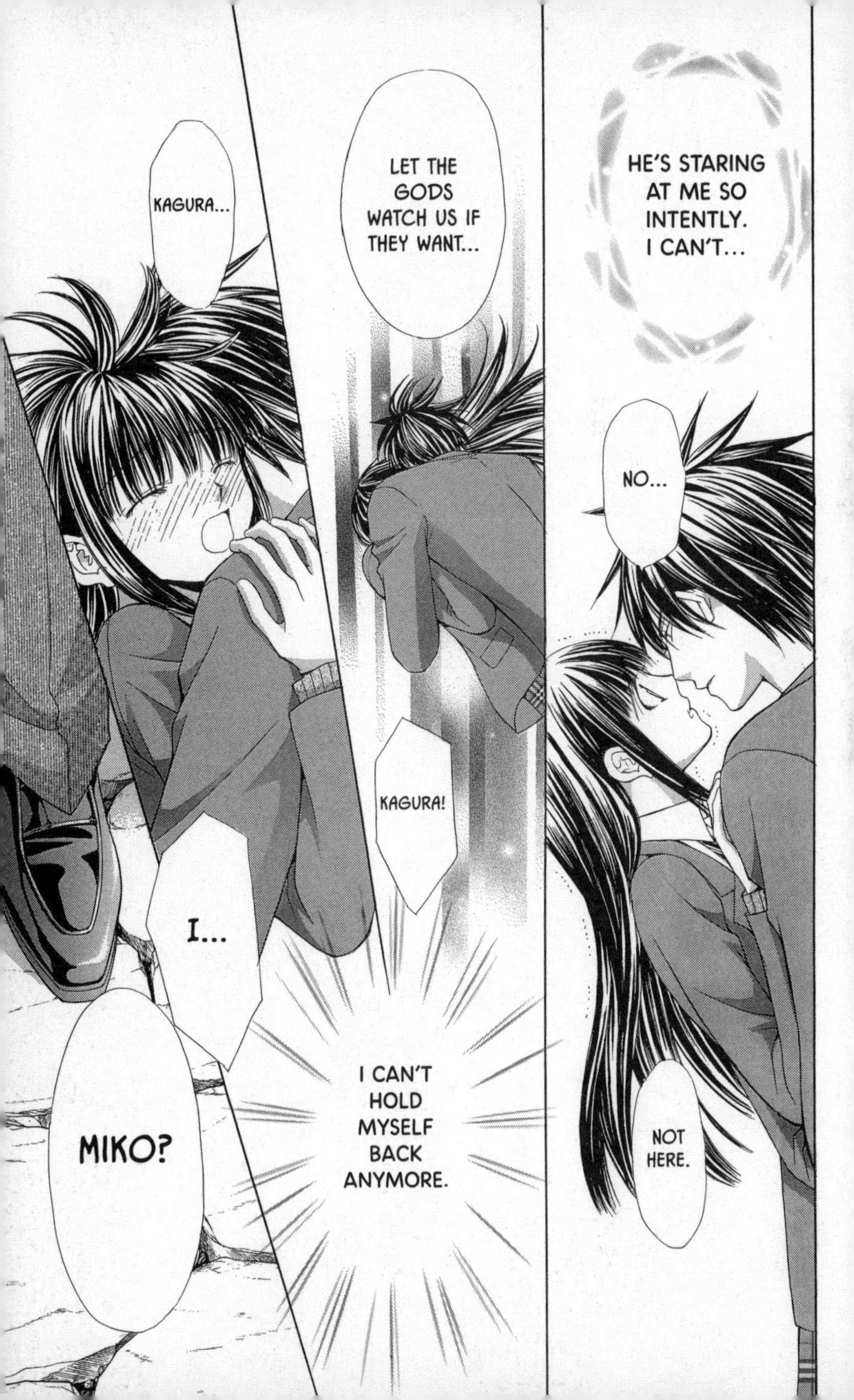
HE'S STARING AT ME SO INTENTLY. I CAN'T...
NO...
NOT HERE.
LET THE GODS WATCH US IF THEY WANT...
KAGURA!
I CAN'T HOLD MYSELF BACK ANYMORE.
KAGURA...
I...
MIKO?

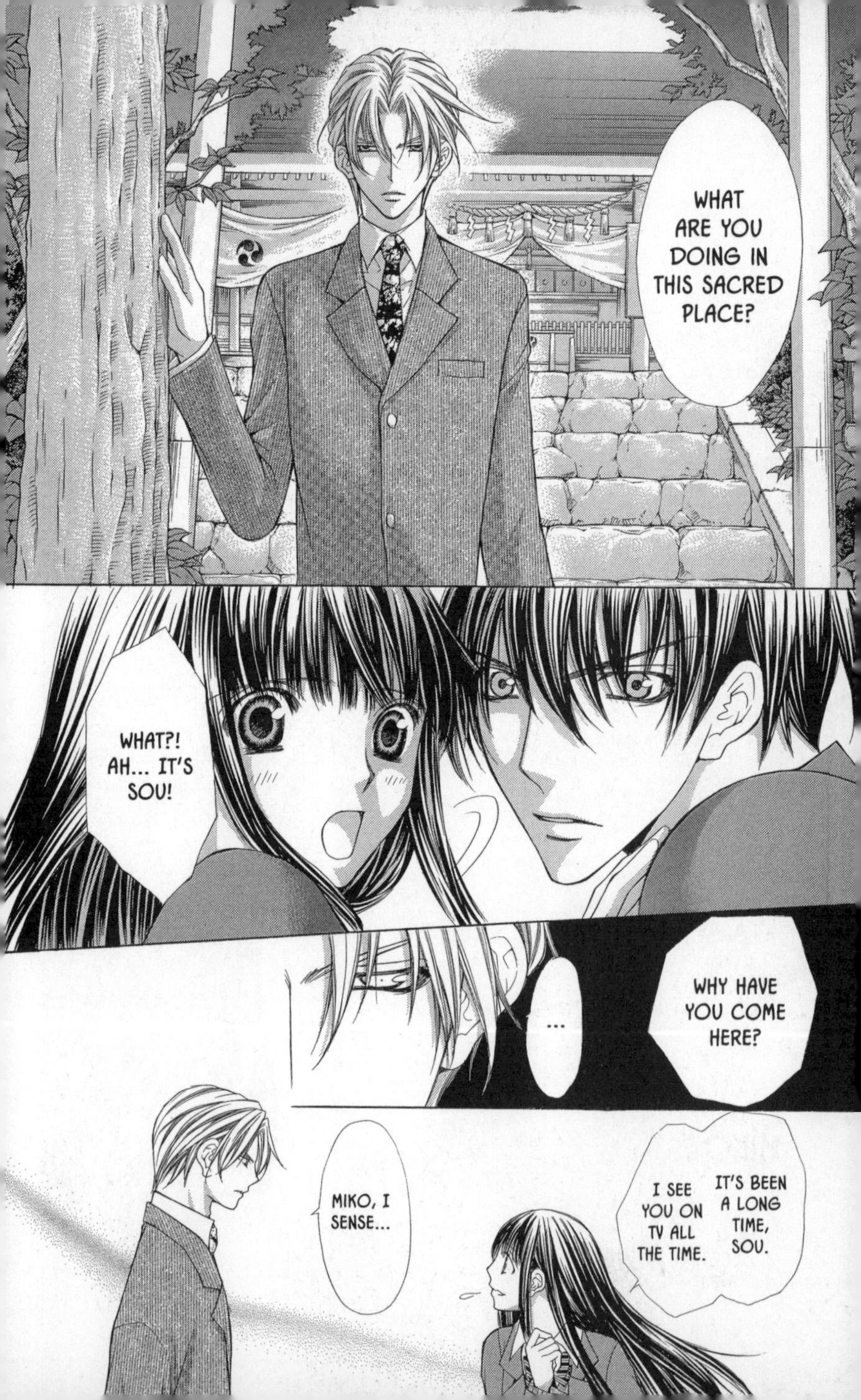
WHAT ARE YOU DOING IN THIS SACRED PLACE?
WHAT?! AH... IT'S SOU!
WHY HAVE YOU COME HERE?
...
IT'S BEEN A LONG TIME, SOU.
I SEE YOU ON TV ALL THE TIME.
MIKO, I SENSE...

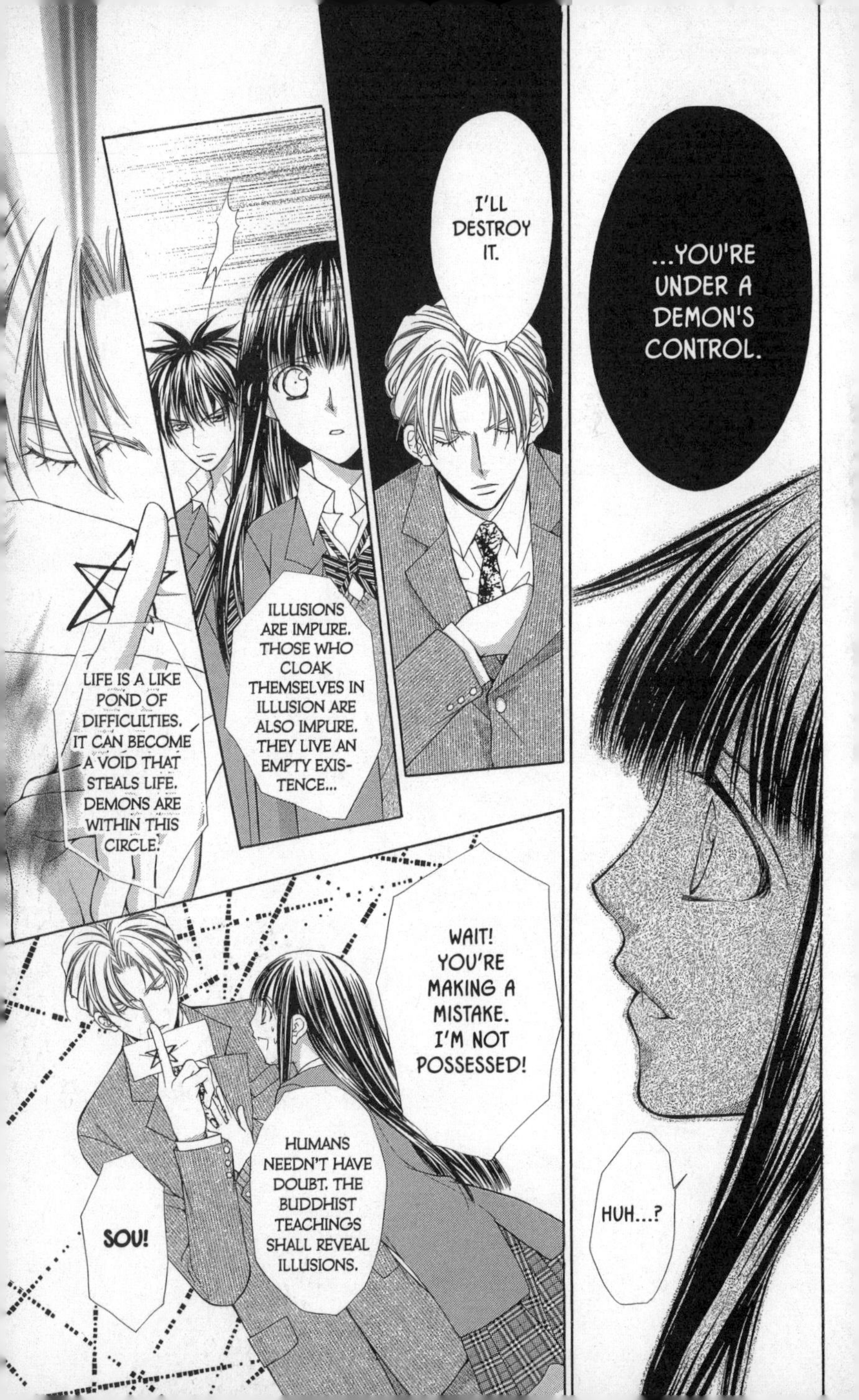
...YOU'RE UNDER A DEMON'S CONTROL.
HUH...?
I'LL DESTROY IT.
ILLUSIONS ARE IMPURE. THOSE WHO CLOAK THEMSELVES IN ILLUSION ARE ALSO IMPURE. THEY LIVE AN EMPTY EXISTENCE...
LIFE IS A LIKE POND OF DIFFICULTIES. IT CAN BECOME A VOID THAT STEALS LIFE. DEMONS ARE WITHIN THIS CIRCLE.
WAIT! YOU'RE MAKING A MISTAKE. I'M NOT POSSESSED!
HUMANS NEEDN'T HAVE DOUBT. THE BUDDHIST TEACHINGS SHALL REVEAL ILLUSIONS.
SOU!

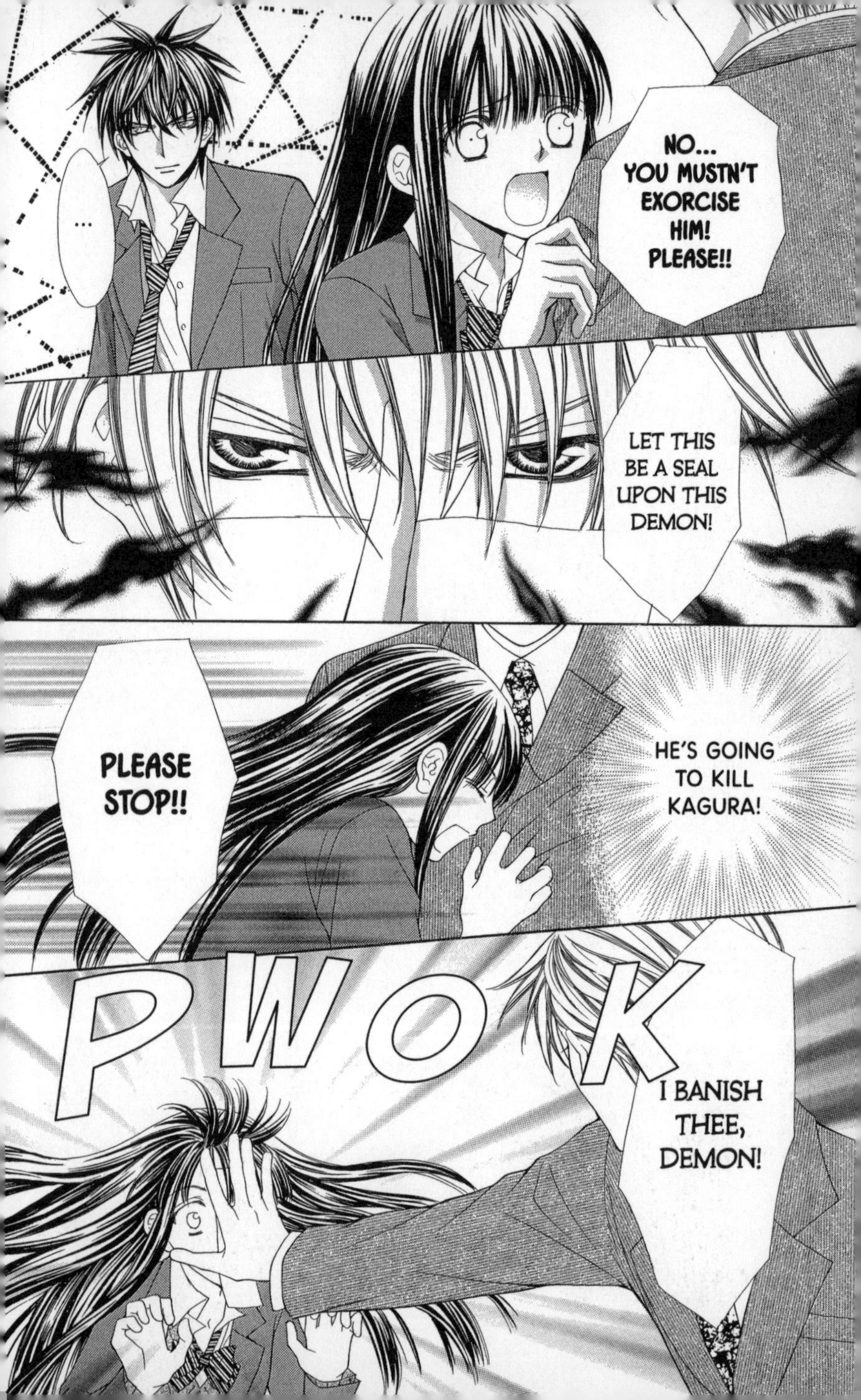
NO... YOU MUSTN'T EXORCISE HIM! PLEASE!!
...
LET THIS BE A SEAL UPON THIS DEMON!
HE'S GOING TO KILL KAGURA!
PLEASE STOP!!
PWOK
I BANISH THEE, DEMON!

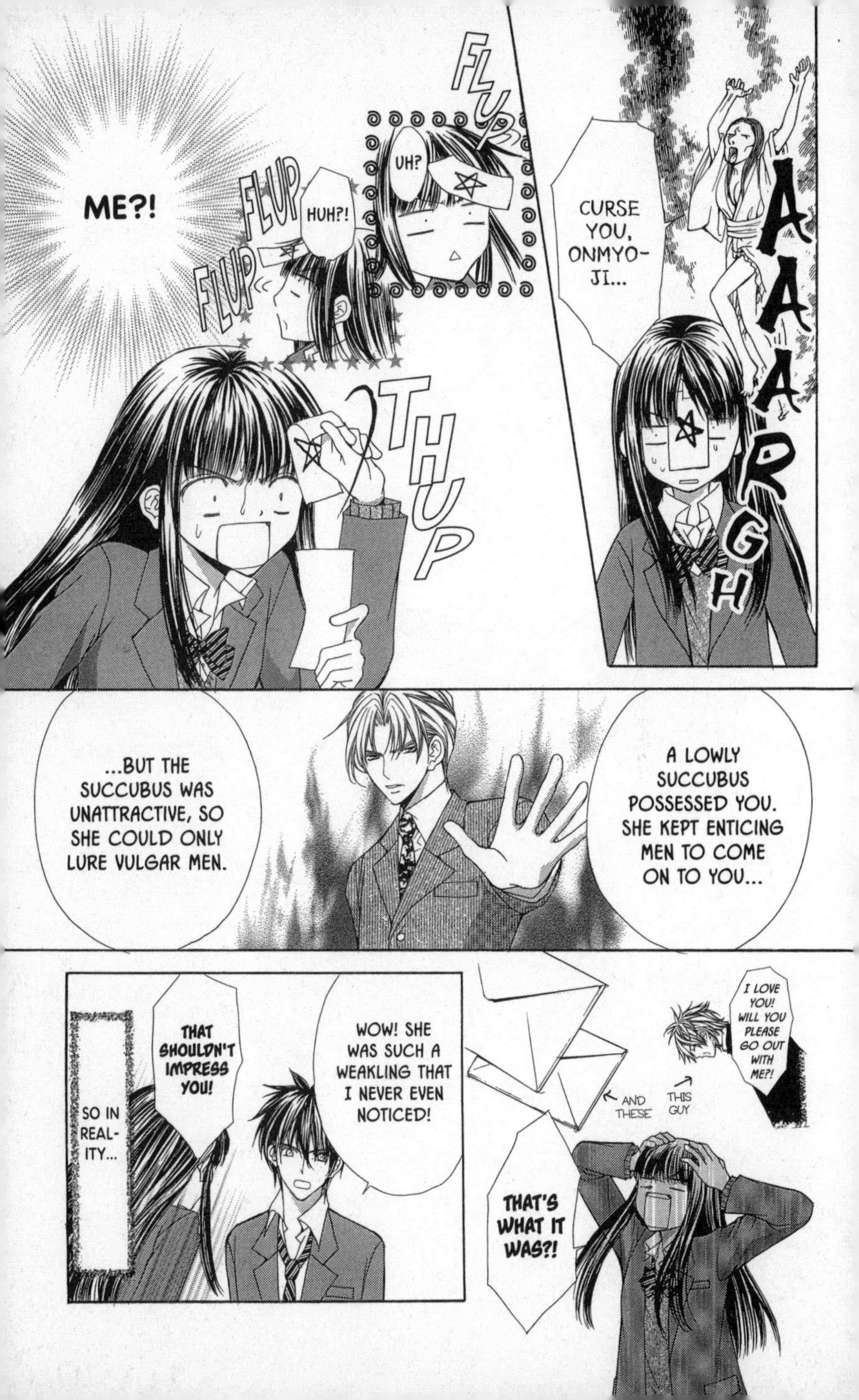
CURSE YOU, ONMYO-JI...
AAARGH
FLUP
UH?
HUH?!
FLUP FLUP
THUP
ME?!
A LOWLY SUCCUBUS POSSESSED YOU. SHE KEPT ENTICING MEN TO COME ON TO YOU...
...BUT THE SUCCUBUS WAS UNATTRACTIVE, SO SHE COULD ONLY LURE VULGAR MEN.
I LOVE YOU! WILL YOU PLEASE GO OUT WITH ME?!
THIS GUY
AND THESE
THAT'S WHAT IT WAS?!
WOW! SHE WAS SUCH A WEAKLING THAT I NEVER EVEN NOTICED!
THAT SHOULDN'T IMPRESS YOU!
SO IN REALITY...

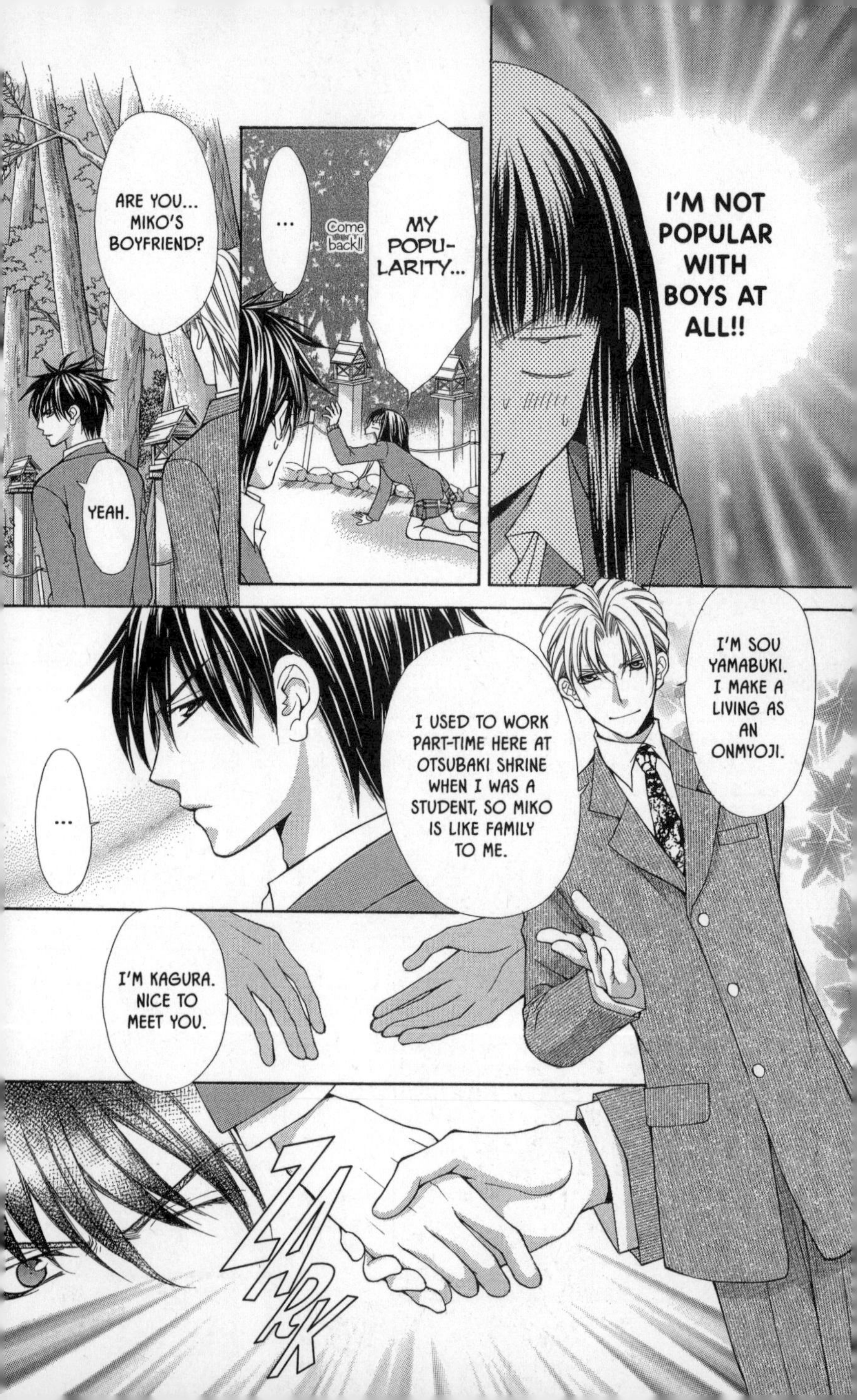
I'M NOT POPULAR WITH BOYS AT ALL!!
MY POPU-LARITY...
Come back!!
...
ARE YOU... MIKO'S BOYFRIEND?
YEAH.
I'M SOU YAMABUKI. I MAKE A LIVING AS AN ONMYOJI.
I USED TO WORK PART-TIME HERE AT OTSUBAKI SHRINE WHEN I WAS A STUDENT, SO MIKO IS LIKE FAMILY TO ME.
...
I'M KAGURA. NICE TO MEET YOU.
ZARK

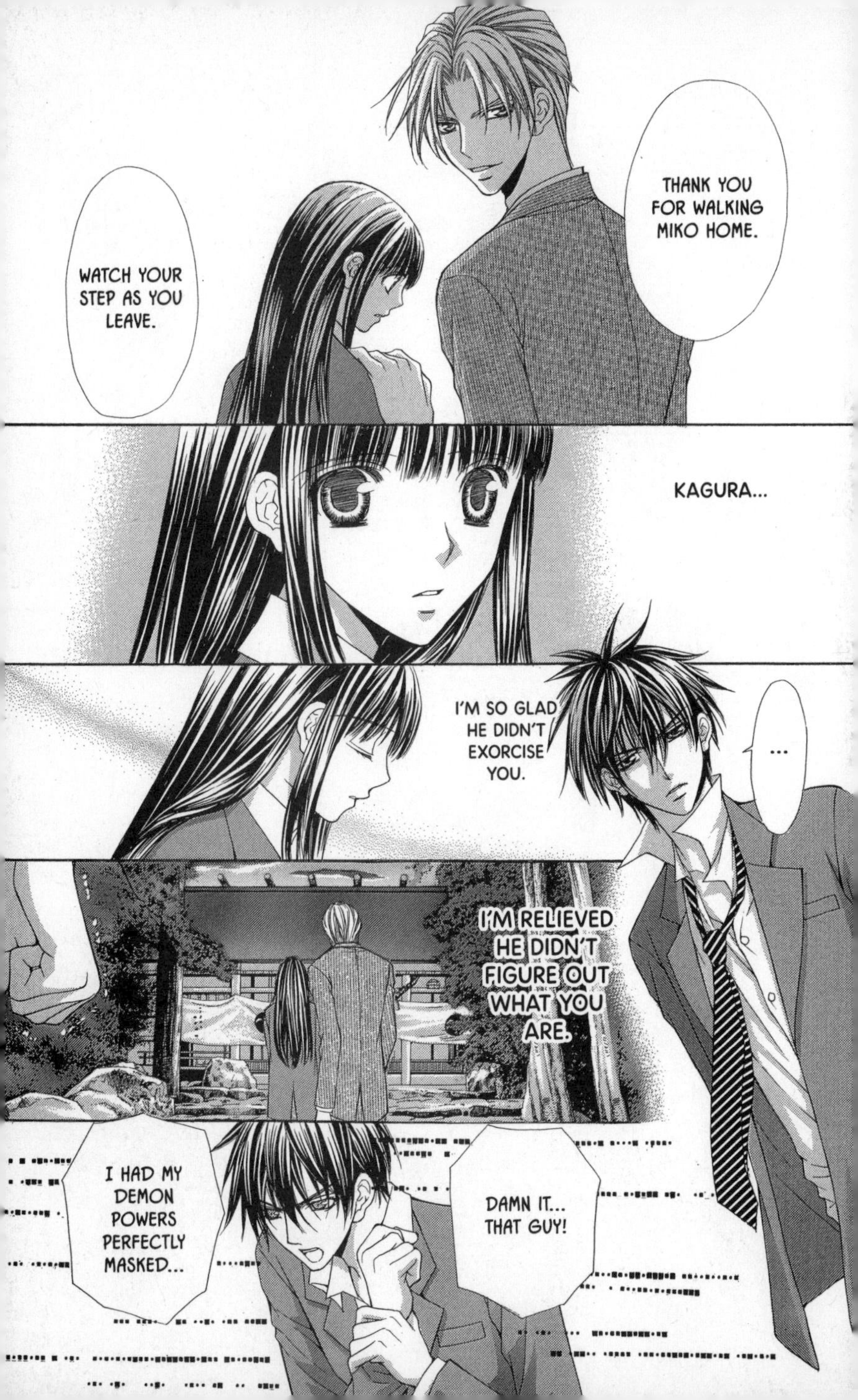
THANK YOU FOR WALKING MIKO HOME.
WATCH YOUR STEP AS YOU LEAVE.
KAGURA...
...
I'M SO GLAD HE DIDN'T EXORCISE YOU.
I'M RELIEVED HE DIDN'T FIGURE OUT WHAT YOU ARE.
DAMN IT... THAT GUY!
I HAD MY DEMON POWERS PERFECTLY MASKED...

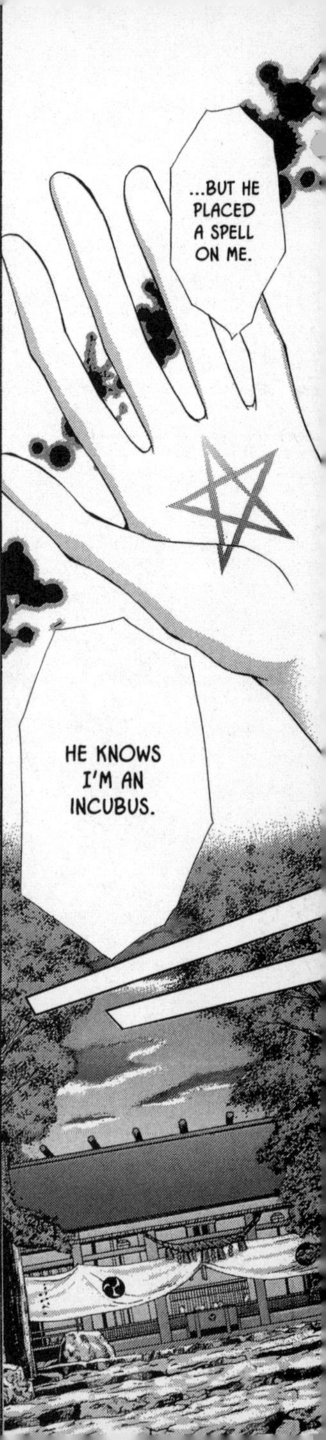
...BUT HE PLACED A SPELL ON ME.
HE KNOWS I'M AN INCUBUS.
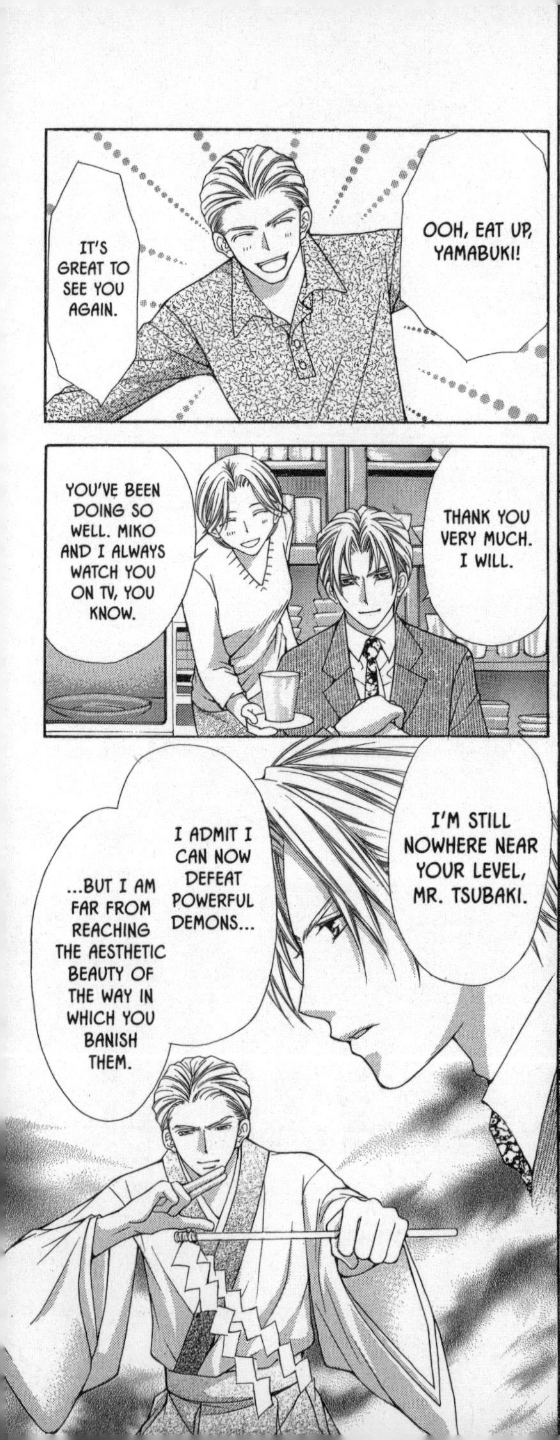
OOH, EAT UP, YAMABUKI!
IT'S GREAT TO SEE YOU AGAIN.
THANK YOU VERY MUCH. I WILL.
YOU'VE BEEN DOING SO WELL. MIKO AND I ALWAYS WATCH YOU ON TV, YOU KNOW.
I'M STILL NOWHERE NEAR YOUR LEVEL, MR. TSUBAKI.
I ADMIT I CAN NOW DEFEAT POWERFUL DEMONS...
...BUT I AM FAR FROM REACHING THE AESTHETIC BEAUTY OF THE WAY IN WHICH YOU BANISH THEM.

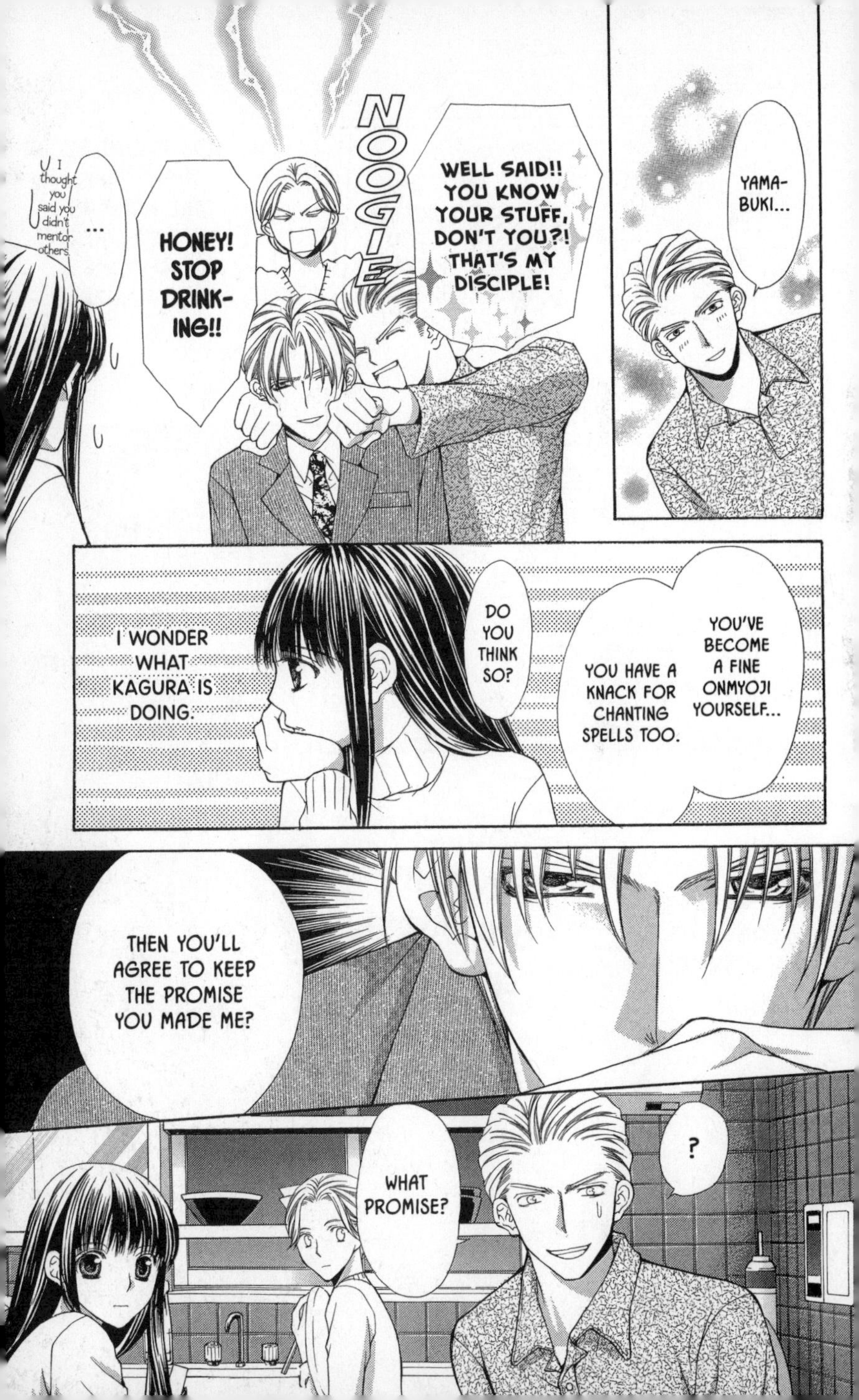
YAMA-BUKI...
WELL SAID!! YOU KNOW YOUR STUFF, DON'T YOU?! THAT'S MY DISCIPLE!
NOOGIE
HONEY! STOP DRINK-ING!!
I thought you said you didn't mentor others.
...
YOU'VE BECOME A FINE ONMYOJI YOURSELF...
YOU HAVE A KNACK FOR CHANTING SPELLS TOO.
DO YOU THINK SO?
I WONDER WHAT KAGURA IS DOING.
THEN YOU'LL AGREE TO KEEP THE PROMISE YOU MADE ME?
?
WHAT PROMISE?

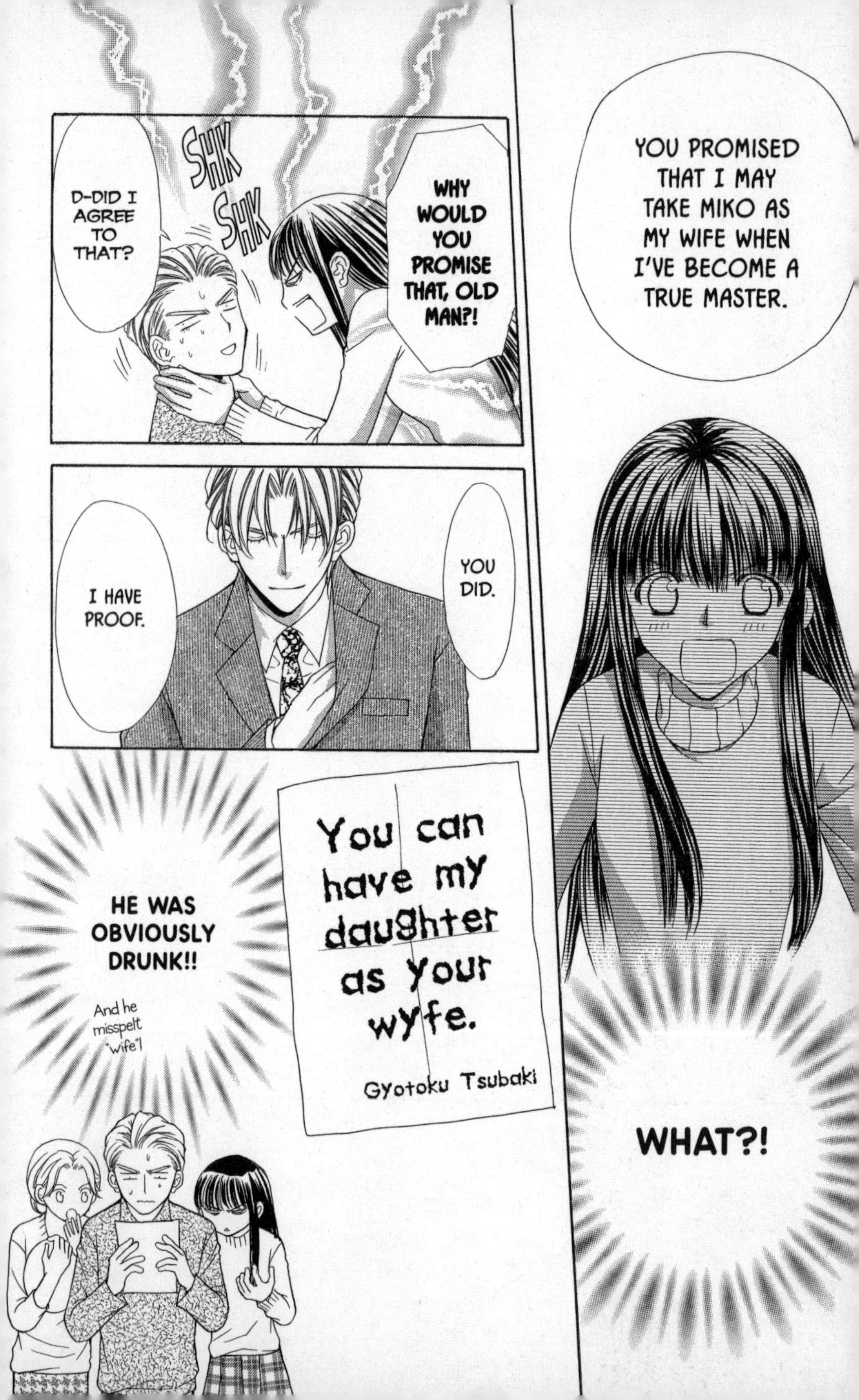
YOU PROMISED THAT I MAY TAKE MIKO AS MY WIFE WHEN I'VE BECOME A TRUE MASTER.
WHAT?!
WHY WOULD YOU PROMISE THAT, OLD MAN?!
SHK SHK
D-DID I AGREE TO THAT?
YOU DID.
I HAVE PROOF.
You can have my daughter as your wyfe.
Gyotoku Tsubaki
HE WAS OBVIOUSLY DRUNK!!
And he misspelt "wife"!

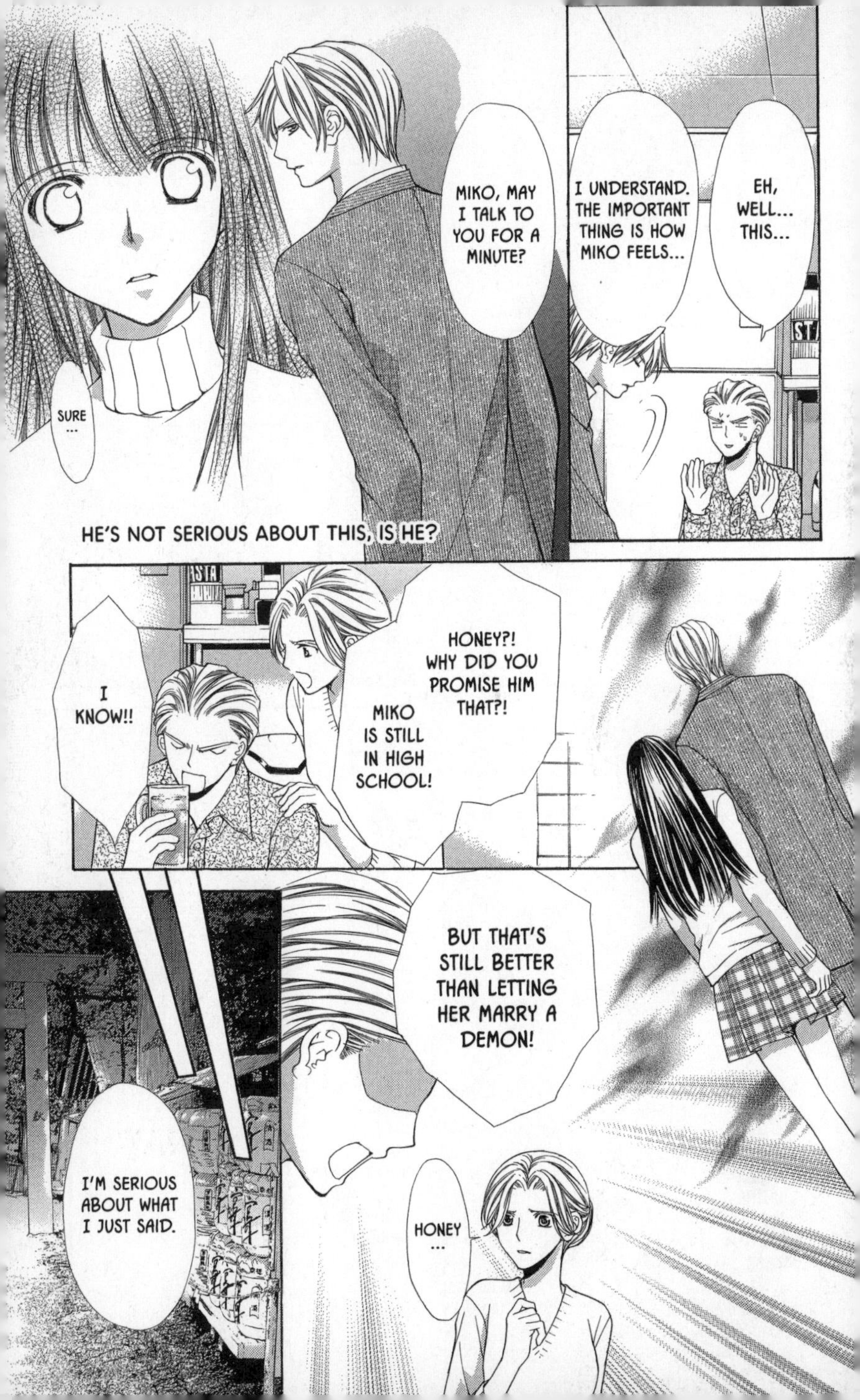
EH, WELL... THIS...
I UNDERSTAND. THE IMPORTANT THING IS HOW MIKO FEELS...
MIKO, MAY I TALK TO YOU FOR A MINUTE?
SURE ...
HE'S NOT SERIOUS ABOUT THIS, IS HE?
HONEY?! WHY DID YOU PROMISE HIM THAT?!
MIKO IS STILL IN HIGH SCHOOL!
I KNOW!!
BUT THAT'S STILL BETTER THAN LETTING HER MARRY A DEMON!
HONEY ...
I'M SERIOUS ABOUT WHAT I JUST SAID.

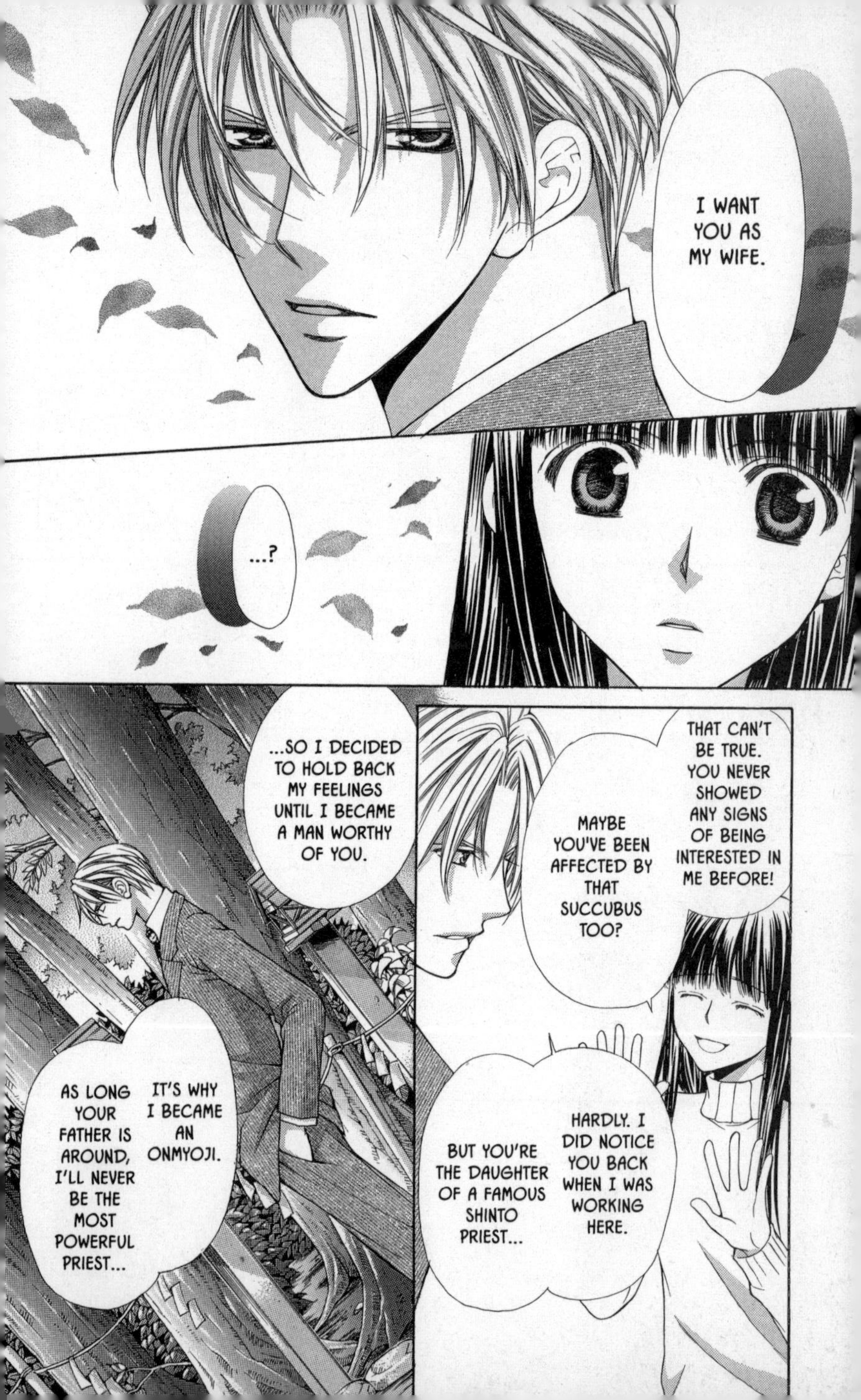
I WANT YOU AS MY WIFE.
...?
THAT CAN'T BE TRUE. YOU NEVER SHOWED ANY SIGNS OF BEING INTERESTED IN ME BEFORE!
MAYBE YOU'VE BEEN AFFECTED BY THAT SUCCUBUS TOO?
HARDLY. I DID NOTICE YOU BACK WHEN I WAS WORKING HERE.
BUT YOU'RE THE DAUGHTER OF A FAMOUS SHINTO PRIEST...
...SO I DECIDED TO HOLD BACK MY FEELINGS UNTIL I BECAME A MAN WORTHY OF YOU.
IT'S WHY I BECAME AN ONMYOJI.
AS LONG YOUR FATHER IS AROUND, I'LL NEVER BE THE MOST POWERFUL PRIEST...

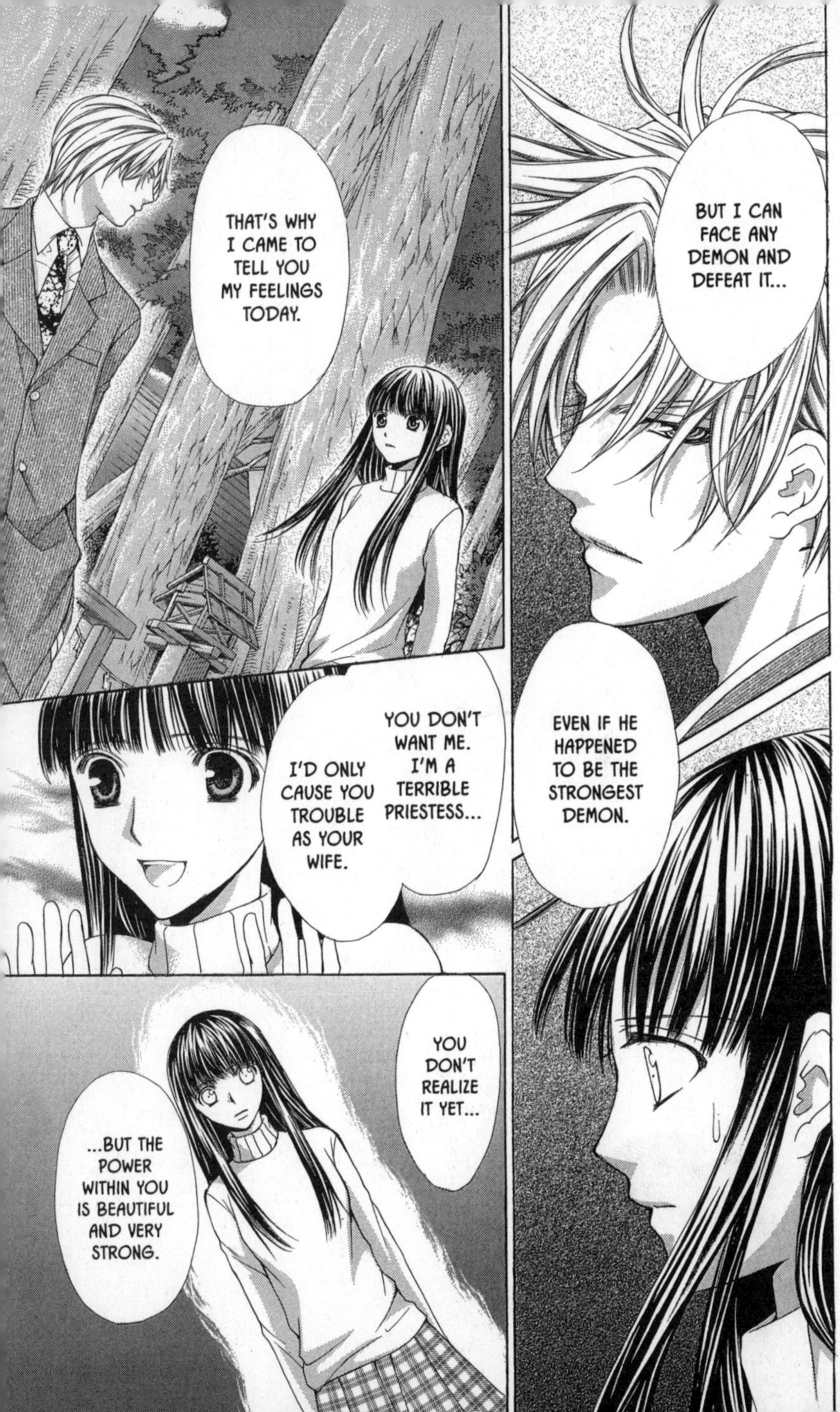
BUT I CAN FACE ANY DEMON AND DEFEAT IT...
EVEN IF HE HAPPENED TO BE THE STRONGEST DEMON.
THAT'S WHY I CAME TO TELL YOU MY FEELINGS TODAY.
YOU DON'T WANT ME. I'M A TERRIBLE PRIESTESS...
I'D ONLY CAUSE YOU TROUBLE AS YOUR WIFE.
YOU DON'T REALIZE IT YET...
...BUT THE POWER WITHIN YOU IS BEAUTIFUL AND VERY STRONG.

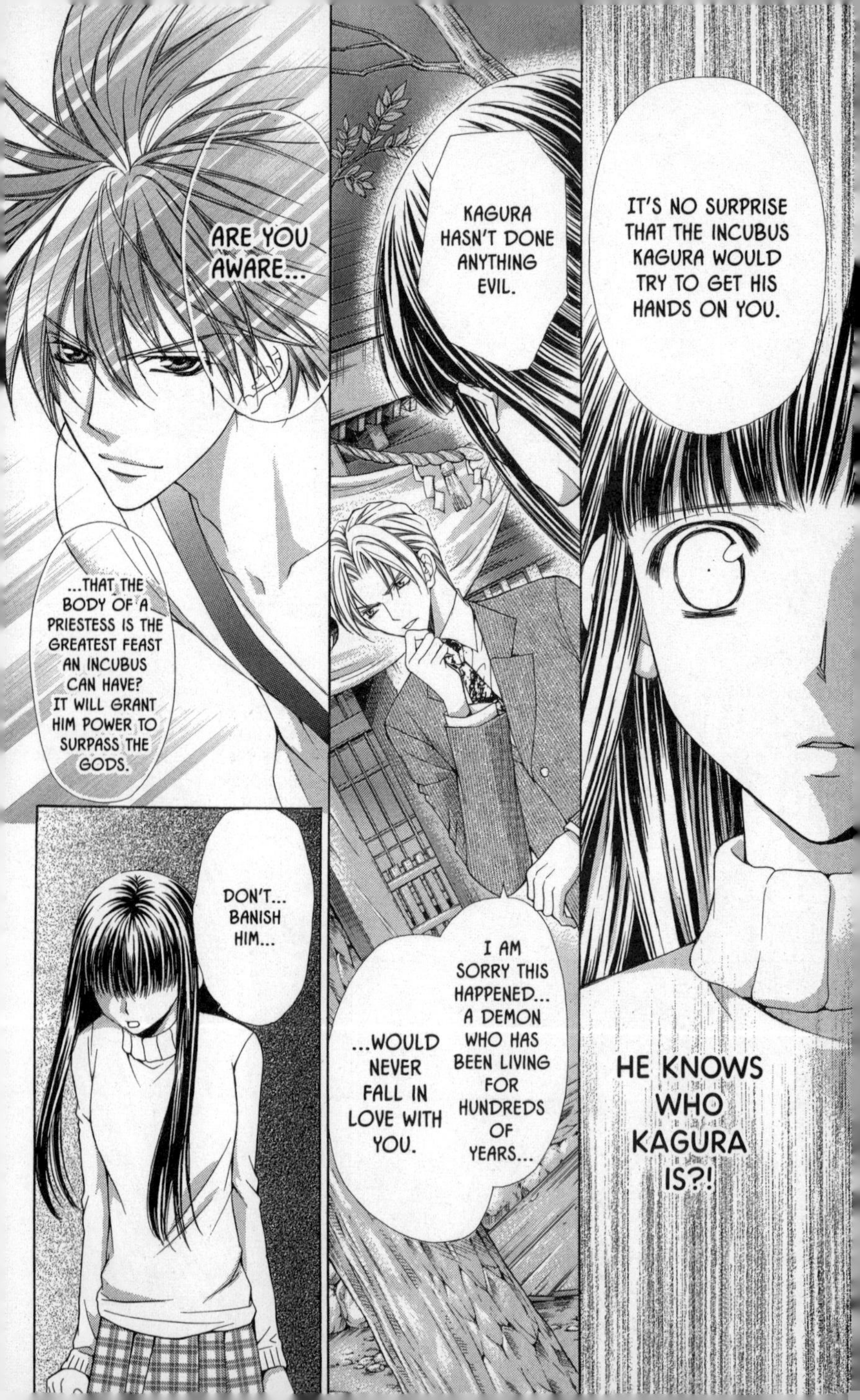

IT'S NO SURPRISE THAT THE INCUBUS KAGURA WOULD TRY TO GET HIS HANDS ON YOU.
HE KNOWS WHO KAGURA IS?!
KAGURA HASN'T DONE ANYTHING EVIL.
I AM SORRY THIS HAPPENED... A DEMON WHO HAS BEEN LIVING FOR HUNDREDS OF YEARS...
...WOULD NEVER FALL IN LOVE WITH YOU.
ARE YOU AWARE...
...THAT THE BODY OF A PRIESTESS IS THE GREATEST FEAST AN INCUBUS CAN HAVE? IT WILL GRANT HIM POWER TO SURPASS THE GODS.
DON'T... BANISH HIM...

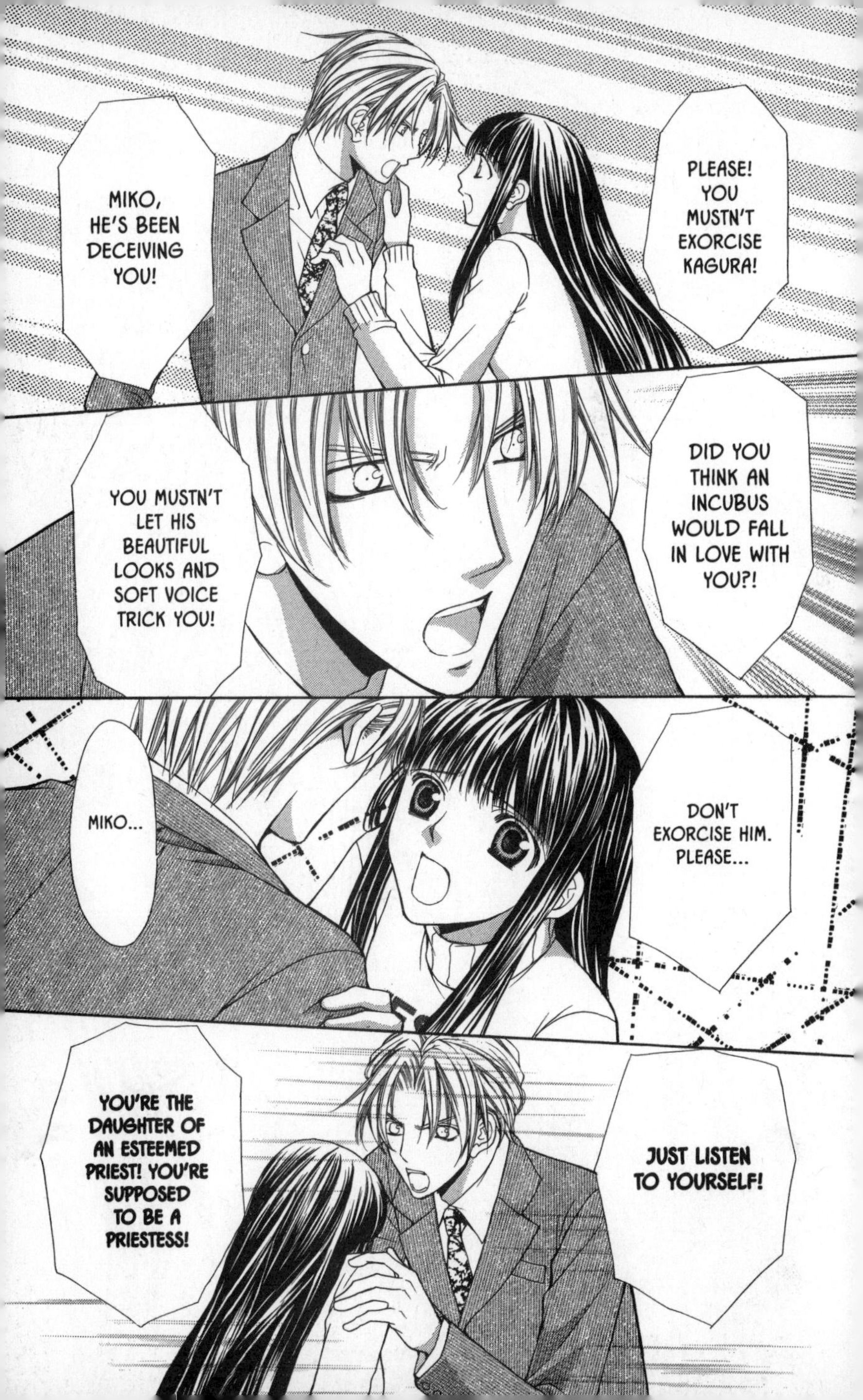
PLEASE! YOU MUSTN'T EXORCISE KAGURA!
MIKO, HE'S BEEN DECEIVING YOU!
DID YOU THINK AN INCUBUS WOULD FALL IN LOVE WITH YOU?!
YOU MUSTN'T LET HIS BEAUTIFUL LOOKS AND SOFT VOICE TRICK YOU!
DON'T EXORCISE HIM. PLEASE...
MIKO...
JUST LISTEN TO YOURSELF!
YOU'RE THE DAUGHTER OF AN ESTEEMED PRIEST! YOU'RE SUPPOSED TO BE A PRIESTESS!

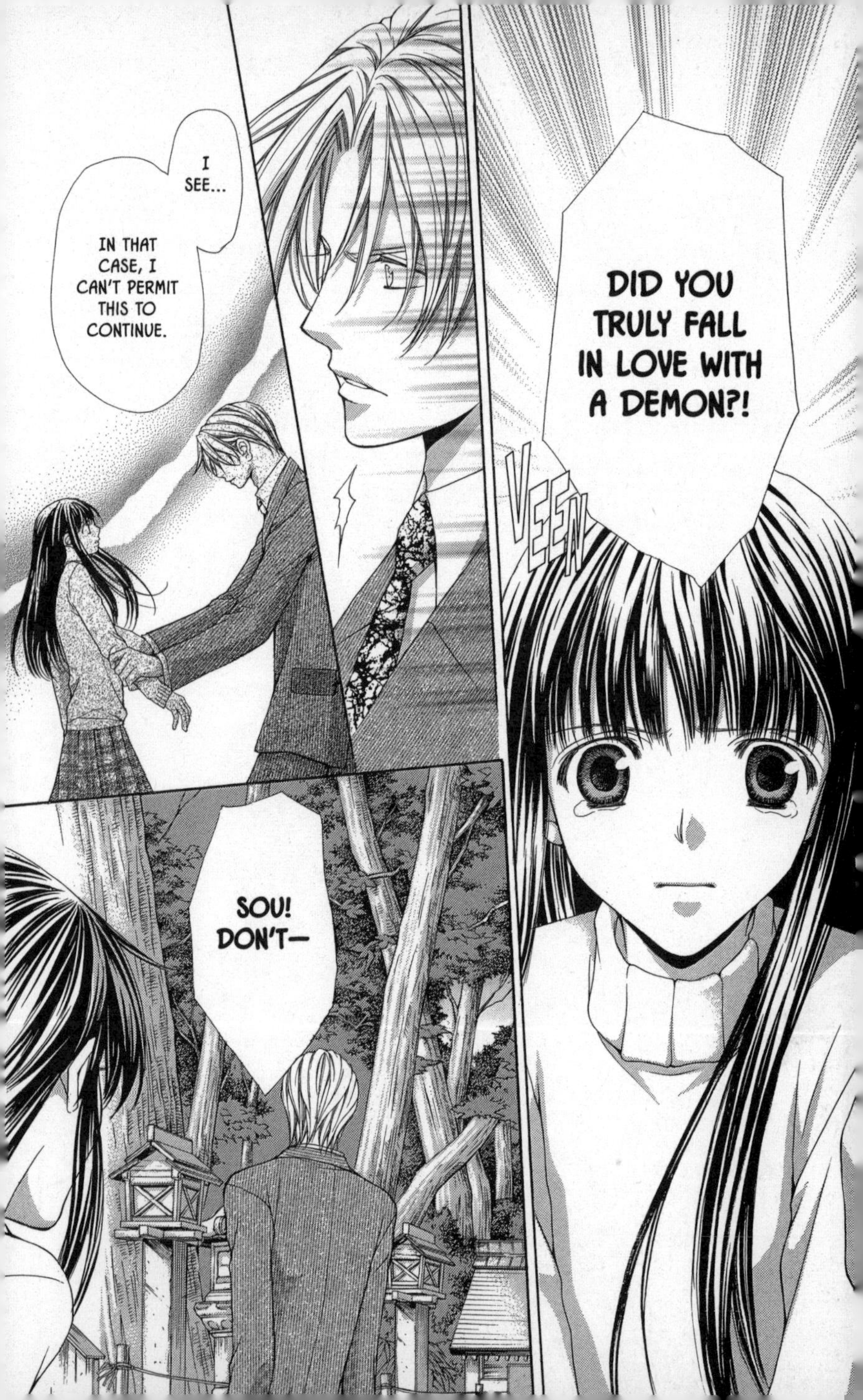
DID YOU TRULY FALL IN LOVE WITH A DEMON?!
VEEN
I SEE...
IN THAT CASE, I CAN'T PERMIT THIS TO CONTINUE.
SOU! DON'T—

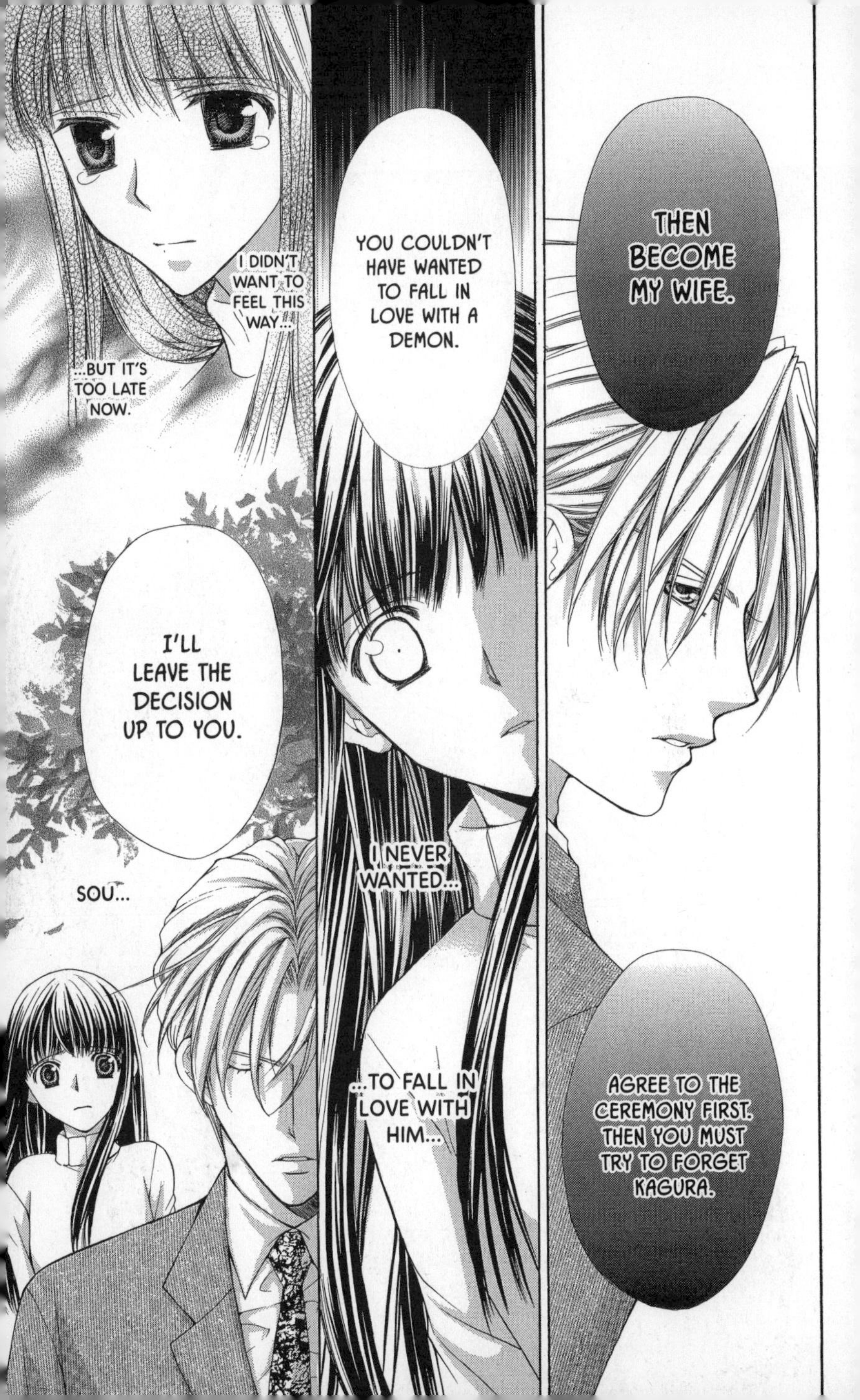
THEN BECOME MY WIFE.
AGREE TO THE CEREMONY FIRST. THEN YOU MUST TRY TO FORGET KAGURA.
YOU COULDN'T HAVE WANTED TO FALL IN LOVE WITH A DEMON.
I NEVER WANTED...
...TO FALL IN LOVE WITH HIM...
I DIDN'T WANT TO FEEL THIS WAY...
...BUT IT'S TOO LATE NOW.
I'LL LEAVE THE DECISION UP TO YOU.
SOU...

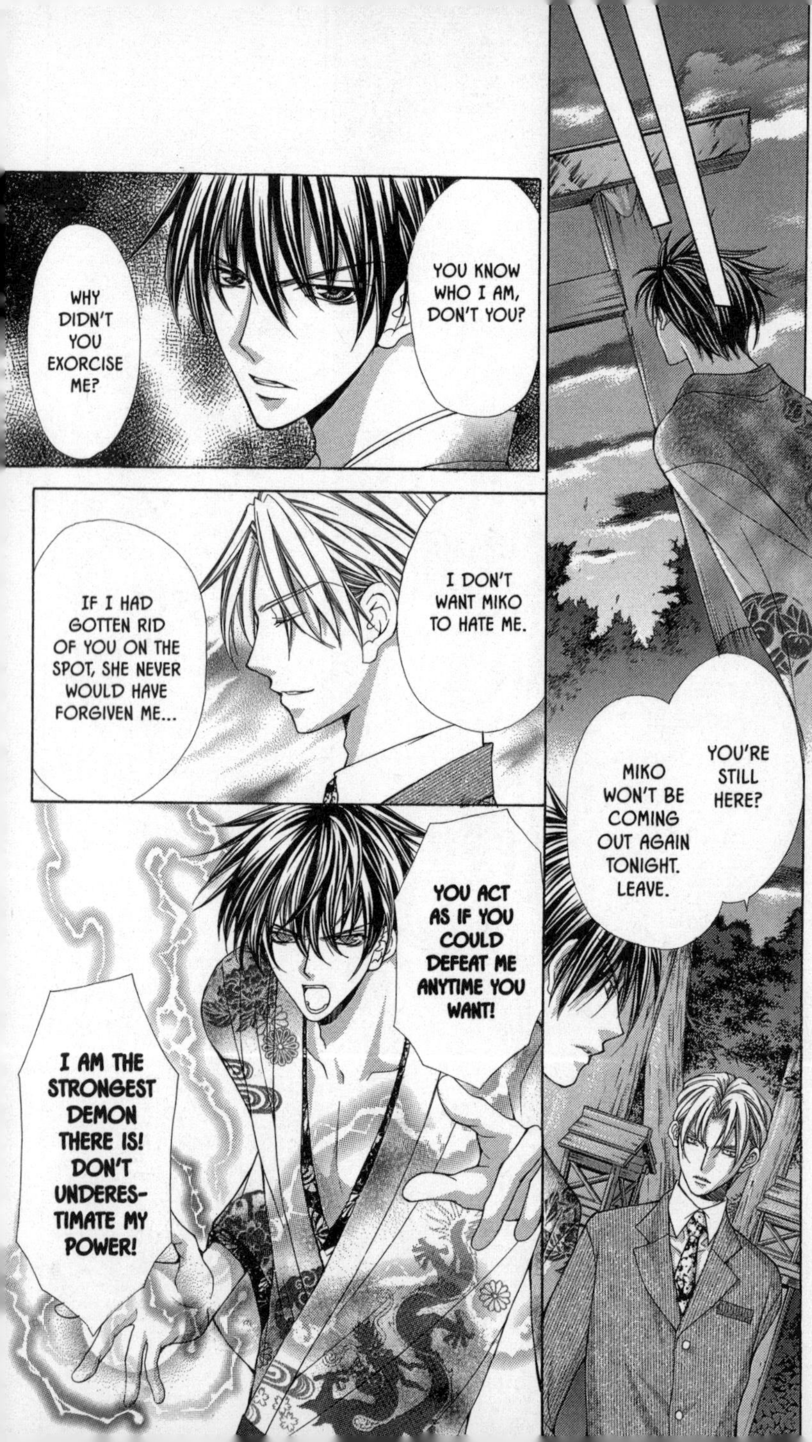
YOU'RE STILL HERE? MIKO WON'T BE COMING OUT AGAIN TONIGHT. LEAVE.
YOU KNOW WHO I AM, DON'T YOU?
WHY DIDN'T YOU EXORCISE ME?
I DON'T WANT MIKO TO HATE ME.
IF I HAD GOTTEN RID OF YOU ON THE SPOT, SHE NEVER WOULD HAVE FORGIVEN ME...
YOU ACT AS IF YOU COULD DEFEAT ME ANYTIME YOU WANT!
I AM THE STRONGEST DEMON THERE IS! DON'T UNDERES- TIMATE MY POWER!

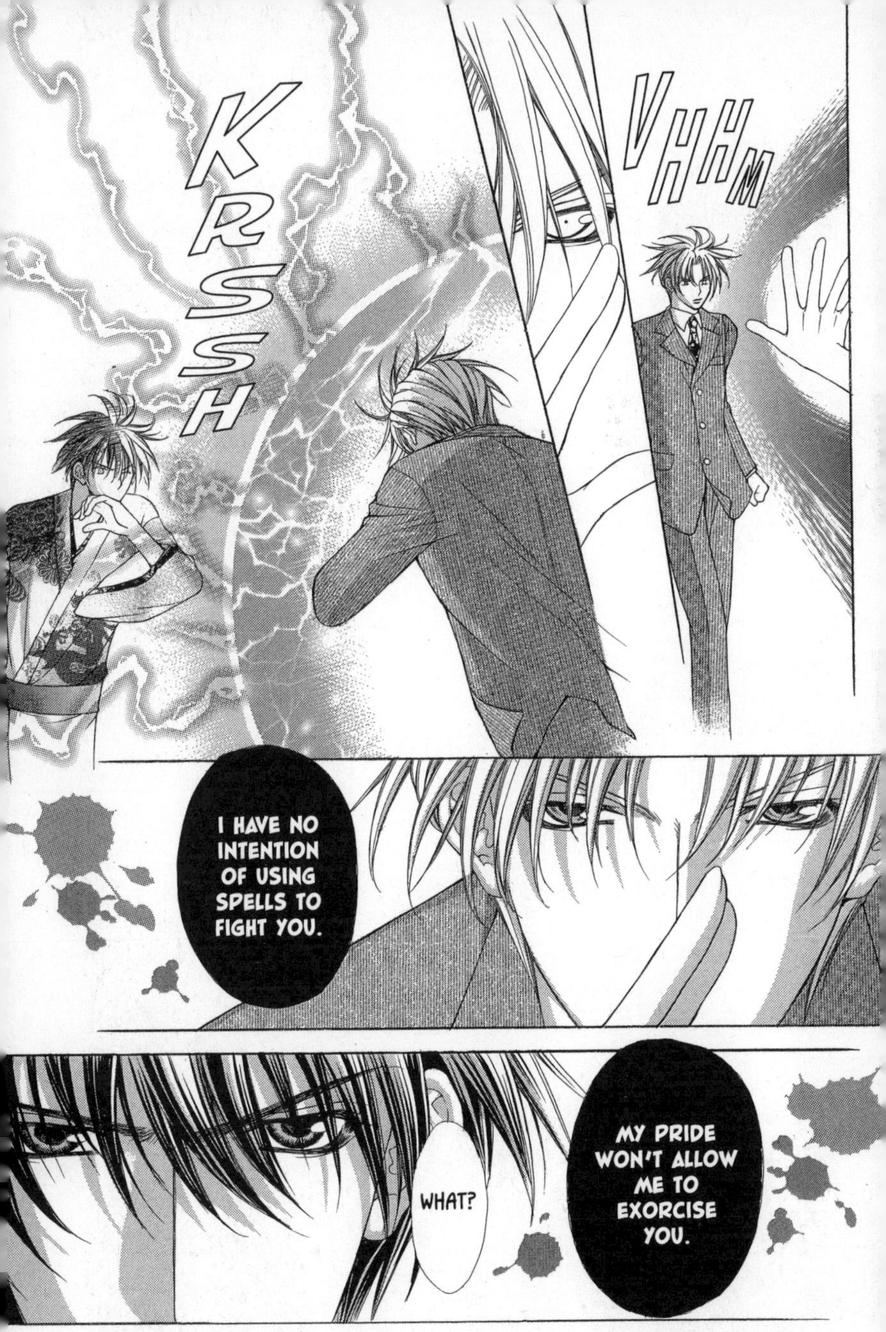
VHHM
KRSSH
I HAVE NO INTENTION OF USING SPELLS TO FIGHT YOU.
MY PRIDE WON'T ALLOW ME TO EXORCISE YOU.
WHAT?

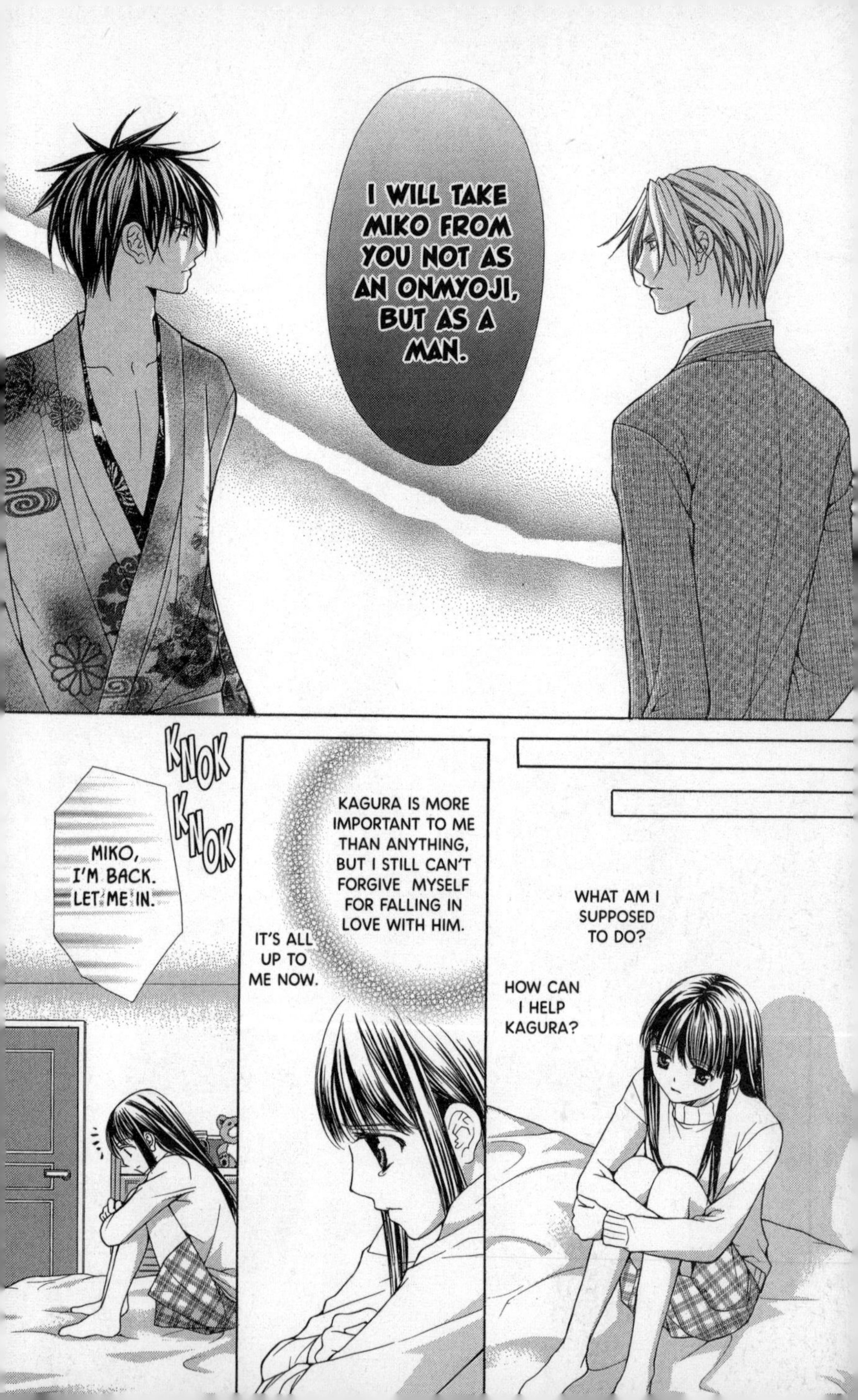
I WILL TAKE MIKO FROM YOU NOT AS AN ONMYOJI, BUT AS A MAN.
WHAT AM I SUPPOSED TO DO?
HOW CAN I HELP KAGURA?
KAGURA IS MORE IMPORTANT TO ME THAN ANYTHING, BUT I STILL CAN'T FORGIVE MYSELF FOR FALLING IN LOVE WITH HIM.
IT'S ALL UP TO ME NOW.
KNOK KNOK
MIKO, I'M BACK. LET ME IN.

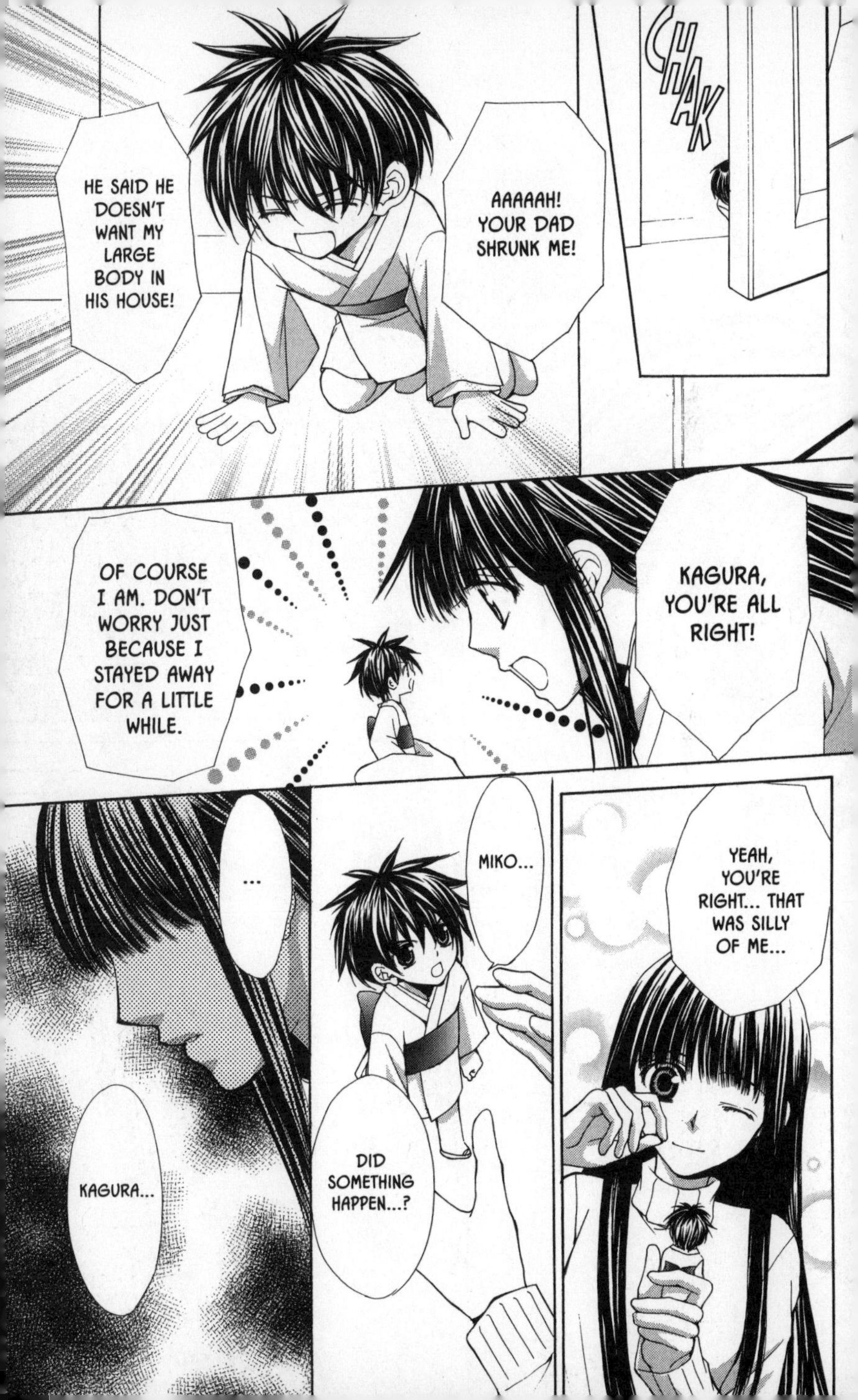
CHAK
AAAAAH! YOUR DAD SHRUNK ME!
HE SAID HE DOESN'T WANT MY LARGE BODY IN HIS HOUSE!
KAGURA, YOU'RE ALL RIGHT!
OF COURSE I AM. DON'T WORRY JUST BECAUSE I STAYED AWAY FOR A LITTLE WHILE.
YEAH, YOU'RE RIGHT... THAT WAS SILLY OF ME...
MIKO...
DID SOMETHING HAPPEN...?
...
KAGURA...

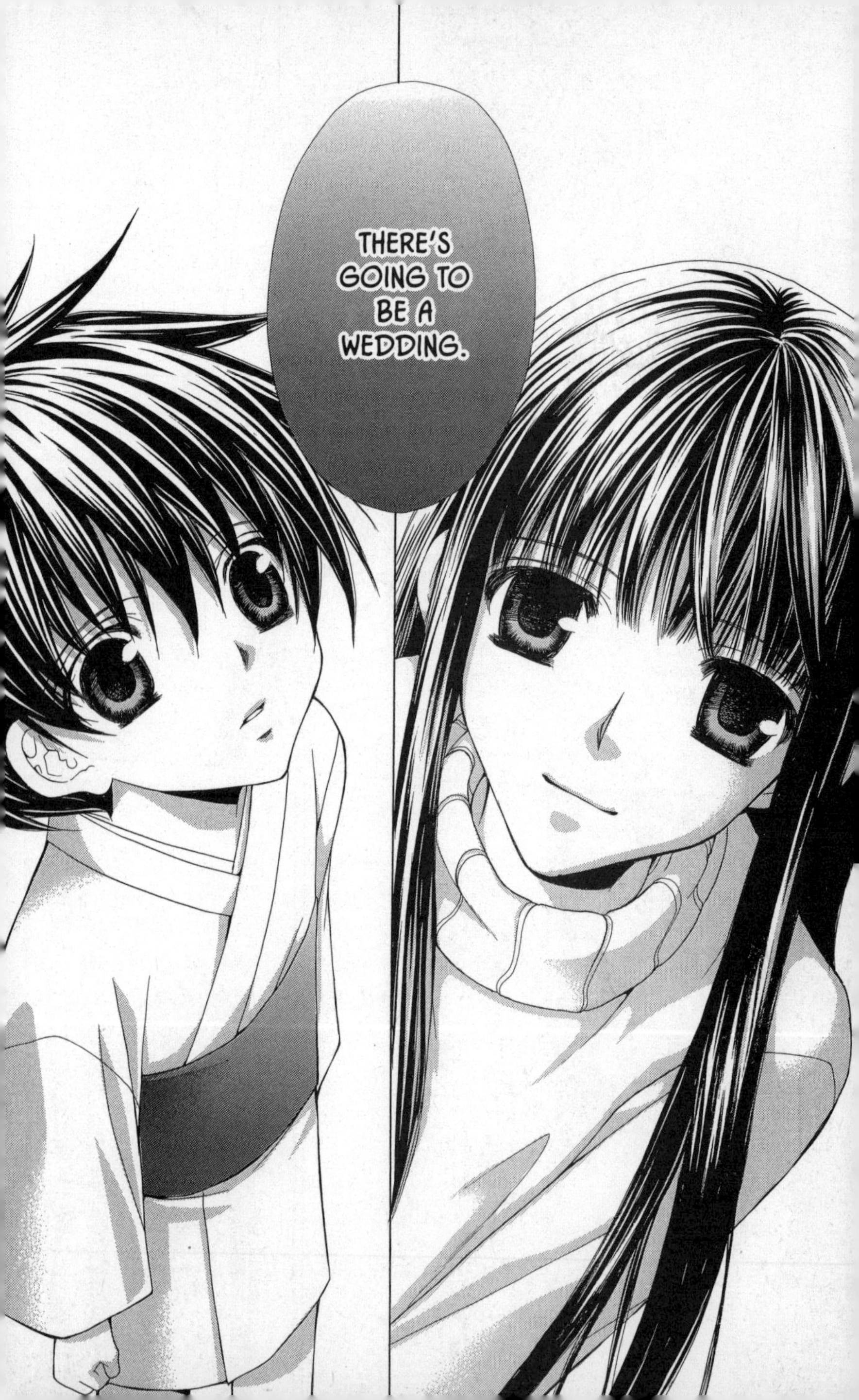
THERE'S GOING TO BE A WEDDING.

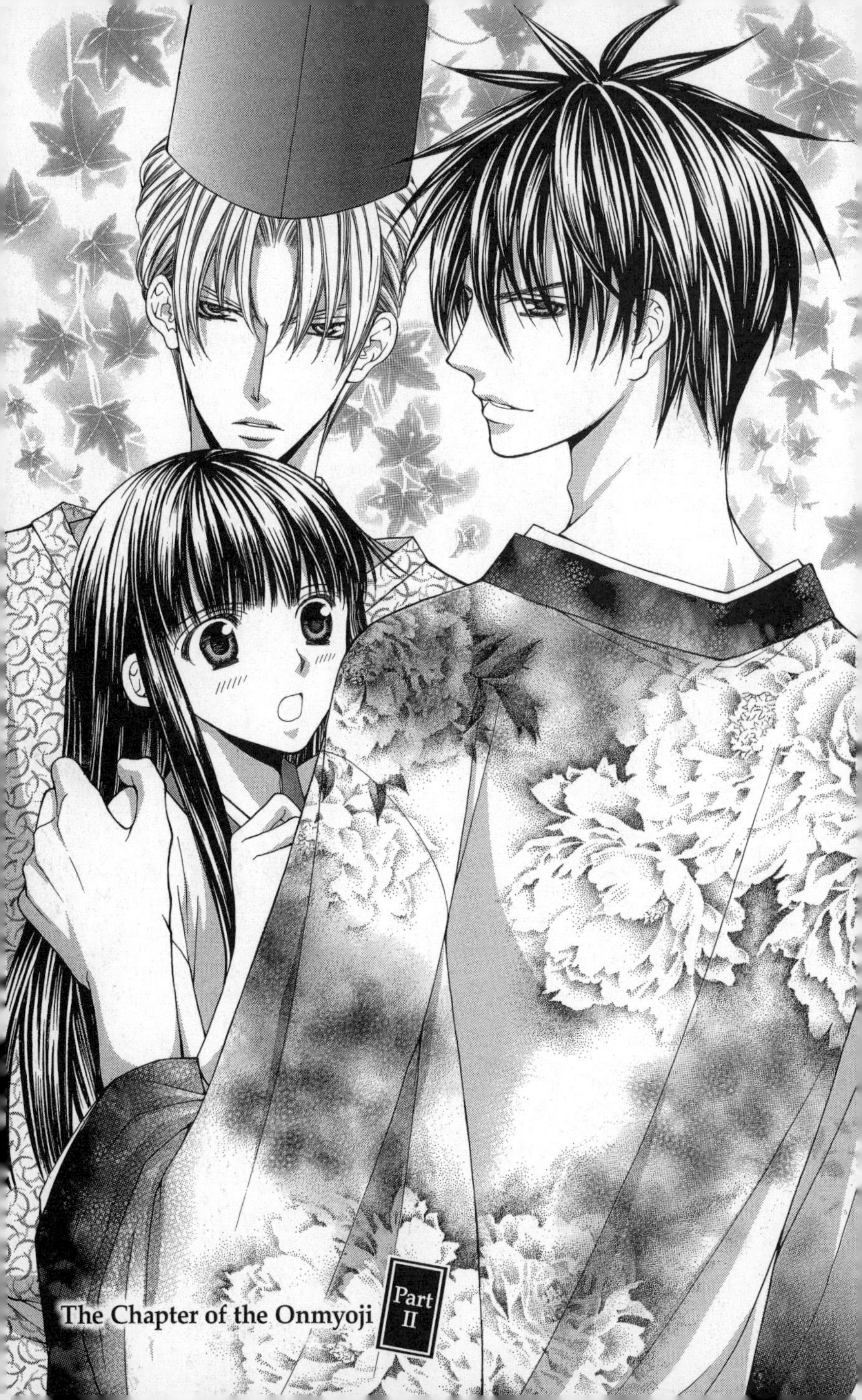
The Chapter of the Onmyoji
Part II

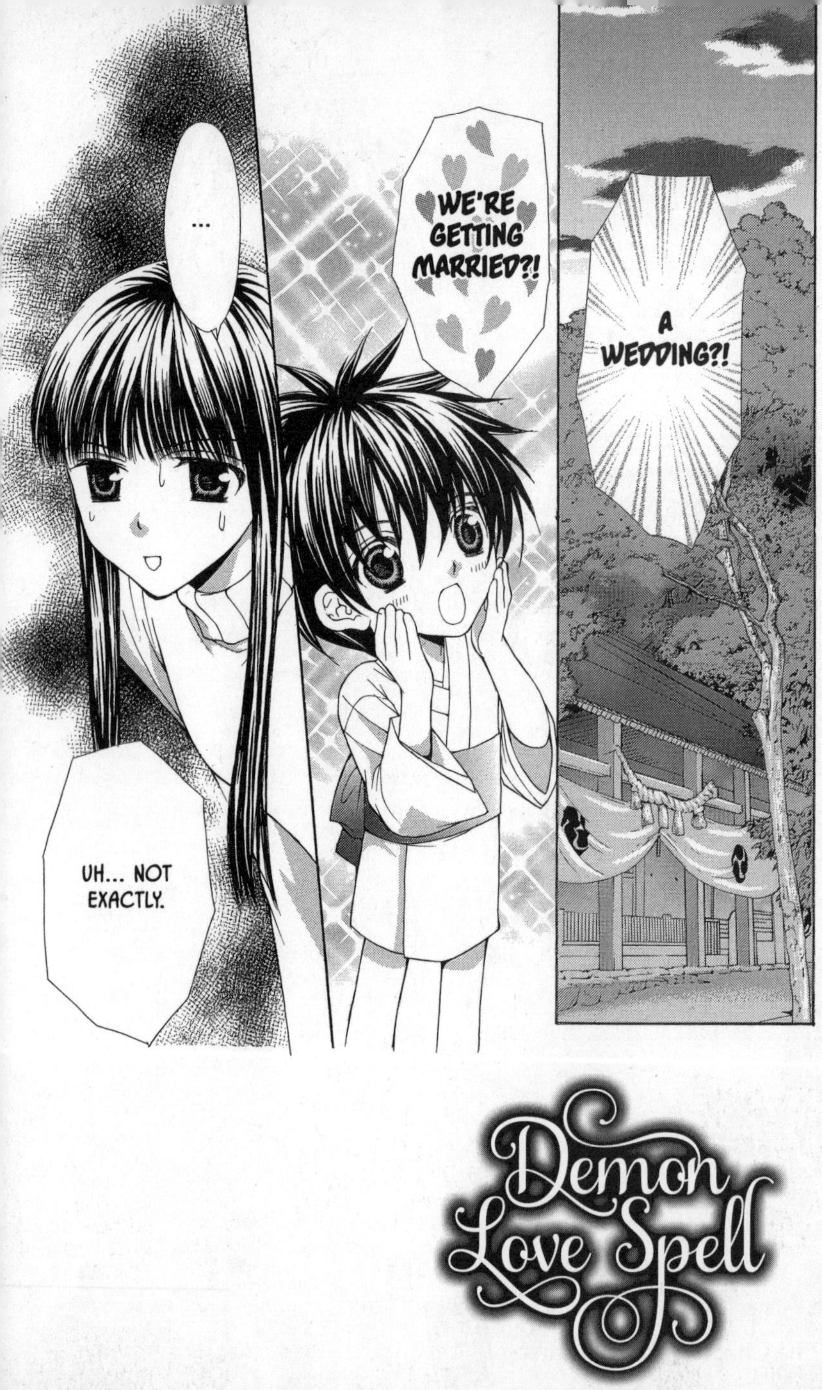
A WEDDING?!
WE'RE GETTING MARRIED?!
...
UH... NOT EXACTLY.

Demon Love Spell

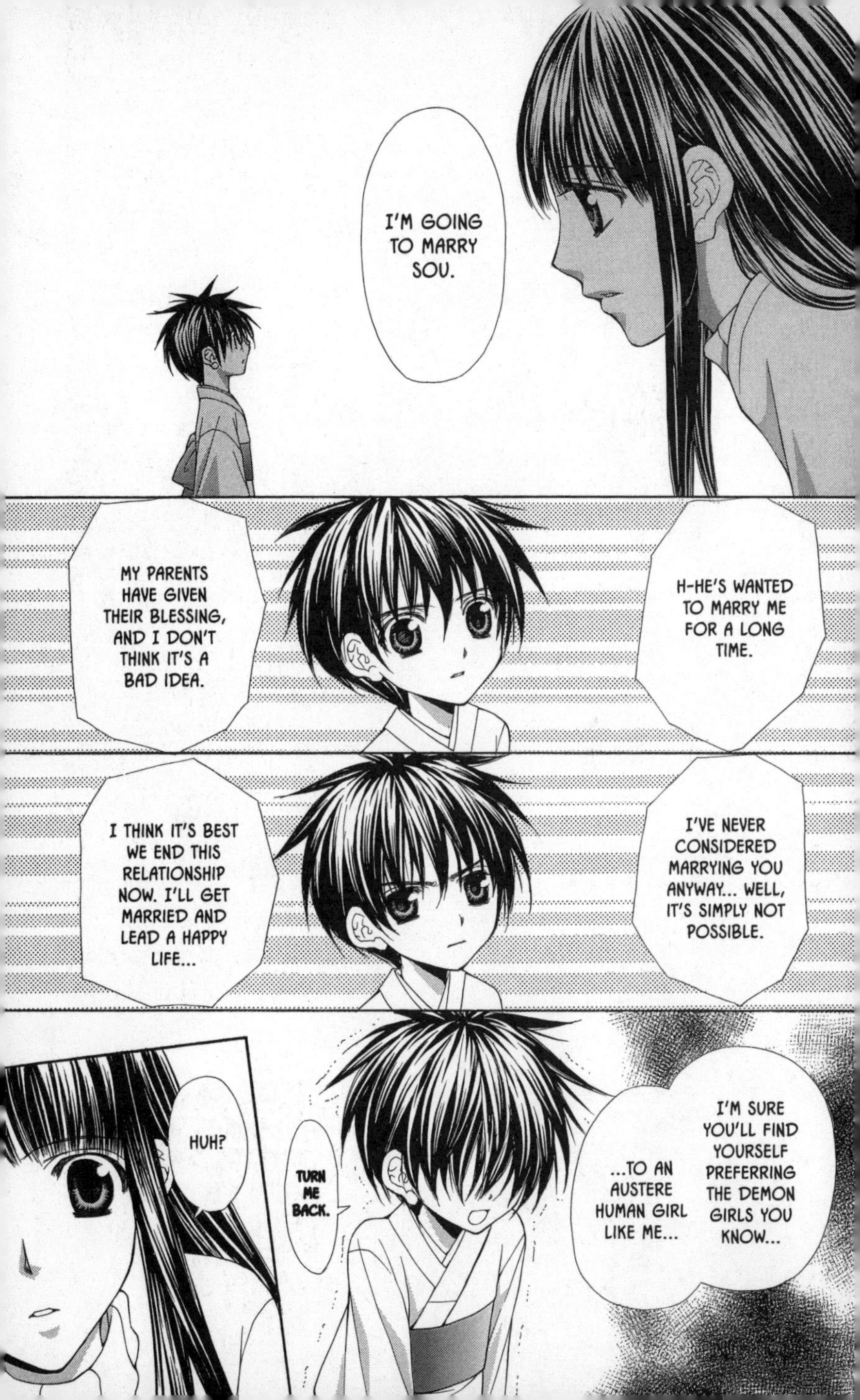
I'M GOING TO MARRY SOU.
H-HE'S WANTED TO MARRY ME FOR A LONG TIME.
MY PARENTS HAVE GIVEN THEIR BLESSING, AND I DON'T THINK IT'S A BAD IDEA.
I'VE NEVER CONSIDERED MARRYING YOU ANYWAY... WELL, IT'S SIMPLY NOT POSSIBLE.
I THINK IT'S BEST WE END THIS RELATIONSHIP NOW. I'LL GET MARRIED AND LEAD A HAPPY LIFE...
I'M SURE YOU'LL FIND YOURSELF PREFERRING THE DEMON GIRLS YOU KNOW...
...TO AN AUSTERE HUMAN GIRL LIKE ME...
TURN ME BACK.
HUH?

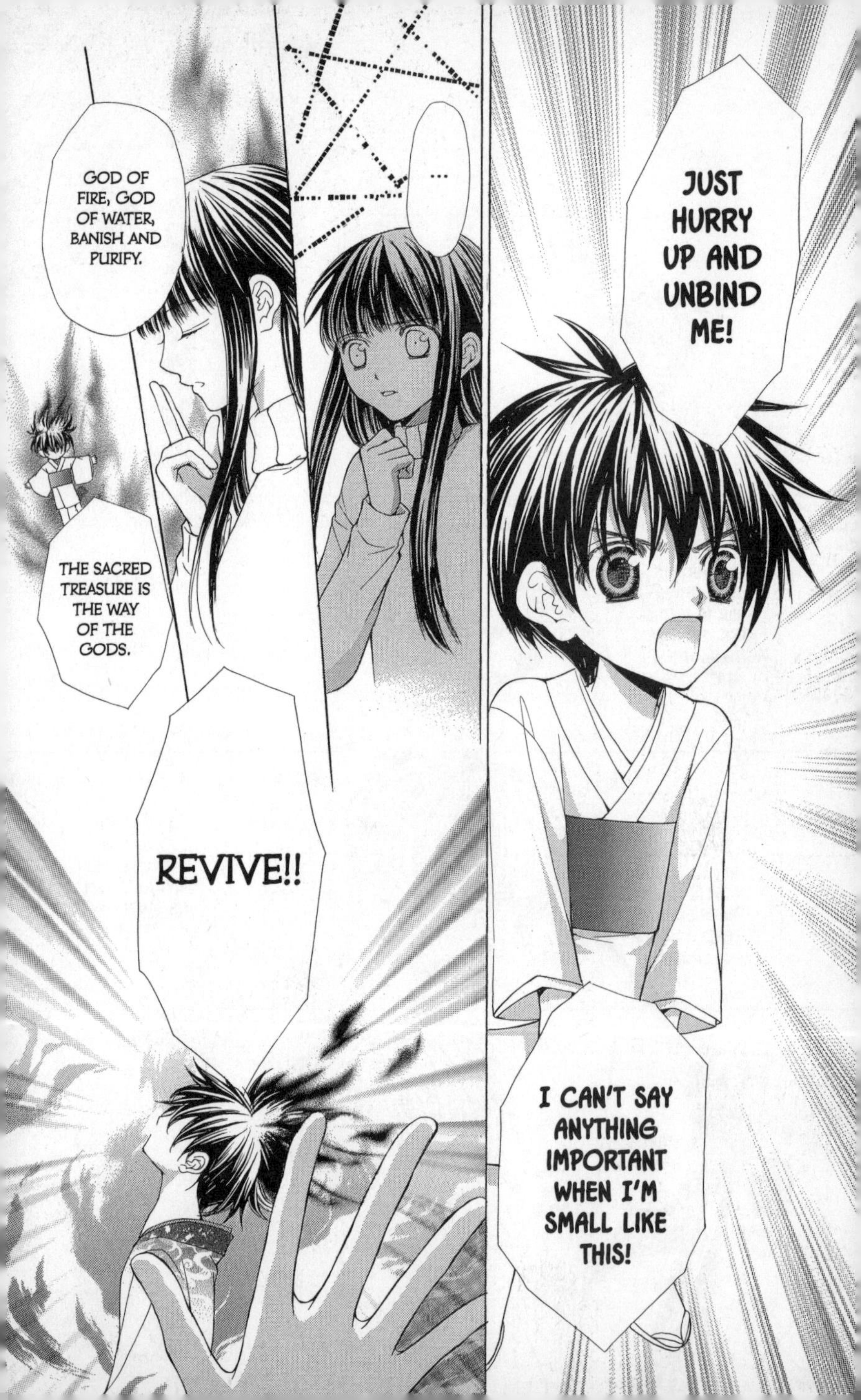
JUST HURRY UP AND UNBIND ME!
I CAN'T SAY ANYTHING IMPORTANT WHEN I'M SMALL LIKE THIS!
...
GOD OF FIRE, GOD OF WATER, BANISH AND PURIFY.
THE SACRED TREASURE IS THE WAY OF THE GODS.
REVIVE!!

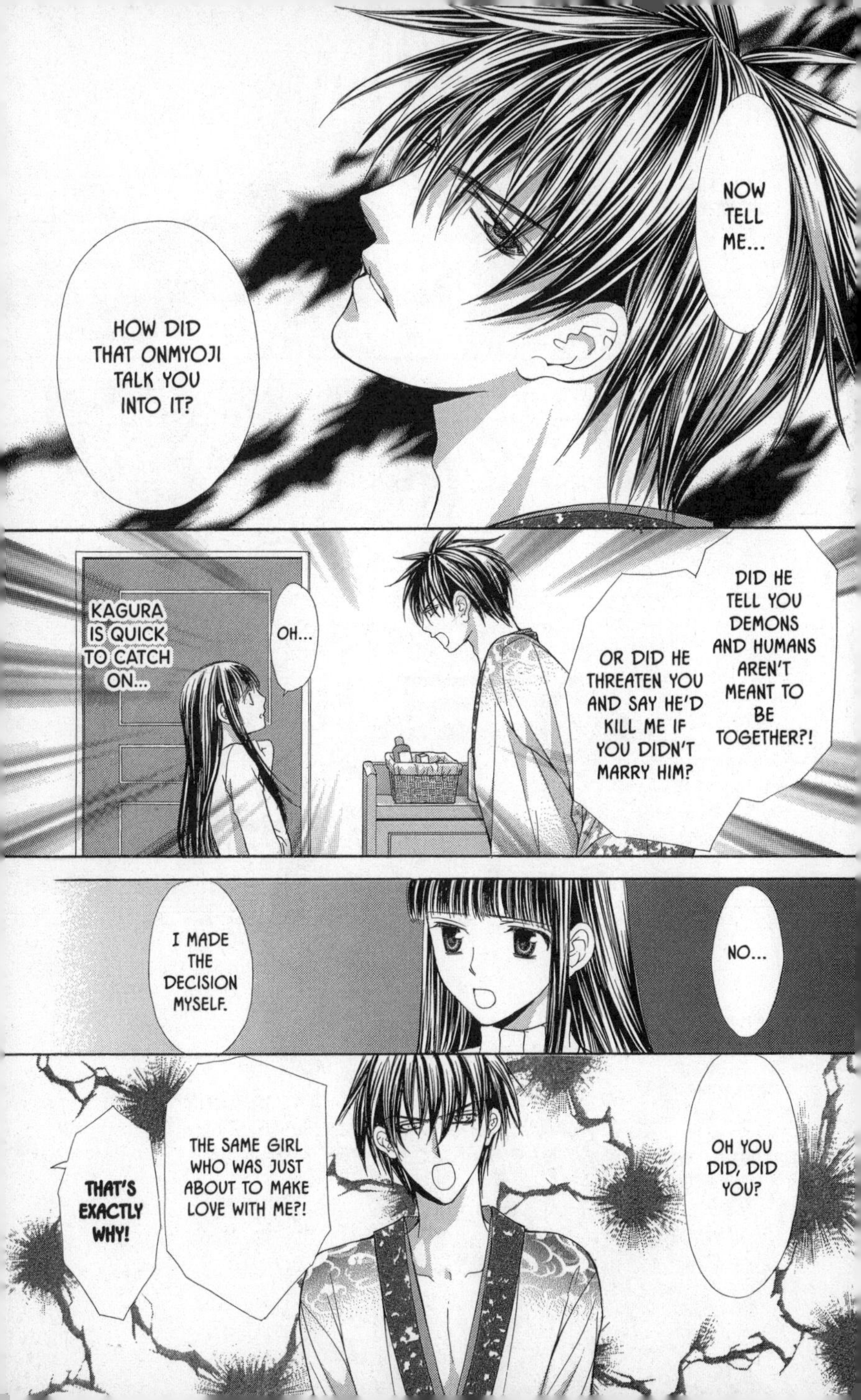
NOW TELL ME...
HOW DID THAT ONMYOJI TALK YOU INTO IT?
DID HE TELL YOU DEMONS AND HUMANS AREN'T MEANT TO BE TOGETHER?!
OR DID HE THREATEN YOU AND SAY HE'D KILL ME IF YOU DIDN'T MARRY HIM?
OH...
KAGURA IS QUICK TO CATCH ON...
NO...
I MADE THE DECISION MYSELF.
OH YOU DID, DID YOU?
THE SAME GIRL WHO WAS JUST ABOUT TO MAKE LOVE WITH ME?!
THAT'S EXACTLY WHY!

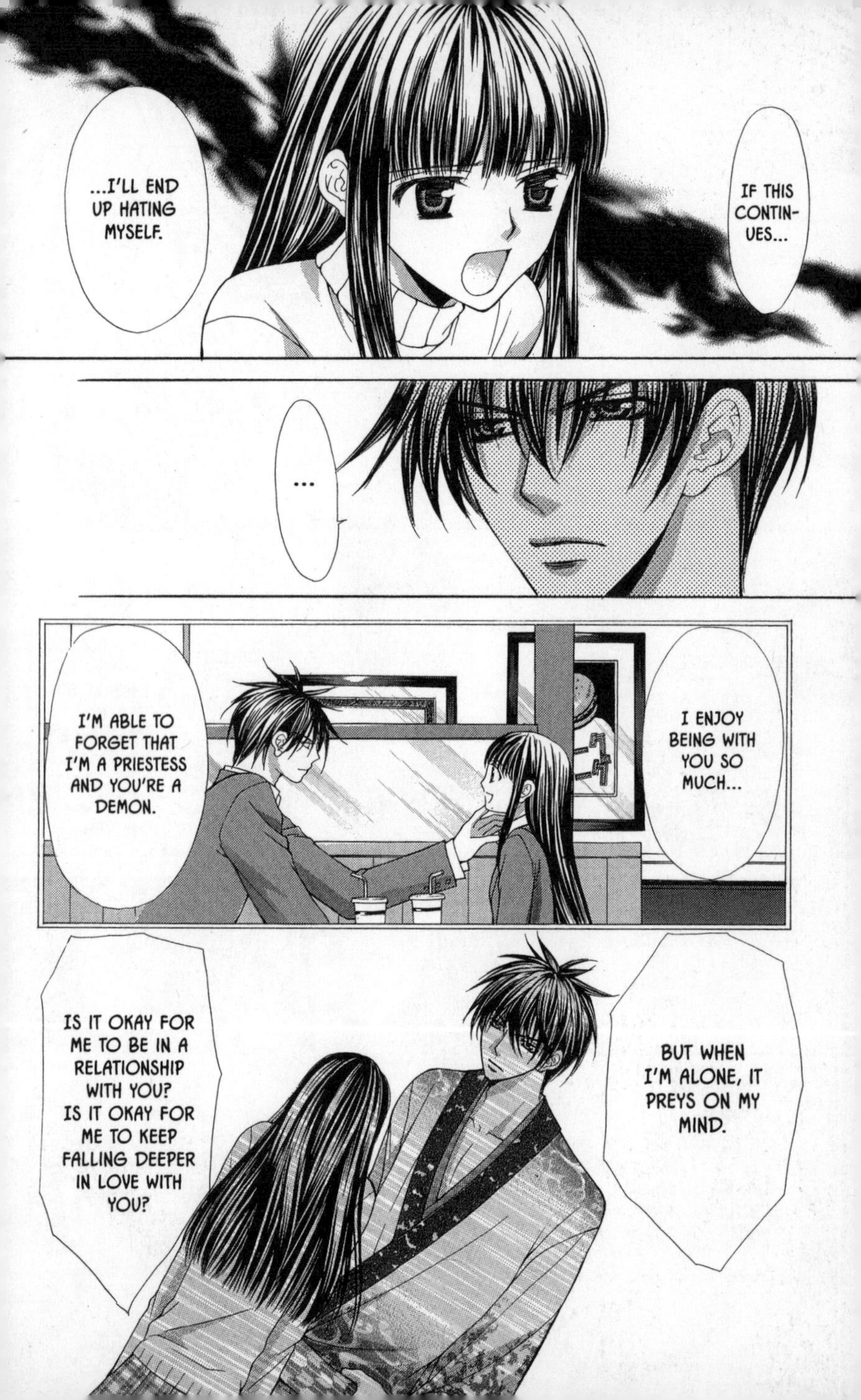
IF THIS CONTIN-UES...
...I'LL END UP HATING MYSELF.
...
I ENJOY BEING WITH YOU SO MUCH...
I'M ABLE TO FORGET THAT I'M A PRIESTESS AND YOU'RE A DEMON.
BUT WHEN I'M ALONE, IT PREYS ON MY MIND.
IS IT OKAY FOR ME TO BE IN A RELATIONSHIP WITH YOU? IS IT OKAY FOR ME TO KEEP FALLING DEEPER IN LOVE WITH YOU?

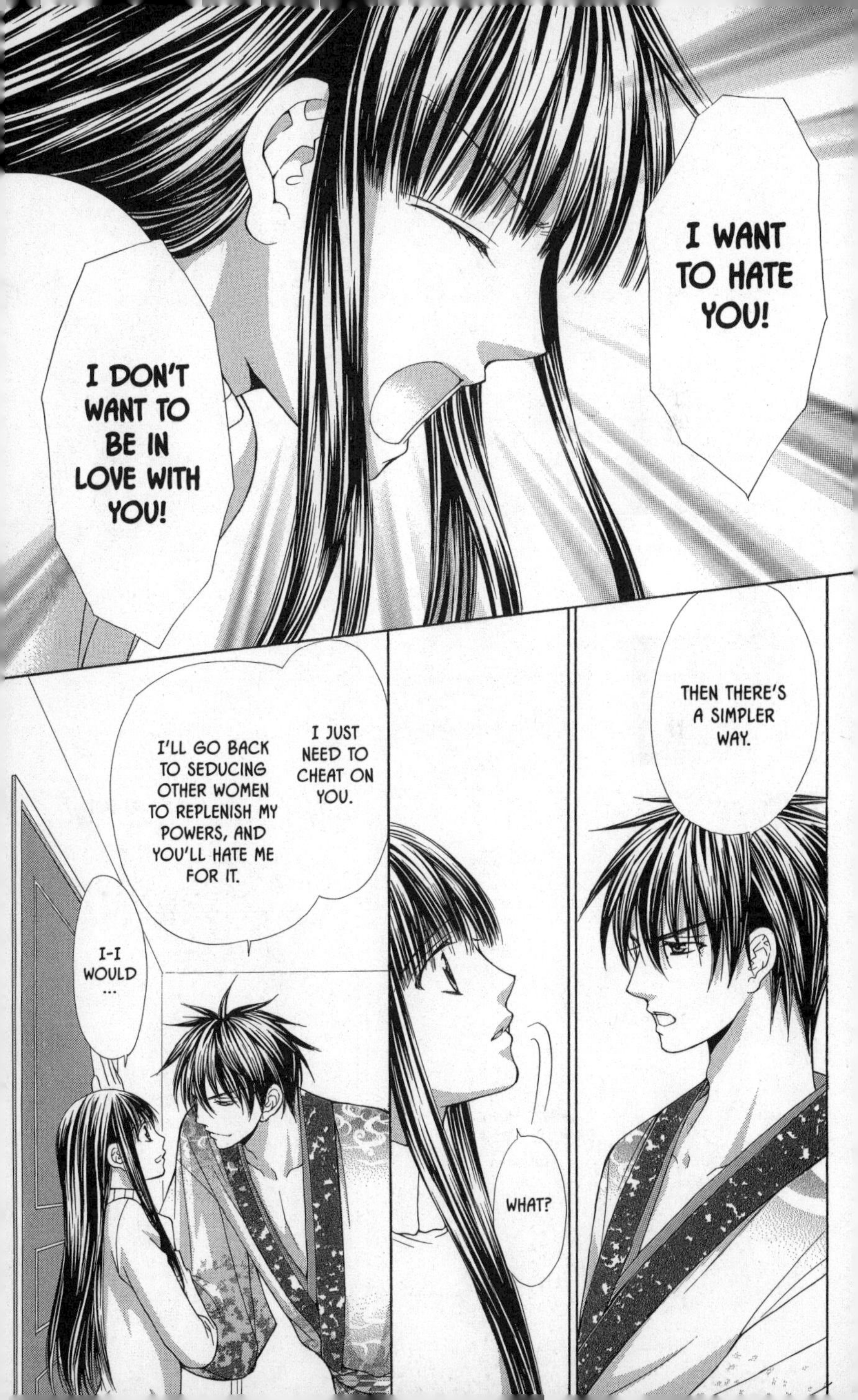
I WANT TO HATE YOU!
I DON'T WANT TO BE IN LOVE WITH YOU!
THEN THERE'S A SIMPLER WAY.
WHAT?
I JUST NEED TO CHEAT ON YOU.
I'LL GO BACK TO SEDUCING OTHER WOMEN TO REPLENISH MY POWERS, AND YOU'LL HATE ME FOR IT.
I-I WOULD ...

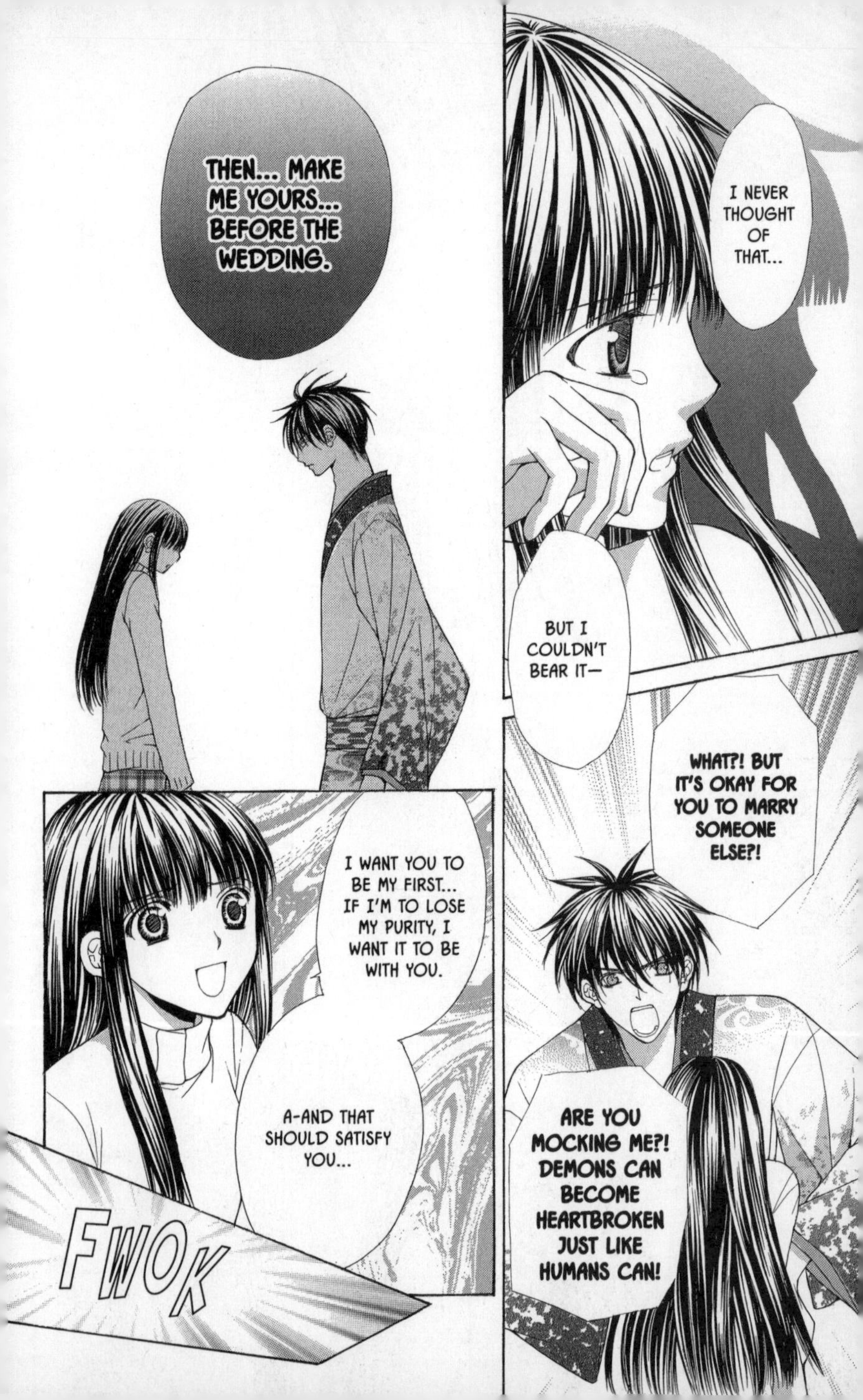
I NEVER THOUGHT OF THAT...
BUT I COULDN'T BEAR IT—
WHAT?! BUT IT'S OKAY FOR YOU TO MARRY SOMEONE ELSE?!
ARE YOU MOCKING ME?! DEMONS CAN BECOME HEARTBROKEN JUST LIKE HUMANS CAN!
THEN... MAKE ME YOURS... BEFORE THE WEDDING.
I WANT YOU TO BE MY FIRST... IF I'M TO LOSE MY PURITY, I WANT IT TO BE WITH YOU.
A-AND THAT SHOULD SATISFY YOU...
FWOK

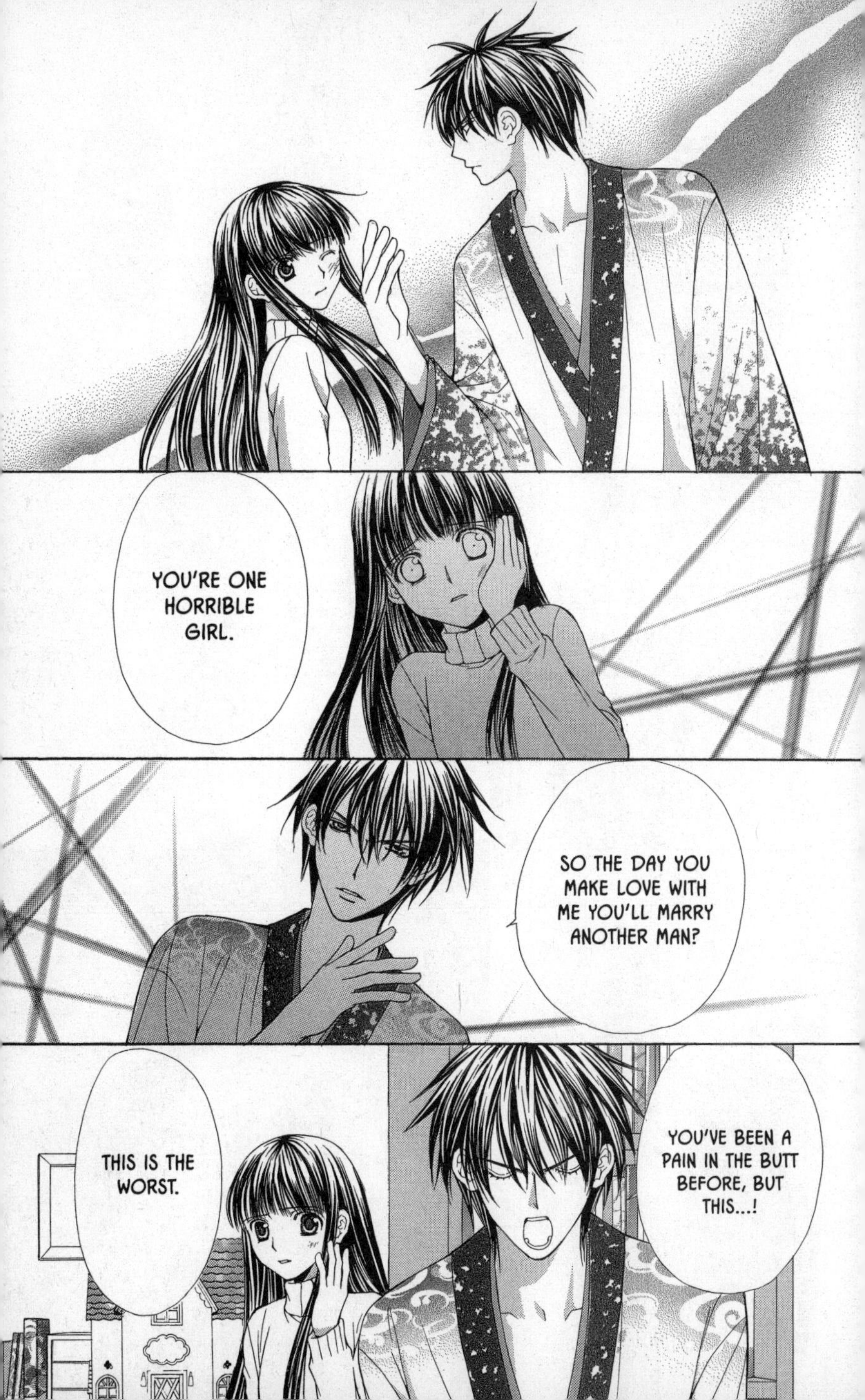
YOU'RE ONE HORRIBLE GIRL.
SO THE DAY YOU MAKE LOVE WITH ME YOU'LL MARRY ANOTHER MAN?
YOU'VE BEEN A PAIN IN THE BUTT BEFORE, BUT THIS...!
THIS IS THE WORST.

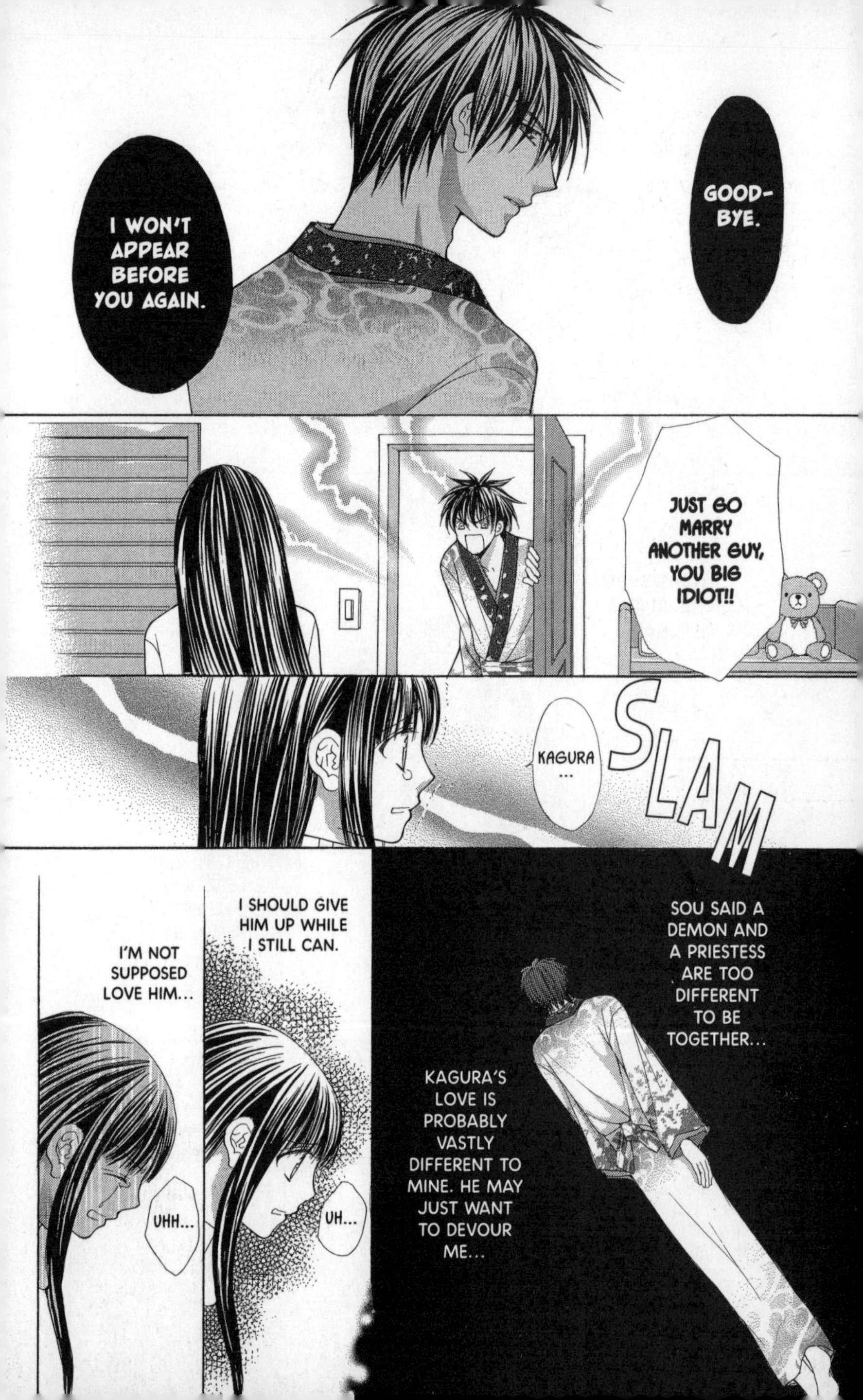
GOOD-BYE.
I WON'T APPEAR BEFORE YOU AGAIN.
JUST GO MARRY ANOTHER GUY, YOU BIG IDIOT!!
SLAM
KAGURA...
SOU SAID A DEMON AND A PRIESTESS ARE TOO DIFFERENT TO BE TOGETHER...
KAGURA'S LOVE IS PROBABLY VASTLY DIFFERENT TO MINE. HE MAY JUST WANT TO DEVOUR ME...
I SHOULD GIVE HIM UP WHILE I STILL CAN.
UH...
I'M NOT SUPPOSED LOVE HIM...
UHH...

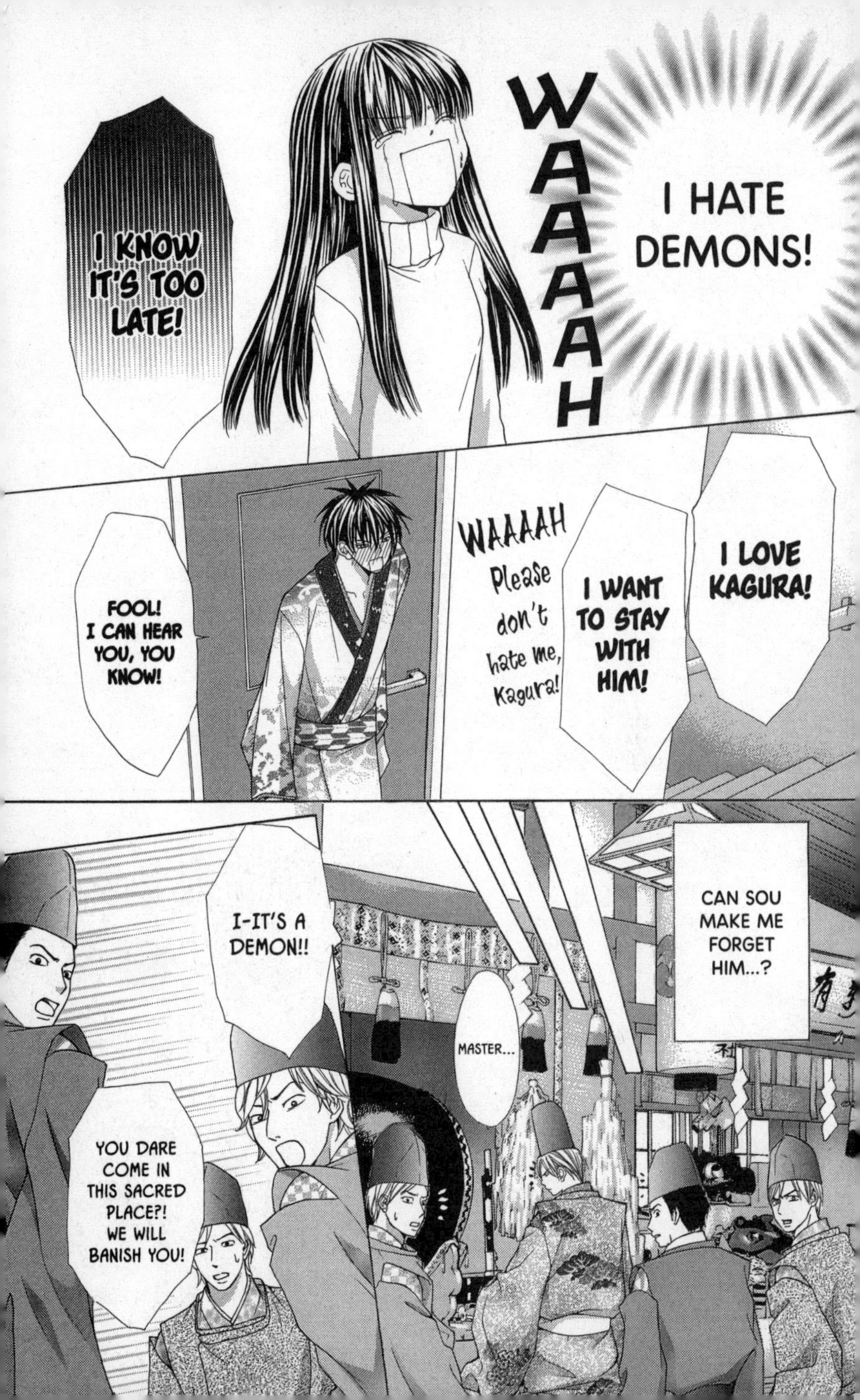
I HATE DEMONS!
WAAAAAH
I KNOW IT'S TOO LATE!
I LOVE KAGURA!
I WANT TO STAY WITH HIM!
WAAAAH
Please don't hate me, Kagura!
FOOL! I CAN HEAR YOU, YOU KNOW!
CAN SOU MAKE ME FORGET HIM...?
MASTER...
I-IT'S A DEMON!!
YOU DARE COME IN THIS SACRED PLACE?! WE WILL BANISH YOU!

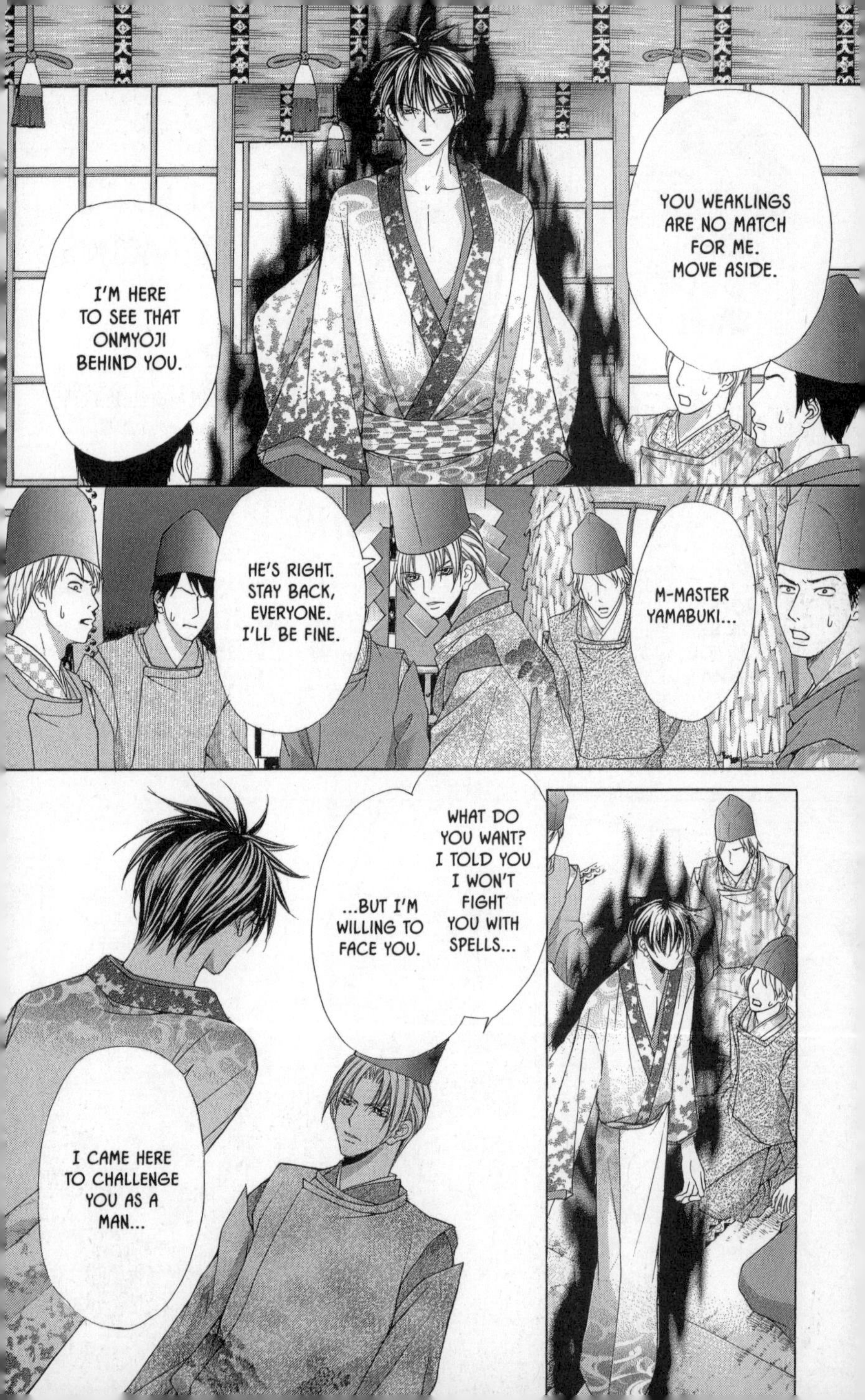
YOU WEAKLINGS ARE NO MATCH FOR ME. MOVE ASIDE.
I'M HERE TO SEE THAT ONMYOJI BEHIND YOU.
M-MASTER YAMABUKI...
HE'S RIGHT. STAY BACK, EVERYONE. I'LL BE FINE.
WHAT DO YOU WANT? I TOLD YOU I WON'T FIGHT YOU WITH SPELLS...
...BUT I'M WILLING TO FACE YOU.
I CAME HERE TO CHALLENGE YOU AS A MAN...

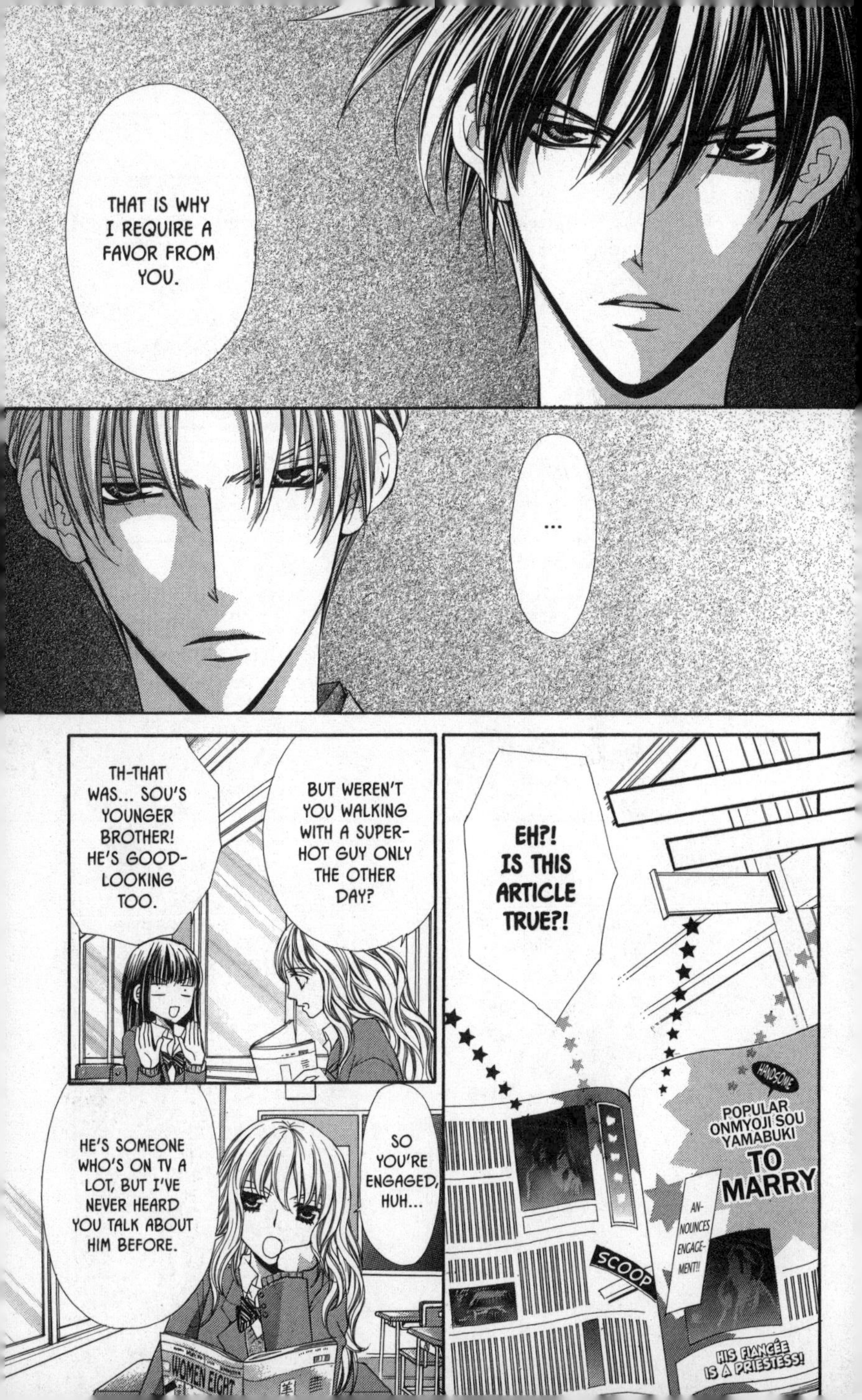
THAT IS WHY I REQUIRE A FAVOR FROM YOU.
...
EH?! IS THIS ARTICLE TRUE?!
HANDSOME
POPULAR ONMYOJI SOU YAMABUKI TO MARRY
AN-NOUNCES ENGAGE-MENT!!
SCOOP
HIS FIANCÉE IS A PRIESTESS!
BUT WEREN'T YOU WALKING WITH A SUPER-HOT GUY ONLY THE OTHER DAY?
TH-THAT WAS... SOU'S YOUNGER BROTHER! HE'S GOOD-LOOKING TOO.
SO YOU'RE ENGAGED, HUH...
HE'S SOMEONE WHO'S ON TV A LOT, BUT I'VE NEVER HEARD YOU TALK ABOUT HIM BEFORE.
WOMEN EIGHT

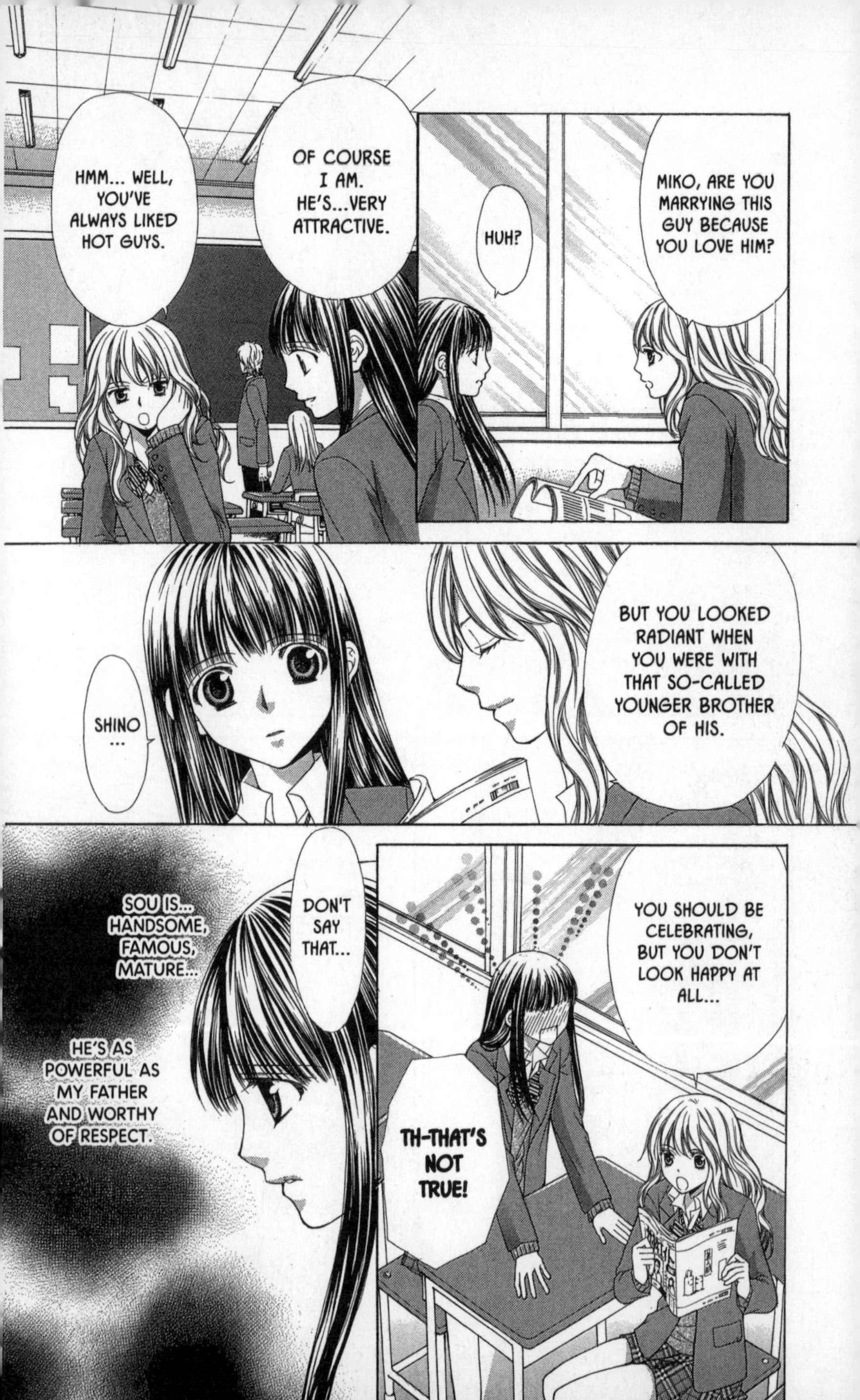
MIKO, ARE YOU MARRYING THIS GUY BECAUSE YOU LOVE HIM?
HUH?
OF COURSE I AM. HE'S...VERY ATTRACTIVE.
HMM... WELL, YOU'VE ALWAYS LIKED HOT GUYS.
BUT YOU LOOKED RADIANT WHEN YOU WERE WITH THAT SO-CALLED YOUNGER BROTHER OF HIS.
SHINO ...
YOU SHOULD BE CELEBRATING, BUT YOU DON'T LOOK HAPPY AT ALL...
TH-THAT'S NOT TRUE!
DON'T SAY THAT...
SOU IS... HANDSOME, FAMOUS, MATURE...
HE'S AS POWERFUL AS MY FATHER AND WORTHY OF RESPECT.

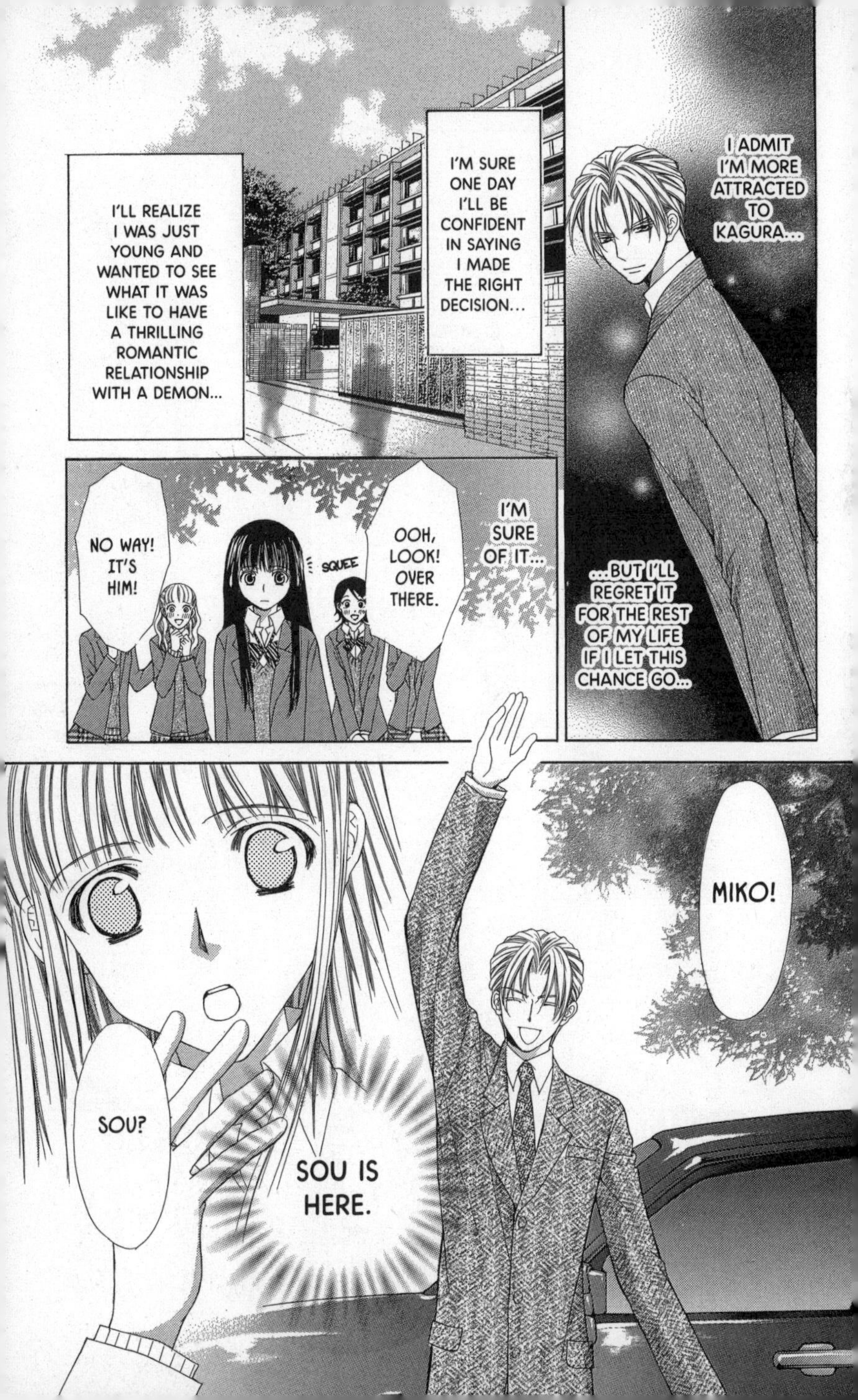
I ADMIT I'M MORE ATTRACTED TO KAGURA...
...BUT I'LL REGRET IT FOR THE REST OF MY LIFE IF I LET THIS CHANCE GO...
I'M SURE ONE DAY I'LL BE CONFIDENT IN SAYING I MADE THE RIGHT DECISION...
I'LL REALIZE I WAS JUST YOUNG AND WANTED TO SEE WHAT IT WAS LIKE TO HAVE A THRILLING ROMANTIC RELATIONSHIP WITH A DEMON...
I'M SURE OF IT...
OOH, LOOK! OVER THERE.
SQUEE
NO WAY! IT'S HIM!
MIKO!
SOU IS HERE.
SOU?

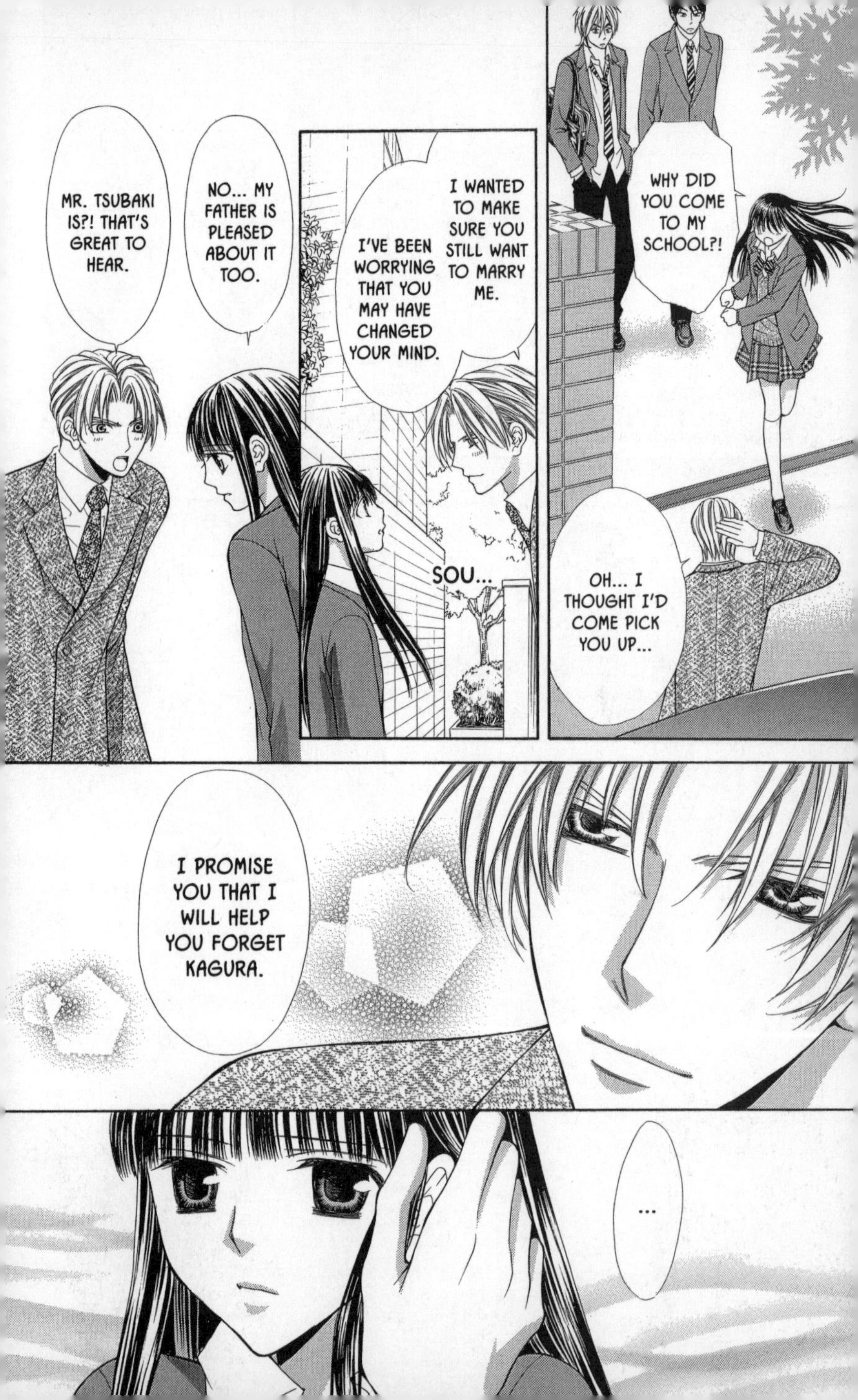
WHY DID YOU COME TO MY SCHOOL?!
OH... I THOUGHT I'D COME PICK YOU UP...
I WANTED TO MAKE SURE YOU STILL WANT TO MARRY ME.
I'VE BEEN WORRYING THAT YOU MAY HAVE CHANGED YOUR MIND.
SOU...
NO... MY FATHER IS PLEASED ABOUT IT TOO.
MR. TSUBAKI IS?! THAT'S GREAT TO HEAR.
I PROMISE YOU THAT I WILL HELP YOU FORGET KAGURA.
...

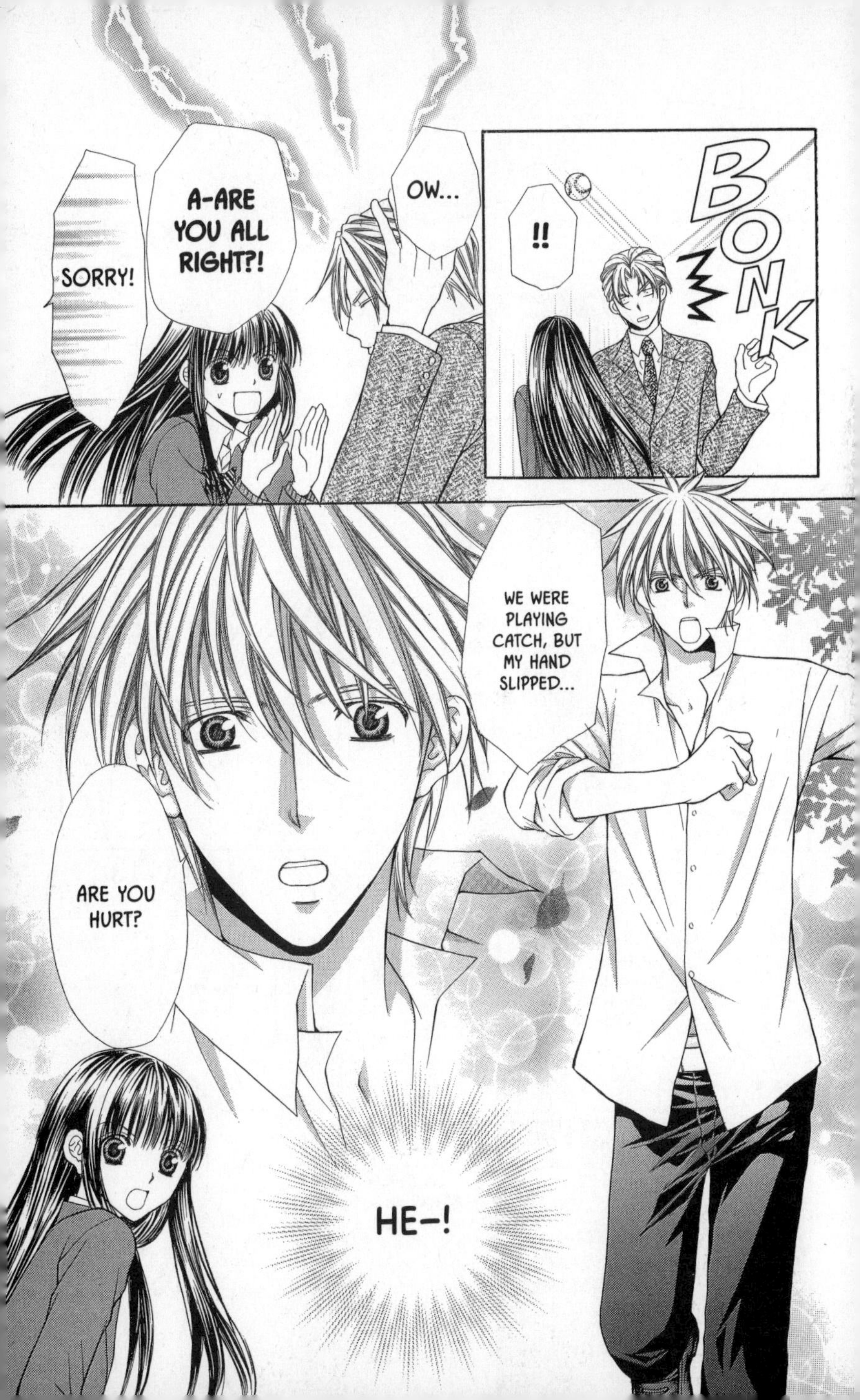
BONK
!!
OW...
A-ARE YOU ALL RIGHT?!
SORRY!
WE WERE PLAYING CATCH, BUT MY HAND SLIPPED...
ARE YOU HURT?
HE-!

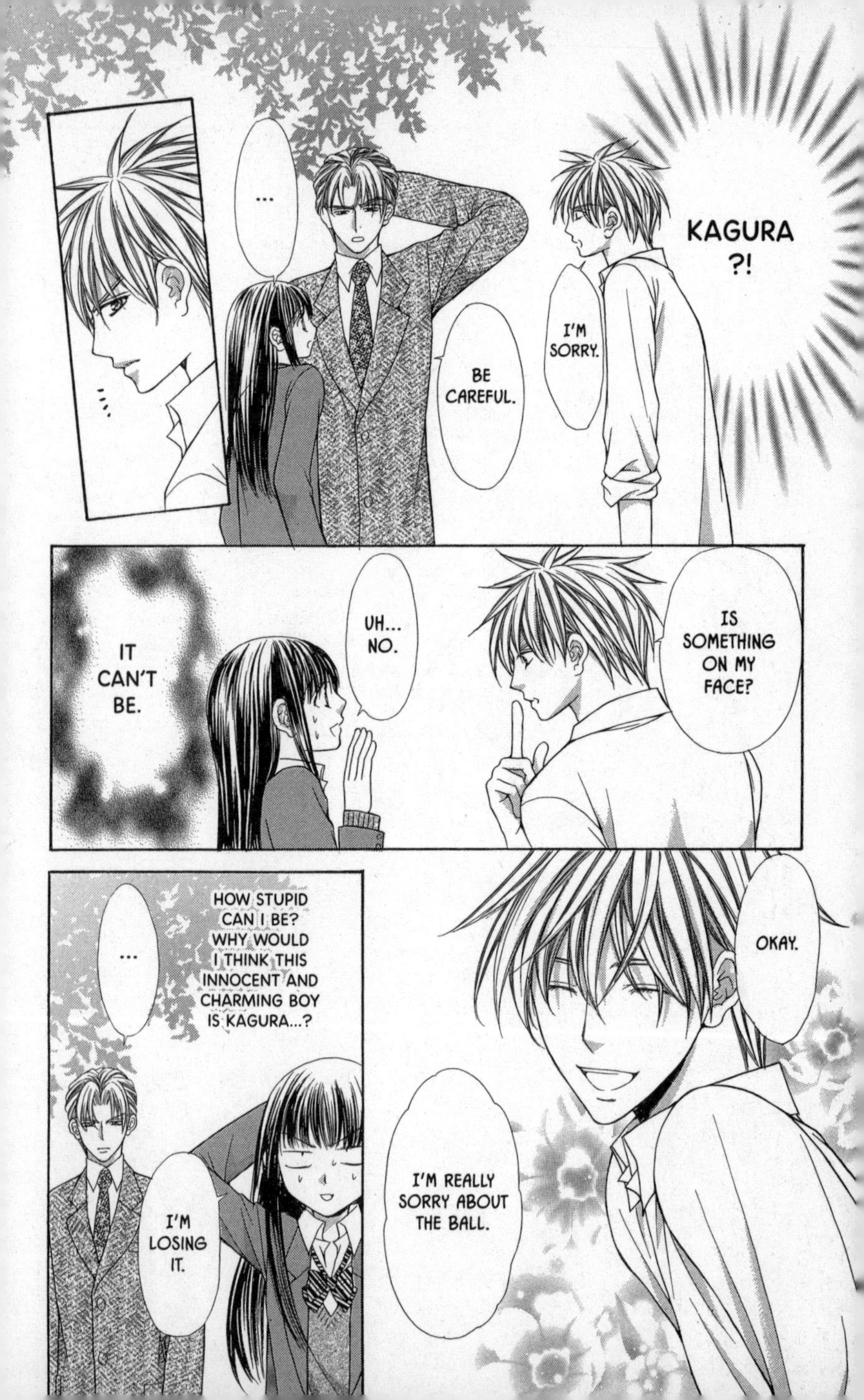
KAGURA ?!
I'M SORRY.
BE CAREFUL.
...
IS SOMETHING ON MY FACE?
UH... NO.
IT CAN'T BE.
OKAY.
I'M REALLY SORRY ABOUT THE BALL.
HOW STUPID CAN I BE? WHY WOULD I THINK THIS INNOCENT AND CHARMING BOY IS KAGURA...?
...
I'M LOSING IT.

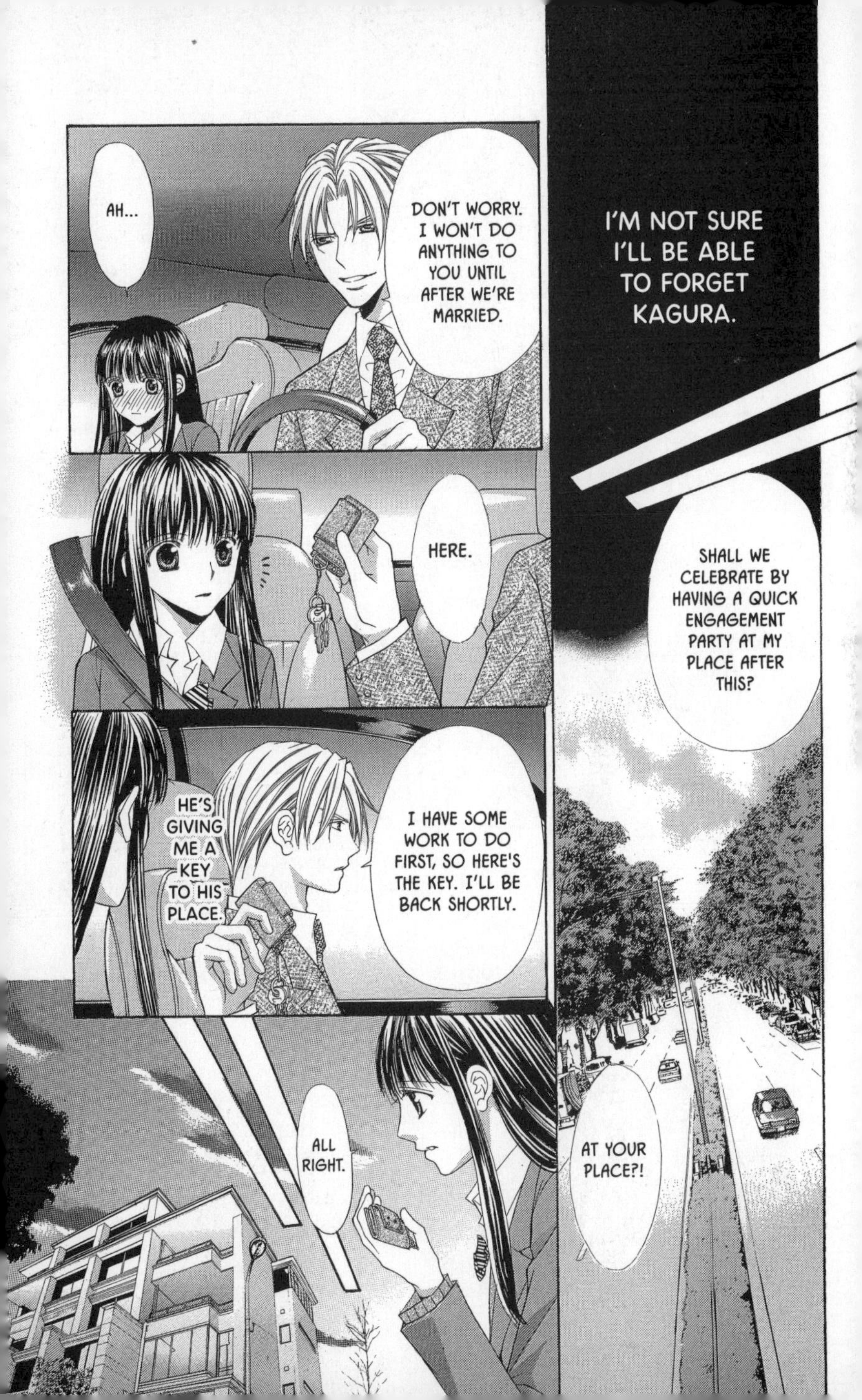
I'M NOT SURE I'LL BE ABLE TO FORGET KAGURA.
SHALL WE CELEBRATE BY HAVING A QUICK ENGAGEMENT PARTY AT MY PLACE AFTER THIS?
AT YOUR PLACE?!
DON'T WORRY. I WON'T DO ANYTHING TO YOU UNTIL AFTER WE'RE MARRIED.
AH...
HERE.
I HAVE SOME WORK TO DO FIRST, SO HERE'S THE KEY. I'LL BE BACK SHORTLY.
HE'S GIVING ME A KEY TO HIS PLACE.
ALL RIGHT.

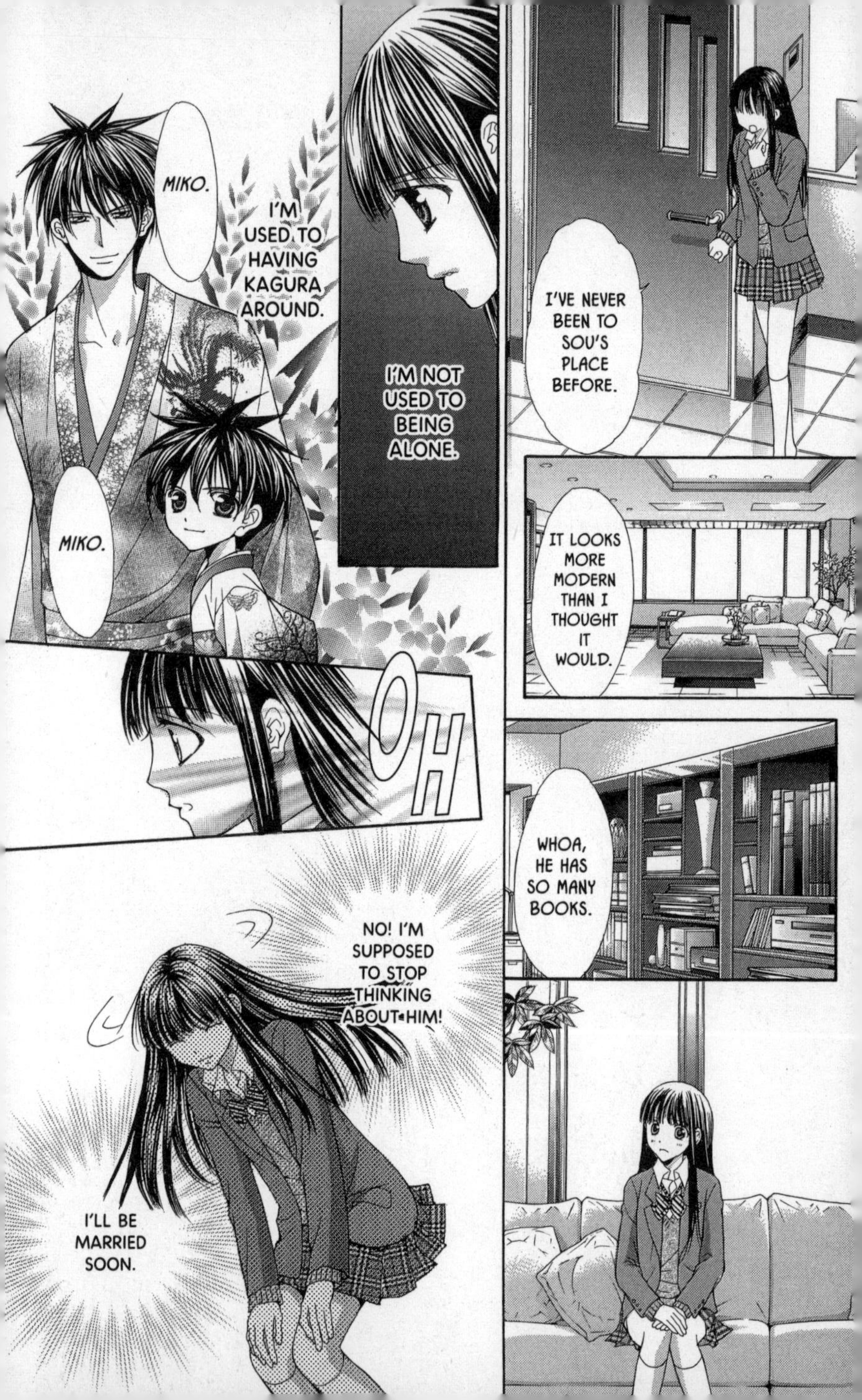
I'VE NEVER BEEN TO SOU'S PLACE BEFORE.
IT LOOKS MORE MODERN THAN I THOUGHT IT WOULD.
WHOA, HE HAS SO MANY BOOKS.
I'M NOT USED TO BEING ALONE.
MIKO.
I'M USED TO HAVING KAGURA AROUND.
MIKO.
OH
NO! I'M SUPPOSED TO STOP THINKING ABOUT HIM!
I'LL BE MARRIED SOON.

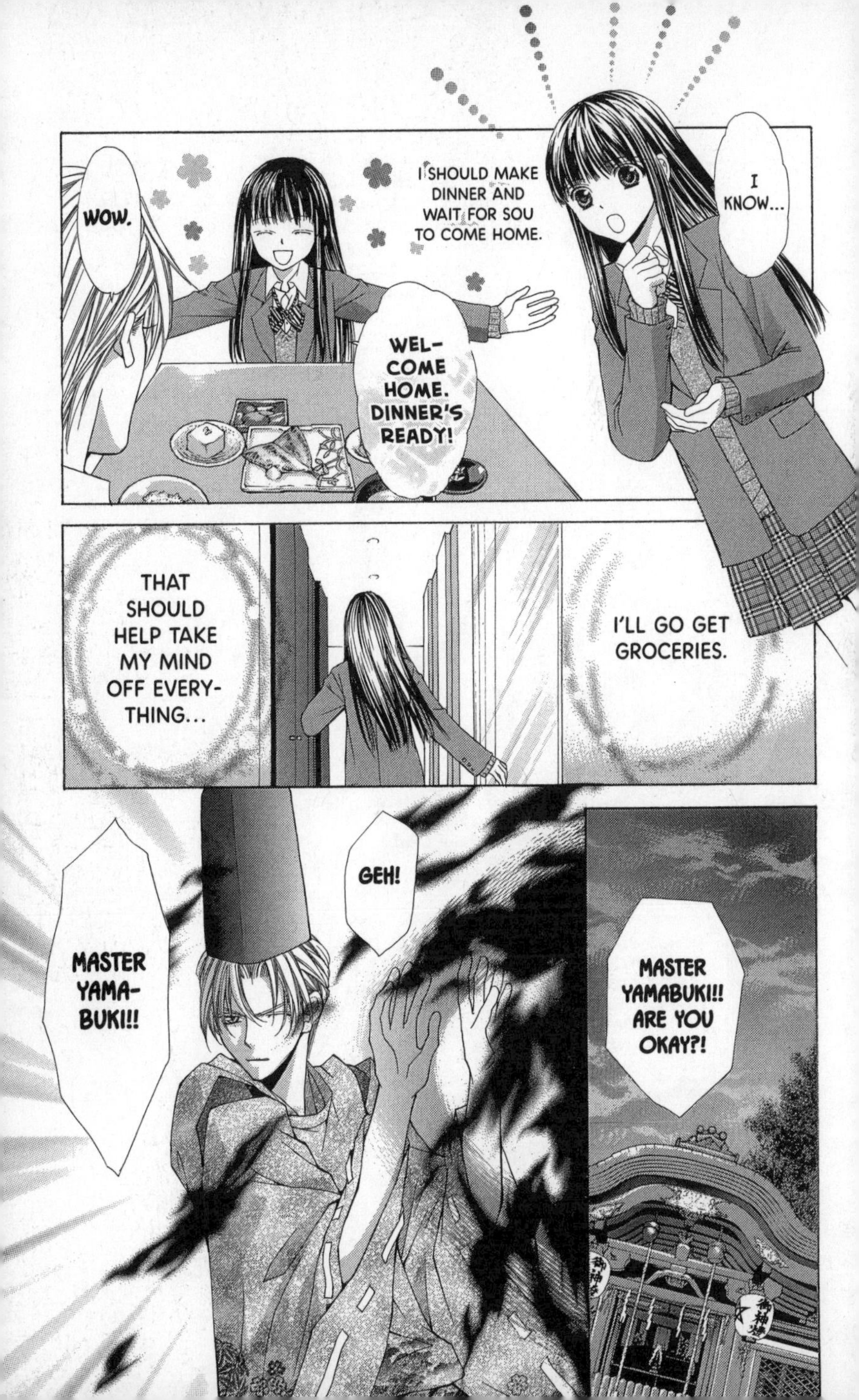
I KNOW...
I SHOULD MAKE DINNER AND WAIT FOR SOU TO COME HOME.
WEL-COME HOME. DINNER'S READY!
WOW.
I'LL GO GET GROCERIES.
THAT SHOULD HELP TAKE MY MIND OFF EVERY-THING...
MASTER YAMABUKI!! ARE YOU OKAY?!
GEH!
MASTER YAMA-BUKI!!

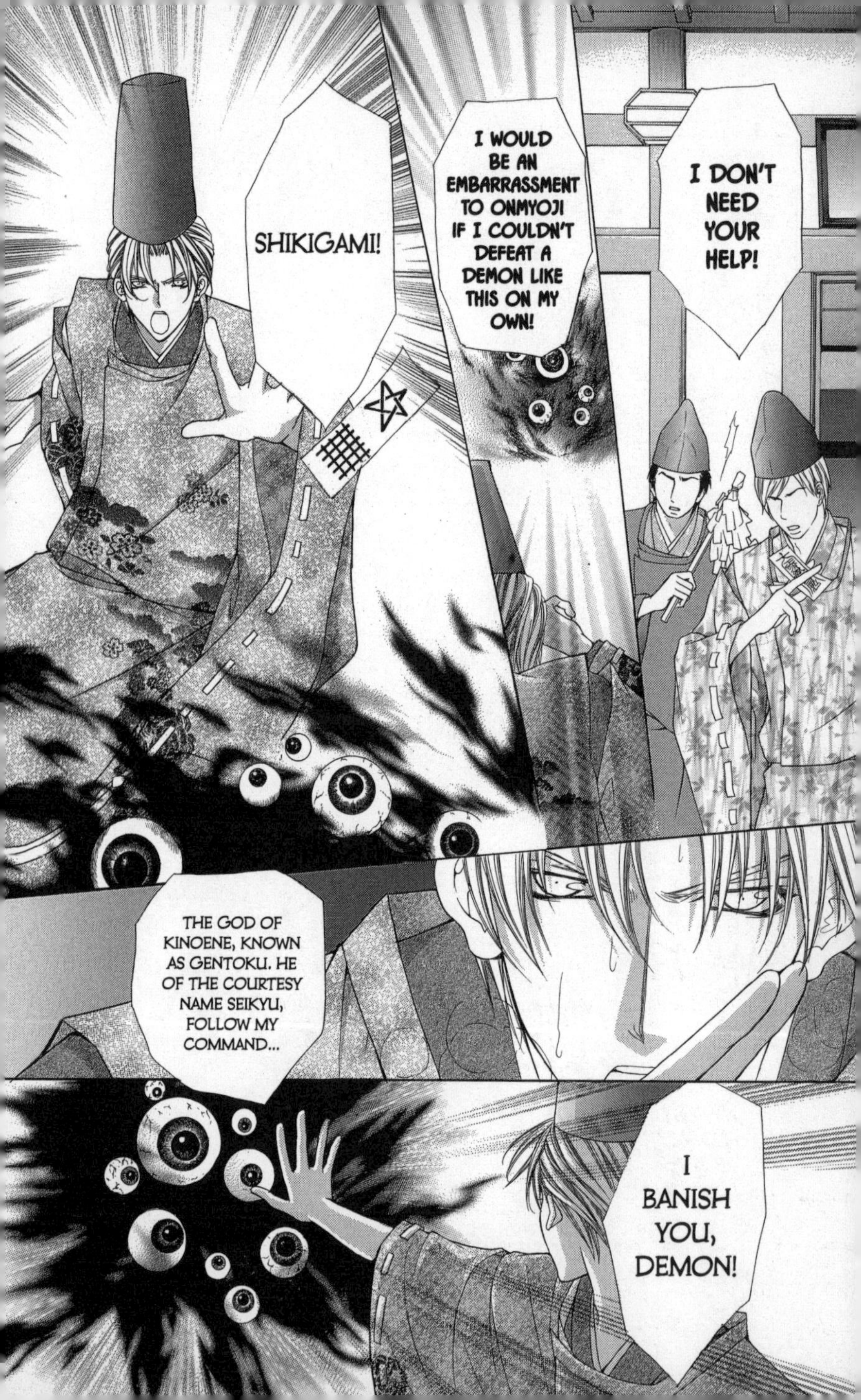
I DON'T NEED YOUR HELP!
I WOULD BE AN EMBARRASSMENT TO ONMYOJI IF I COULDN'T DEFEAT A DEMON LIKE THIS ON MY OWN!
SHIKIGAMI!
THE GOD OF KINOENE, KNOWN AS GENTOKU. HE OF THE COURTESY NAME SEIKYU, FOLLOW MY COMMAND...
I BANISH YOU, DEMON!

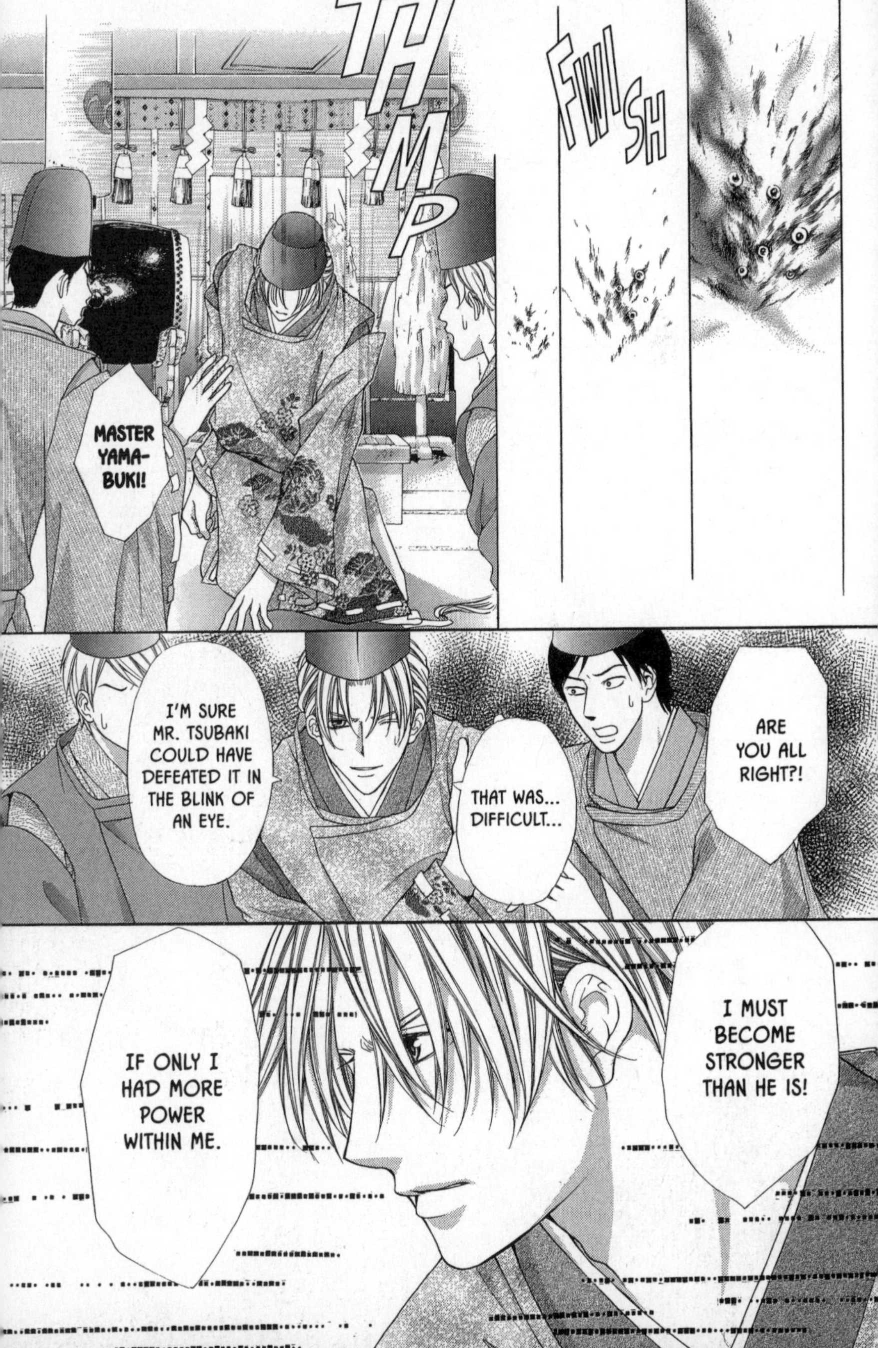
FWISH
THMP
MASTER YAMABUKI!
ARE YOU ALL RIGHT?!
THAT WAS... DIFFICULT...
I'M SURE MR. TSUBAKI COULD HAVE DEFEATED IT IN THE BLINK OF AN EYE.
I MUST BECOME STRONGER THAN HE IS!
IF ONLY I HAD MORE POWER WITHIN ME.

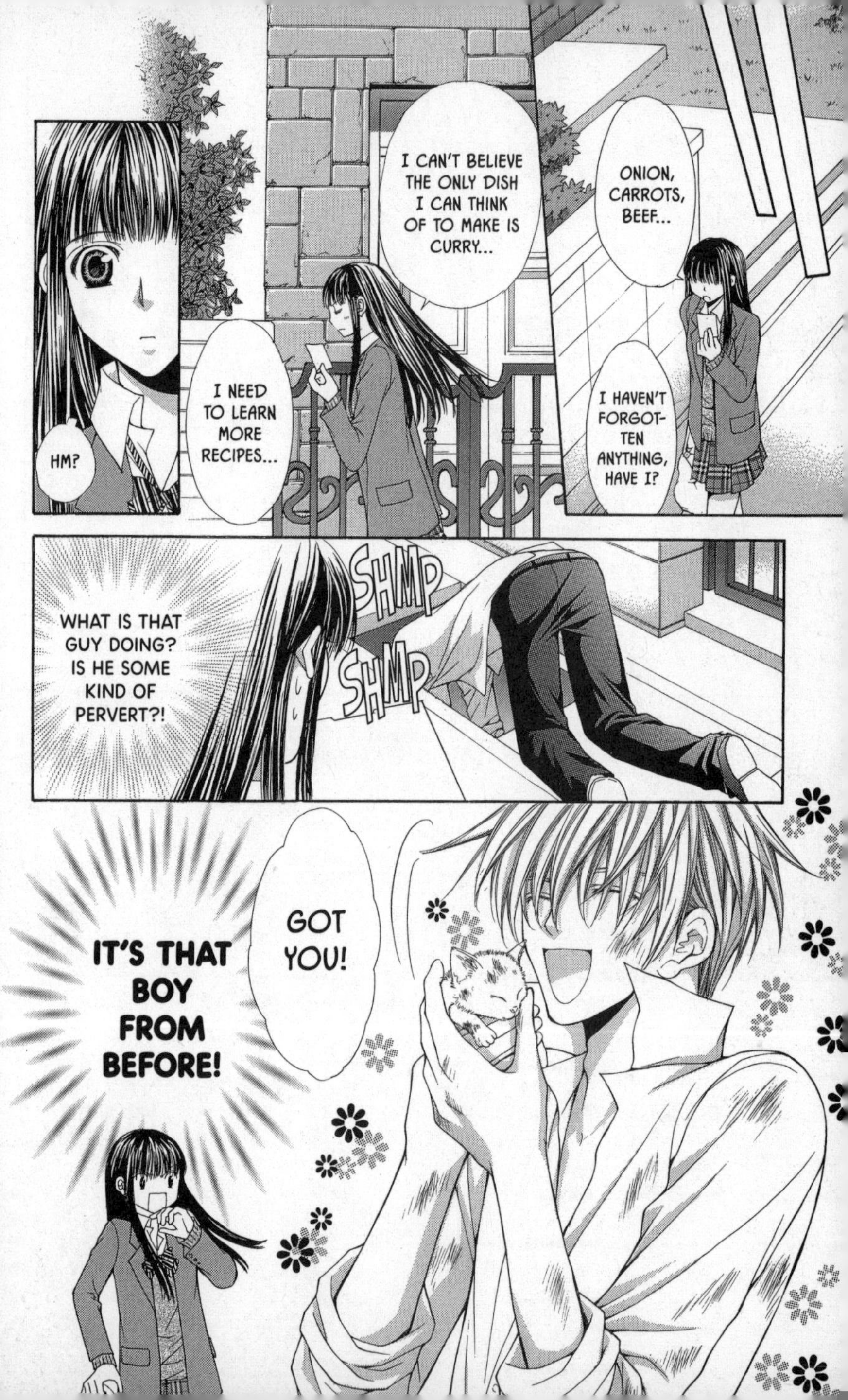
ONION, CARROTS, BEEF...
I HAVEN'T FORGOT-TEN ANYTHING, HAVE I?
I CAN'T BELIEVE THE ONLY DISH I CAN THINK OF TO MAKE IS CURRY...
I NEED TO LEARN MORE RECIPES...
HM?
SHMP
SHMP
WHAT IS THAT GUY DOING? IS HE SOME KIND OF PERVERT?!
GOT YOU!
IT'S THAT BOY FROM BEFORE!

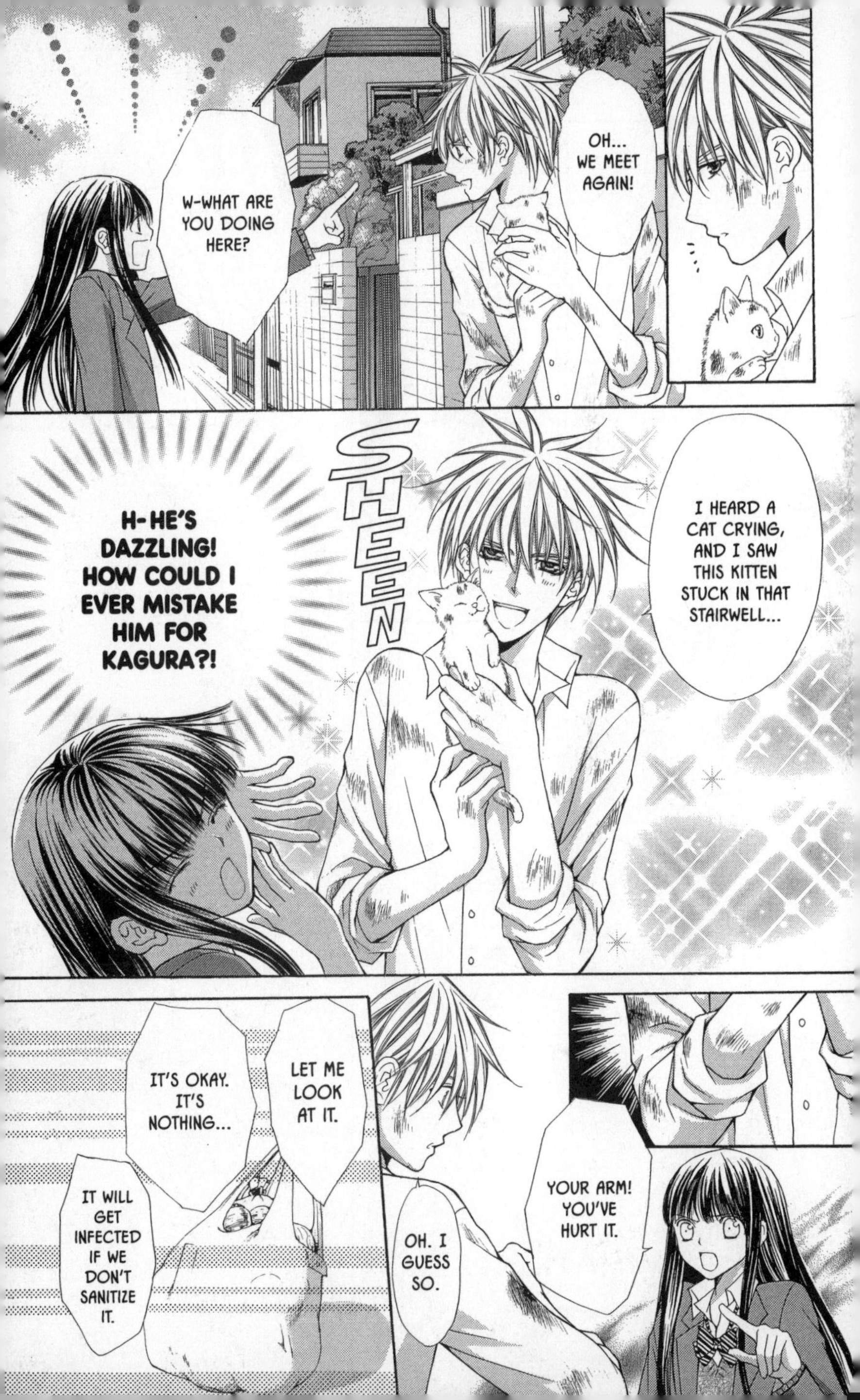
OH... WE MEET AGAIN!
W-WHAT ARE YOU DOING HERE?
SHEEN
I HEARD A CAT CRYING, AND I SAW THIS KITTEN STUCK IN THAT STAIRWELL...
H-HE'S DAZZLING! HOW COULD I EVER MISTAKE HIM FOR KAGURA?!
YOUR ARM! YOU'VE HURT IT.
OH. I GUESS SO.
LET ME LOOK AT IT.
IT'S OKAY. IT'S NOTHING...
IT WILL GET INFECTED IF WE DON'T SANITIZE IT.

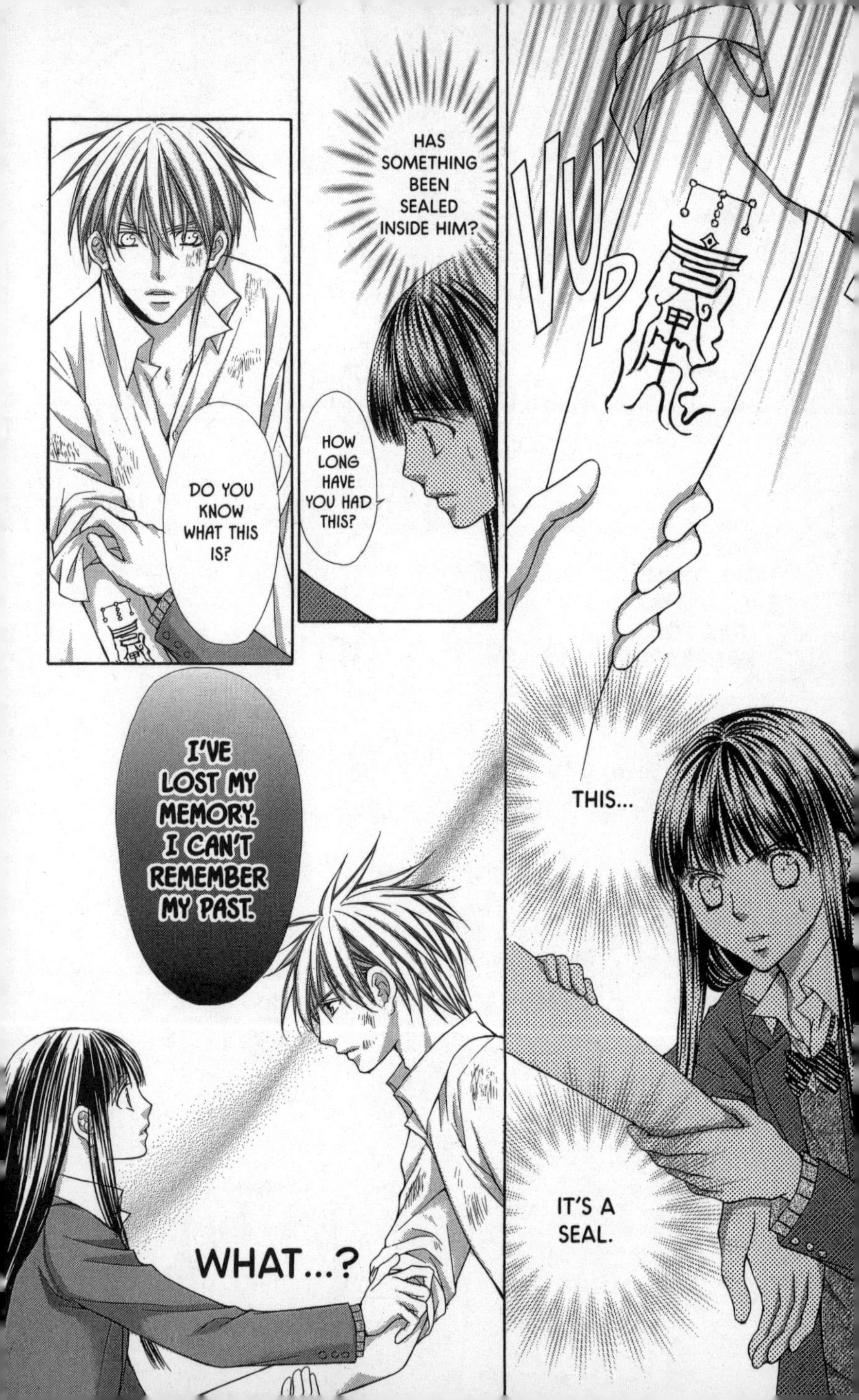
VUP
THIS...
IT'S A SEAL.
HAS SOMETHING BEEN SEALED INSIDE HIM?
HOW LONG HAVE YOU HAD THIS?
DO YOU KNOW WHAT THIS IS?
I'VE LOST MY MEMORY. I CAN'T REMEMBER MY PAST.
WHAT...?

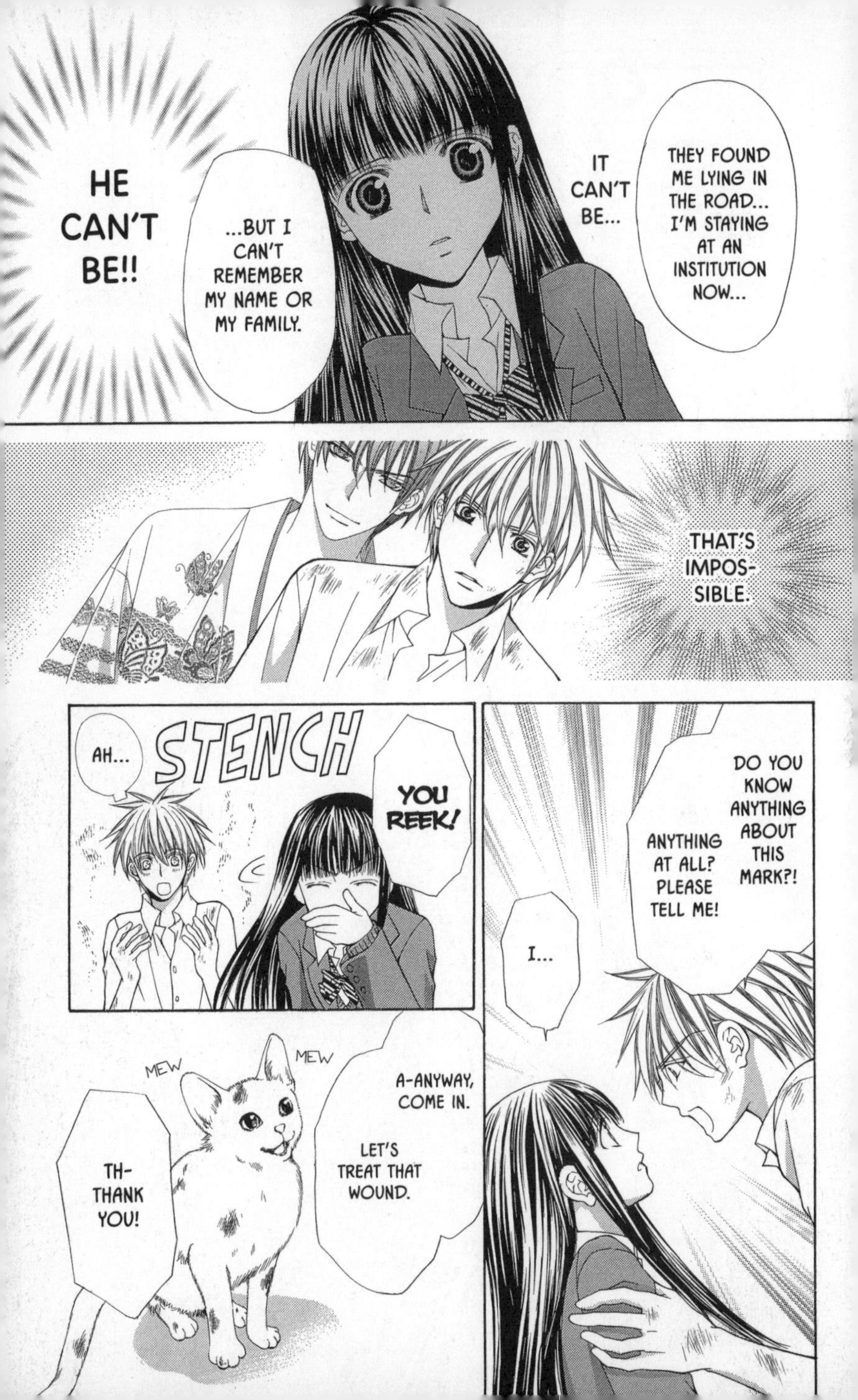
THEY FOUND ME LYING IN THE ROAD... I'M STAYING AT AN INSTITUTION NOW...
IT CAN'T BE...
...BUT I CAN'T REMEMBER MY NAME OR MY FAMILY.
HE CAN'T BE!!
THAT'S IMPOS-SIBLE.
DO YOU KNOW ANYTHING ABOUT THIS MARK?!
ANYTHING AT ALL? PLEASE TELL ME!
I...
YOU REEK!
STENCH
AH...
MEW
A-ANYWAY, COME IN.
LET'S TREAT THAT WOUND.
MEW
TH-THANK YOU!

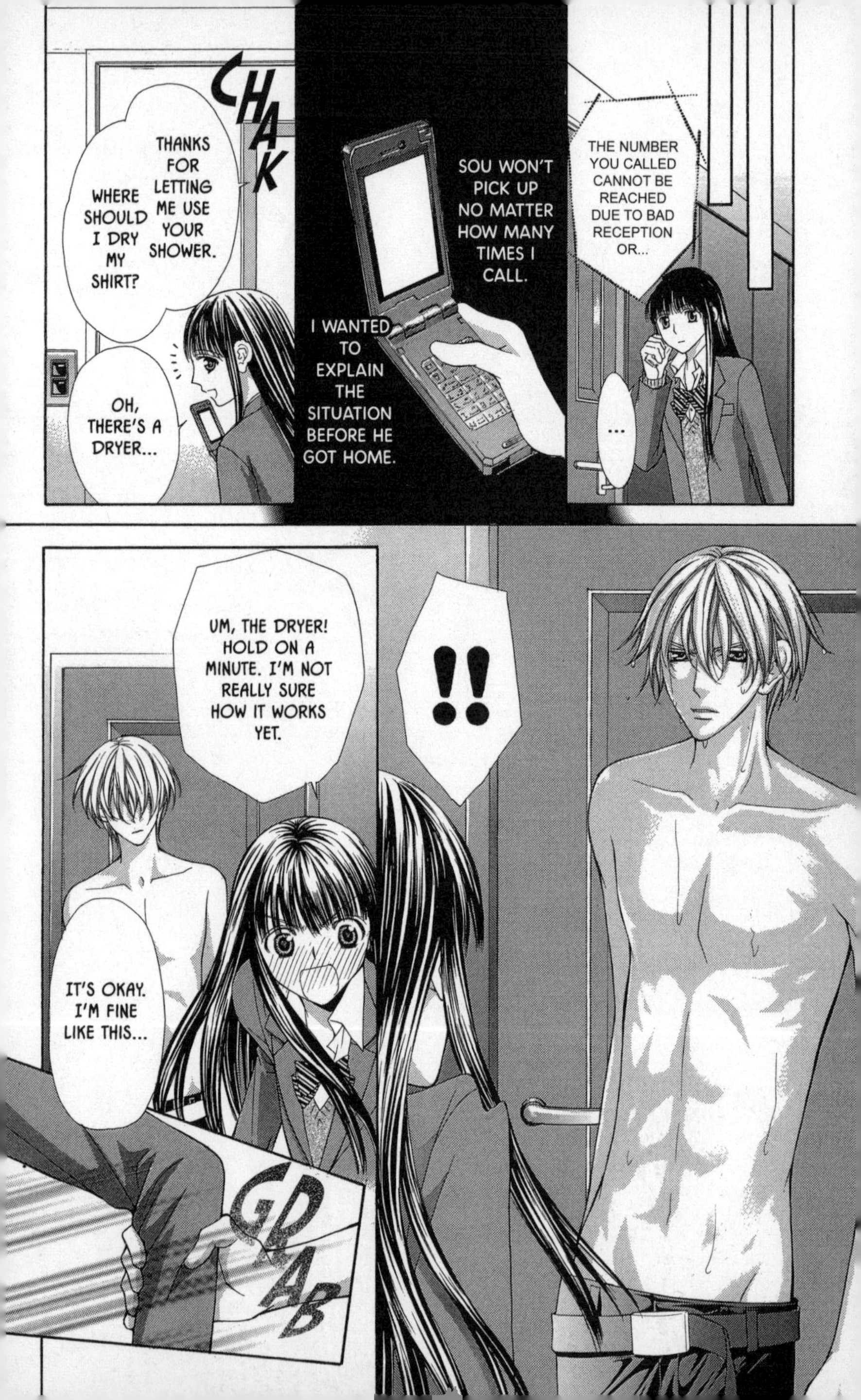
THE NUMBER YOU CALLED CANNOT BE REACHED DUE TO BAD RECEPTION OR...
...
SOU WON'T PICK UP NO MATTER HOW MANY TIMES I CALL.
I WANTED TO EXPLAIN THE SITUATION BEFORE HE GOT HOME.
CHAK
THANKS FOR LETTING ME USE YOUR SHOWER.
WHERE SHOULD I DRY MY SHIRT?
OH, THERE'S A DRYER...
UM, THE DRYER! HOLD ON A MINUTE. I'M NOT REALLY SURE HOW IT WORKS YET.
!!
IT'S OKAY. I'M FINE LIKE THIS...
GRAB

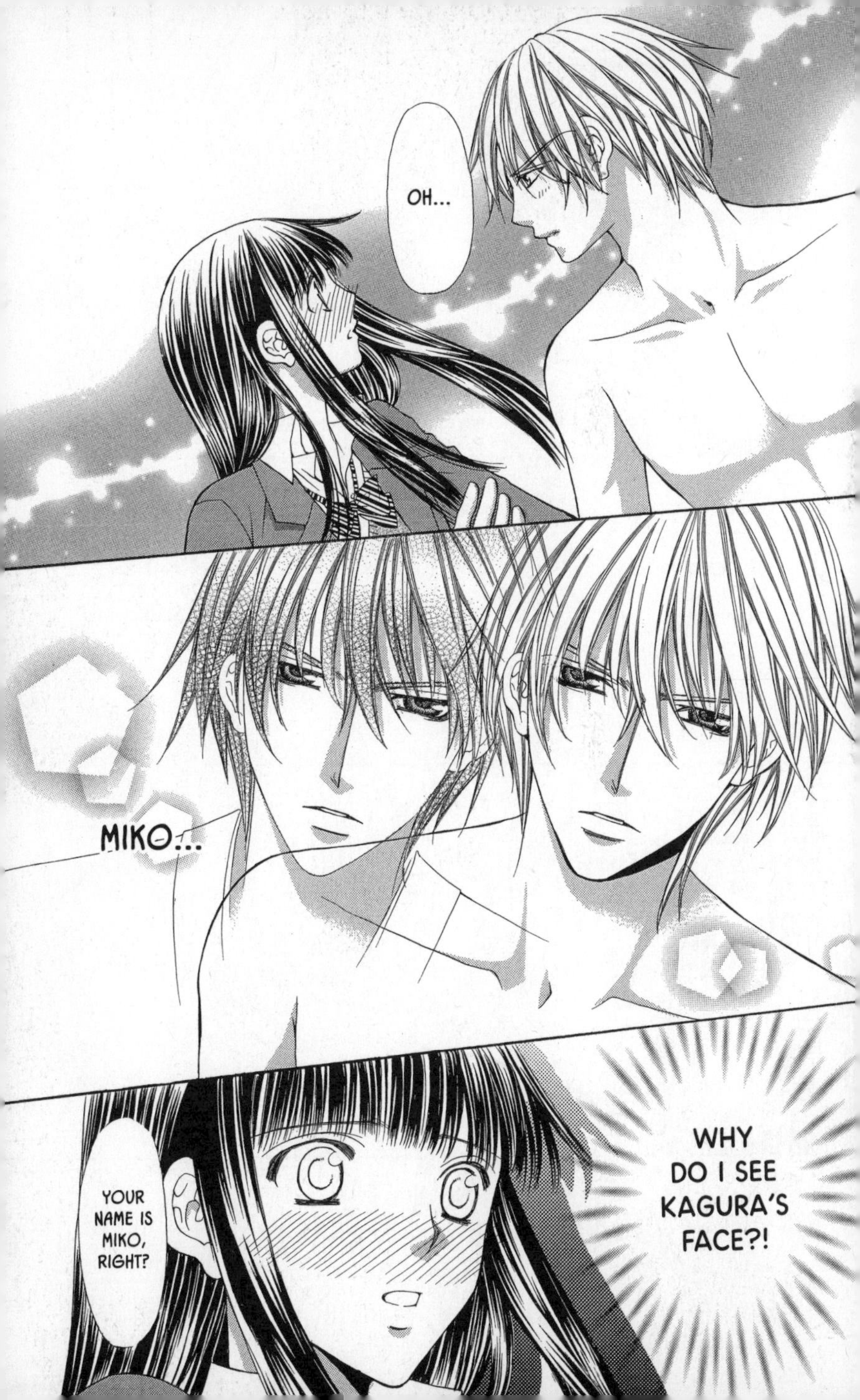
OH...
MIKO...
WHY DO I SEE KAGURA'S FACE?!
YOUR NAME IS MIKO, RIGHT?

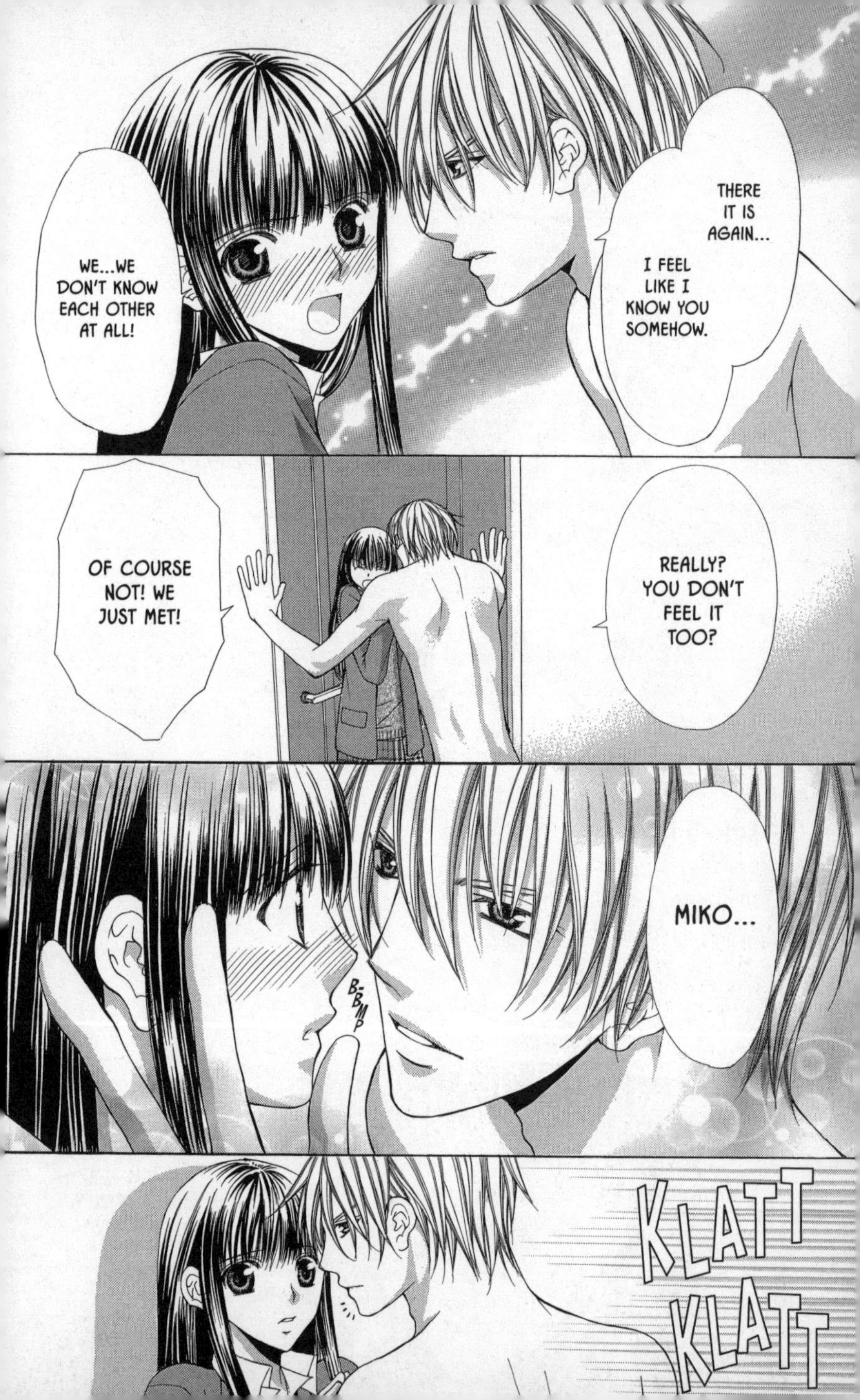
THERE IT IS AGAIN...
I FEEL LIKE I KNOW YOU SOMEHOW.
WE...WE DON'T KNOW EACH OTHER AT ALL!
REALLY? YOU DON'T FEEL IT TOO?
OF COURSE NOT! WE JUST MET!
MIKO...
B-BMP
KLATT KLATT

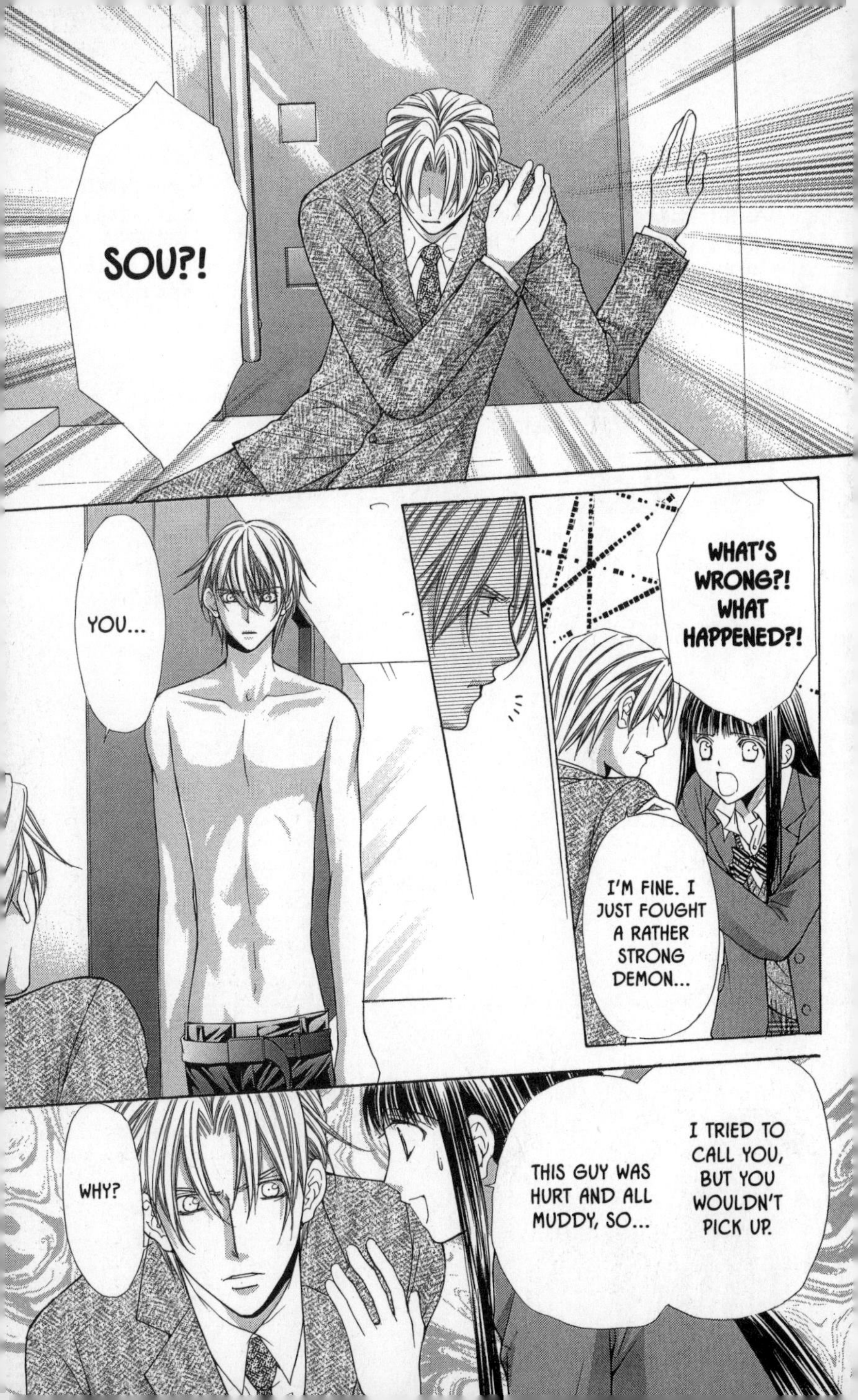
SOU?!
WHAT'S WRONG?! WHAT HAPPENED?!
I'M FINE. I JUST FOUGHT A RATHER STRONG DEMON...
YOU...
I TRIED TO CALL YOU, BUT YOU WOULDN'T PICK UP.
THIS GUY WAS HURT AND ALL MUDDY, SO...
WHY?

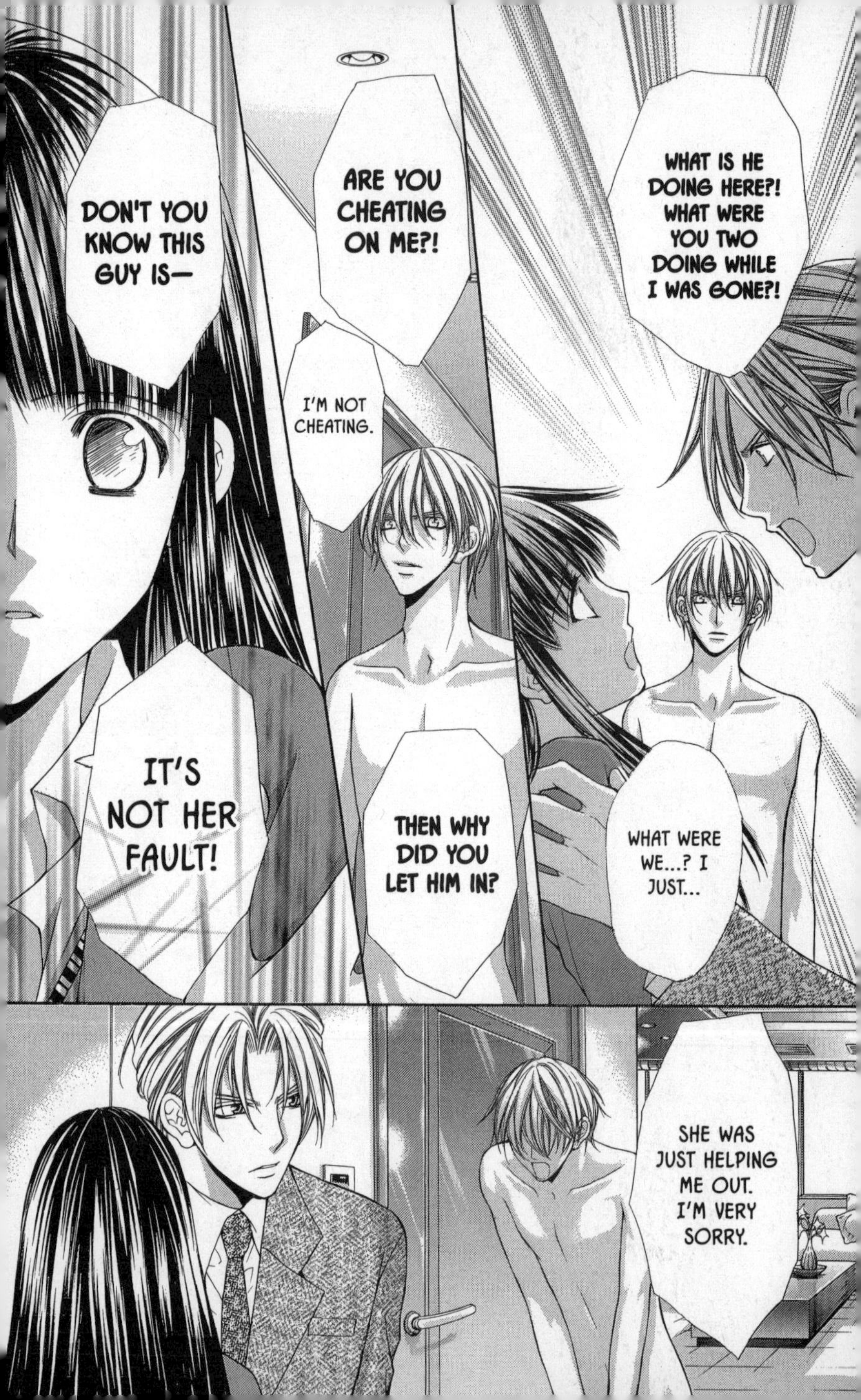
WHAT IS HE DOING HERE?! WHAT WERE YOU TWO DOING WHILE I WAS GONE?!
WHAT WERE WE...? I JUST...
ARE YOU CHEATING ON ME?!
I'M NOT CHEATING.
THEN WHY DID YOU LET HIM IN?
DON'T YOU KNOW THIS GUY IS—
IT'S NOT HER FAULT!
SHE WAS JUST HELPING ME OUT. I'M VERY SORRY.

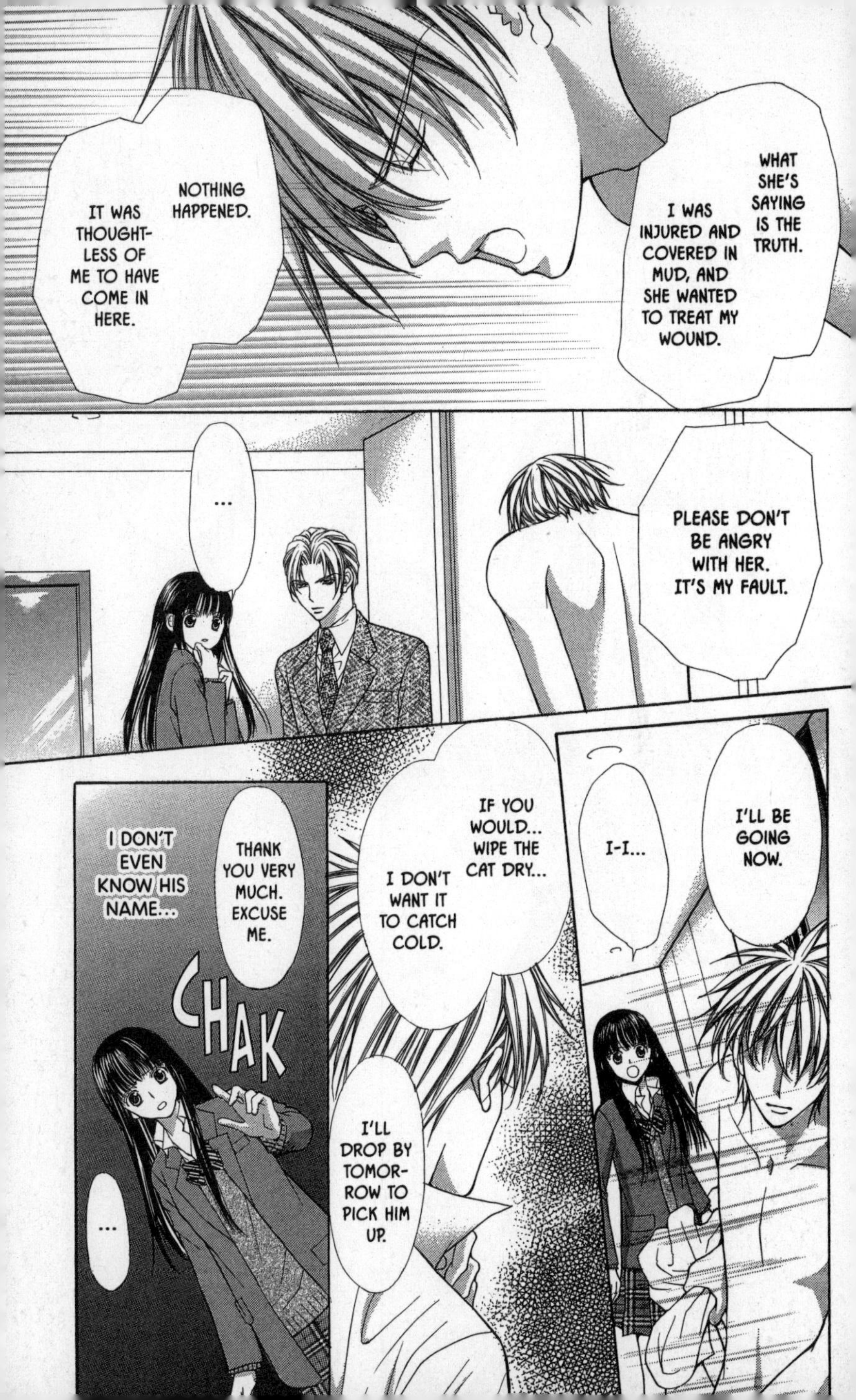

WHAT SHE'S SAYING IS THE TRUTH.
I WAS INJURED AND COVERED IN MUD, AND SHE WANTED TO TREAT MY WOUND.
NOTHING HAPPENED.
IT WAS THOUGHTLESS OF ME TO HAVE COME IN HERE.
PLEASE DON'T BE ANGRY WITH HER. IT'S MY FAULT.
...
I'LL BE GOING NOW.
I-I...
IF YOU WOULD... WIPE THE CAT DRY...
I DON'T WANT IT TO CATCH COLD.
I'LL DROP BY TOMORROW TO PICK HIM UP.
THANK YOU VERY MUCH. EXCUSE ME.
CHAK
I DON'T EVEN KNOW HIS NAME...
...

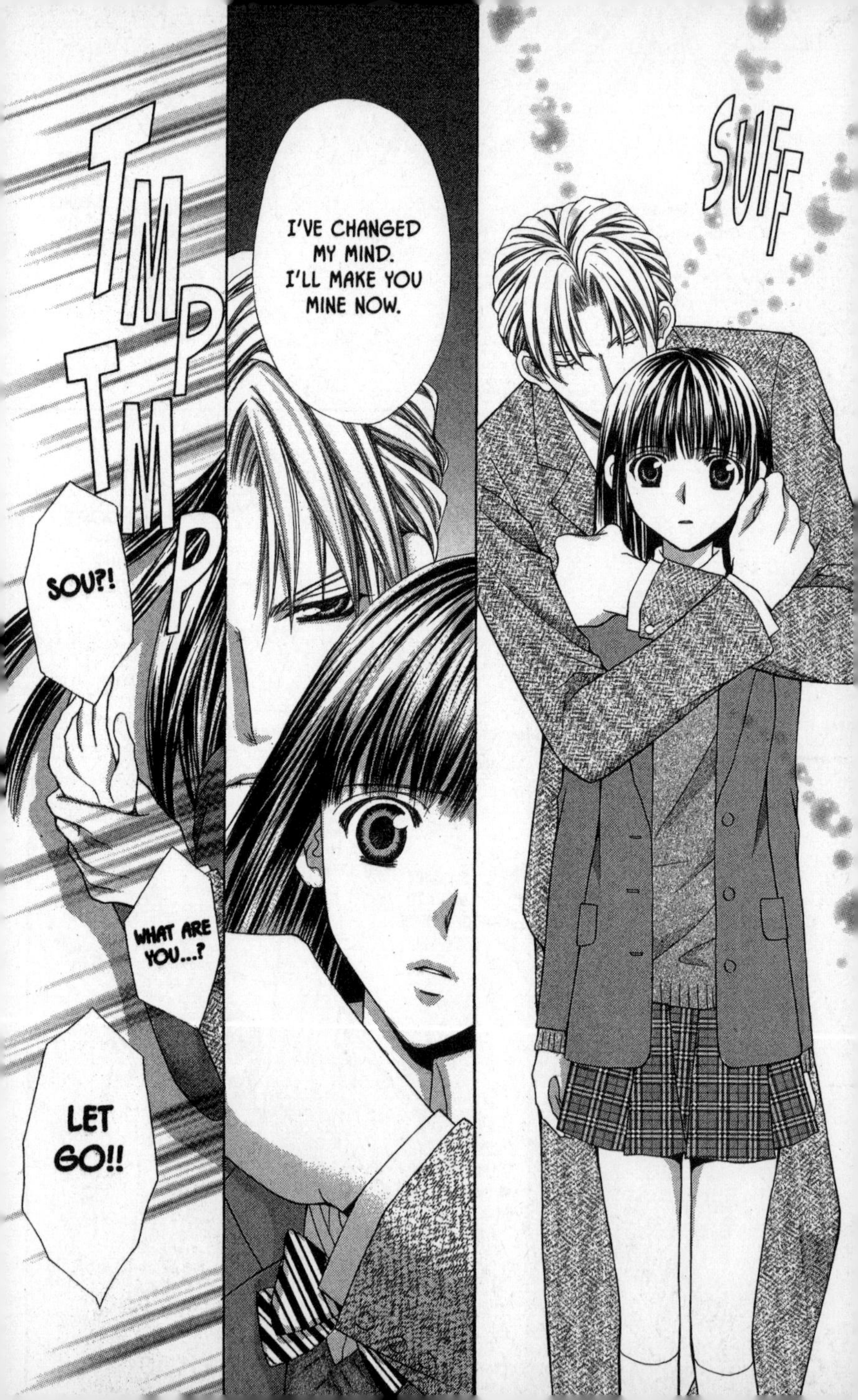
SUFF
I'VE CHANGED MY MIND. I'LL MAKE YOU MINE NOW.
TMP TMP
SOU?!
WHAT ARE YOU...?
LET GO!!

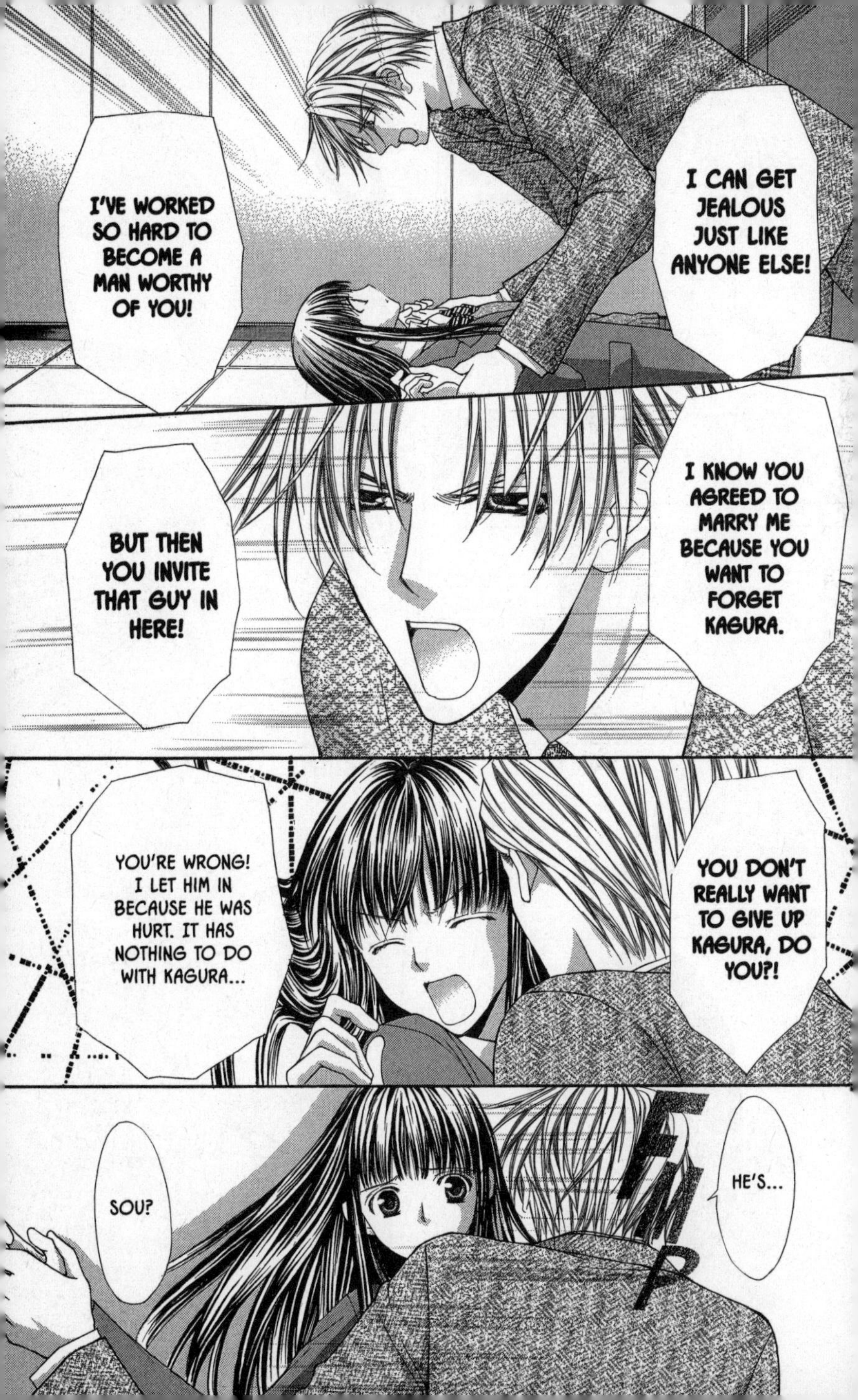
I CAN GET JEALOUS JUST LIKE ANYONE ELSE!
I'VE WORKED SO HARD TO BECOME A MAN WORTHY OF YOU!
I KNOW YOU AGREED TO MARRY ME BECAUSE YOU WANT TO FORGET KAGURA.
BUT THEN YOU INVITE THAT GUY IN HERE!
YOU DON'T REALLY WANT TO GIVE UP KAGURA, DO YOU?!
YOU'RE WRONG! I LET HIM IN BECAUSE HE WAS HURT. IT HAS NOTHING TO DO WITH KAGURA...
HE'S...
SOU?

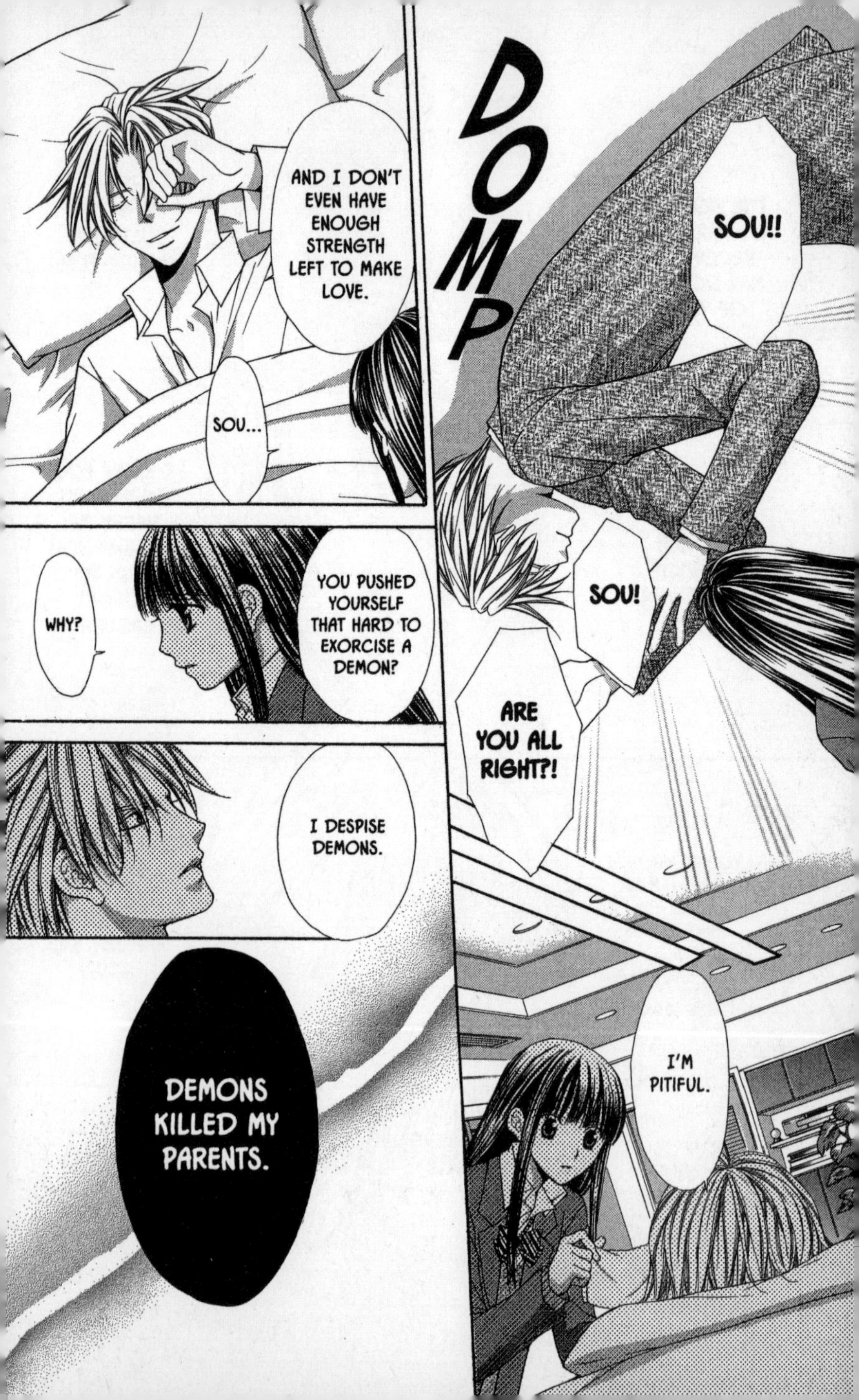
DOMP
SOU!!
SOU!
ARE YOU ALL RIGHT?!
I'M PITIFUL.
AND I DON'T EVEN HAVE ENOUGH STRENGTH LEFT TO MAKE LOVE.
SOU...
YOU PUSHED YOURSELF THAT HARD TO EXORCISE A DEMON?
WHY?
I DESPISE DEMONS.
DEMONS KILLED MY PARENTS.

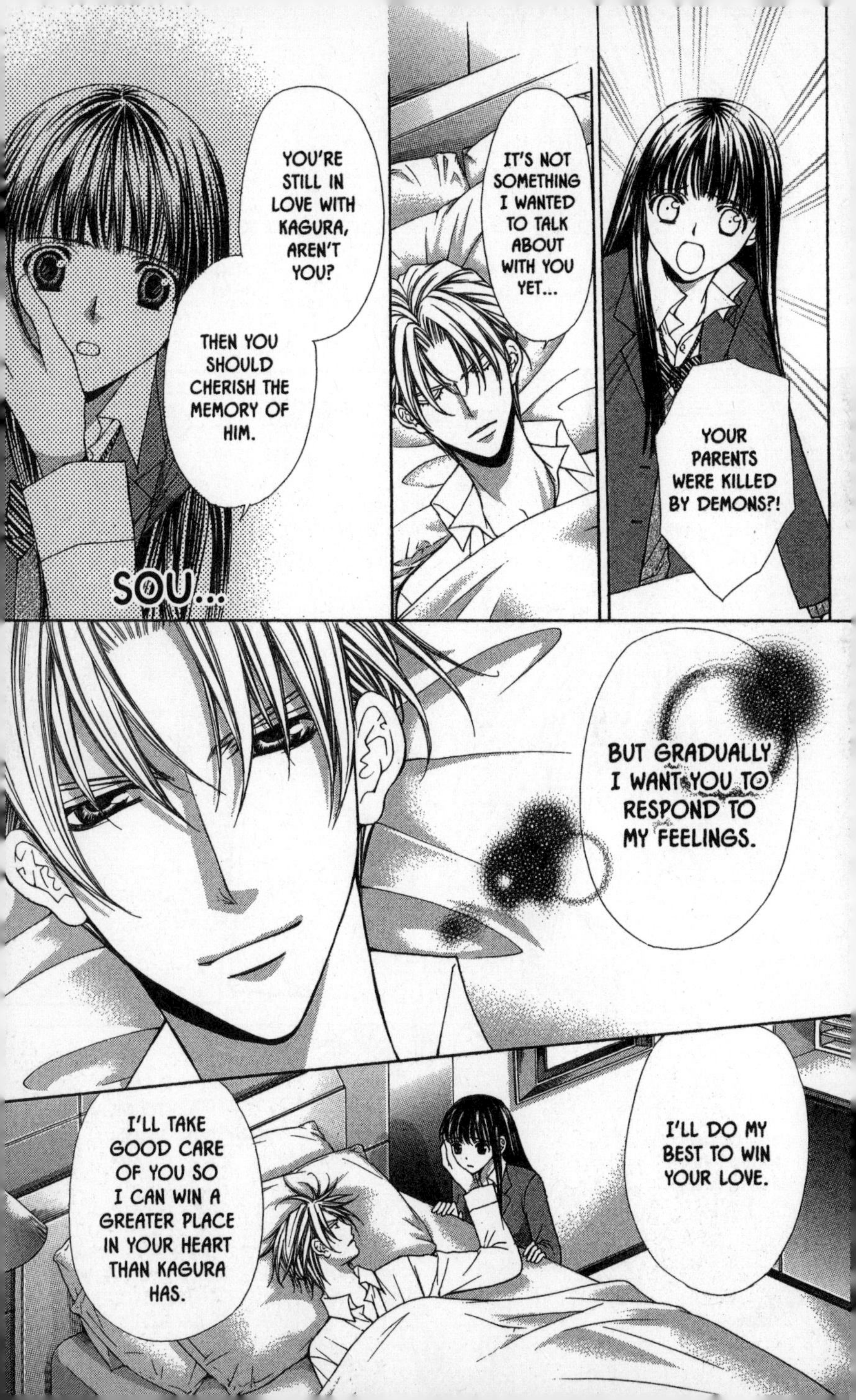
YOUR PARENTS WERE KILLED BY DEMONS?!
IT'S NOT SOMETHING I WANTED TO TALK ABOUT WITH YOU YET...
YOU'RE STILL IN LOVE WITH KAGURA, AREN'T YOU?
THEN YOU SHOULD CHERISH THE MEMORY OF HIM.
SOU...
BUT GRADUALLY I WANT YOU TO RESPOND TO MY FEELINGS.
I'LL DO MY BEST TO WIN YOUR LOVE.
I'LL TAKE GOOD CARE OF YOU SO I CAN WIN A GREATER PLACE IN YOUR HEART THAN KAGURA HAS.

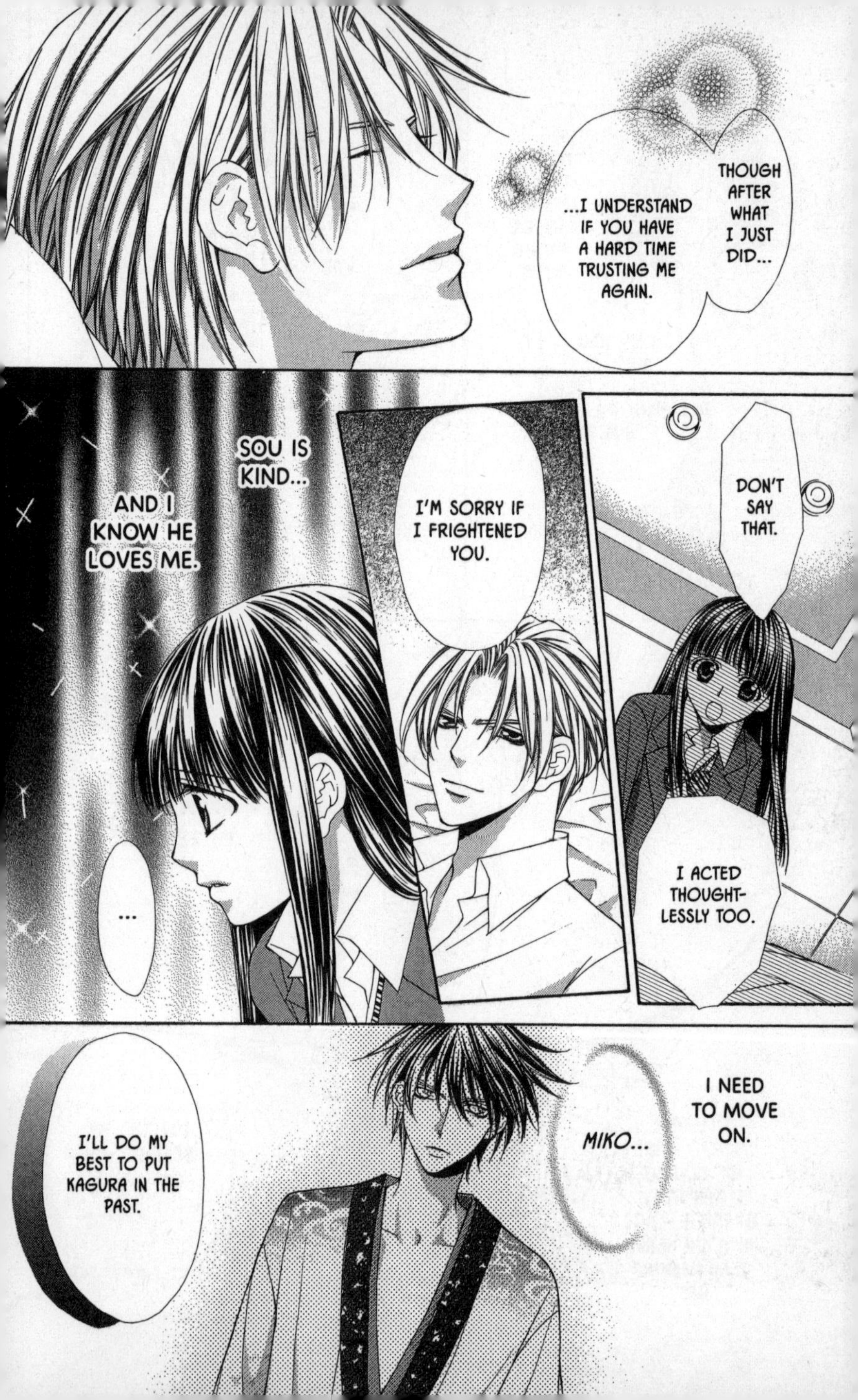
THOUGH AFTER WHAT I JUST DID...
...I UNDERSTAND IF YOU HAVE A HARD TIME TRUSTING ME AGAIN.
DON'T SAY THAT.
I ACTED THOUGHT-LESSLY TOO.
I'M SORRY IF I FRIGHTENED YOU.
SOU IS KIND...
AND I KNOW HE LOVES ME.
...
I NEED TO MOVE ON.
MIKO...
I'LL DO MY BEST TO PUT KAGURA IN THE PAST.

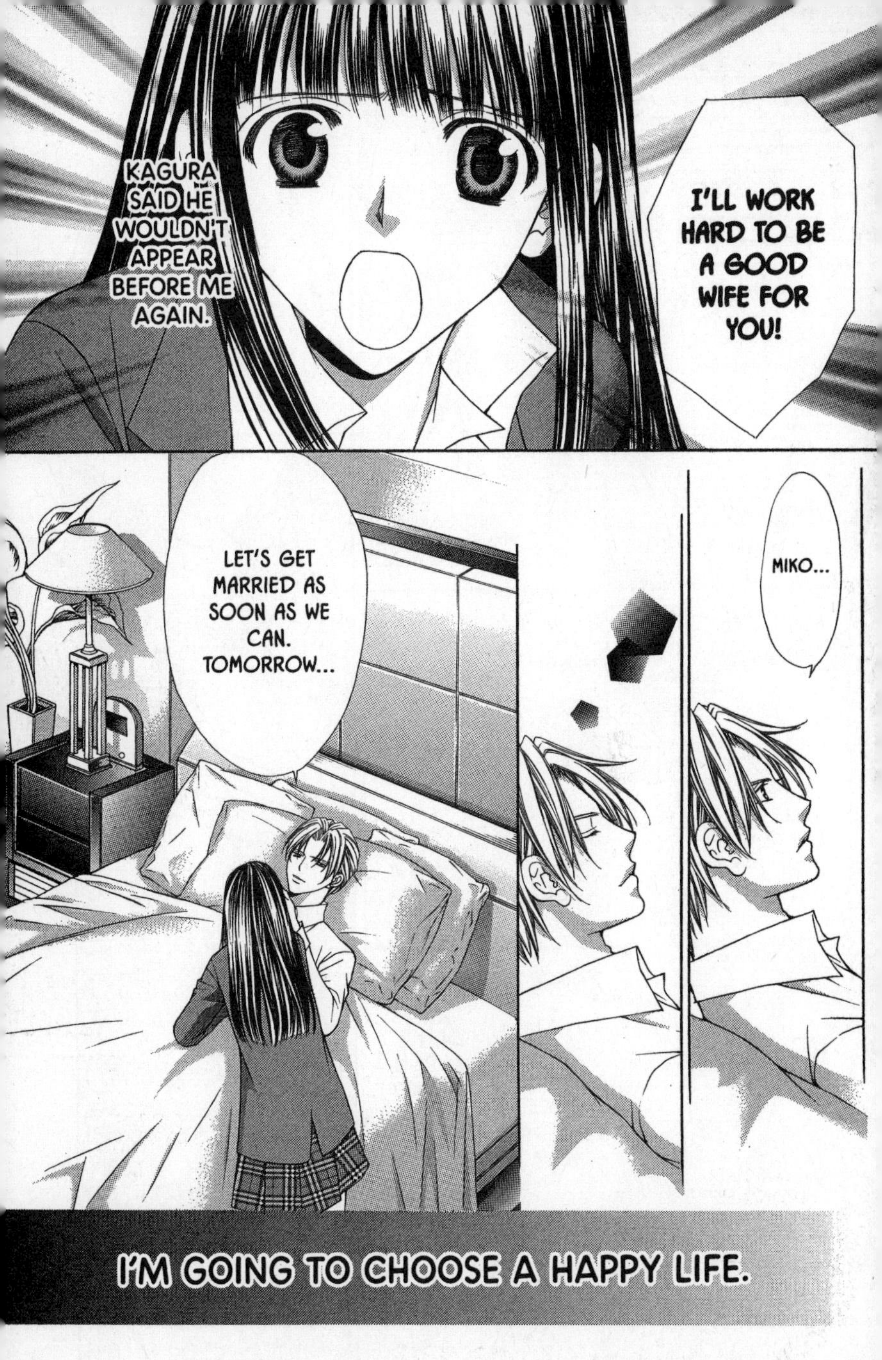
I'LL WORK HARD TO BE A GOOD WIFE FOR YOU!
KAGURA SAID HE WOULDN'T APPEAR BEFORE ME AGAIN.
MIKO...
LET'S GET MARRIED AS SOON AS WE CAN. TOMORROW...
I'M GOING TO CHOOSE A HAPPY LIFE.

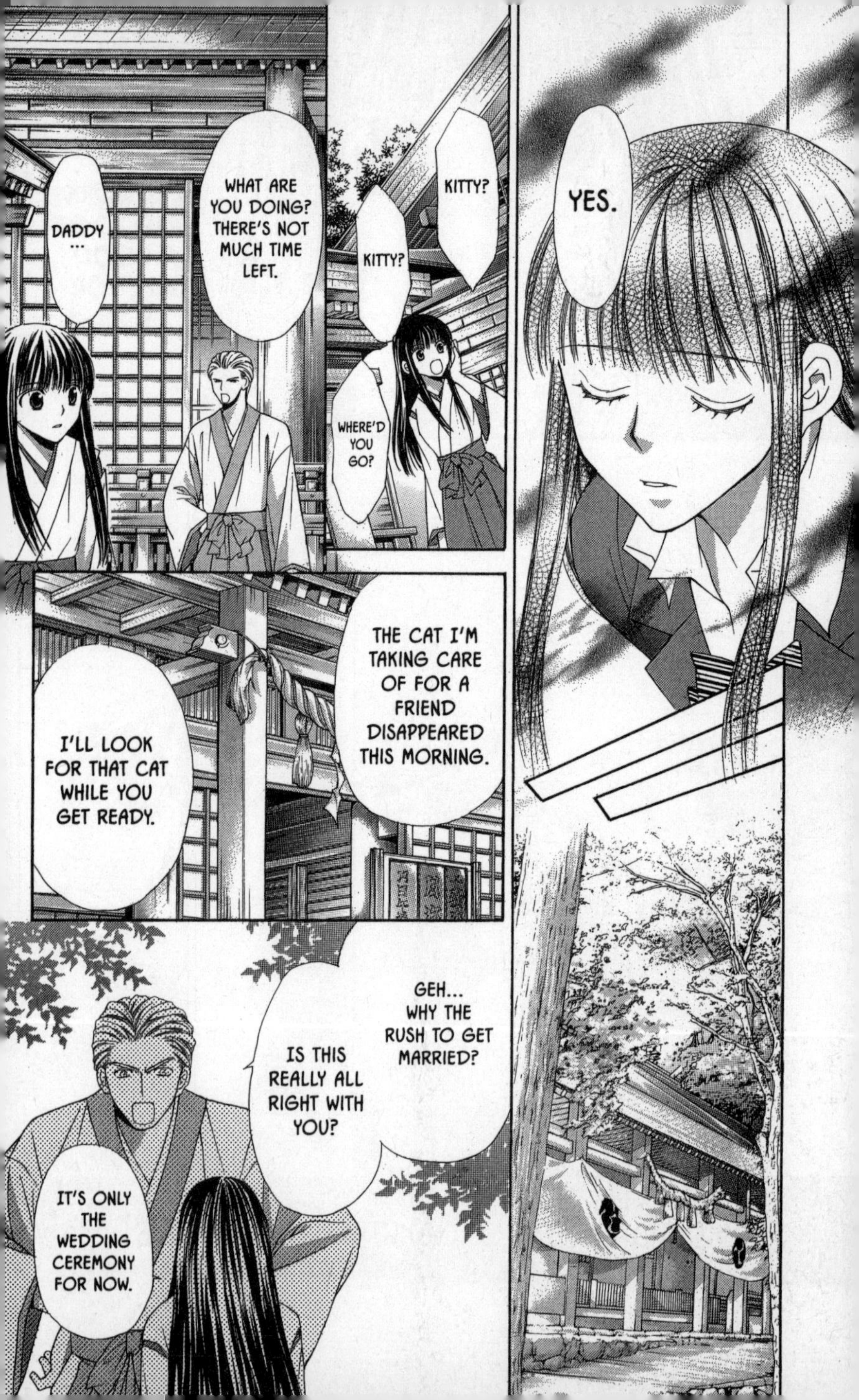
KITTY?
KITTY?
WHERE'D YOU GO?
WHAT ARE YOU DOING? THERE'S NOT MUCH TIME LEFT.
DADDY ...
THE CAT I'M TAKING CARE OF FOR A FRIEND DISAPPEARED THIS MORNING.
I'LL LOOK FOR THAT CAT WHILE YOU GET READY.
GEH... WHY THE RUSH TO GET MARRIED?
IS THIS REALLY ALL RIGHT WITH YOU?
IT'S ONLY THE WEDDING CEREMONY FOR NOW.
YES.

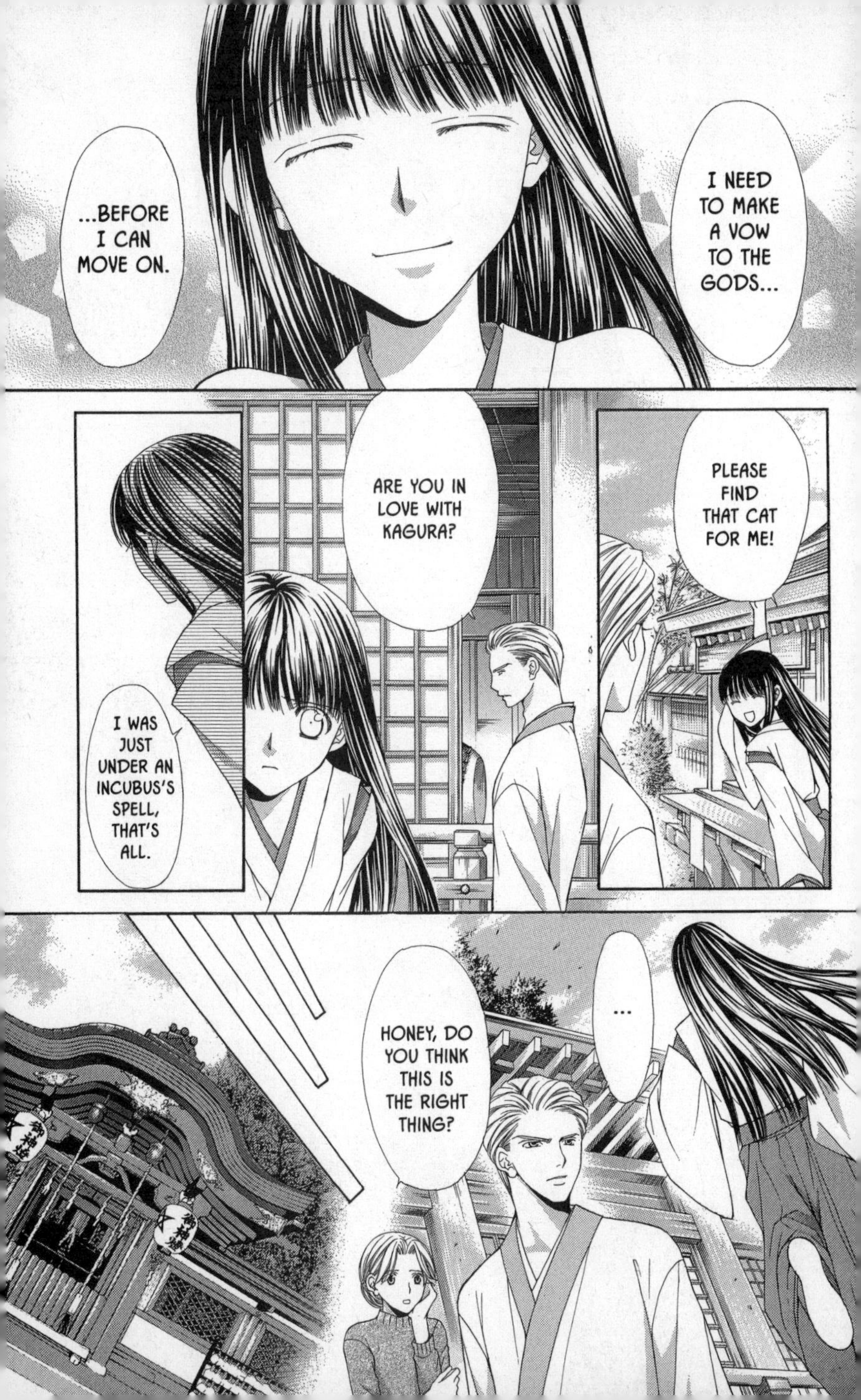
I NEED TO MAKE A VOW TO THE GODS...
...BEFORE I CAN MOVE ON.
PLEASE FIND THAT CAT FOR ME!
ARE YOU IN LOVE WITH KAGURA?
I WAS JUST UNDER AN INCUBUS'S SPELL, THAT'S ALL.
...
HONEY, DO YOU THINK THIS IS THE RIGHT THING?

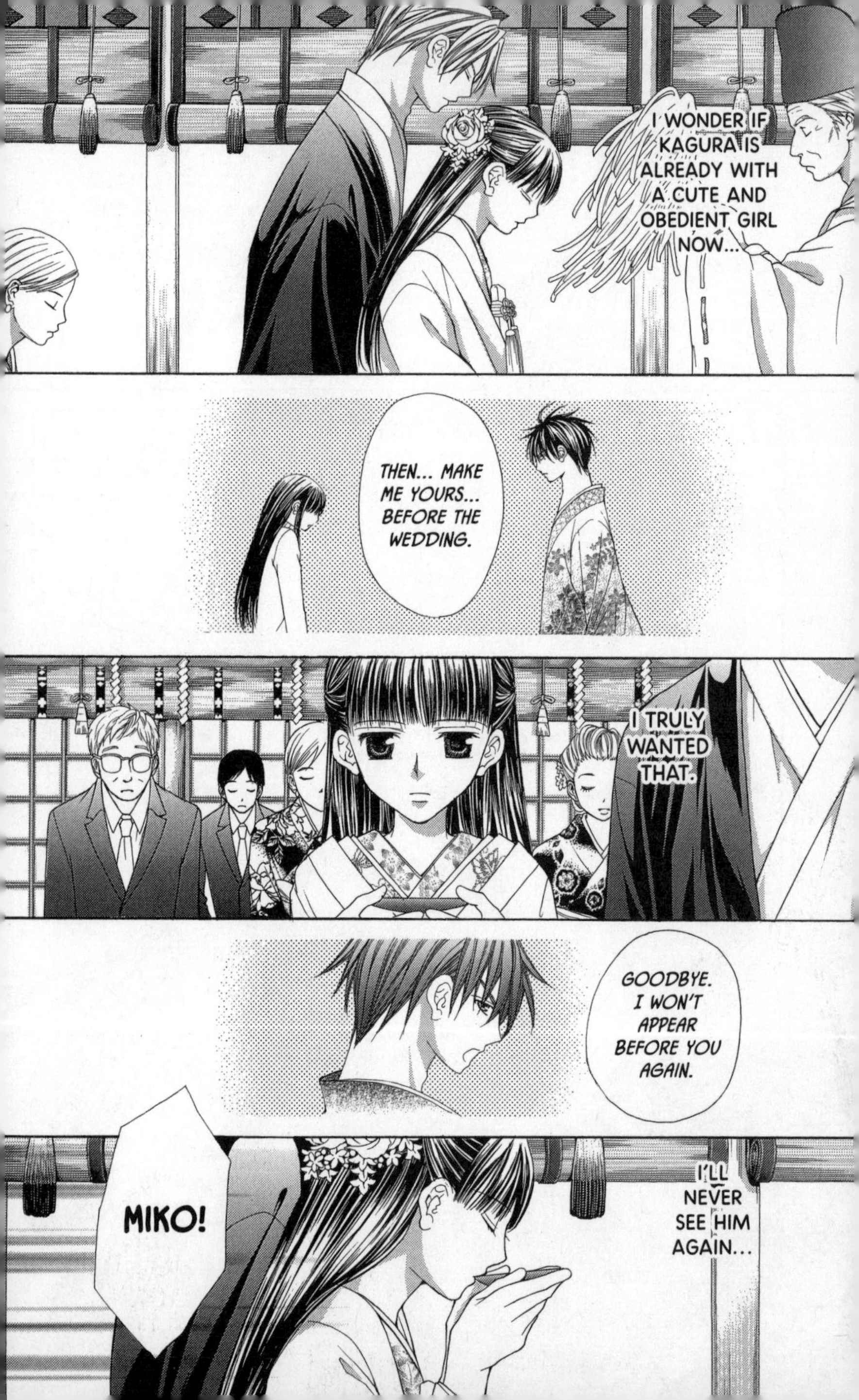
I WONDER IF KAGURA IS ALREADY WITH A CUTE AND OBEDIENT GIRL NOW...
THEN... MAKE ME YOURS... BEFORE THE WEDDING.
I TRULY WANTED THAT.
GOODBYE. I WON'T APPEAR BEFORE YOU AGAIN.
I'LL NEVER SEE HIM AGAIN...
MIKO!

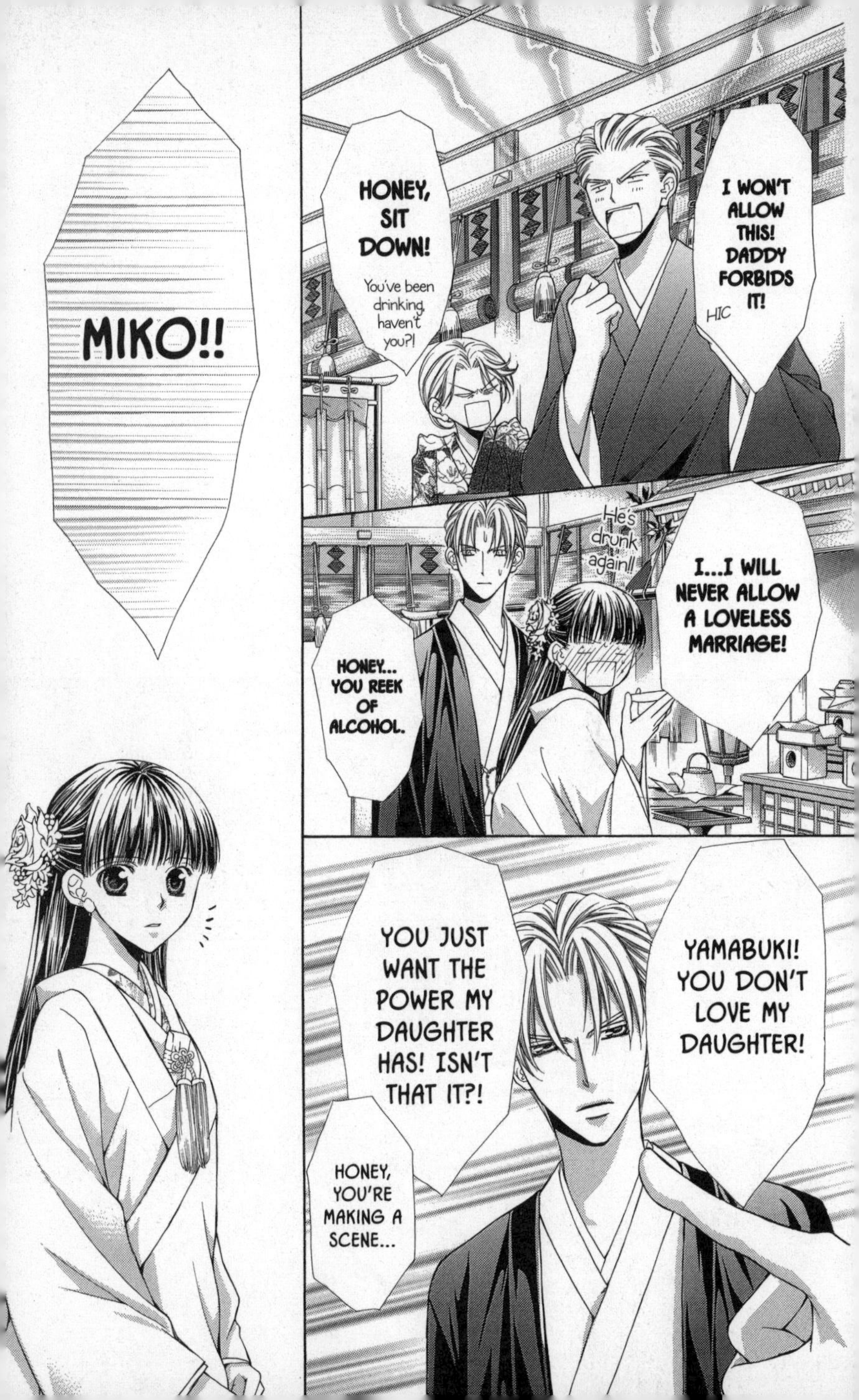
I WON'T ALLOW THIS! DADDY FORBIDS IT!
HIC
HONEY, SIT DOWN!
You've been drinking, haven't you?!
I...I WILL NEVER ALLOW A LOVELESS MARRIAGE!
He's drunk again!!
HONEY... YOU REEK OF ALCOHOL.
YAMABUKI! YOU DON'T LOVE MY DAUGHTER!
YOU JUST WANT THE POWER MY DAUGHTER HAS! ISN'T THAT IT?!
HONEY, YOU'RE MAKING A SCENE...
MIKO!!

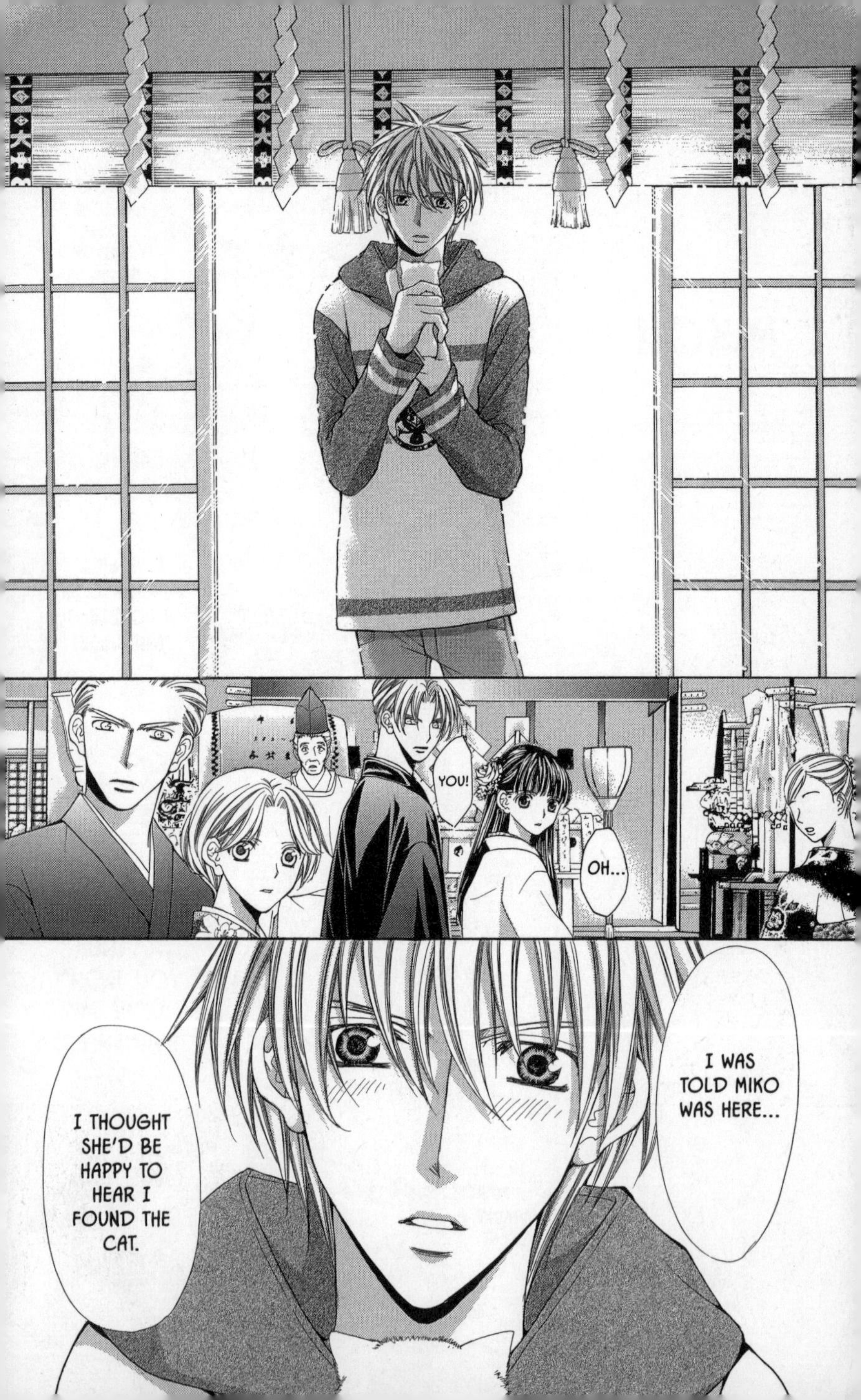
OH...
YOU!
I WAS TOLD MIKO WAS HERE...
I THOUGHT SHE'D BE HAPPY TO HEAR I FOUND THE CAT.

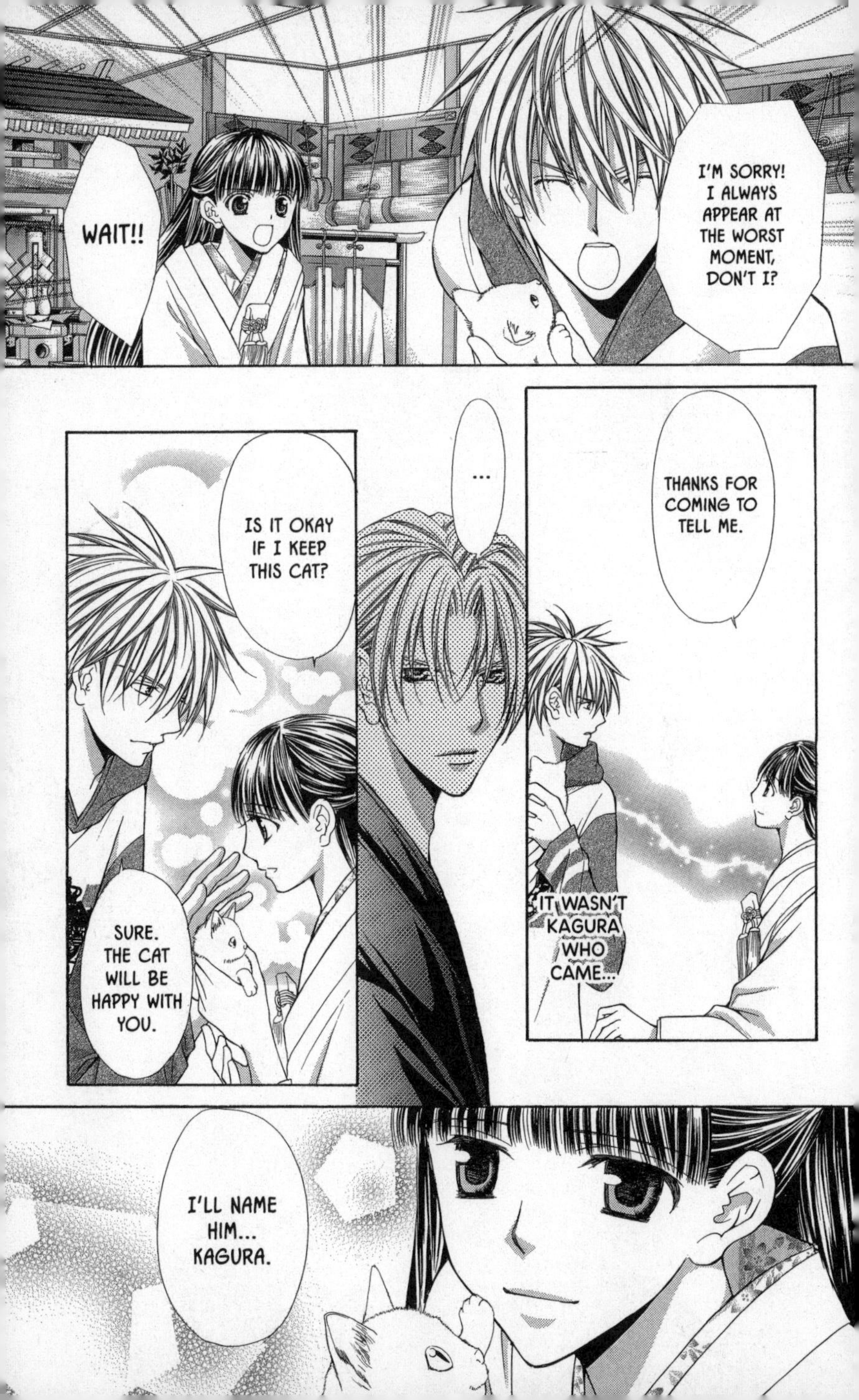
I'M SORRY! I ALWAYS APPEAR AT THE WORST MOMENT, DON'T I?
WAIT!!
THANKS FOR COMING TO TELL ME.
IT WASN'T KAGURA WHO CAME...
...
IS IT OKAY IF I KEEP THIS CAT?
SURE. THE CAT WILL BE HAPPY WITH YOU.
I'LL NAME HIM... KAGURA.

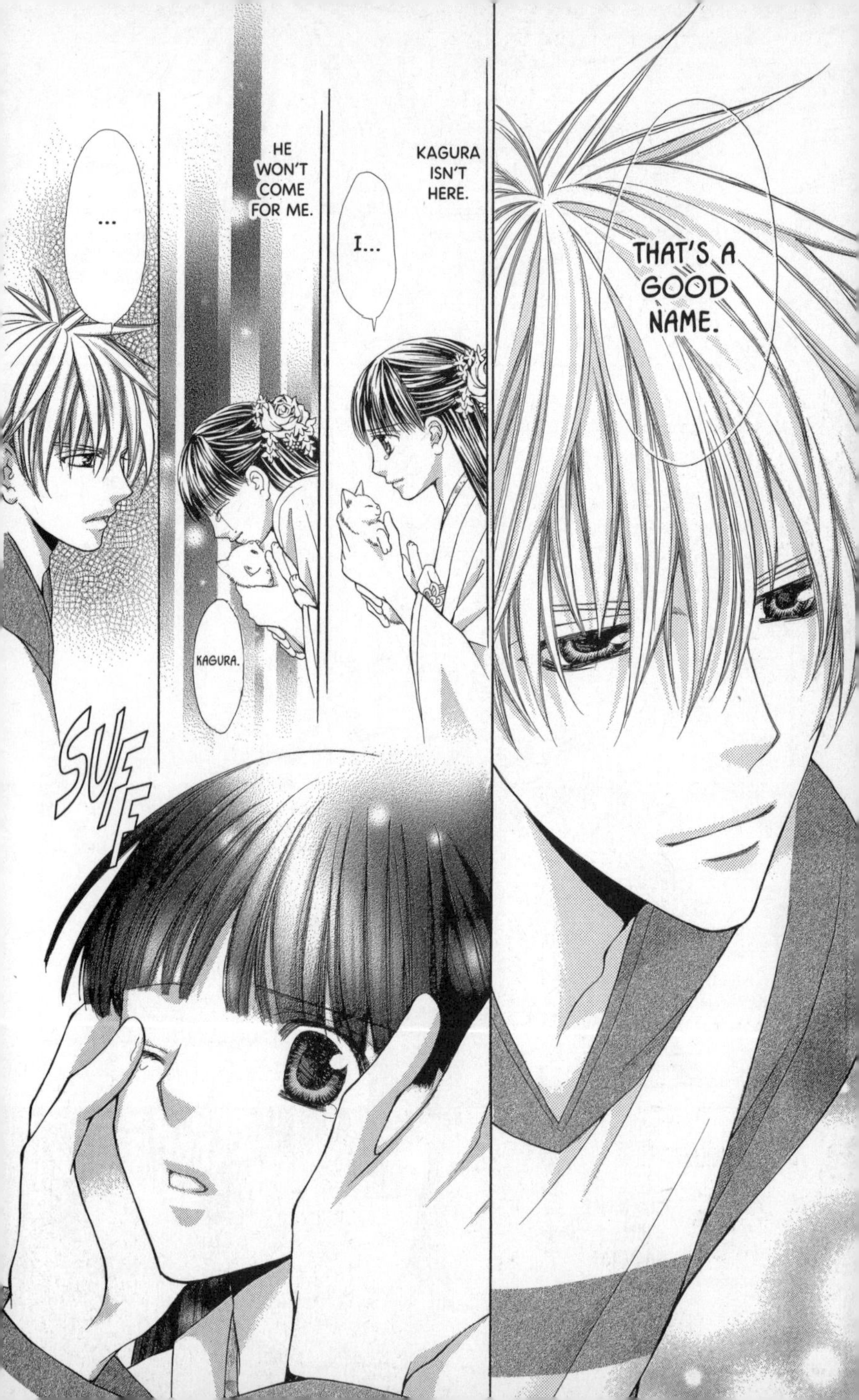
THAT'S A GOOD NAME.
KAGURA ISN'T HERE.
I...
HE WON'T COME FOR ME.
KAGURA.
...
SUFF

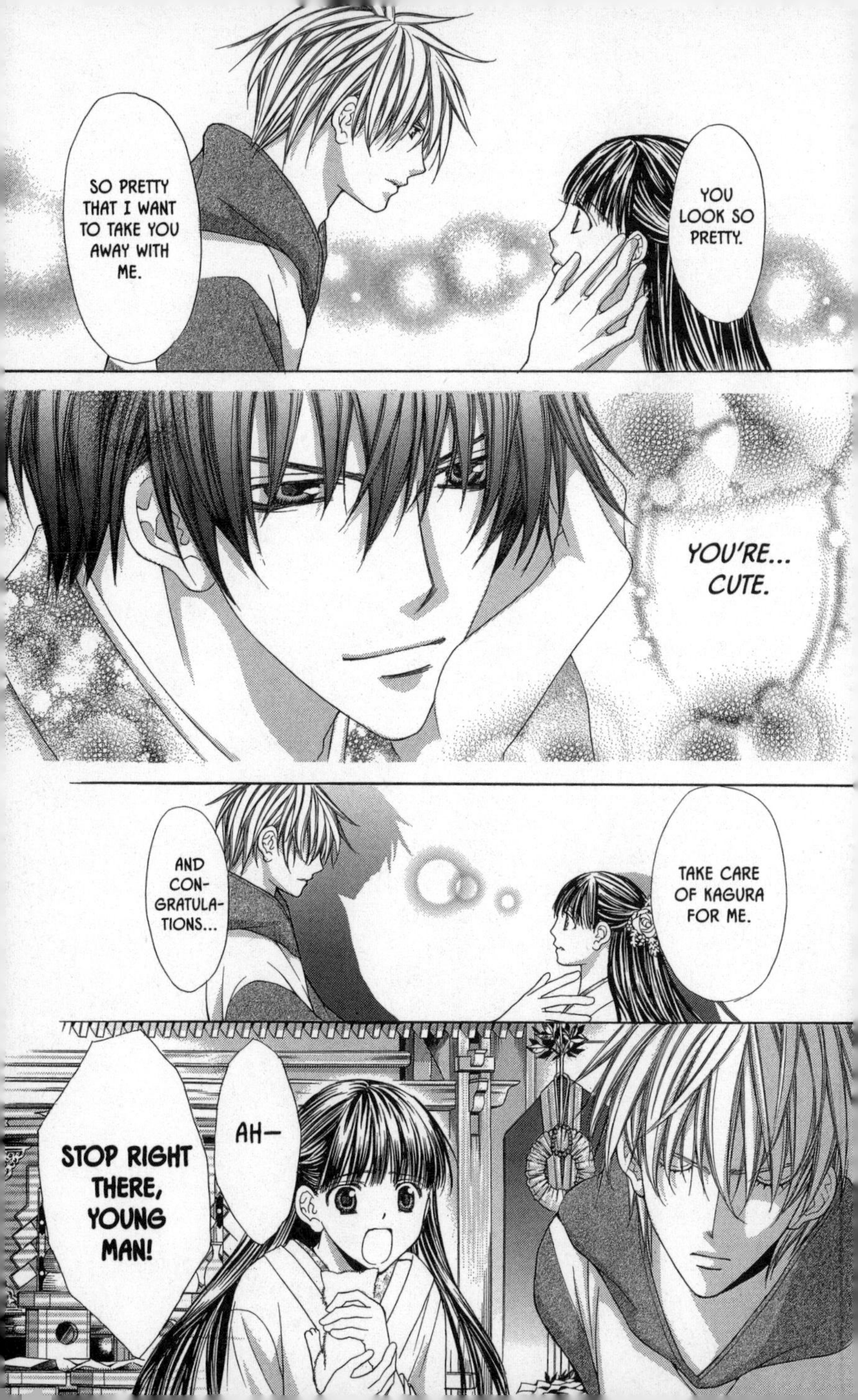
YOU LOOK SO PRETTY.
SO PRETTY THAT I WANT TO TAKE YOU AWAY WITH ME.
YOU'RE... CUTE.
TAKE CARE OF KAGURA FOR ME.
AND CON-GRATULA-TIONS...
AH—
STOP RIGHT THERE, YOUNG MAN!

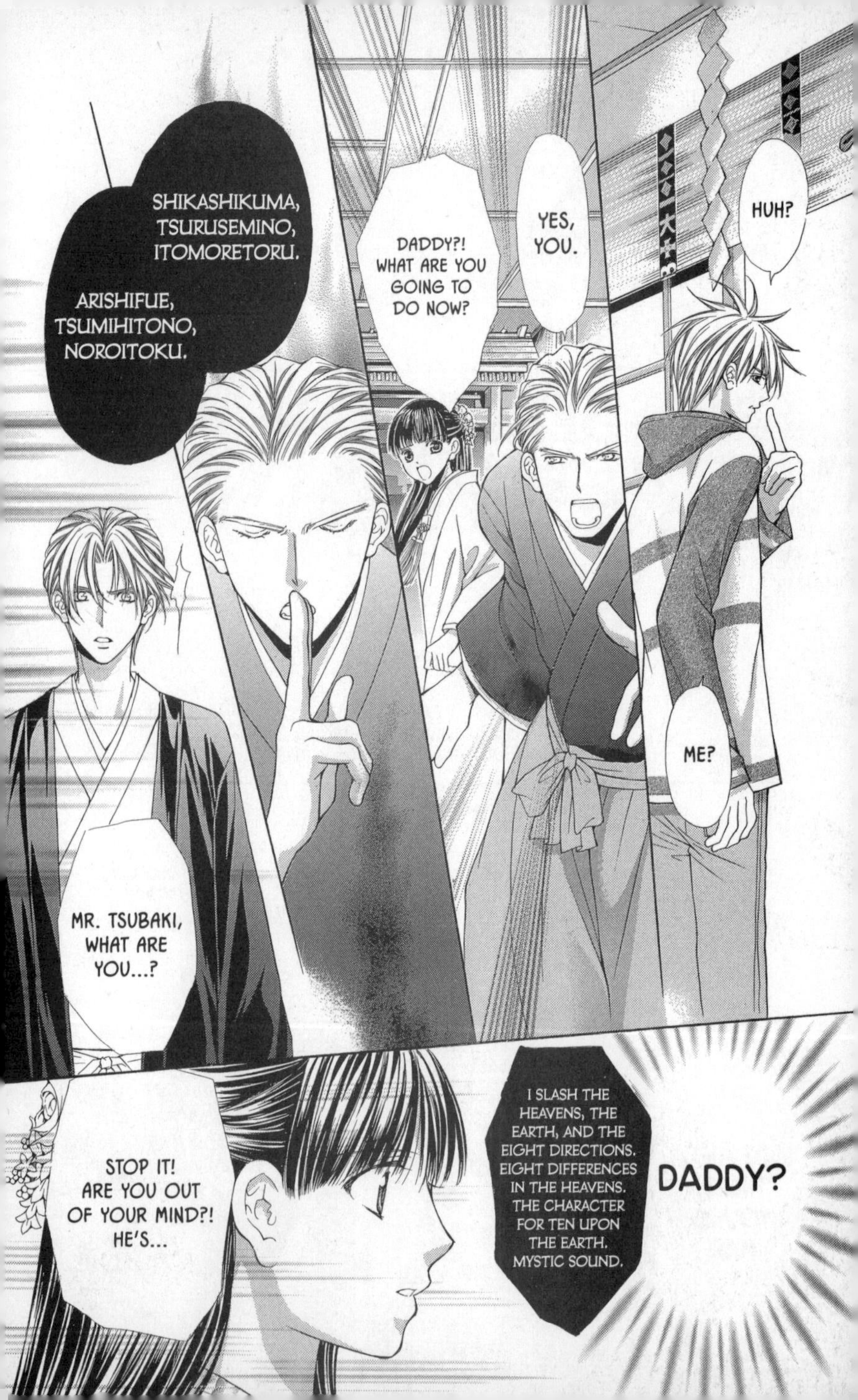
HUH?
ME?
YES, YOU.
DADDY?! WHAT ARE YOU GOING TO DO NOW?
SHIKASHIKUMA, TSURUSEMINO, ITOMORETORU.
ARISHIFUE, TSUMIHITONO, NOROITOKU.
MR. TSUBAKI, WHAT ARE YOU...?
DADDY?
I SLASH THE HEAVENS, THE EARTH, AND THE EIGHT DIRECTIONS. EIGHT DIFFERENCES IN THE HEAVENS. THE CHARACTER FOR TEN UPON THE EARTH. MYSTIC SOUND.
STOP IT! ARE YOU OUT OF YOUR MIND?! HE'S...

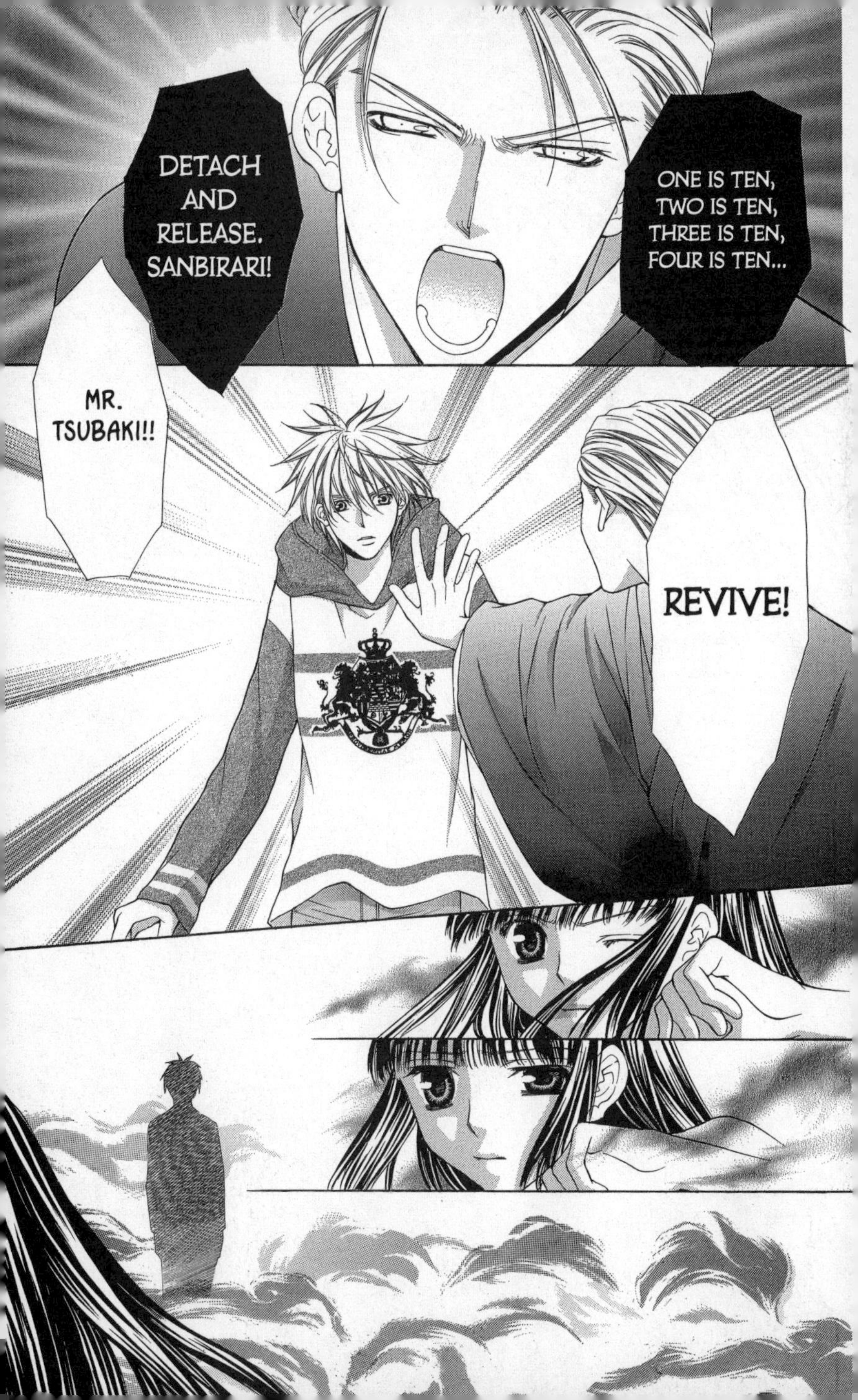
ONE IS TEN, TWO IS TEN, THREE IS TEN, FOUR IS TEN...
DETACH AND RELEASE. SANBIRARI!
REVIVE!
MR. TSUBAKI!!

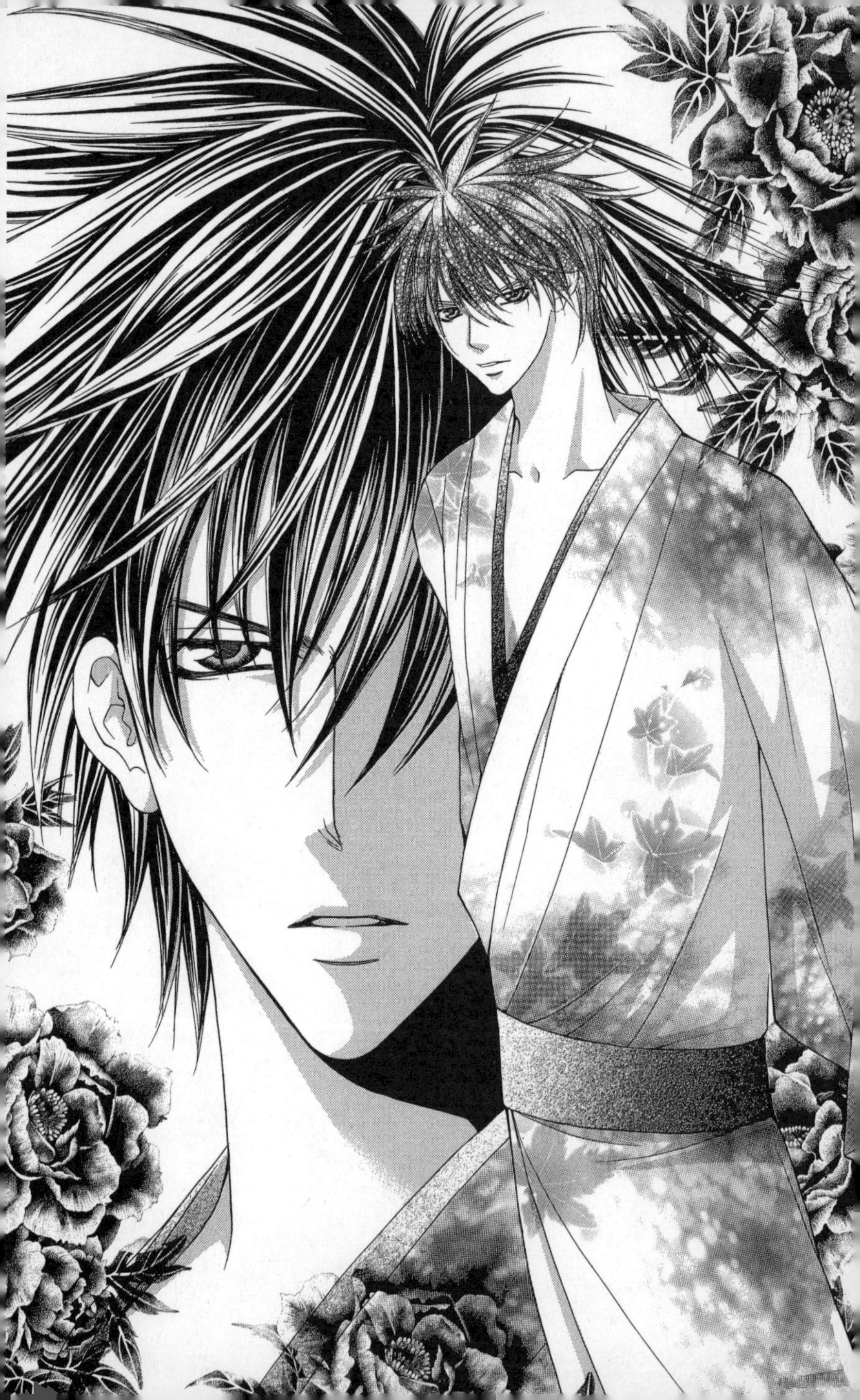

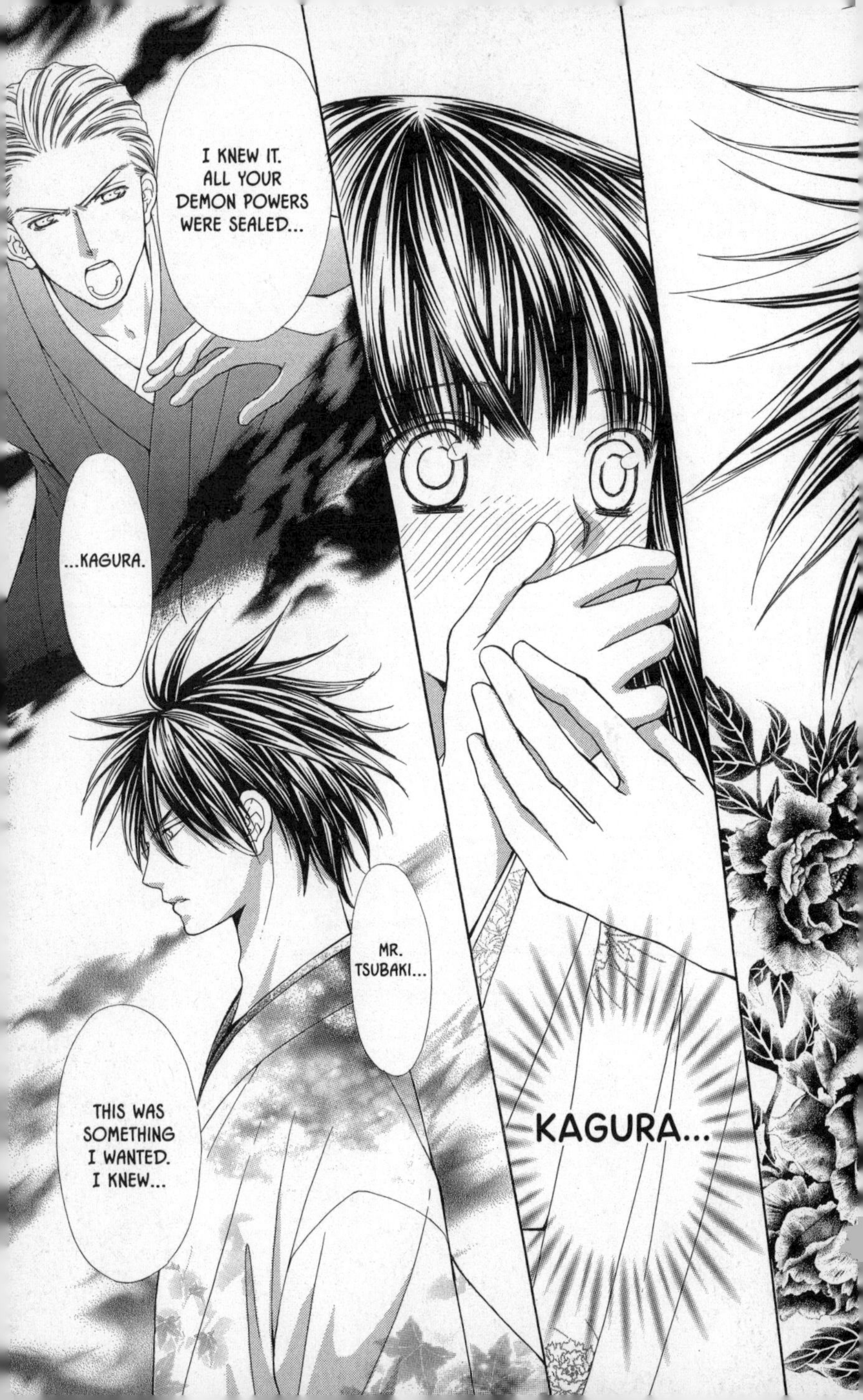
KAGURA...
I KNEW IT. ALL YOUR DEMON POWERS WERE SEALED...
...KAGURA.
MR. TSUBAKI...
THIS WAS SOMETHING I WANTED. I KNEW...

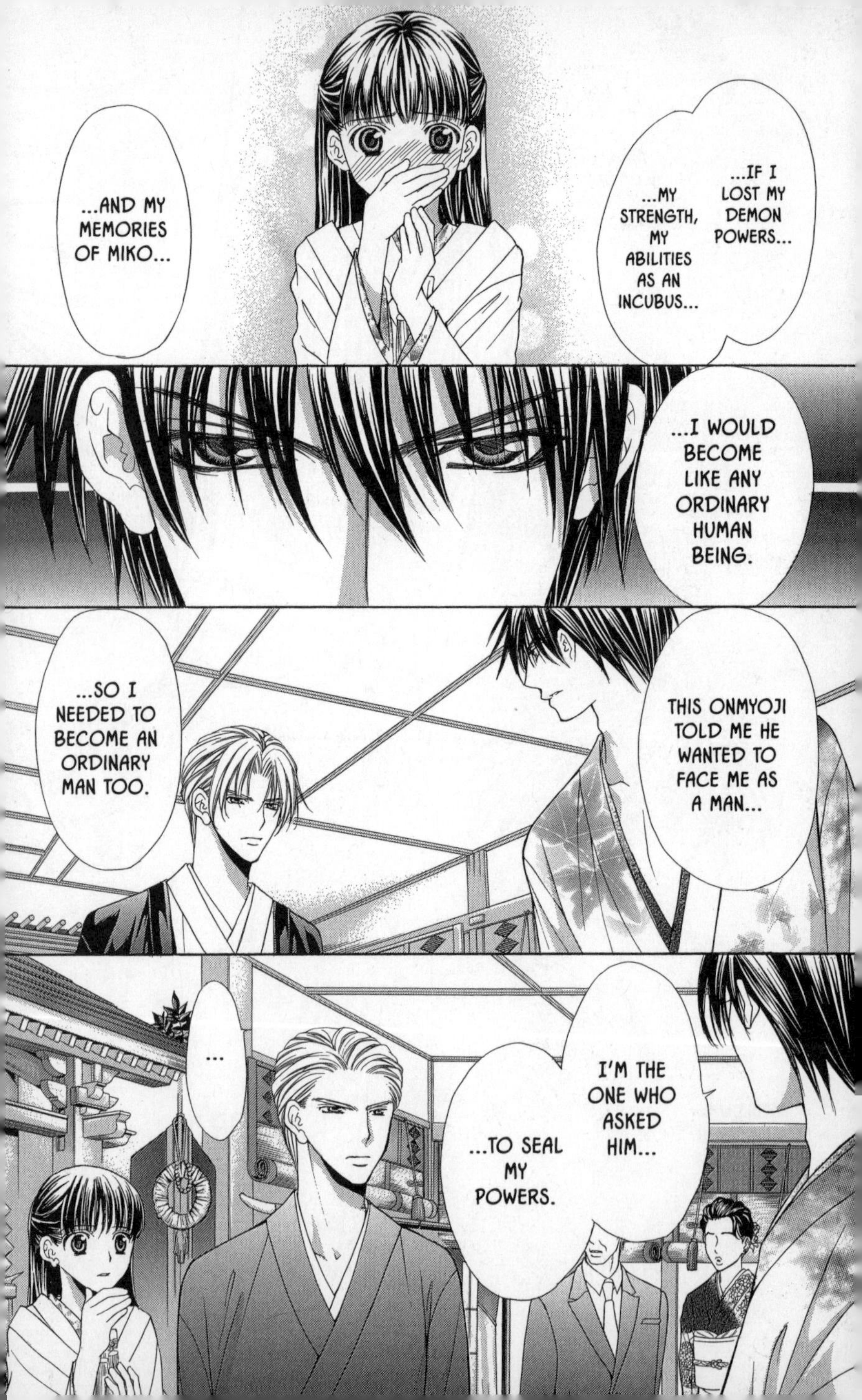
...IF I LOST MY DEMON POWERS...
...MY STRENGTH, MY ABILITIES AS AN INCUBUS...
...AND MY MEMORIES OF MIKO...
...I WOULD BECOME LIKE ANY ORDINARY HUMAN BEING.
THIS ONMYOJI TOLD ME HE WANTED TO FACE ME AS A MAN...
...SO I NEEDED TO BECOME AN ORDINARY MAN TOO.
I'M THE ONE WHO ASKED HIM...
...TO SEAL MY POWERS.
...

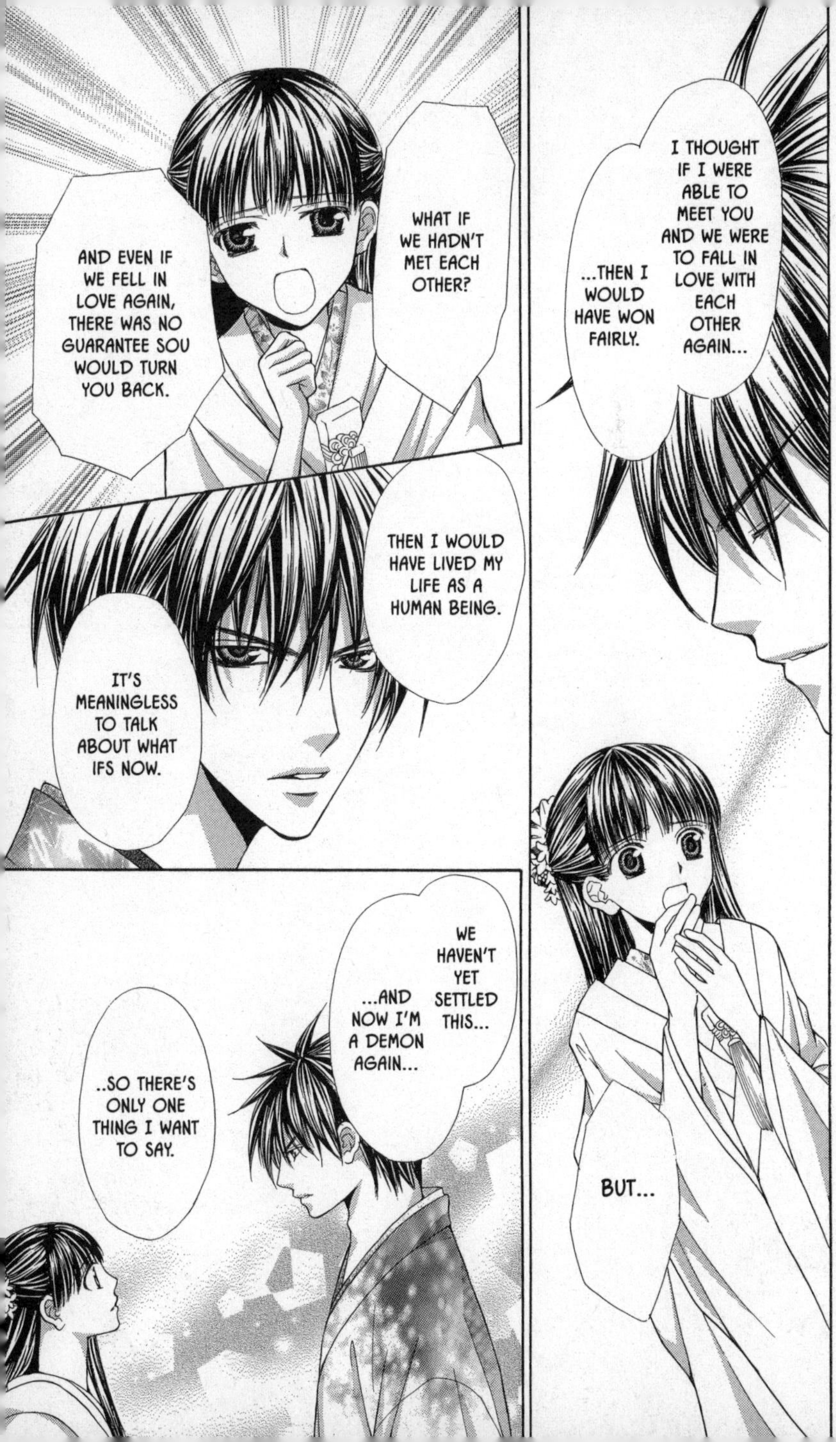
I THOUGHT IF I WERE ABLE TO MEET YOU AND WE WERE TO FALL IN LOVE WITH EACH OTHER AGAIN...
...THEN I WOULD HAVE WON FAIRLY.
BUT...
WHAT IF WE HADN'T MET EACH OTHER?
AND EVEN IF WE FELL IN LOVE AGAIN, THERE WAS NO GUARANTEE SOU WOULD TURN YOU BACK.
THEN I WOULD HAVE LIVED MY LIFE AS A HUMAN BEING.
IT'S MEANINGLESS TO TALK ABOUT WHAT IFS NOW.
WE HAVEN'T YET SETTLED THIS...
...AND NOW I'M A DEMON AGAIN...
..SO THERE'S ONLY ONE THING I WANT TO SAY.

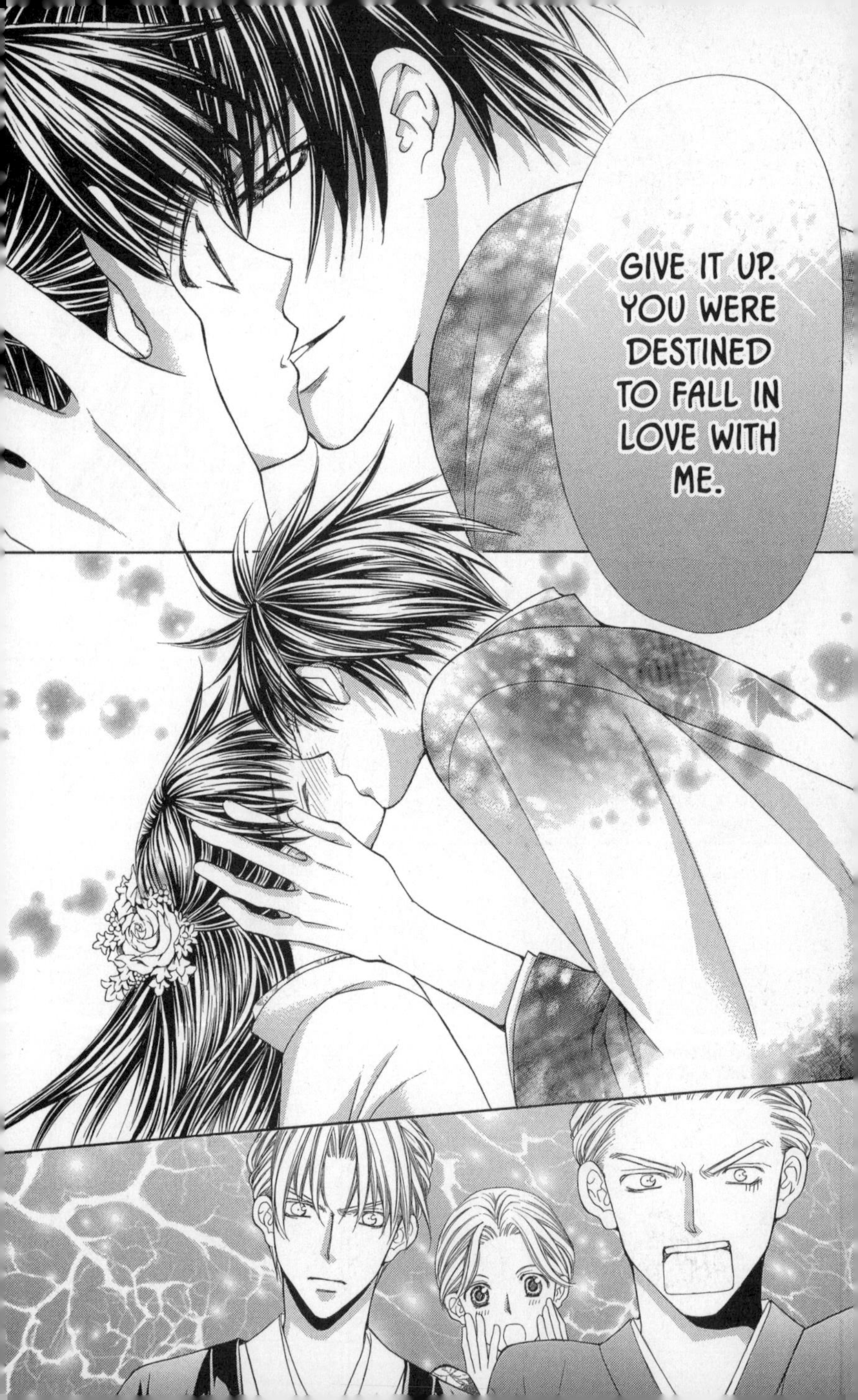
GIVE IT UP. YOU WERE DESTINED TO FALL IN LOVE WITH ME.

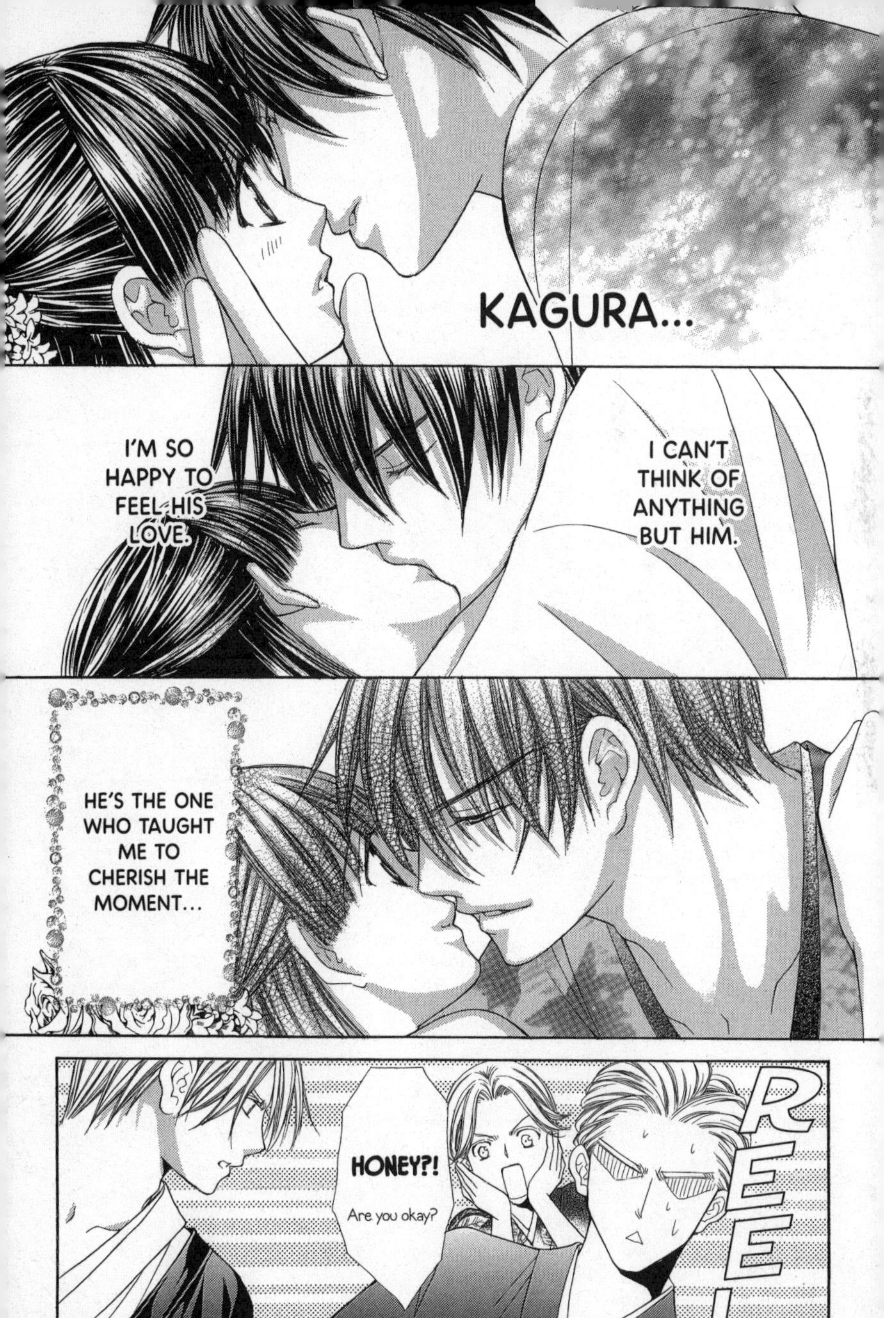
KAGURA...
I CAN'T THINK OF ANYTHING BUT HIM.
I'M SO HAPPY TO FEEL HIS LOVE.
HE'S THE ONE WHO TAUGHT ME TO CHERISH THE MOMENT...
REEL
HONEY?!
Are you okay?

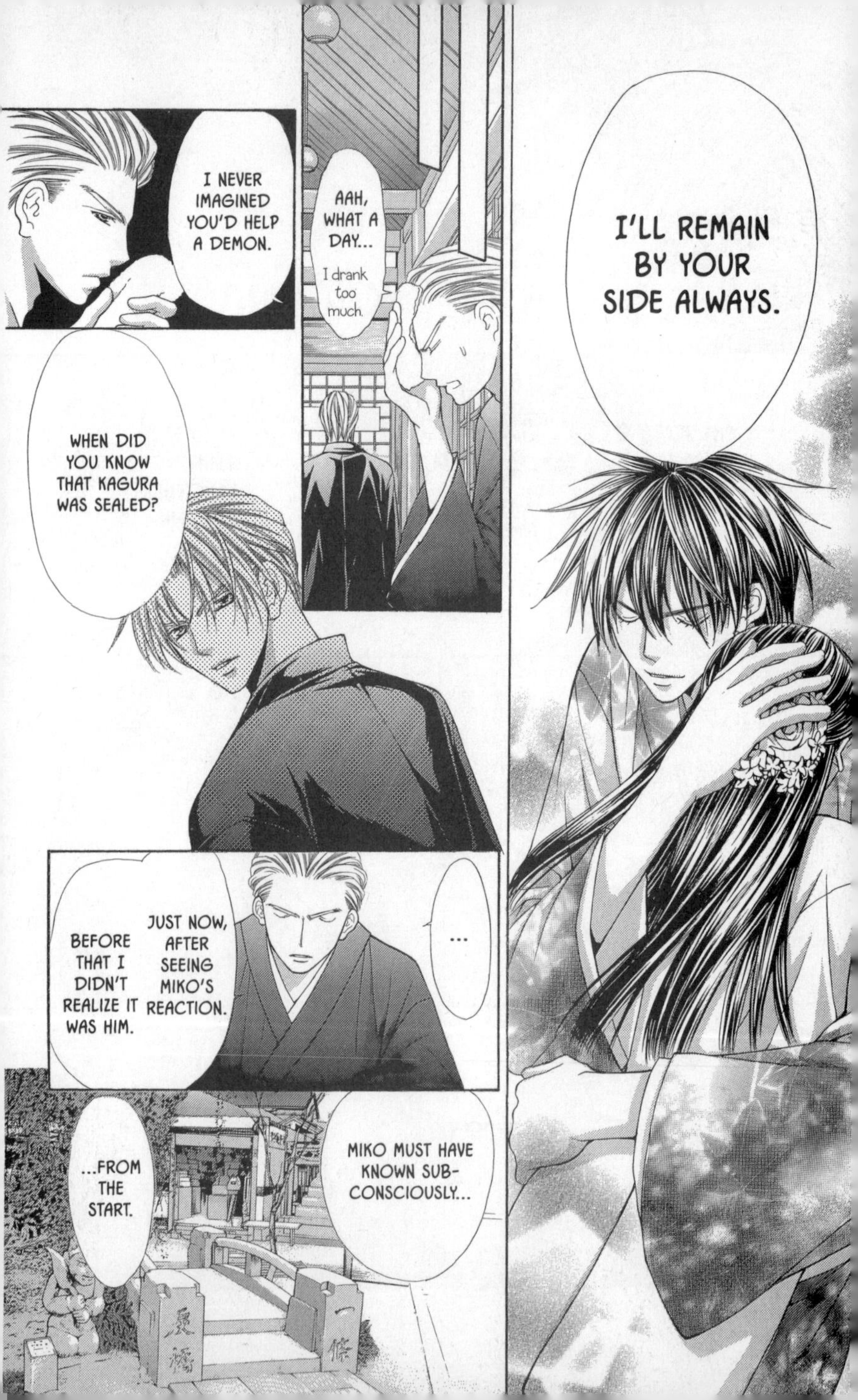
I'LL REMAIN BY YOUR SIDE ALWAYS.
AAH, WHAT A DAY...
I drank too much.
I NEVER IMAGINED YOU'D HELP A DEMON.
WHEN DID YOU KNOW THAT KAGURA WAS SEALED?
...
JUST NOW, AFTER SEEING MIKO'S REACTION.
BEFORE THAT I DIDN'T REALIZE IT WAS HIM.
MIKO MUST HAVE KNOWN SUB-CONSCIOUSLY...
...FROM THE START.

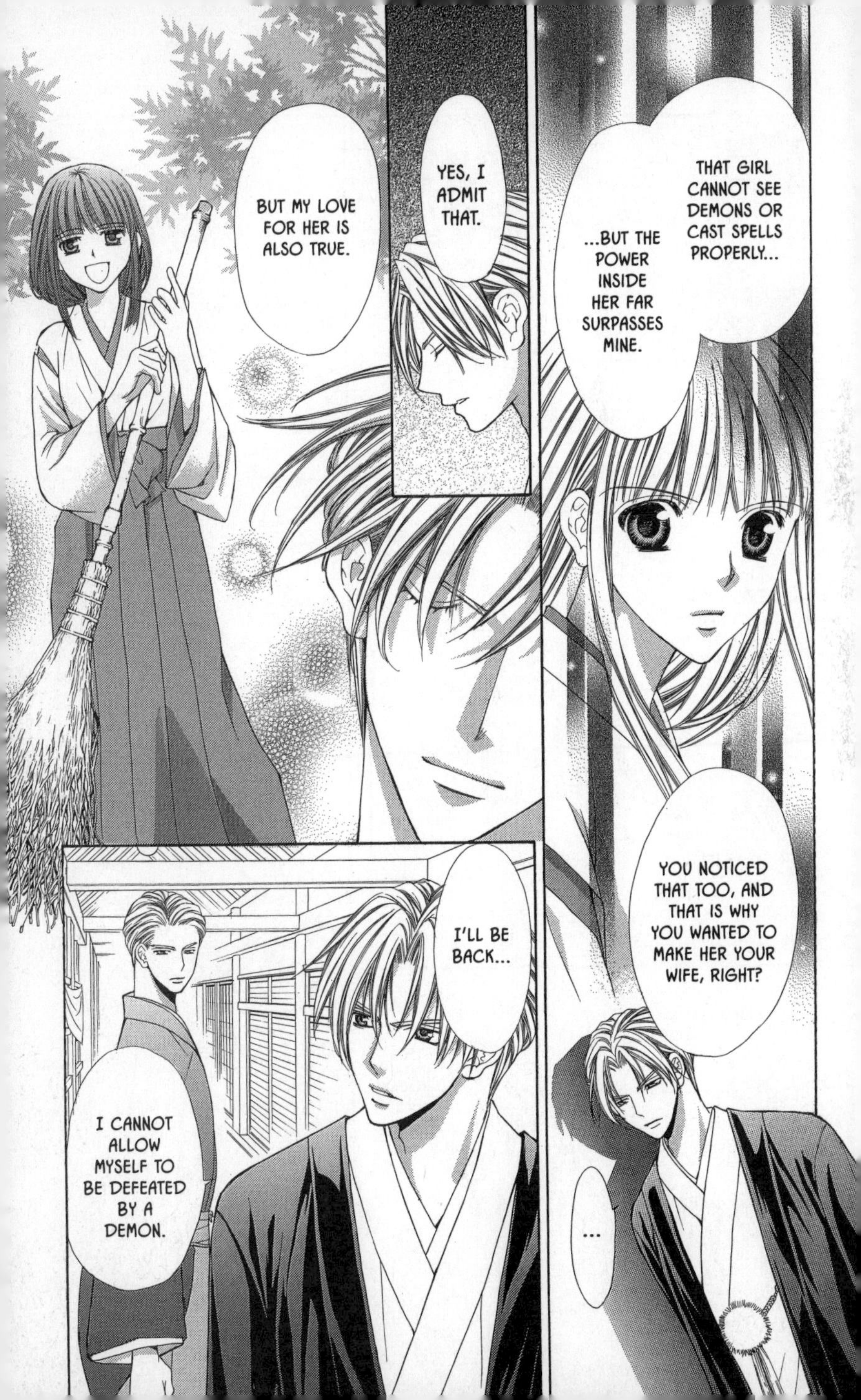
THAT GIRL CANNOT SEE DEMONS OR CAST SPELLS PROPERLY...
...BUT THE POWER INSIDE HER FAR SURPASSES MINE.
YOU NOTICED THAT TOO, AND THAT IS WHY YOU WANTED TO MAKE HER YOUR WIFE, RIGHT?
...
YES, I ADMIT THAT.
BUT MY LOVE FOR HER IS ALSO TRUE.
I'LL BE BACK...
I CANNOT ALLOW MYSELF TO BE DEFEATED BY A DEMON.

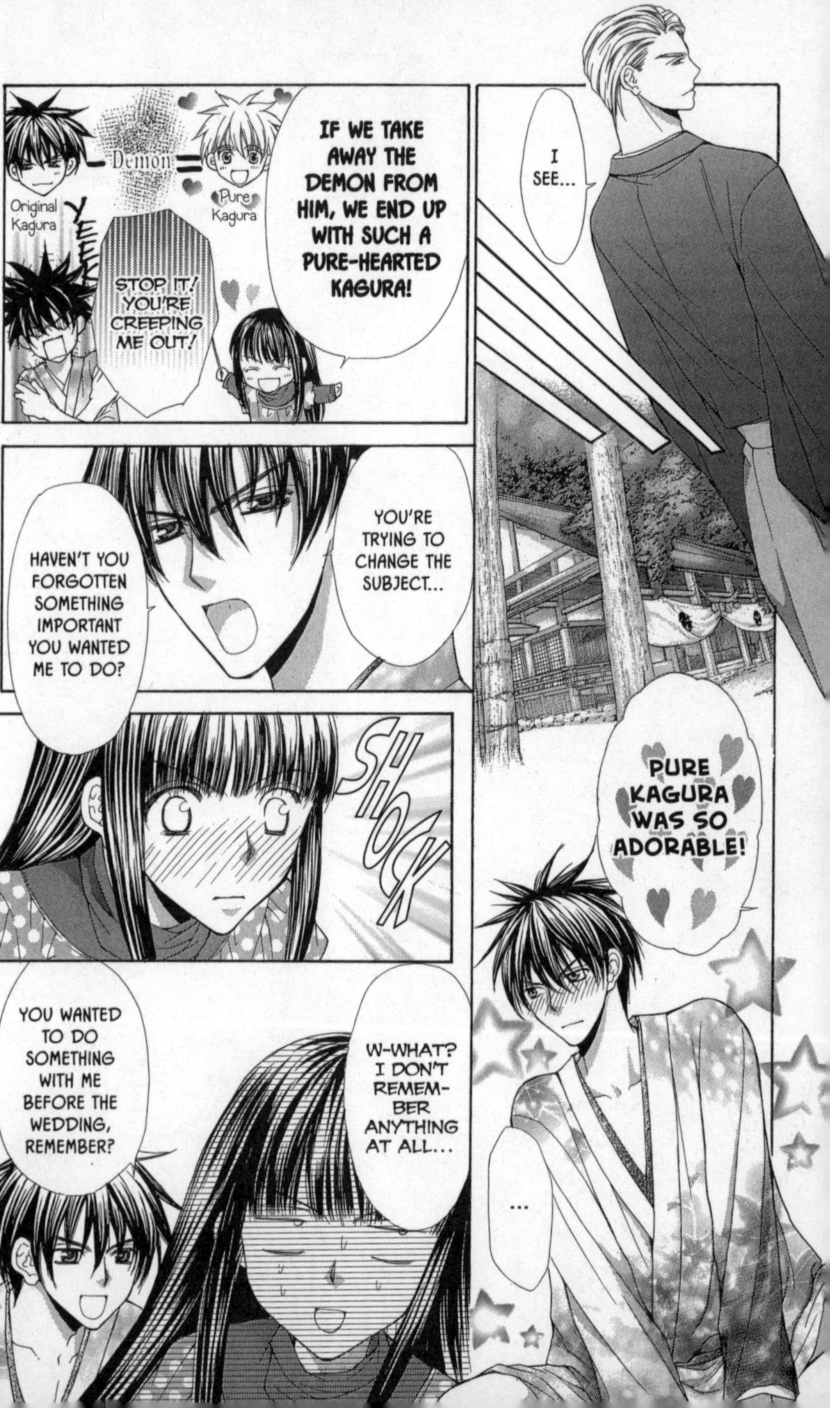
I SEE...
PURE KAGURA WAS SO ADORABLE!
...
IF WE TAKE AWAY THE DEMON FROM HIM, WE END UP WITH SUCH A PURE-HEARTED KAGURA!
Original Kagura
Demon
Pure Kagura
YEEK
STOP IT! YOU'RE CREEPING ME OUT!
YOU'RE TRYING TO CHANGE THE SUBJECT...
HAVEN'T YOU FORGOTTEN SOMETHING IMPORTANT YOU WANTED ME TO DO?
SHOCK
W-WHAT? I DON'T REMEMBER ANYTHING AT ALL...
YOU WANTED TO DO SOMETHING WITH ME BEFORE THE WEDDING, REMEMBER?

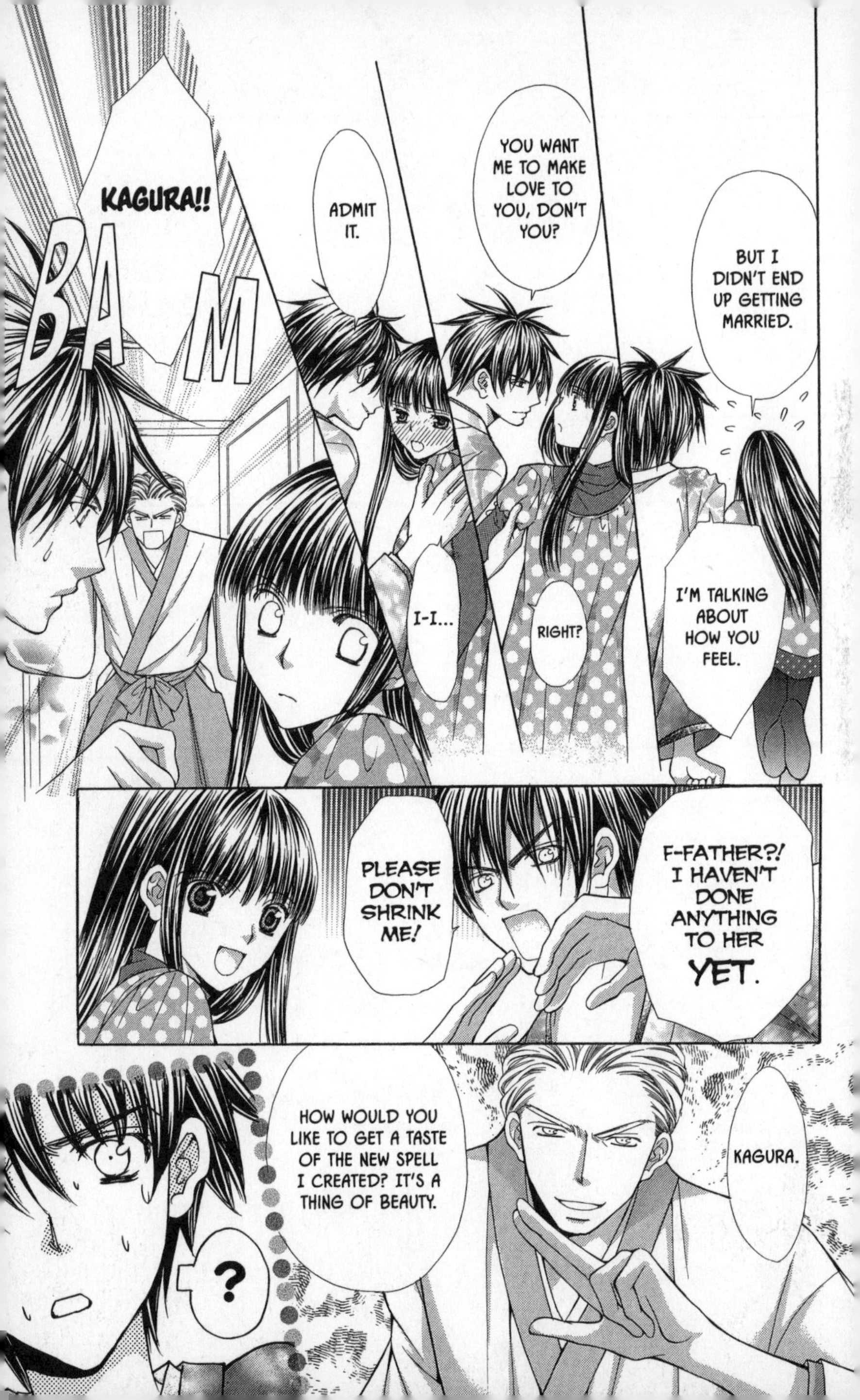
BUT I DIDN'T END UP GETTING MARRIED.
I'M TALKING ABOUT HOW YOU FEEL.
YOU WANT ME TO MAKE LOVE TO YOU, DON'T YOU?
RIGHT?
ADMIT IT.
I-I...
KAGURA!!
BAM
F-FATHER?! I HAVEN'T DONE ANYTHING TO HER YET.
PLEASE DON'T SHRINK ME!
KAGURA.
HOW WOULD YOU LIKE TO GET A TASTE OF THE NEW SPELL I CREATED? IT'S A THING OF BEAUTY.
?

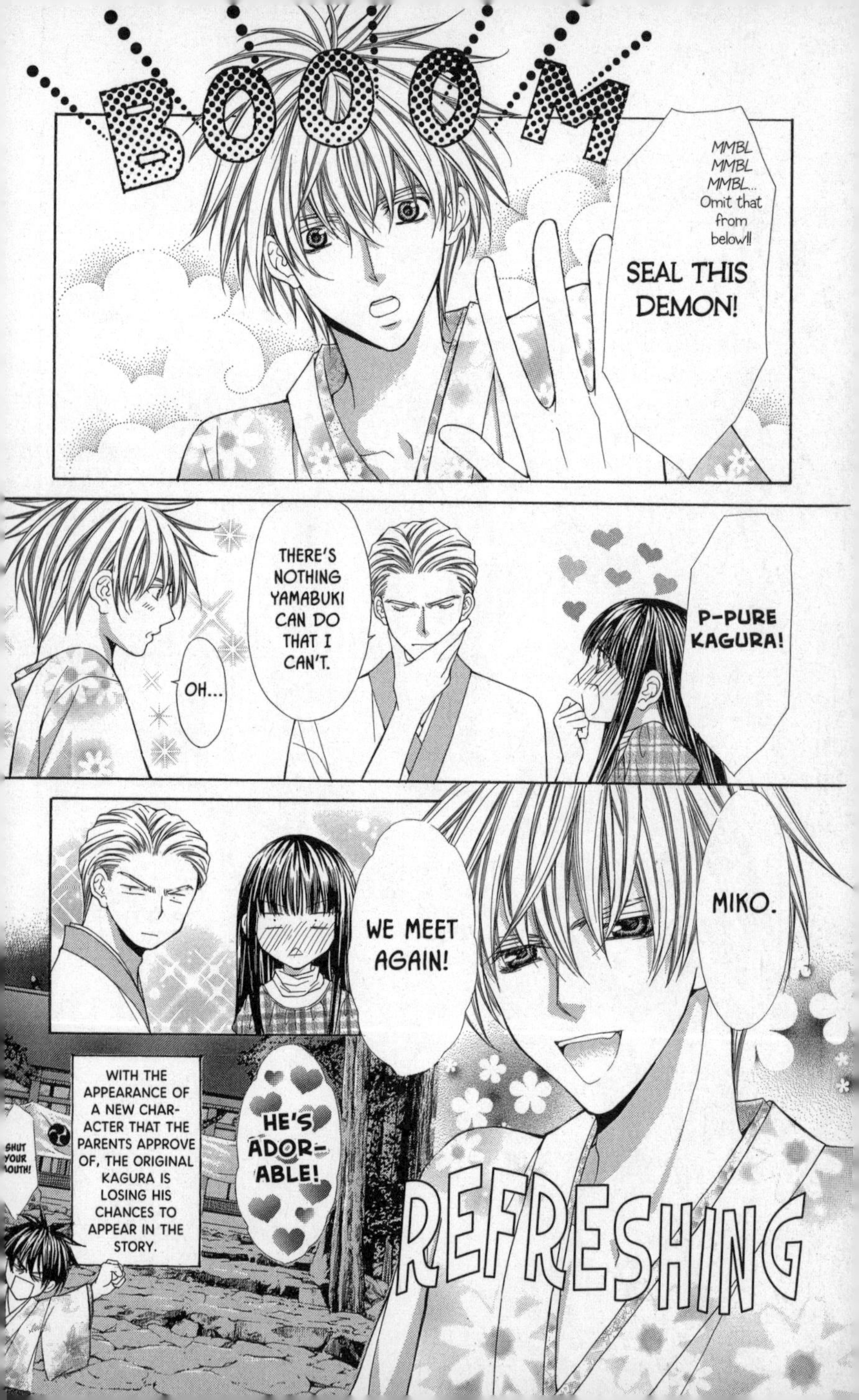
BOOOM
MMBL MMBL MMBL... Omit that from below!!
SEAL THIS DEMON!
P-PURE KAGURA!
THERE'S NOTHING YAMABUKI CAN DO THAT I CAN'T.
OH...
MIKO.
WE MEET AGAIN!
REFRESHING
HE'S ADORABLE!
WITH THE APPEARANCE OF A NEW CHARACTER THAT THE PARENTS APPROVE OF, THE ORIGINAL KAGURA IS LOSING HIS CHANCES TO APPEAR IN THE STORY.
SHUT YOUR MOUTH!

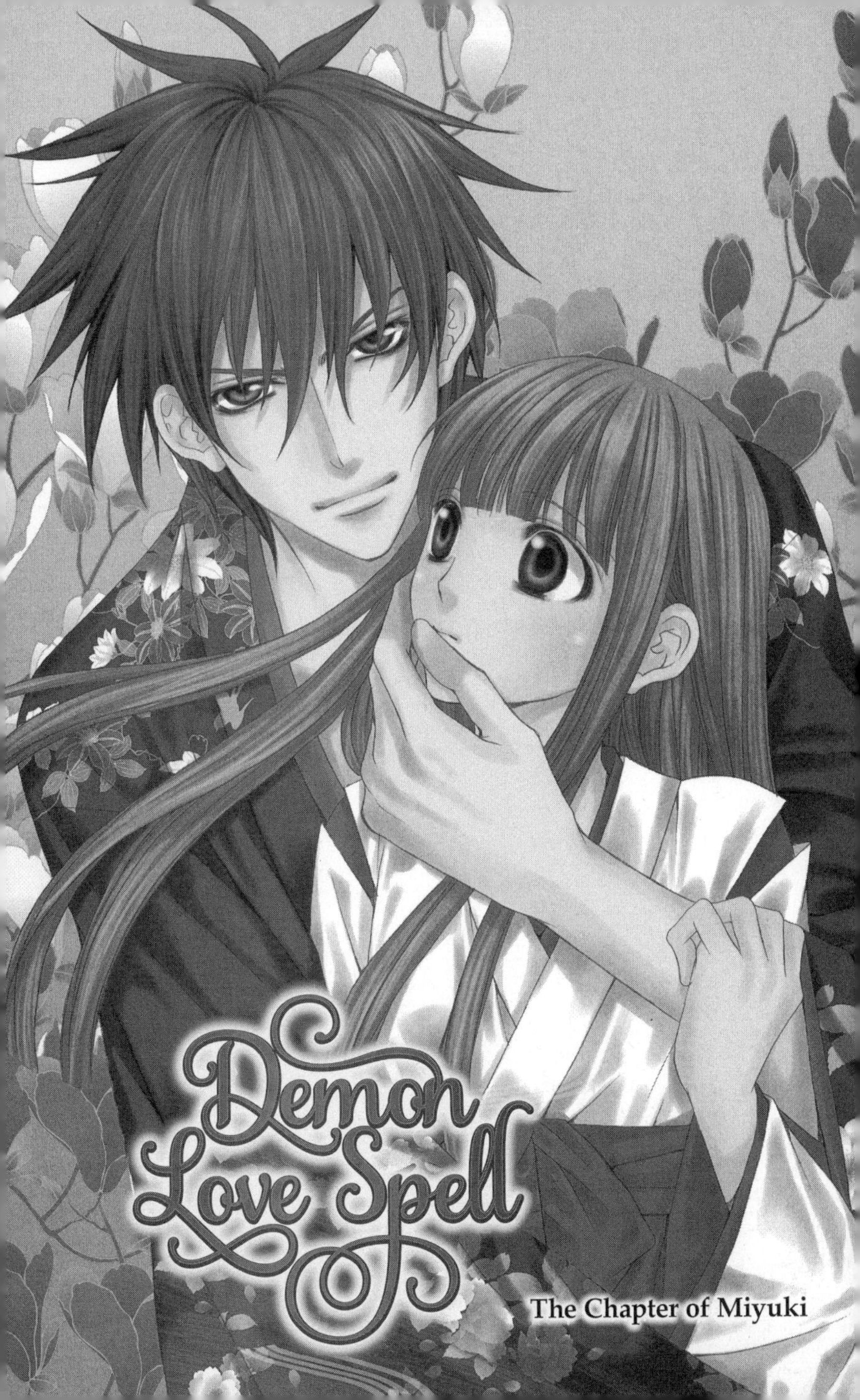
Demon Love Spell
The Chapter of Miyuki

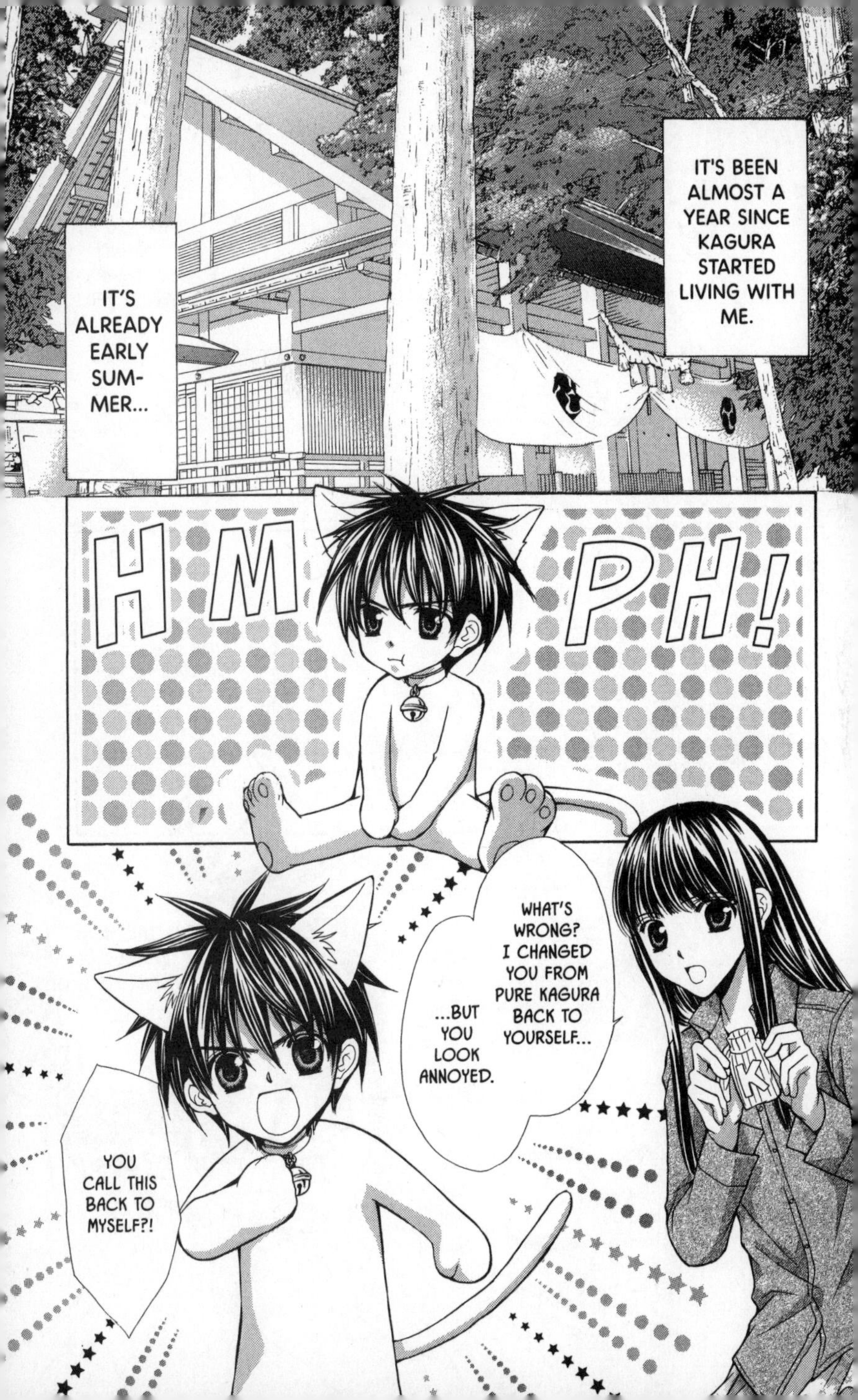
IT'S BEEN ALMOST A YEAR SINCE KAGURA STARTED LIVING WITH ME.
IT'S ALREADY EARLY SUM-MER...
HMPH!
WHAT'S WRONG? I CHANGED YOU FROM PURE KAGURA BACK TO YOURSELF...
...BUT YOU LOOK ANNOYED.
YOU CALL THIS BACK TO MYSELF?!

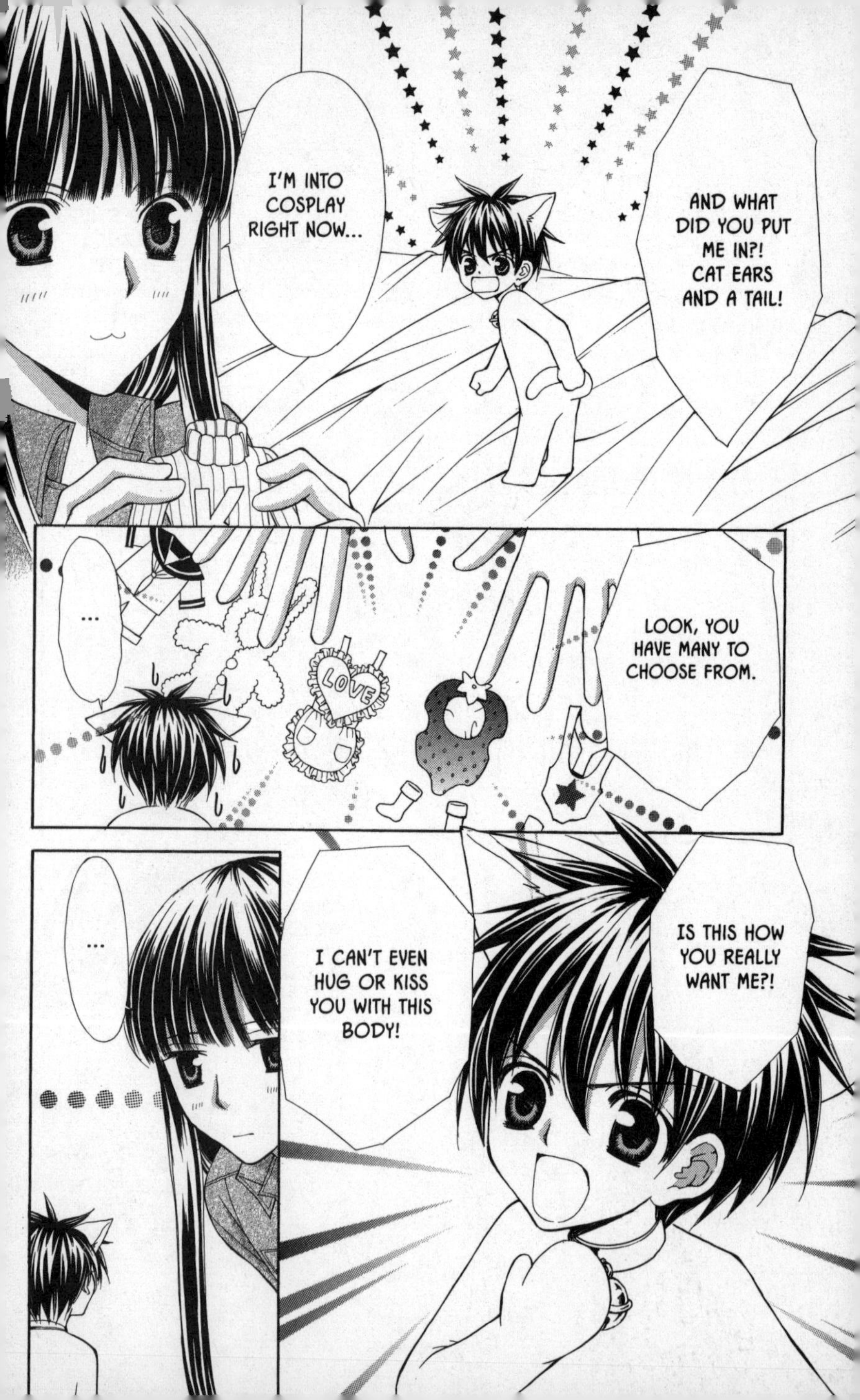
AND WHAT DID YOU PUT ME IN?! CAT EARS AND A TAIL!
I'M INTO COSPLAY RIGHT NOW...
LOOK, YOU HAVE MANY TO CHOOSE FROM.
LOVE
...
IS THIS HOW YOU REALLY WANT ME?!
I CAN'T EVEN HUG OR KISS YOU WITH THIS BODY!
...

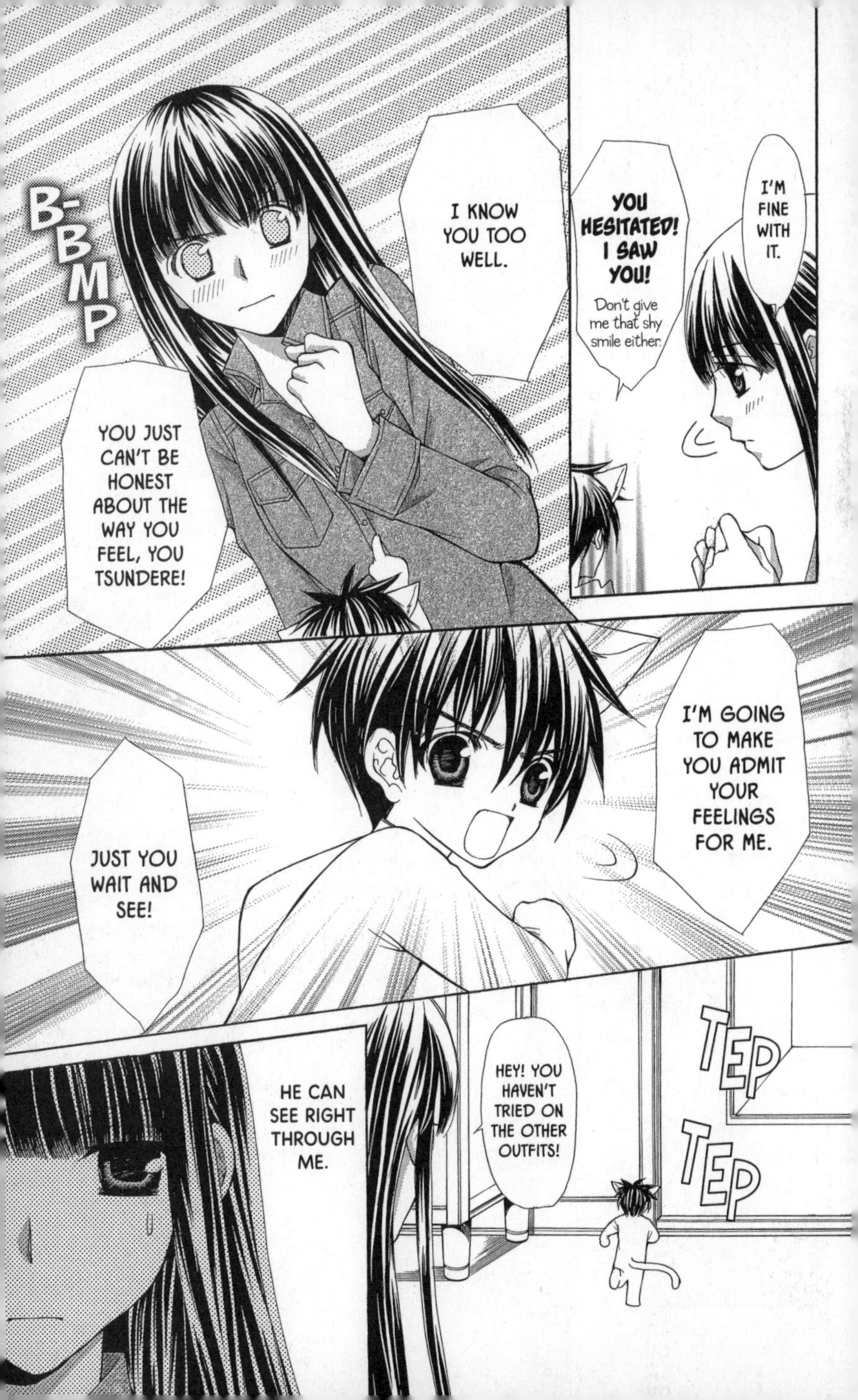
I'M FINE WITH IT.
YOU HESITATED! I SAW YOU!
Don't give me that shy smile either.
I KNOW YOU TOO WELL.
B-BMP
YOU JUST CAN'T BE HONEST ABOUT THE WAY YOU FEEL, YOU TSUNDERE!
I'M GOING TO MAKE YOU ADMIT YOUR FEELINGS FOR ME.
JUST YOU WAIT AND SEE!
TEP
TEP
HEY! YOU HAVEN'T TRIED ON THE OTHER OUTFITS!
HE CAN SEE RIGHT THROUGH ME.

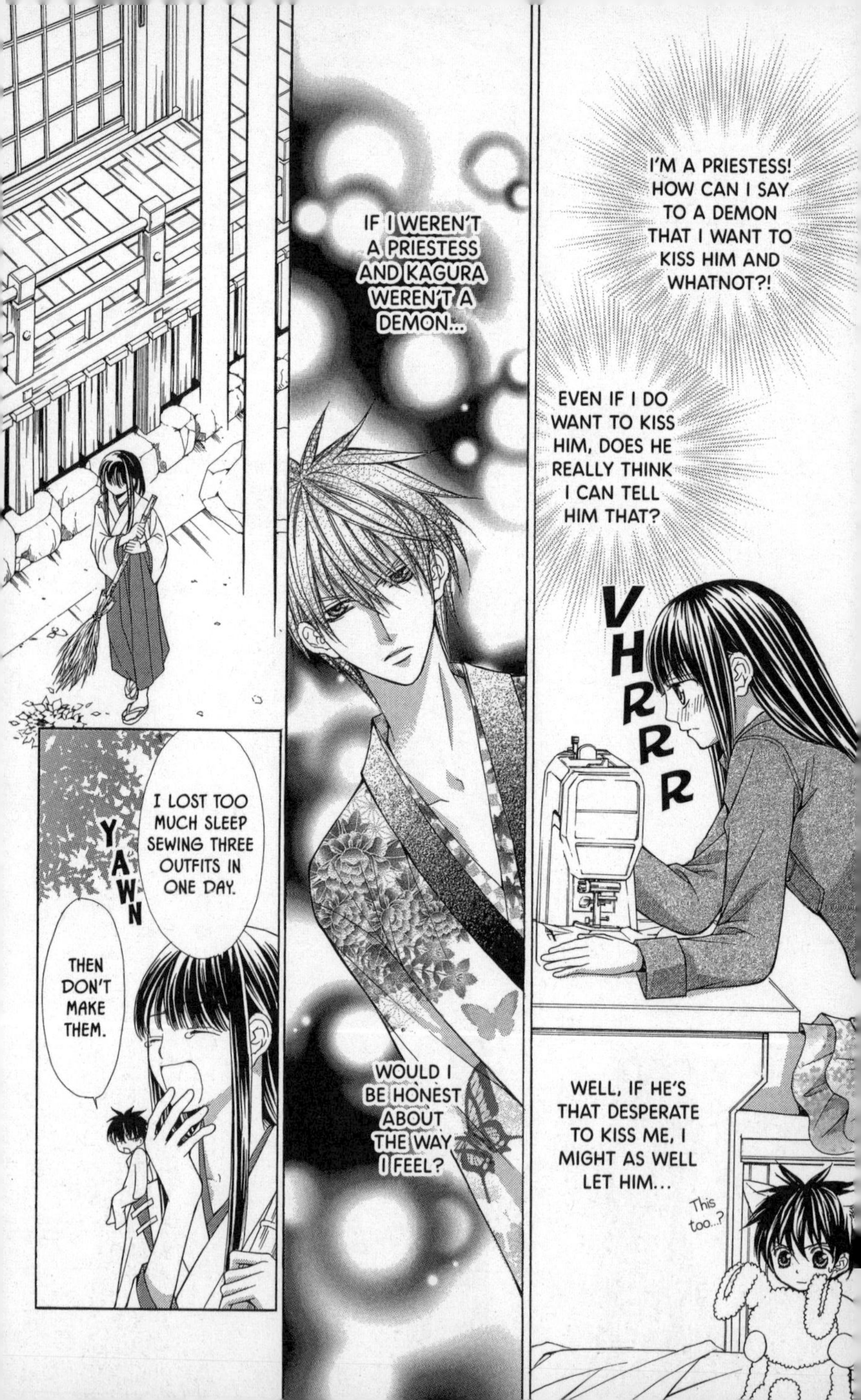
I'M A PRIESTESS! HOW CAN I SAY TO A DEMON THAT I WANT TO KISS HIM AND WHATNOT?!
EVEN IF I DO WANT TO KISS HIM, DOES HE REALLY THINK I CAN TELL HIM THAT?
VHRRR
WELL, IF HE'S THAT DESPERATE TO KISS ME, I MIGHT AS WELL LET HIM...
This too...?
IF I WEREN'T A PRIESTESS AND KAGURA WEREN'T A DEMON...
WOULD I BE HONEST ABOUT THE WAY I FEEL?
I LOST TOO MUCH SLEEP SEWING THREE OUTFITS IN ONE DAY.
YAWN
THEN DON'T MAKE THEM.

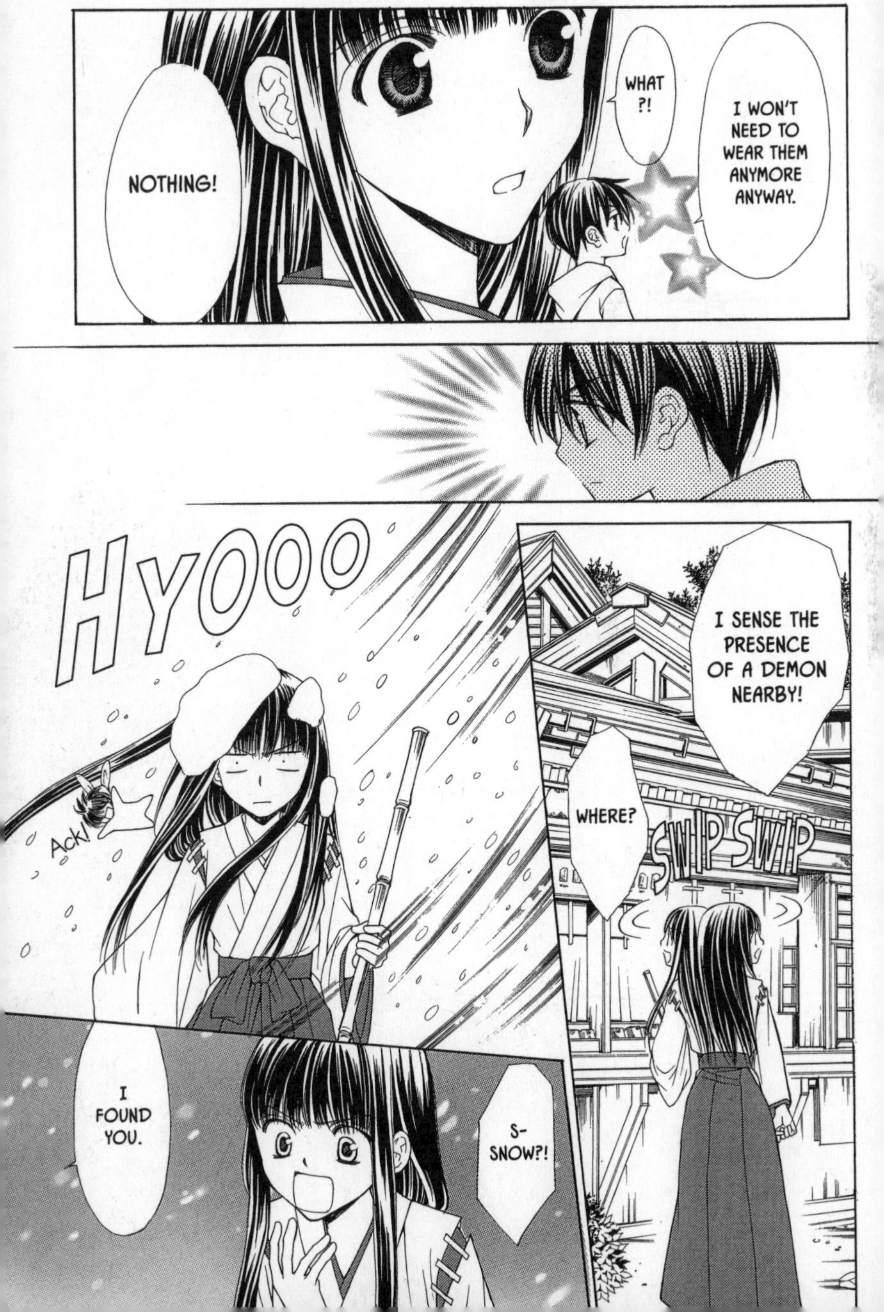
I WON'T NEED TO WEAR THEM ANYMORE ANYWAY.
WHAT?!
NOTHING!
I SENSE THE PRESENCE OF A DEMON NEARBY!
SWIP SWIP
WHERE?
HYOOO
Ack!
S-SNOW?!
I FOUND YOU.

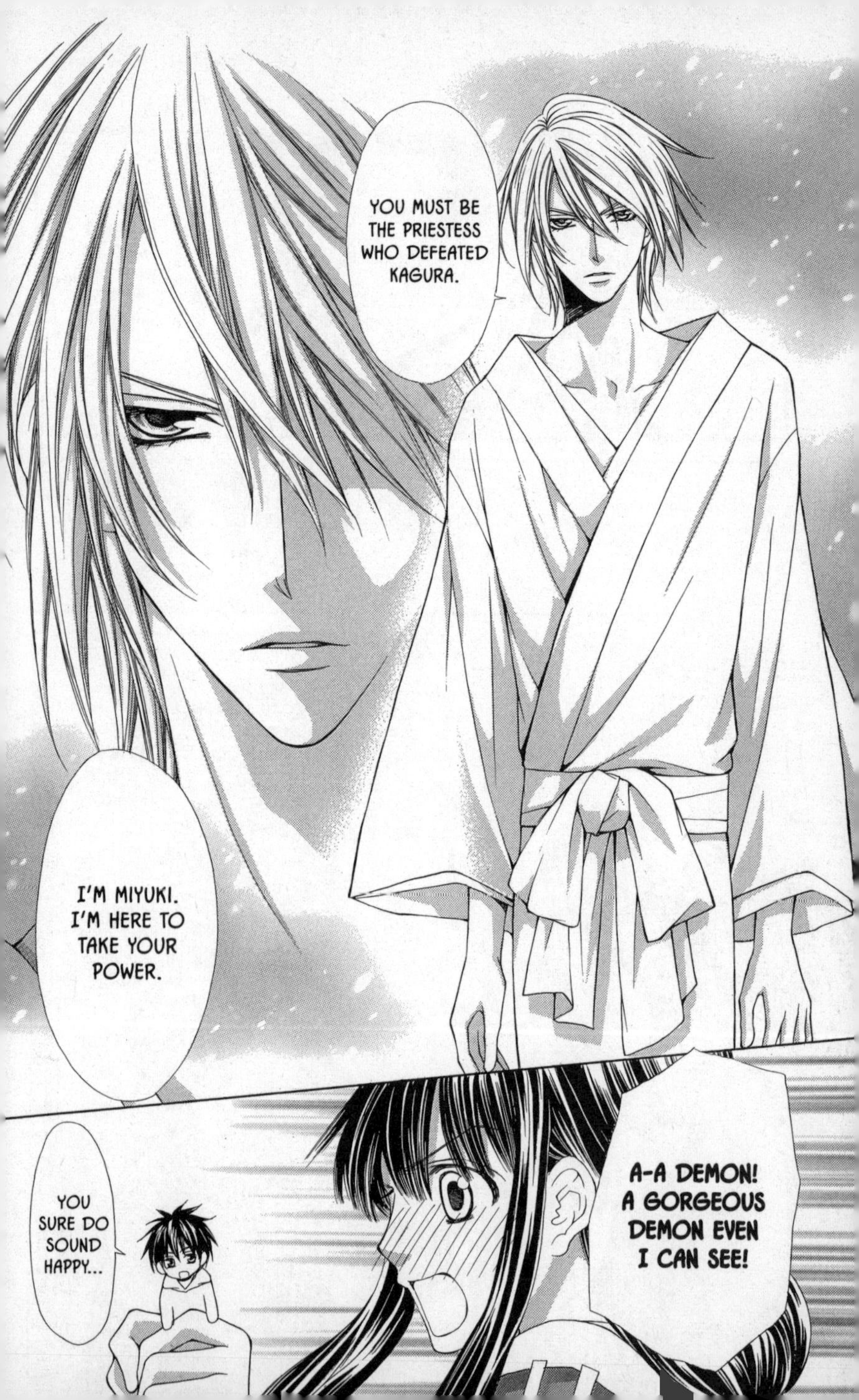
YOU MUST BE THE PRIESTESS WHO DEFEATED KAGURA.
I'M MIYUKI. I'M HERE TO TAKE YOUR POWER.
A-A DEMON! A GORGEOUS DEMON EVEN I CAN SEE!
YOU SURE DO SOUND HAPPY...

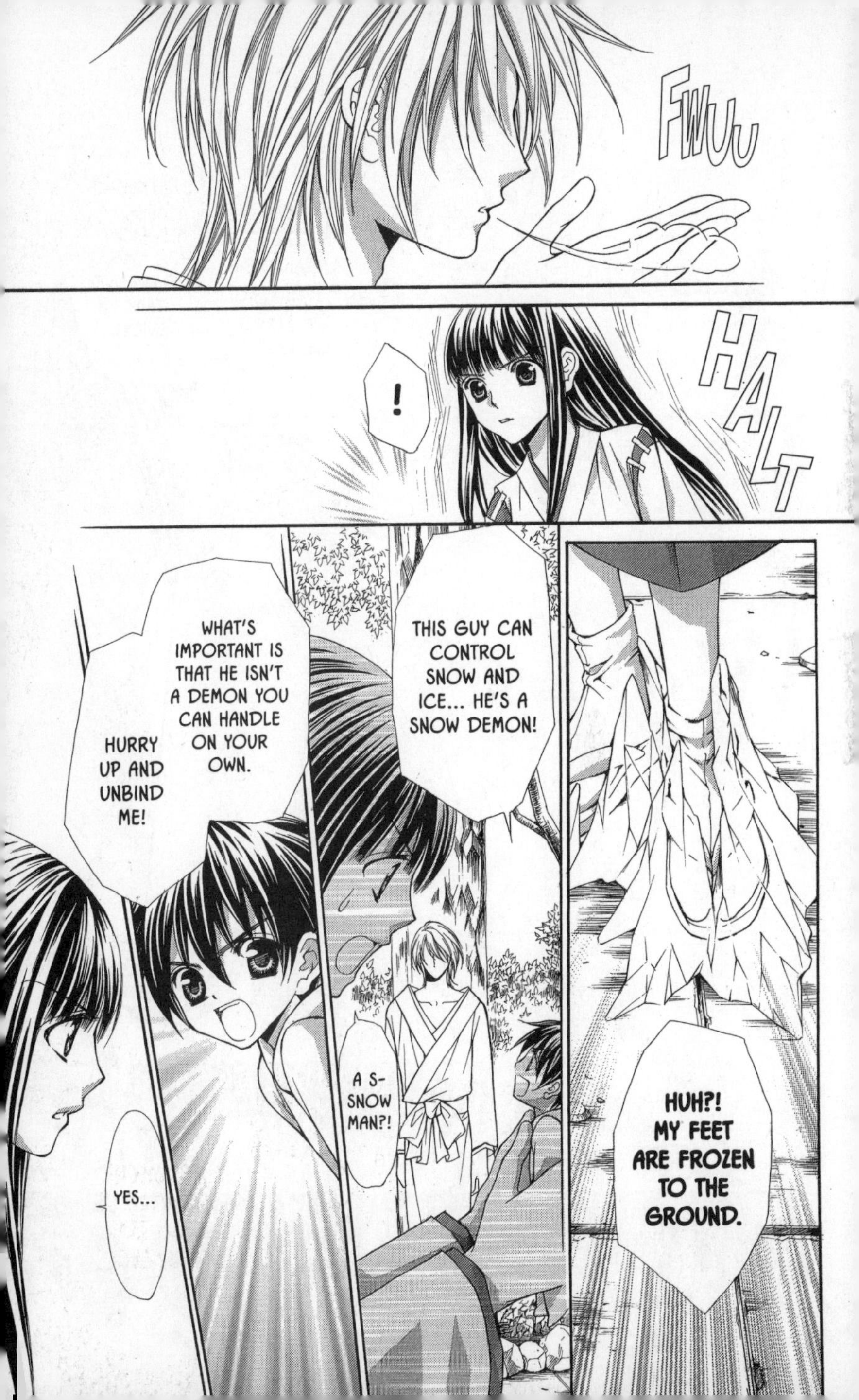
FWUU
HALT
!
HUH?! MY FEET ARE FROZEN TO THE GROUND.
THIS GUY CAN CONTROL SNOW AND ICE... HE'S A SNOW DEMON!
A S-SNOW MAN?!
WHAT'S IMPORTANT IS THAT HE ISN'T A DEMON YOU CAN HANDLE ON YOUR OWN.
HURRY UP AND UNBIND ME!
YES...

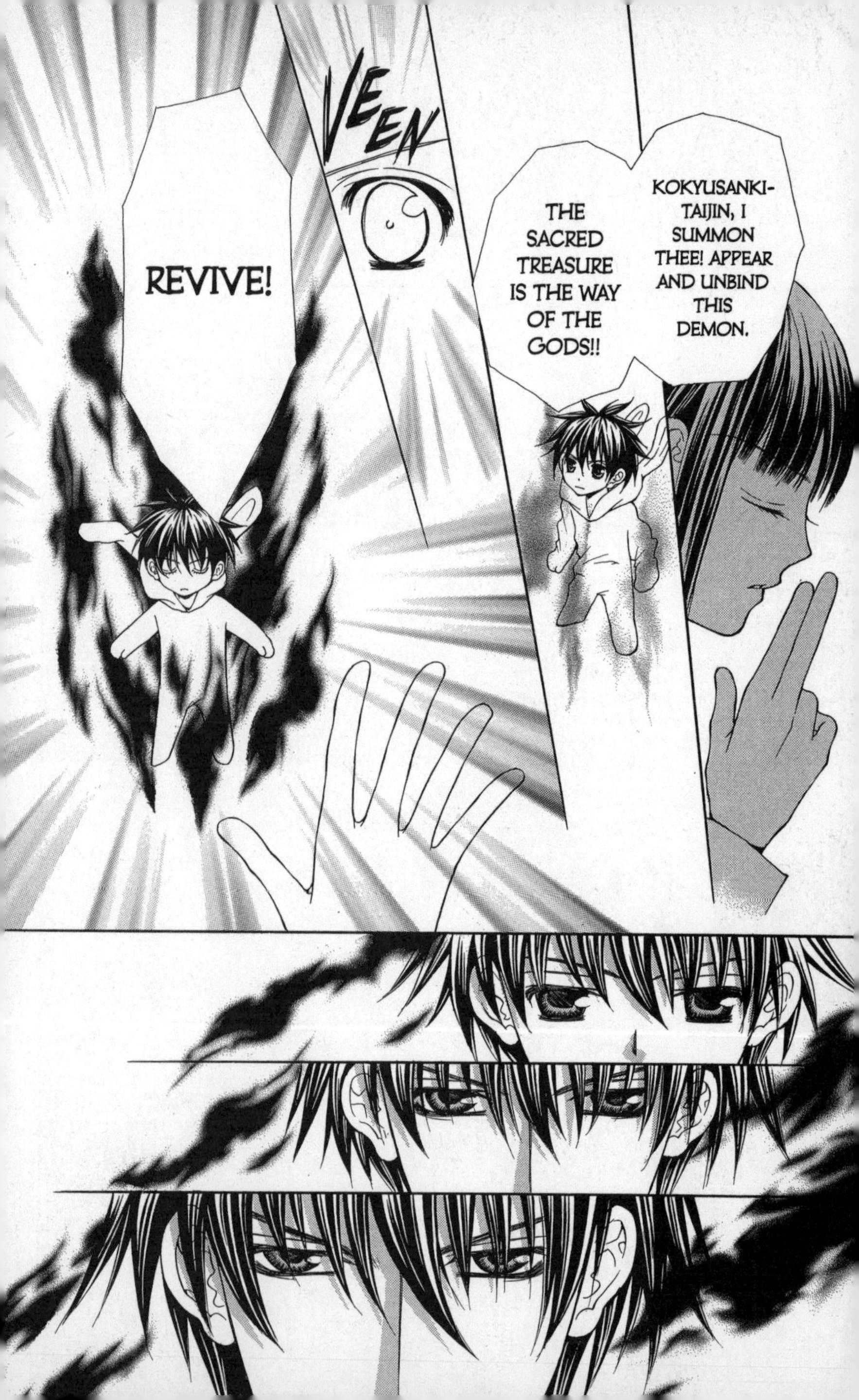
KOKYUSANKI-TAIJIN, I SUMMON THEE! APPEAR AND UNBIND THIS DEMON.
THE SACRED TREASURE IS THE WAY OF THE GODS!!
VEEN
REVIVE!

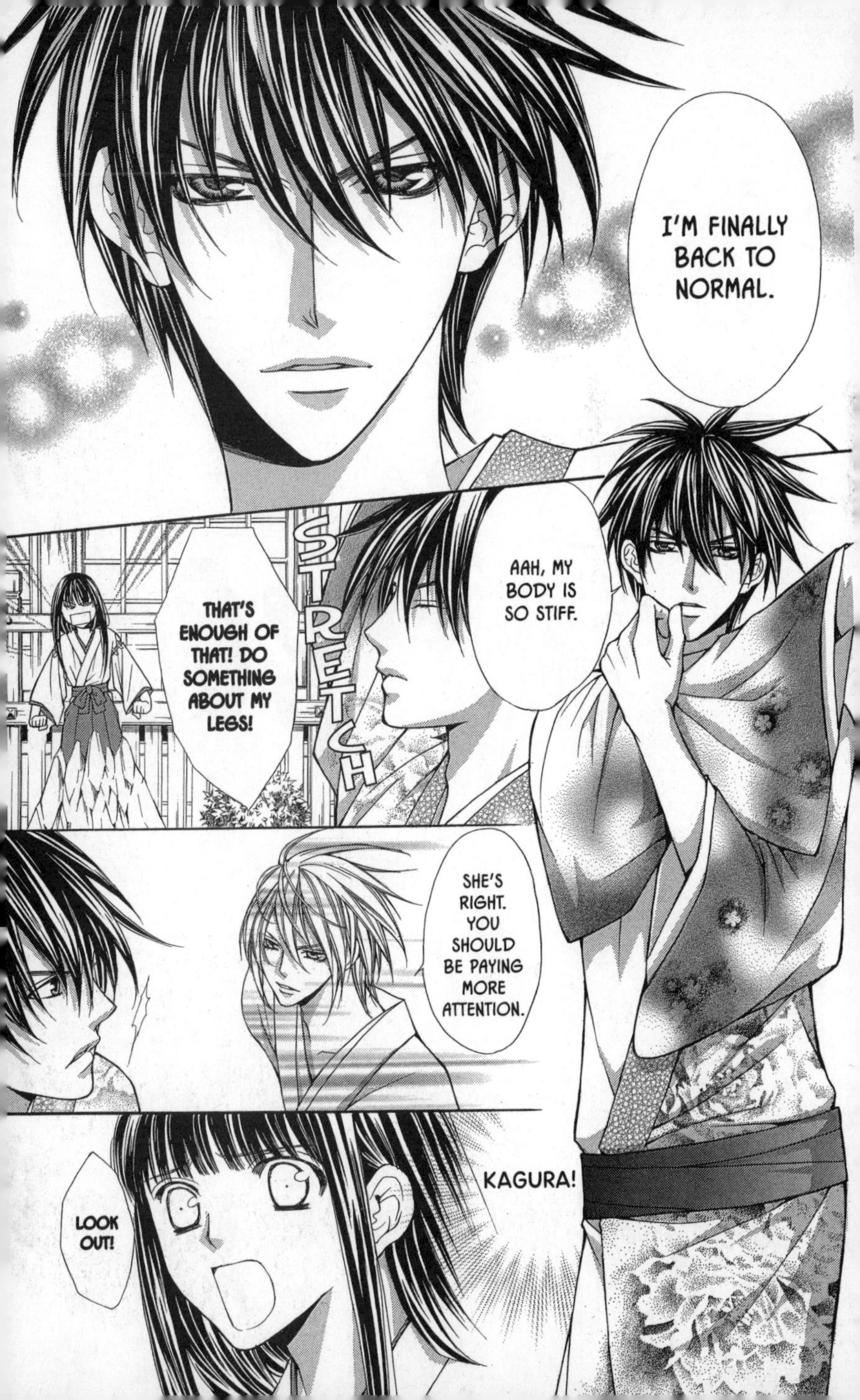
I'M FINALLY BACK TO NORMAL.
AAH, MY BODY IS SO STIFF.
STRETCH
THAT'S ENOUGH OF THAT! DO SOMETHING ABOUT MY LEGS!
SHE'S RIGHT. YOU SHOULD BE PAYING MORE ATTENTION.
KAGURA!
LOOK OUT!

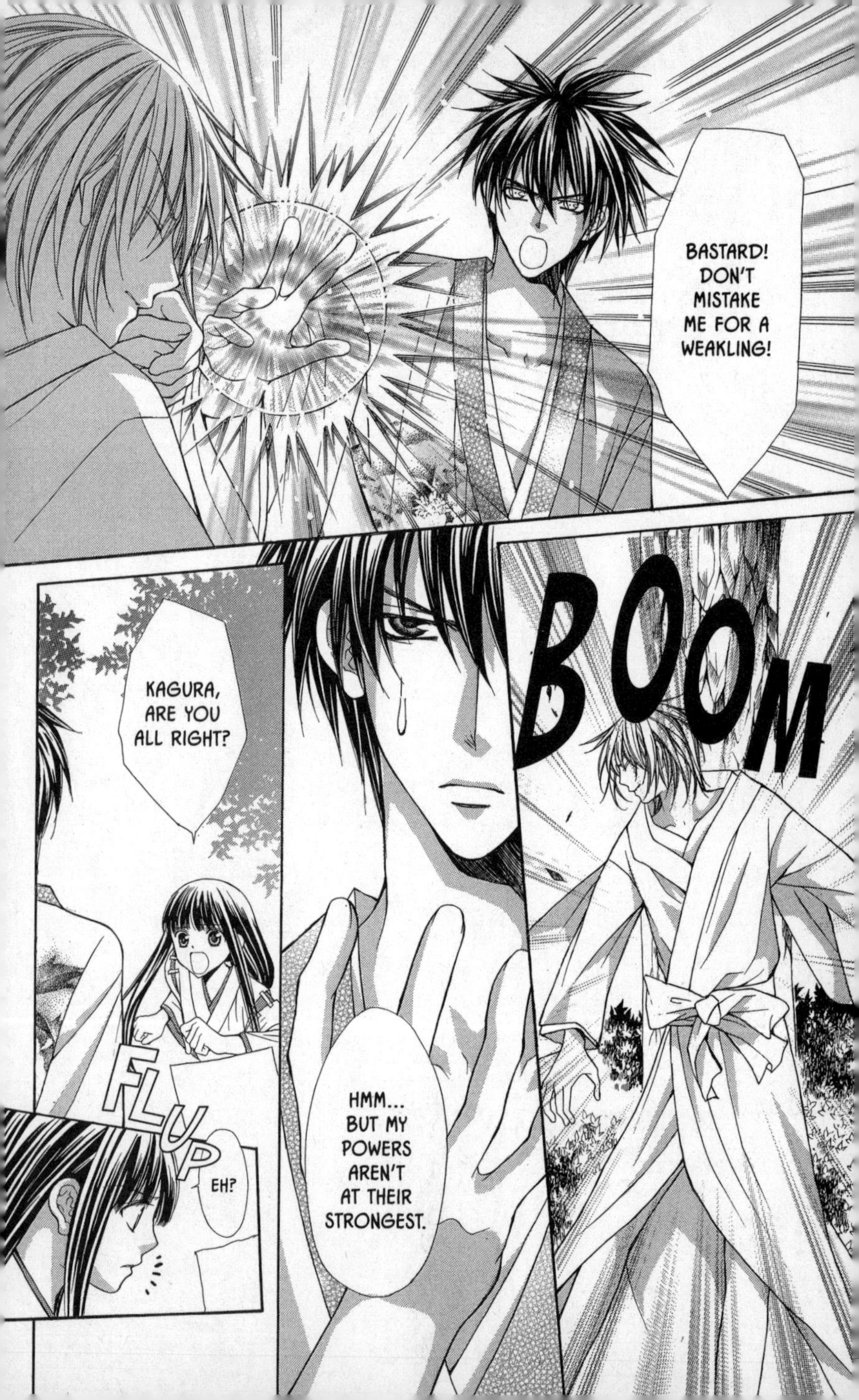
BASTARD! DON'T MISTAKE ME FOR A WEAKLING!
BOOM
HMM... BUT MY POWERS AREN'T AT THEIR STRONGEST.
KAGURA, ARE YOU ALL RIGHT?
FLUP
EH?

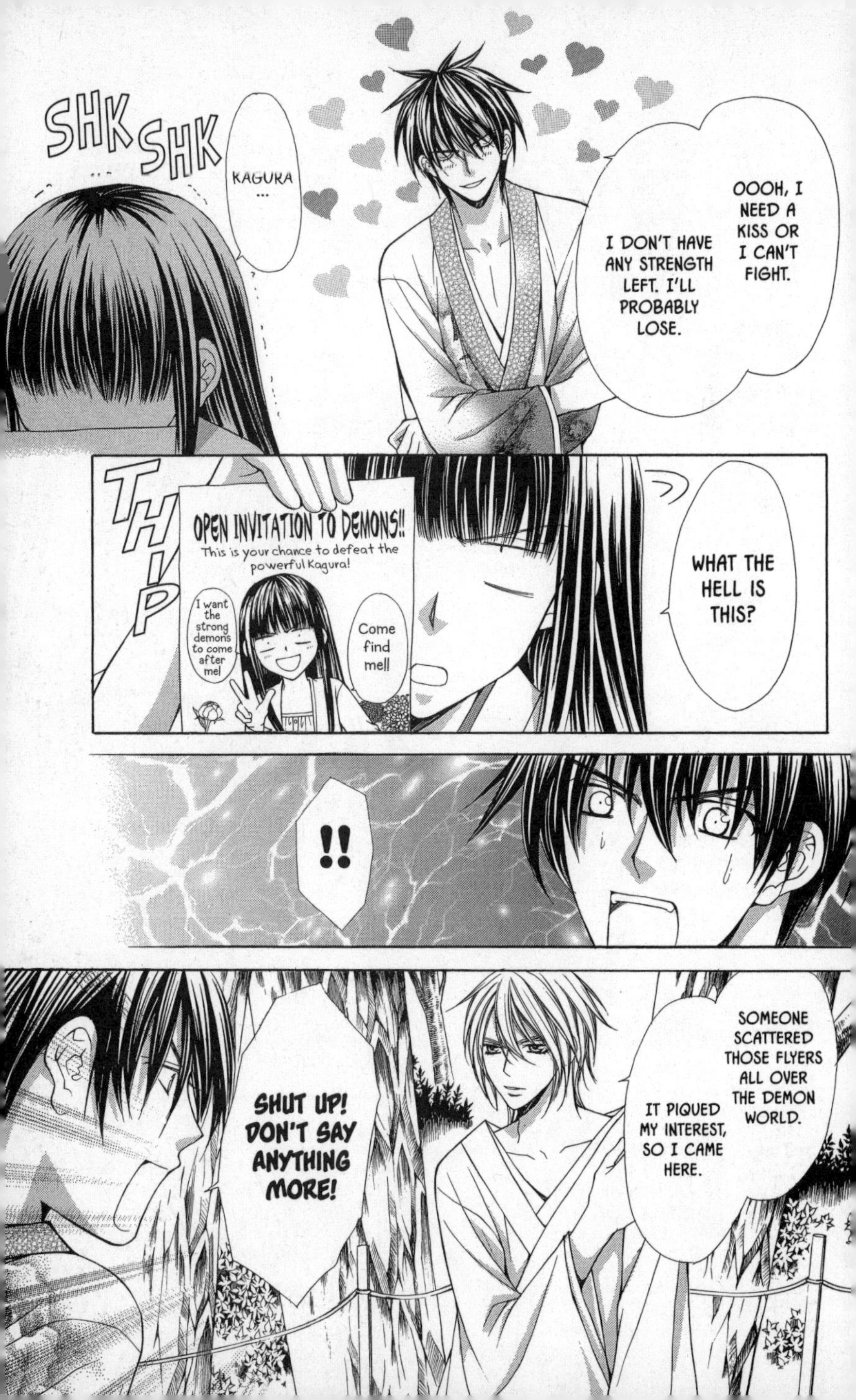

OOOH, I NEED A KISS OR I CAN'T FIGHT.
I DON'T HAVE ANY STRENGTH LEFT. I'LL PROBABLY LOSE.
KAGURA ...
SHK SHK
WHAT THE HELL IS THIS?
THIP
OPEN INVITATION TO DEMONS!!
This is your chance to defeat the powerful Kagura!
Come find me!!
I want the strong demons to come after me!
!!
SOMEONE SCATTERED THOSE FLYERS ALL OVER THE DEMON WORLD.
IT PIQUED MY INTEREST, SO I CAME HERE.
SHUT UP! DON'T SAY ANYTHING MORE!

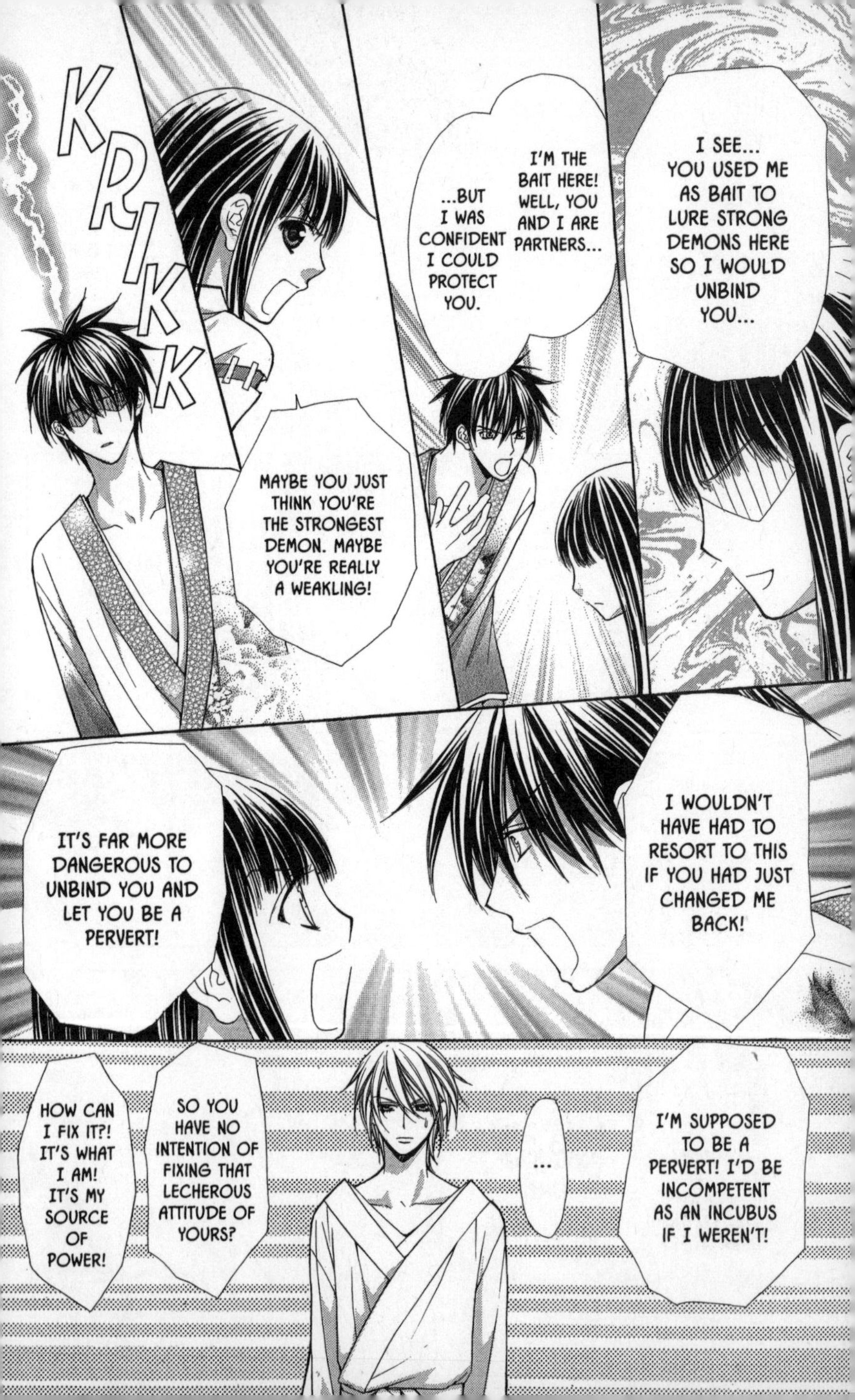
I SEE... YOU USED ME AS BAIT TO LURE STRONG DEMONS HERE SO I WOULD UNBIND YOU...
I'M THE BAIT HERE! WELL, YOU AND I ARE PARTNERS...
...BUT I WAS CONFIDENT I COULD PROTECT YOU.
MAYBE YOU JUST THINK YOU'RE THE STRONGEST DEMON. MAYBE YOU'RE REALLY A WEAKLING!
KRIKK
I WOULDN'T HAVE HAD TO RESORT TO THIS IF YOU HAD JUST CHANGED ME BACK!
IT'S FAR MORE DANGEROUS TO UNBIND YOU AND LET YOU BE A PERVERT!
I'M SUPPOSED TO BE A PERVERT! I'D BE INCOMPETENT AS AN INCUBUS IF I WEREN'T!
...
SO YOU HAVE NO INTENTION OF FIXING THAT LECHEROUS ATTITUDE OF YOURS?
HOW CAN I FIX IT?! IT'S WHAT I AM! IT'S MY SOURCE OF POWER!

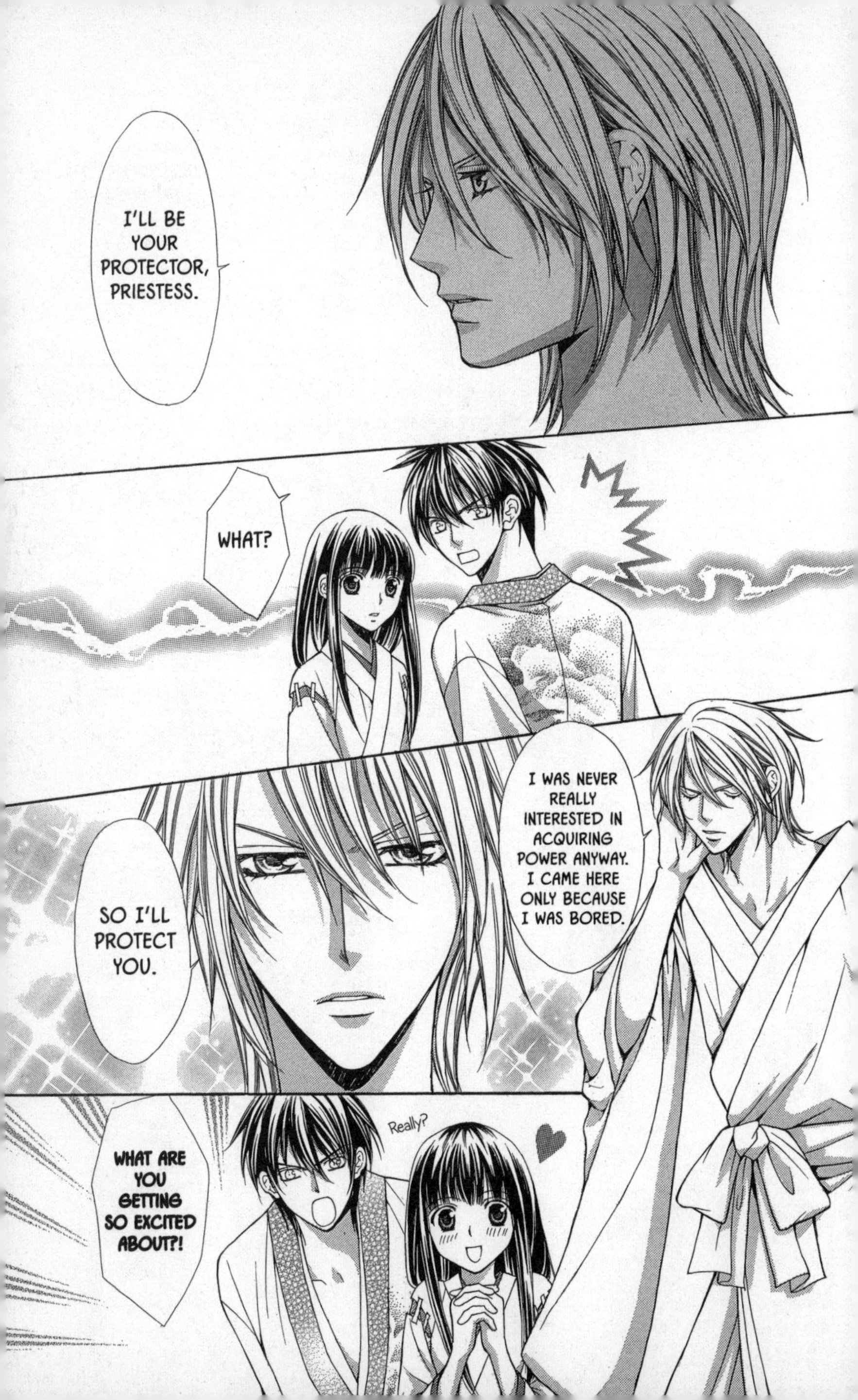
I'LL BE YOUR PROTECTOR, PRIESTESS.
WHAT?
I WAS NEVER REALLY INTERESTED IN ACQUIRING POWER ANYWAY. I CAME HERE ONLY BECAUSE I WAS BORED.
SO I'LL PROTECT YOU.
Really?
WHAT ARE YOU GETTING SO EXCITED ABOUT?!

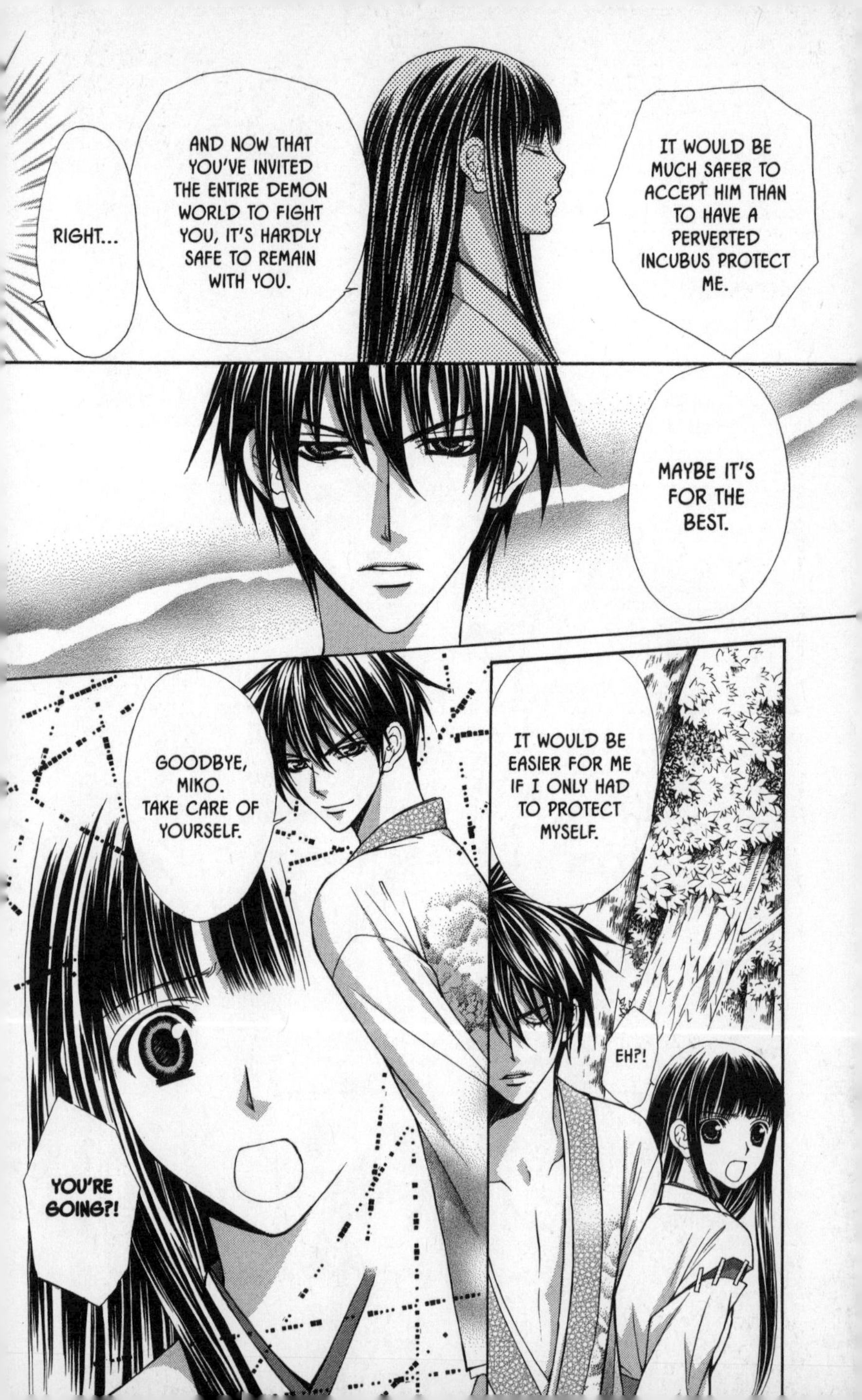
IT WOULD BE MUCH SAFER TO ACCEPT HIM THAN TO HAVE A PERVERTED INCUBUS PROTECT ME.
AND NOW THAT YOU'VE INVITED THE ENTIRE DEMON WORLD TO FIGHT YOU, IT'S HARDLY SAFE TO REMAIN WITH YOU.
RIGHT...
MAYBE IT'S FOR THE BEST.
IT WOULD BE EASIER FOR ME IF I ONLY HAD TO PROTECT MYSELF.
EH?!
GOODBYE, MIKO. TAKE CARE OF YOURSELF.
YOU'RE GOING?!

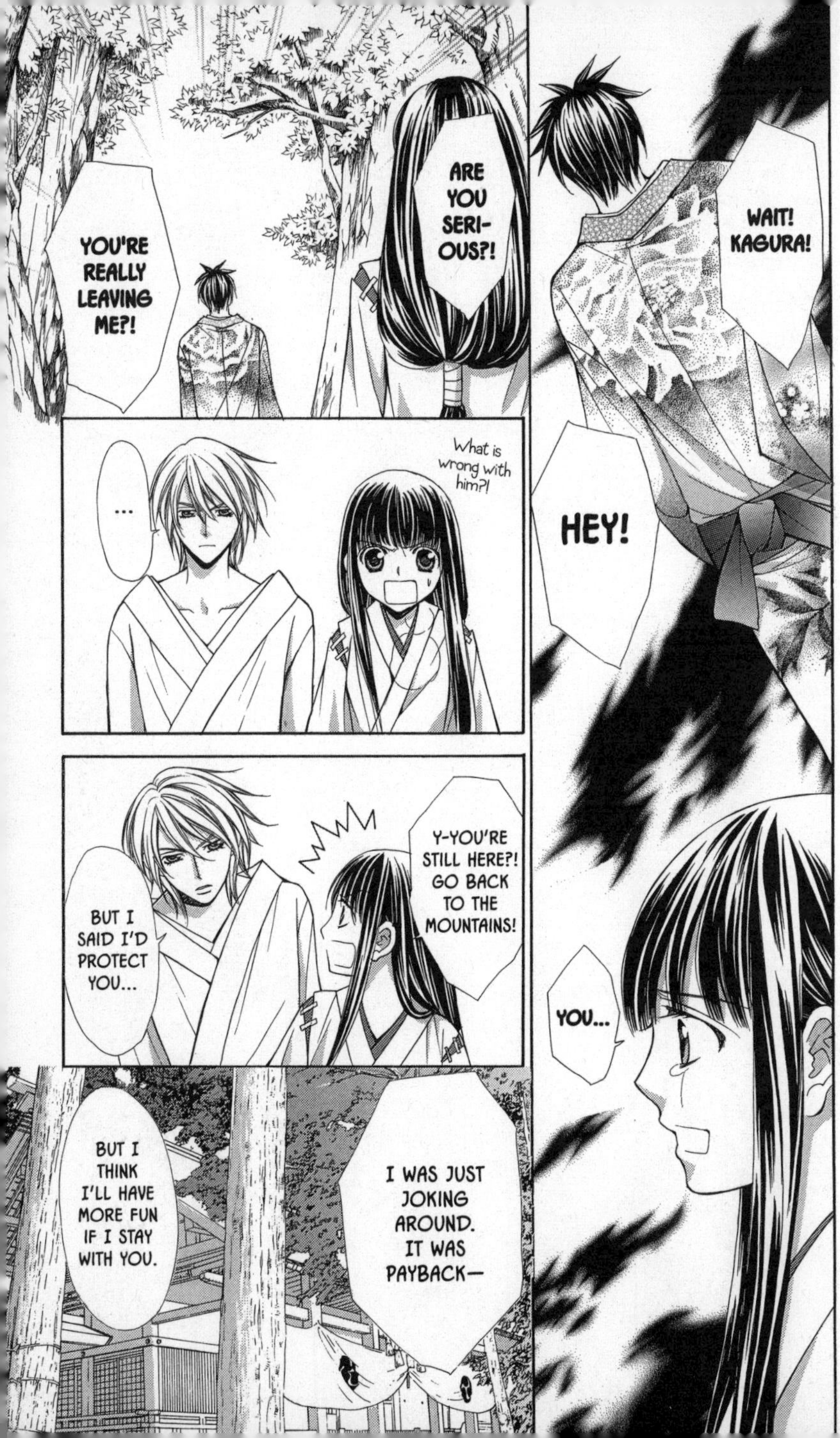
WAIT! KAGURA!
HEY!
YOU...
ARE YOU SERI-OUS?!
YOU'RE REALLY LEAVING ME?!
What is wrong with him?!
...
Y-YOU'RE STILL HERE?! GO BACK TO THE MOUNTAINS!
BUT I SAID I'D PROTECT YOU...
I WAS JUST JOKING AROUND. IT WAS PAYBACK—
BUT I THINK I'LL HAVE MORE FUN IF I STAY WITH YOU.

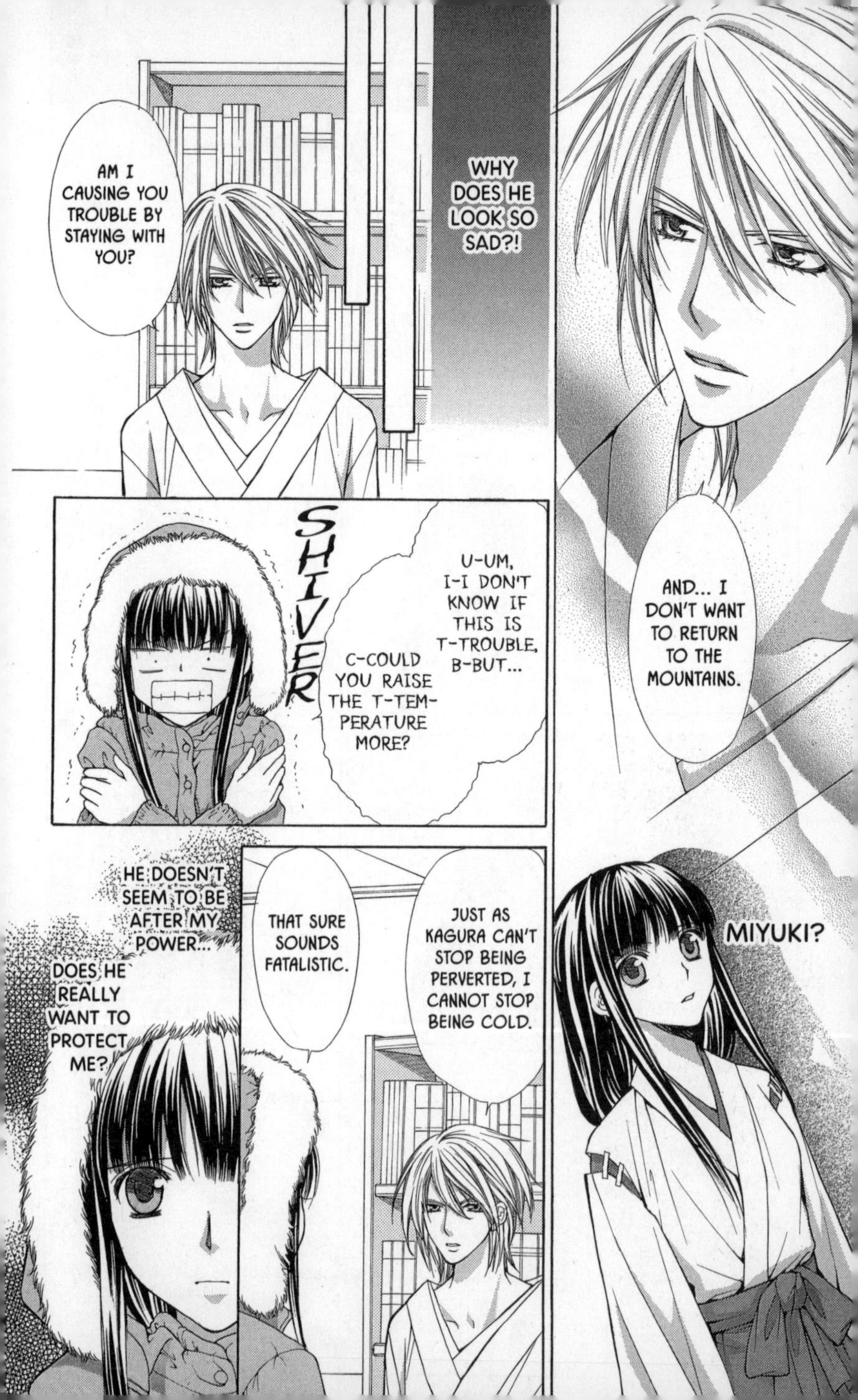
AM I CAUSING YOU TROUBLE BY STAYING WITH YOU?
AND... I DON'T WANT TO RETURN TO THE MOUNTAINS.
WHY DOES HE LOOK SO SAD?!
MIYUKI?
SHIVER
U-UM, I-I DON'T KNOW IF THIS IS T-TROUBLE, B-BUT...
C-COULD YOU RAISE THE T-TEM-PERATURE MORE?
JUST AS KAGURA CAN'T STOP BEING PERVERTED, I CANNOT STOP BEING COLD.
THAT SURE SOUNDS FATALISTIC.
HE DOESN'T SEEM TO BE AFTER MY POWER...
DOES HE REALLY WANT TO PROTECT ME?

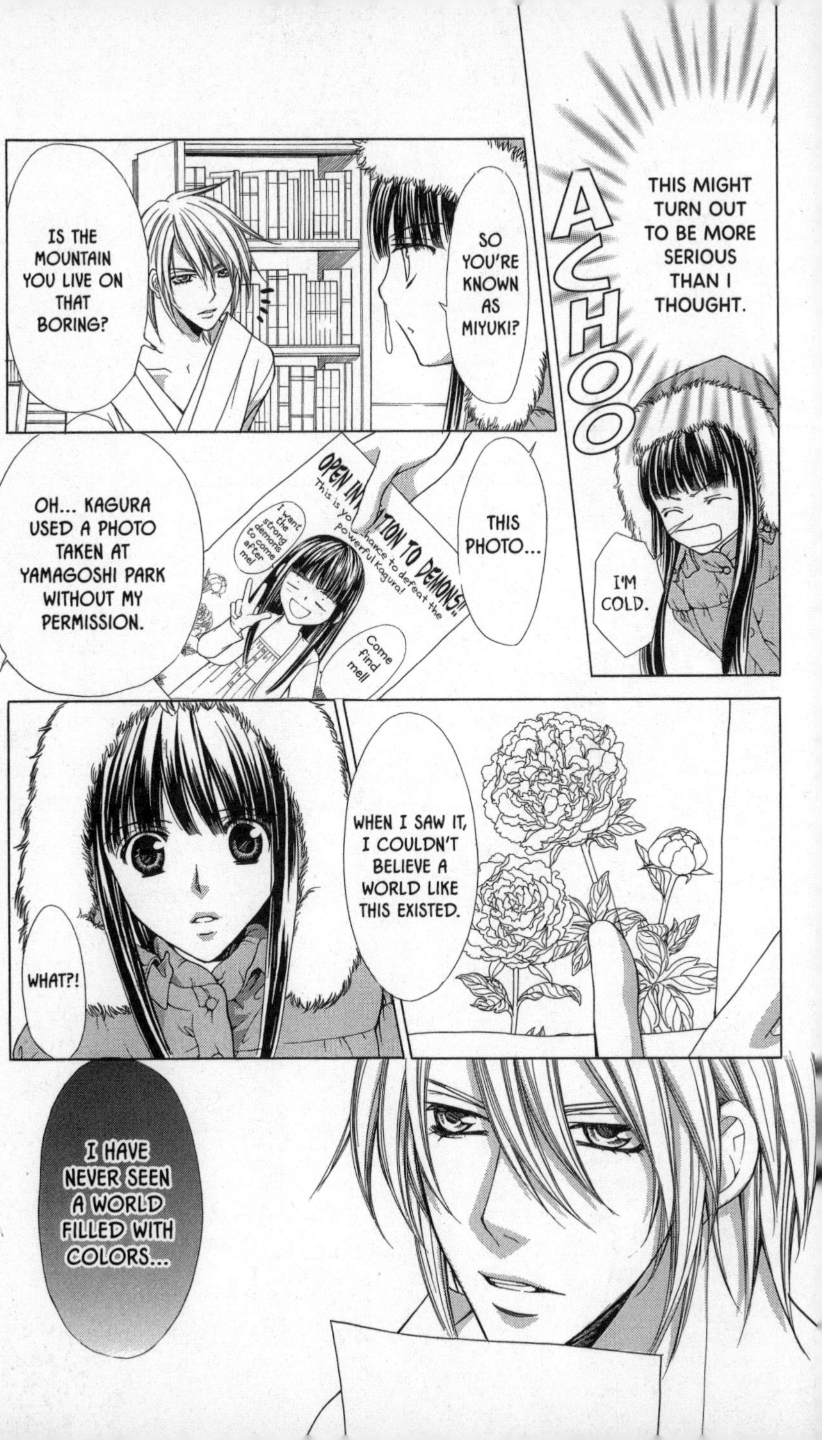
THIS MIGHT TURN OUT TO BE MORE SERIOUS THAN I THOUGHT.
ACHOO
I'M COLD.
SO YOU'RE KNOWN AS MIYUKI?
IS THE MOUNTAIN YOU LIVE ON THAT BORING?
THIS PHOTO...
OPEN IN
TION TO DEMONS!!
This is yo
hance to defeat the powerful Kagura!
I want the strong demons to come after me!
Come find me!
OH... KAGURA USED A PHOTO TAKEN AT YAMAGOSHI PARK WITHOUT MY PERMISSION.
WHEN I SAW IT, I COULDN'T BELIEVE A WORLD LIKE THIS EXISTED.
WHAT?!
I HAVE NEVER SEEN A WORLD FILLED WITH COLORS...

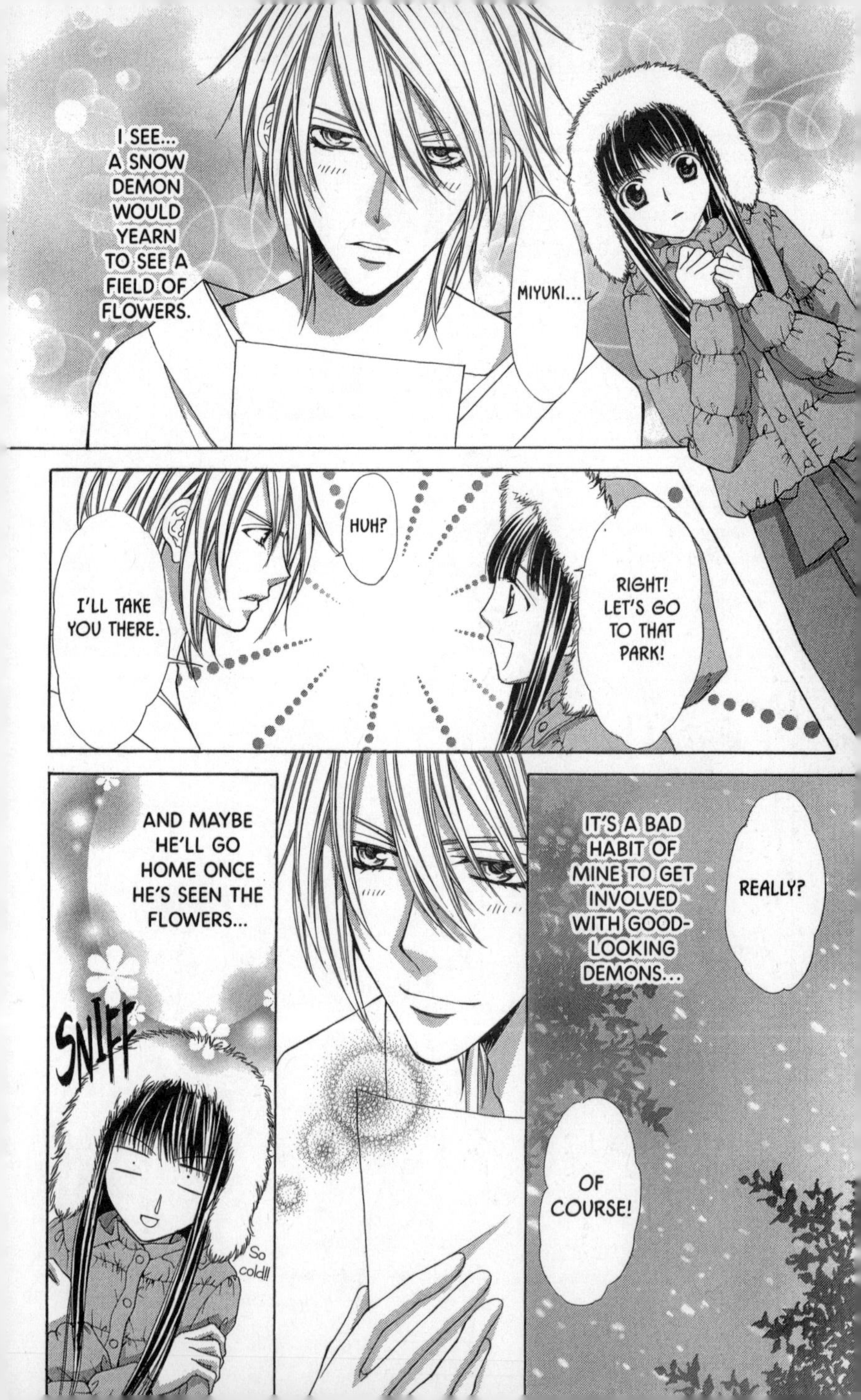
I SEE... A SNOW DEMON WOULD YEARN TO SEE A FIELD OF FLOWERS.
MIYUKI...
HUH?
RIGHT! LET'S GO TO THAT PARK!
I'LL TAKE YOU THERE.
REALLY?
IT'S A BAD HABIT OF MINE TO GET INVOLVED WITH GOOD-LOOKING DEMONS...
OF COURSE!
AND MAYBE HE'LL GO HOME ONCE HE'S SEEN THE FLOWERS...
SNIFF
So cold!!

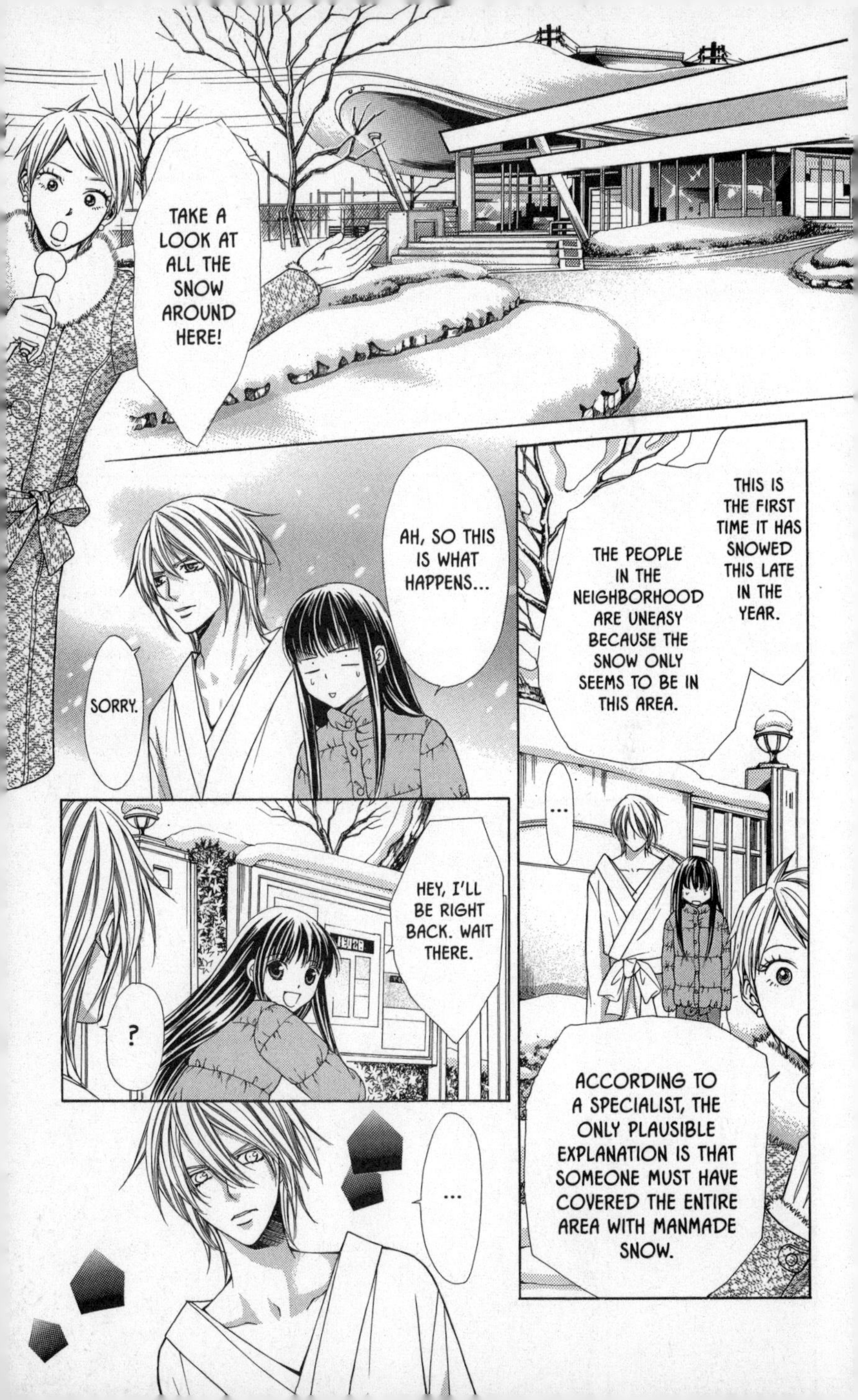
TAKE A LOOK AT ALL THE SNOW AROUND HERE!
THIS IS THE FIRST TIME IT HAS SNOWED THIS LATE IN THE YEAR.
THE PEOPLE IN THE NEIGHBORHOOD ARE UNEASY BECAUSE THE SNOW ONLY SEEMS TO BE IN THIS AREA.
...
ACCORDING TO A SPECIALIST, THE ONLY PLAUSIBLE EXPLANATION IS THAT SOMEONE MUST HAVE COVERED THE ENTIRE AREA WITH MANMADE SNOW.
AH, SO THIS IS WHAT HAPPENS...
SORRY.
HEY, I'LL BE RIGHT BACK. WAIT THERE.
?
...

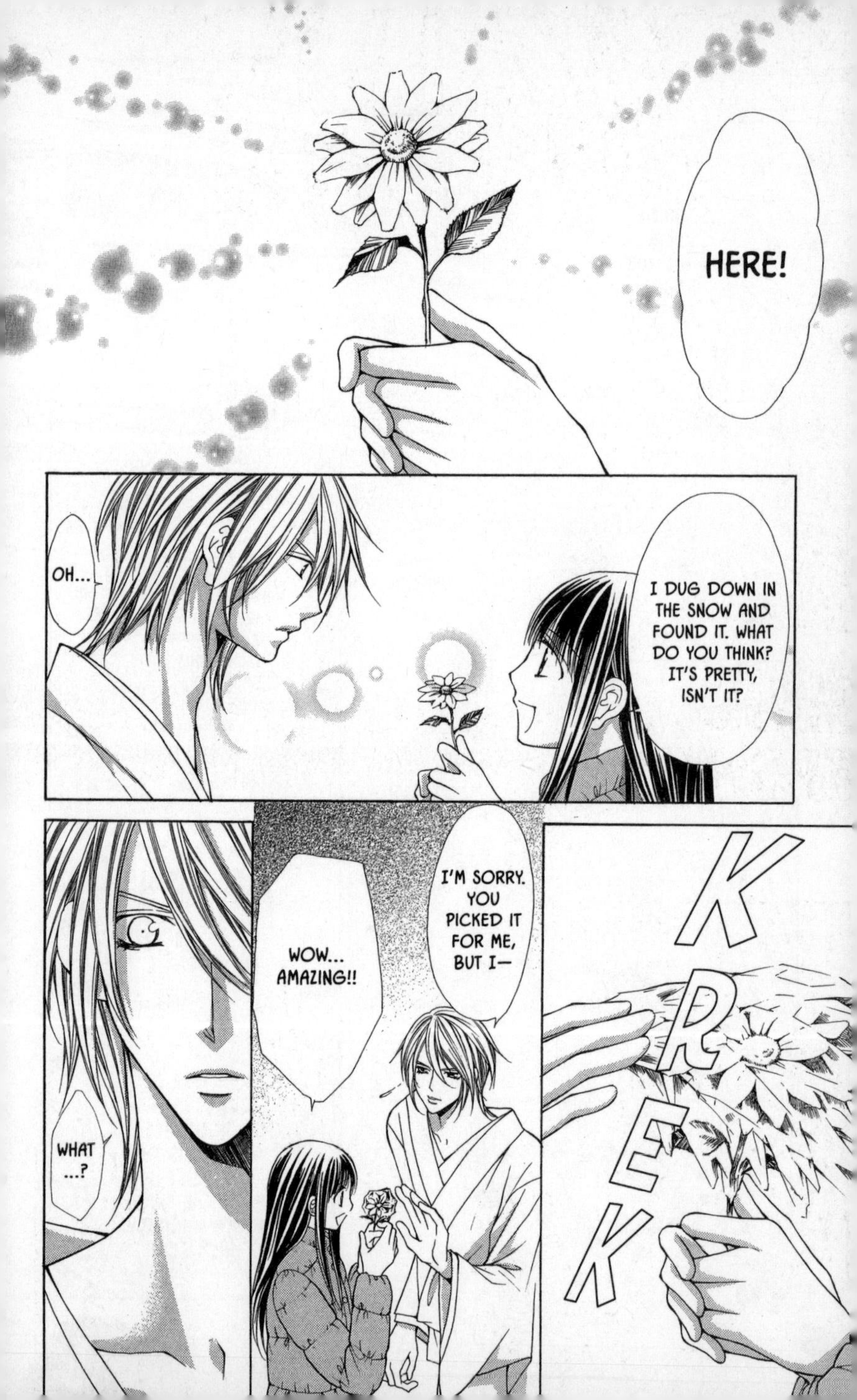
HERE!
I DUG DOWN IN THE SNOW AND FOUND IT. WHAT DO YOU THINK? IT'S PRETTY, ISN'T IT?
OH...
KREEK
I'M SORRY. YOU PICKED IT FOR ME, BUT I—
WOW... AMAZING!!
WHAT ...?

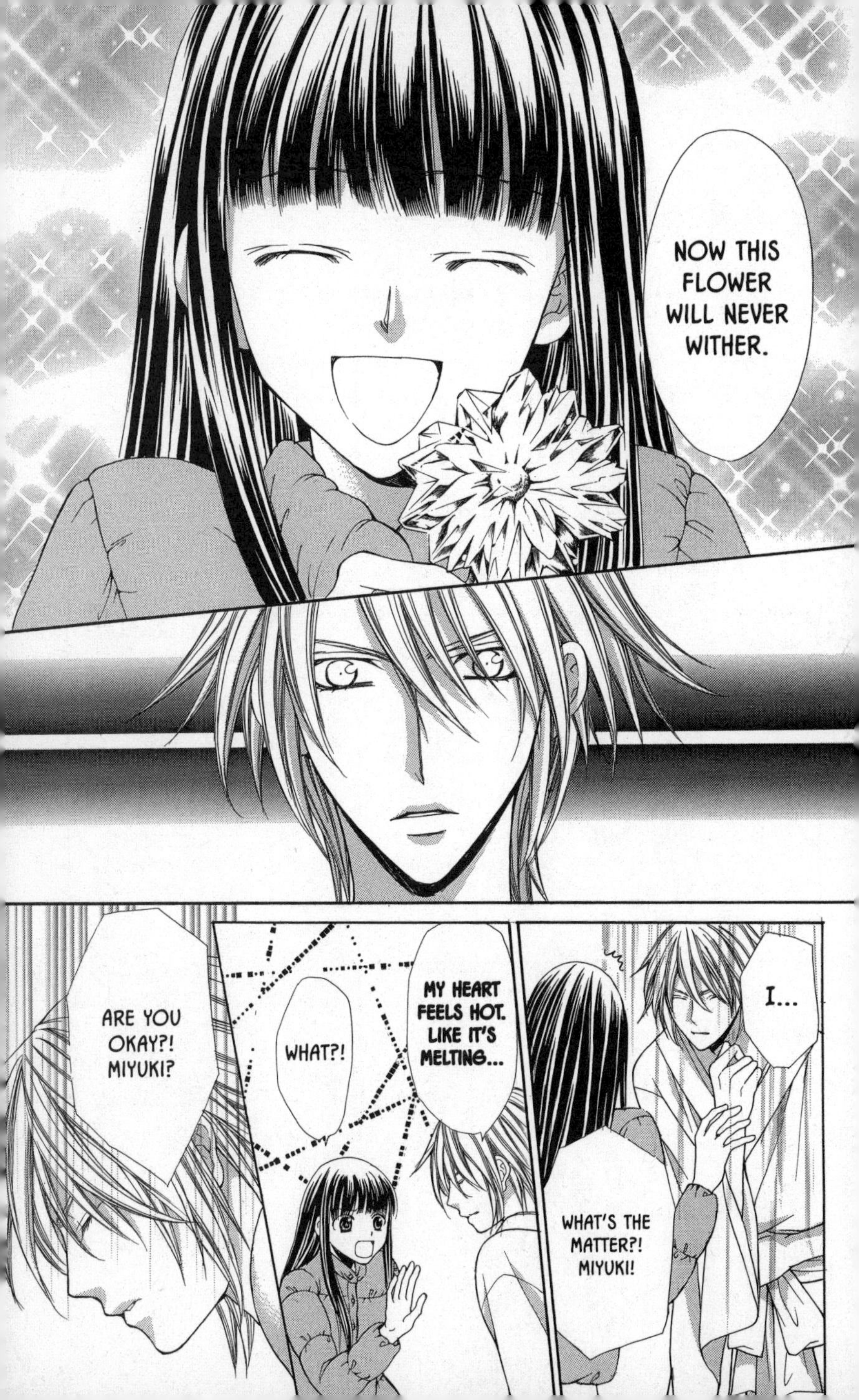
NOW THIS FLOWER WILL NEVER WITHER.
I...
WHAT'S THE MATTER?! MIYUKI!
MY HEART FEELS HOT. LIKE IT'S MELTING...
WHAT?!
ARE YOU OKAY?! MIYUKI?

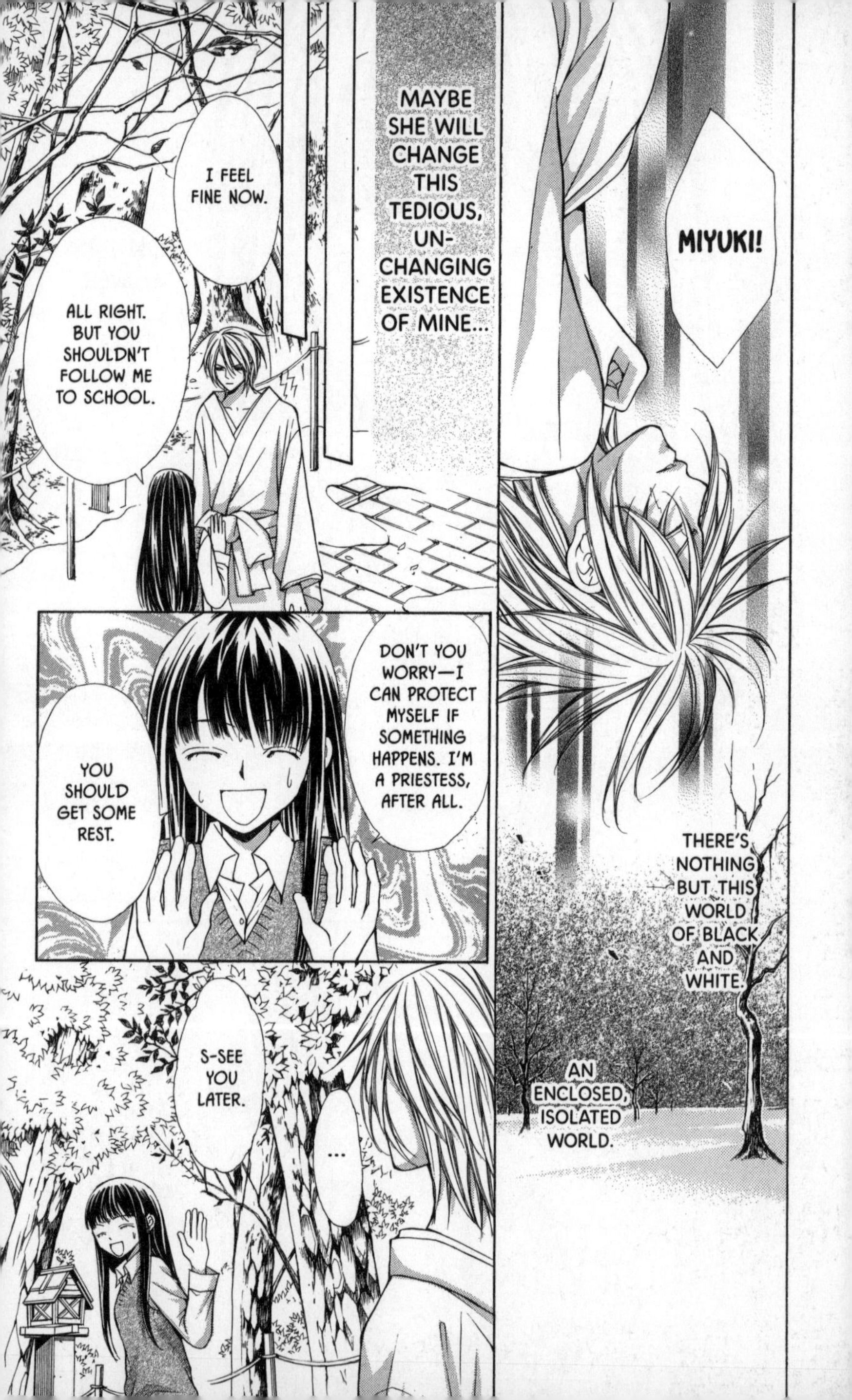
MIYUKI!
THERE'S NOTHING BUT THIS WORLD OF BLACK AND WHITE.
AN ENCLOSED, ISOLATED WORLD.
MAYBE SHE WILL CHANGE THIS TEDIOUS, UN-CHANGING EXISTENCE OF MINE...
I FEEL FINE NOW.
ALL RIGHT. BUT YOU SHOULDN'T FOLLOW ME TO SCHOOL.
DON'T YOU WORRY—I CAN PROTECT MYSELF IF SOMETHING HAPPENS. I'M A PRIESTESS, AFTER ALL.
YOU SHOULD GET SOME REST.
...
S-SEE YOU LATER.

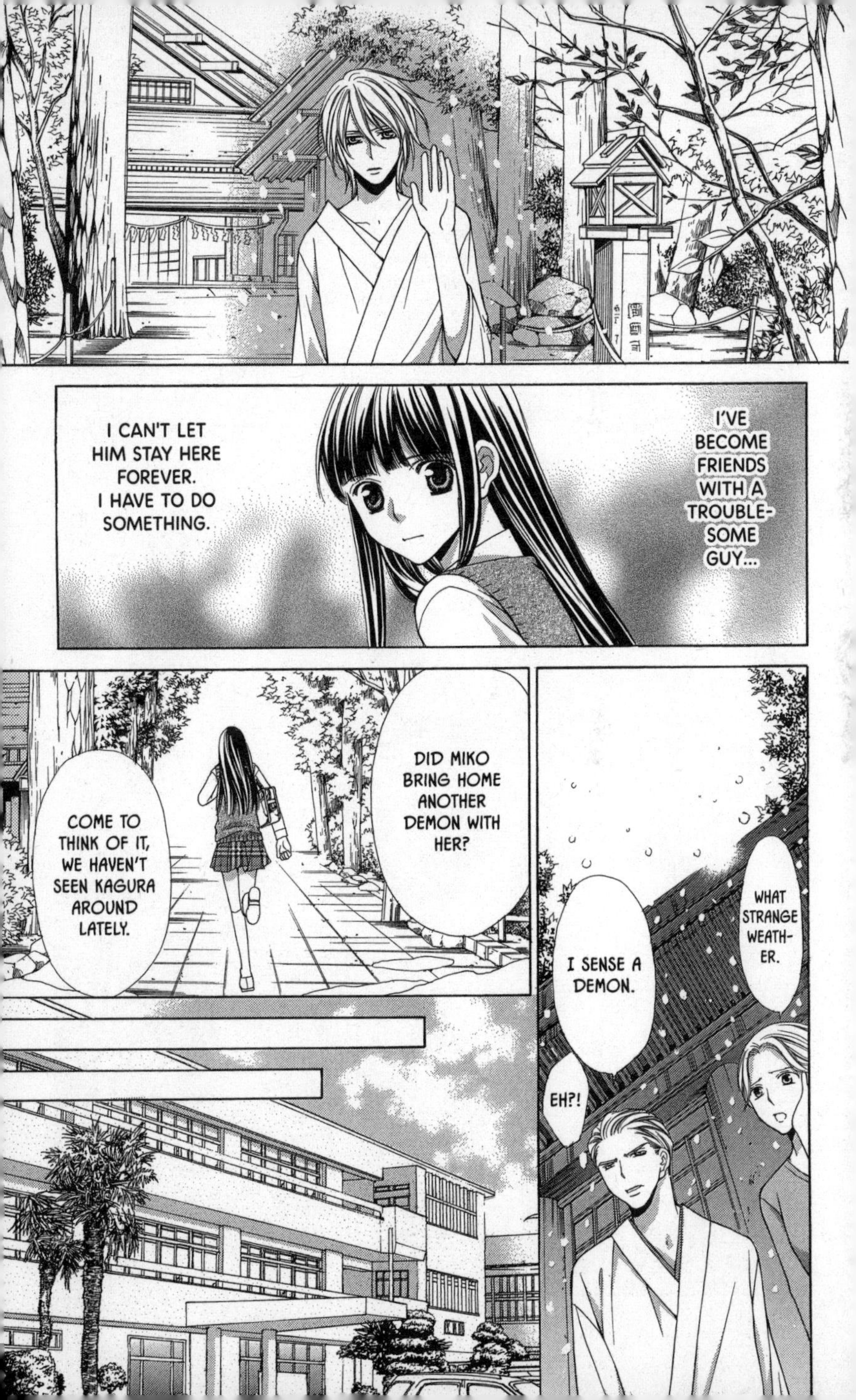
I'VE BECOME FRIENDS WITH A TROUBLE-SOME GUY...
I CAN'T LET HIM STAY HERE FOREVER. I HAVE TO DO SOMETHING.
WHAT STRANGE WEATH-ER.
I SENSE A DEMON.
EH?!
DID MIKO BRING HOME ANOTHER DEMON WITH HER?
COME TO THINK OF IT, WE HAVEN'T SEEN KAGURA AROUND LATELY.

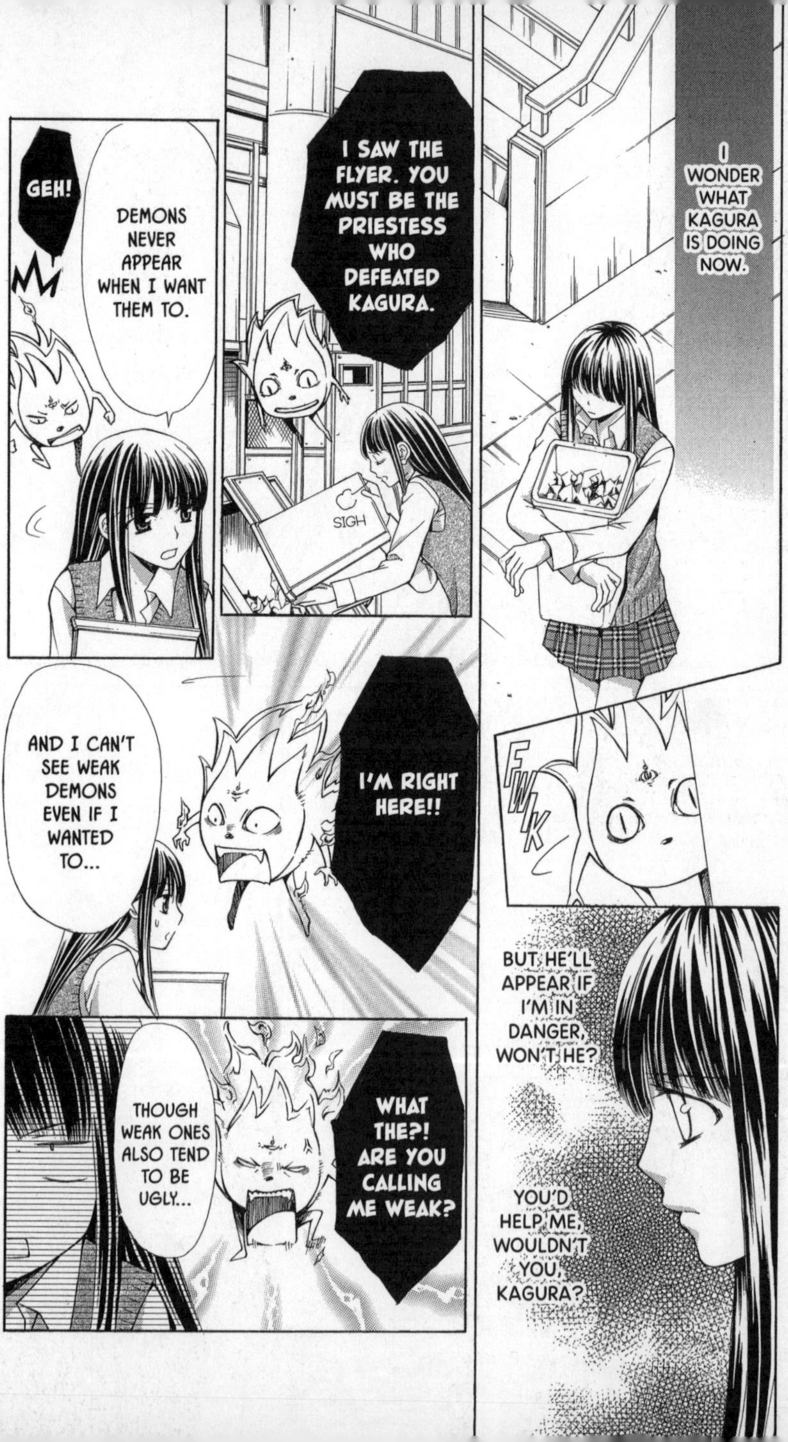
I WONDER WHAT KAGURA IS DOING NOW.
FWIK
I SAW THE FLYER. YOU MUST BE THE PRIESTESS WHO DEFEATED KAGURA.
SIGH
DEMONS NEVER APPEAR WHEN I WANT THEM TO.
GEH!
I'M RIGHT HERE!!
AND I CAN'T SEE WEAK DEMONS EVEN IF I WANTED TO...
WHAT THE?! ARE YOU CALLING ME WEAK?
THOUGH WEAK ONES ALSO TEND TO BE UGLY...
BUT HE'LL APPEAR IF I'M IN DANGER, WON'T HE?
YOU'D HELP ME, WOULDN'T YOU, KAGURA?

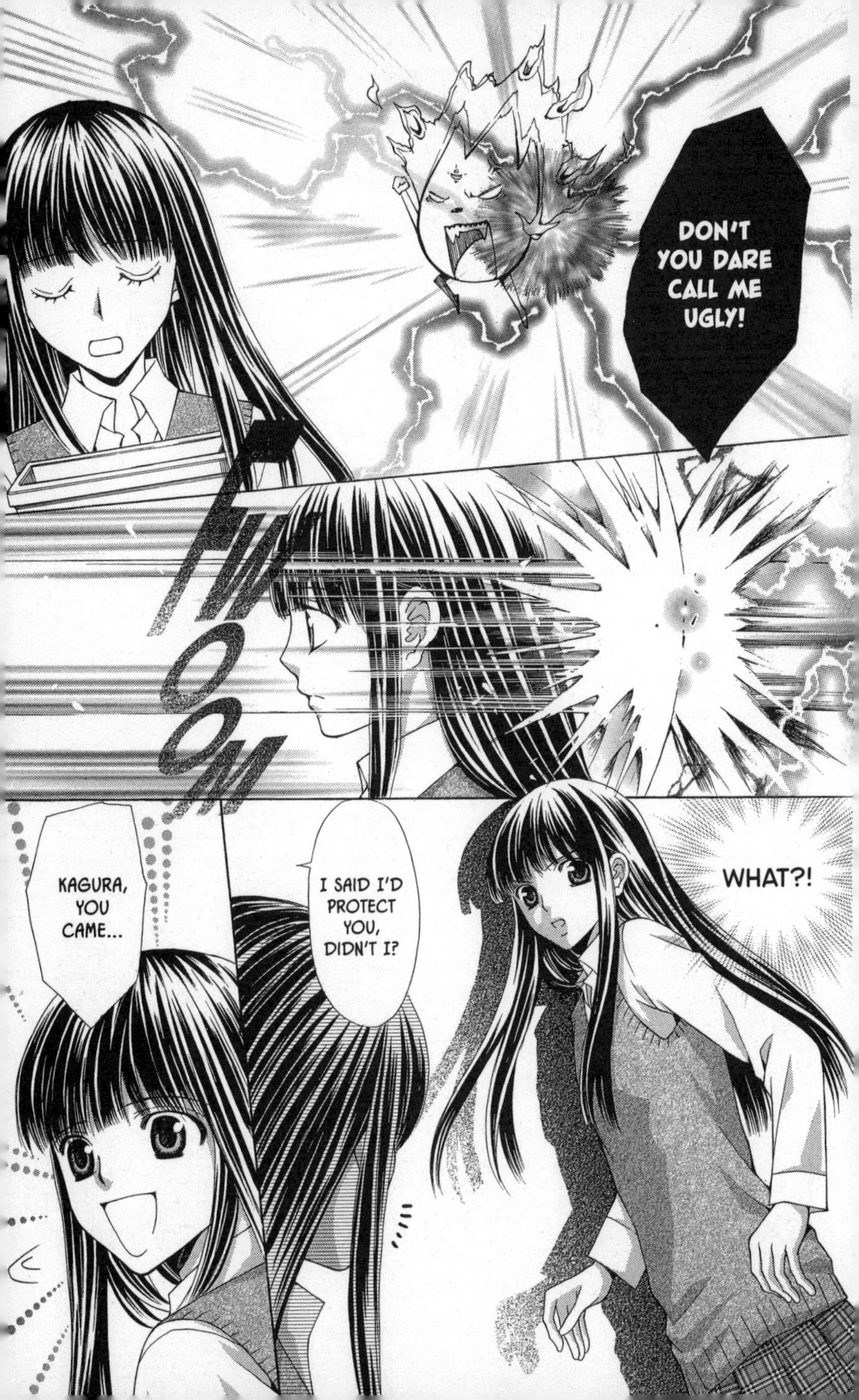
DON'T YOU DARE CALL ME UGLY!
WHOOM
WHAT?!
I SAID I'D PROTECT YOU, DIDN'T I?
KAGURA, YOU CAME...

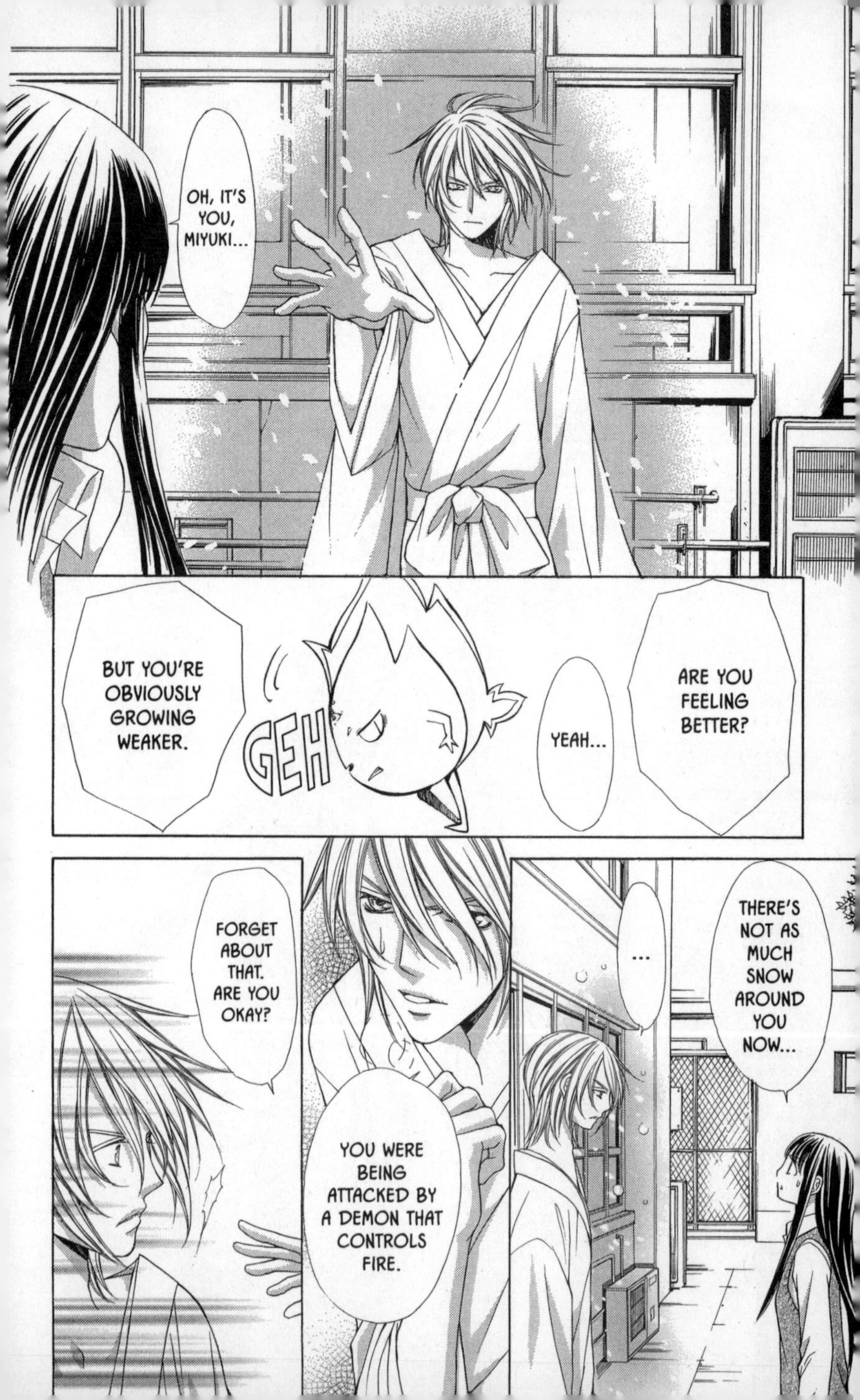
OH, IT'S YOU, MIYUKI...
ARE YOU FEELING BETTER?
YEAH...
GEH
BUT YOU'RE OBVIOUSLY GROWING WEAKER.
THERE'S NOT AS MUCH SNOW AROUND YOU NOW...
...
YOU WERE BEING ATTACKED BY A DEMON THAT CONTROLS FIRE.
FORGET ABOUT THAT. ARE YOU OKAY?

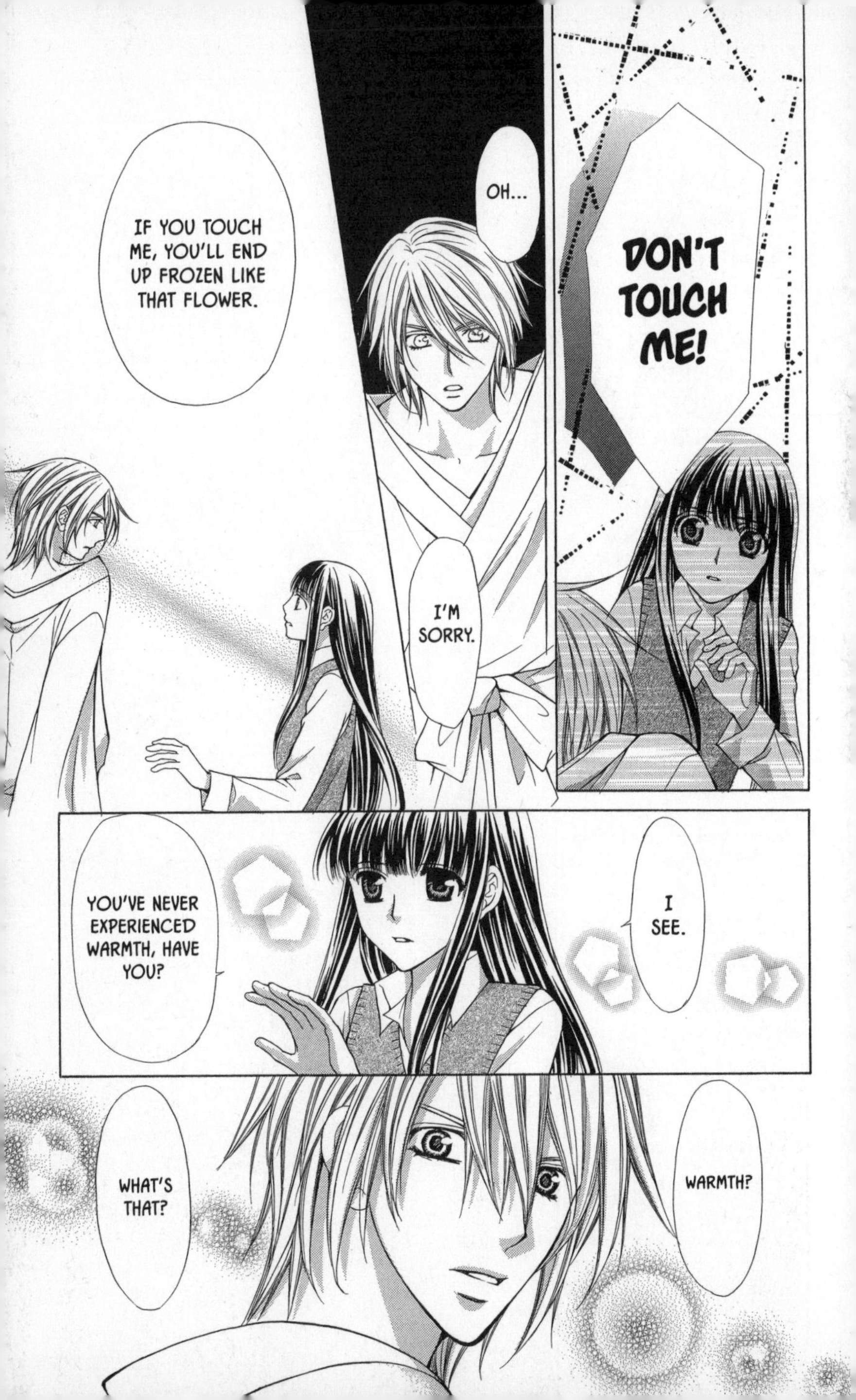
DON'T TOUCH ME!
OH...
I'M SORRY.
IF YOU TOUCH ME, YOU'LL END UP FROZEN LIKE THAT FLOWER.
I SEE.
YOU'VE NEVER EXPERIENCED WARMTH, HAVE YOU?
WARMTH?
WHAT'S THAT?

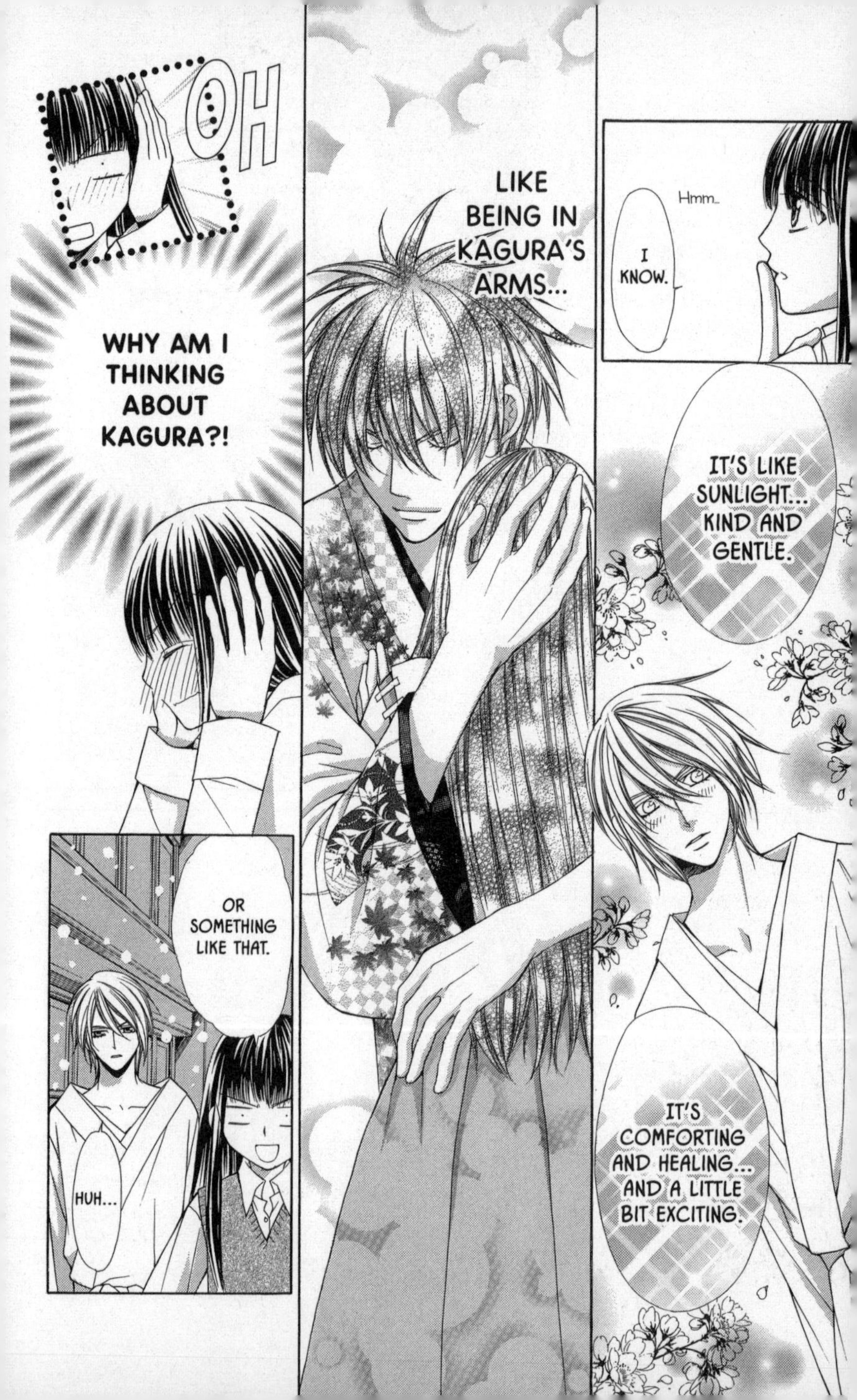
Hmm...
I KNOW.
IT'S LIKE SUNLIGHT... KIND AND GENTLE.
IT'S COMFORTING AND HEALING... AND A LITTLE BIT EXCITING.
LIKE BEING IN KAGURA'S ARMS...
OH
WHY AM I THINKING ABOUT KAGURA?!
OR SOMETHING LIKE THAT.
HUH...

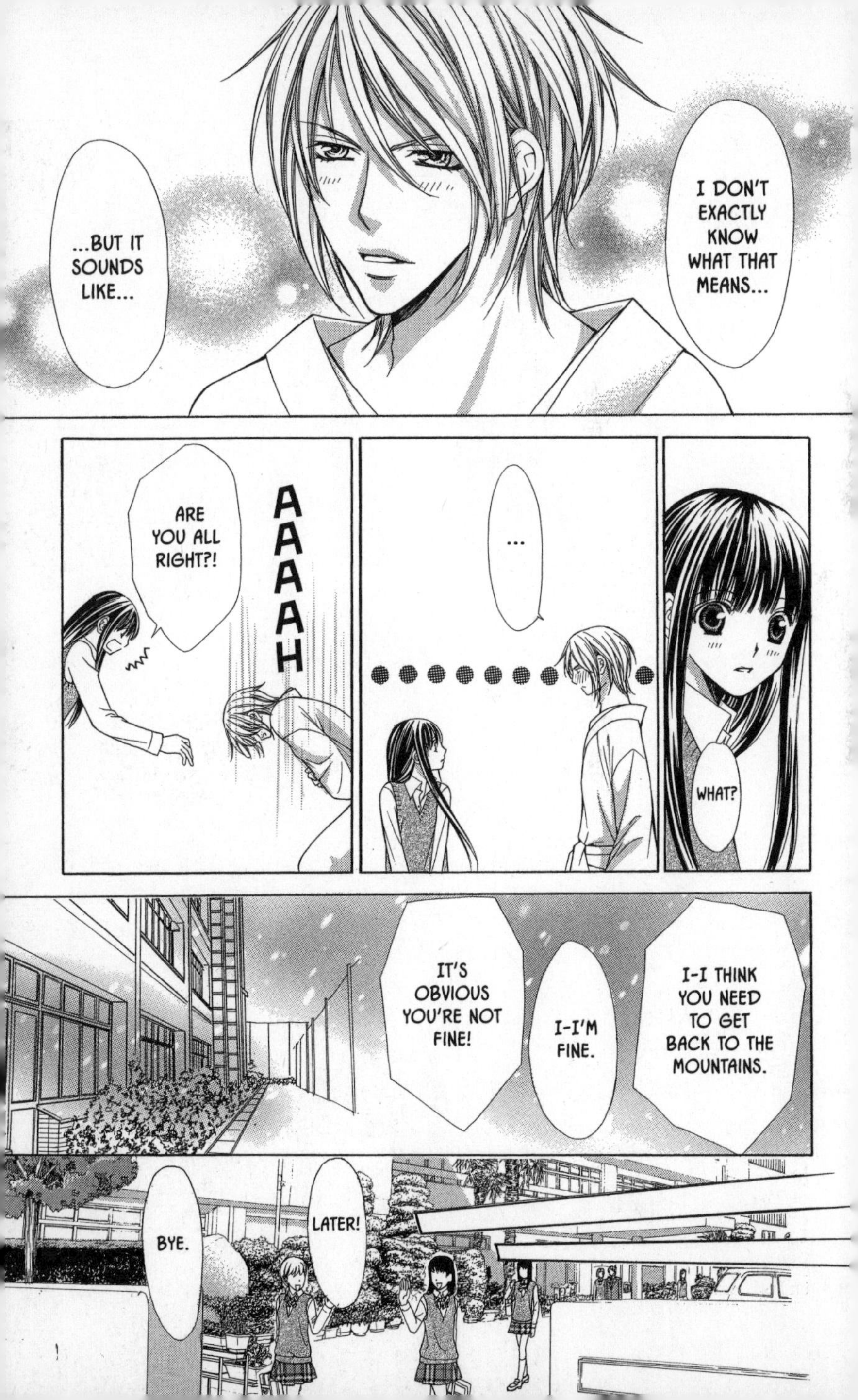
I DON'T EXACTLY KNOW WHAT THAT MEANS...
...BUT IT SOUNDS LIKE...
WHAT?
...
AAAAH
ARE YOU ALL RIGHT?!
I-I THINK YOU NEED TO GET BACK TO THE MOUNTAINS.
I-I'M FINE.
IT'S OBVIOUS YOU'RE NOT FINE!
LATER!
BYE.

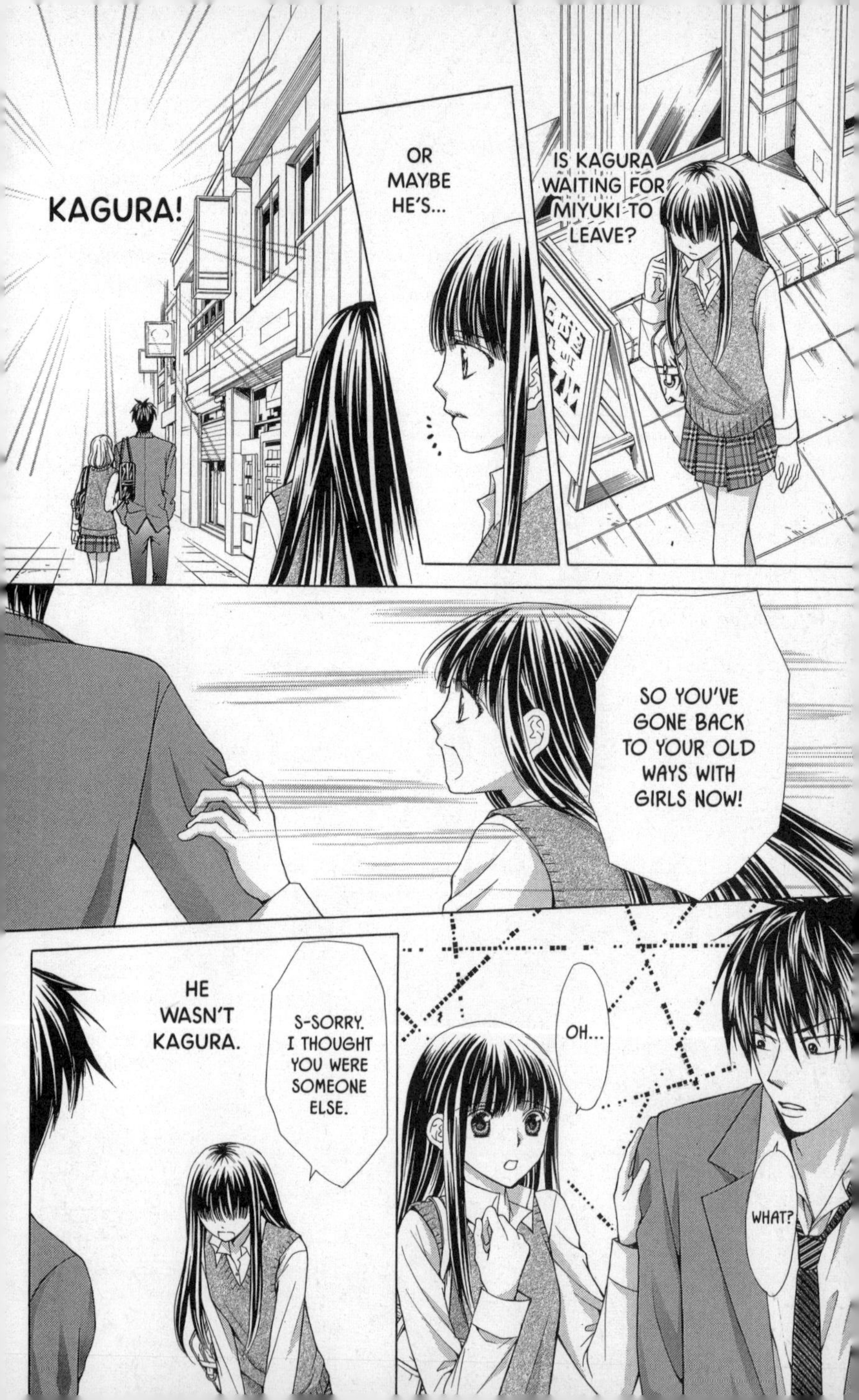
IS KAGURA WAITING FOR MIYUKI TO LEAVE?
OR MAYBE HE'S...
KAGURA!
SO YOU'VE GONE BACK TO YOUR OLD WAYS WITH GIRLS NOW!
WHAT?
OH...
S-SORRY. I THOUGHT YOU WERE SOMEONE ELSE.
HE WASN'T KAGURA.

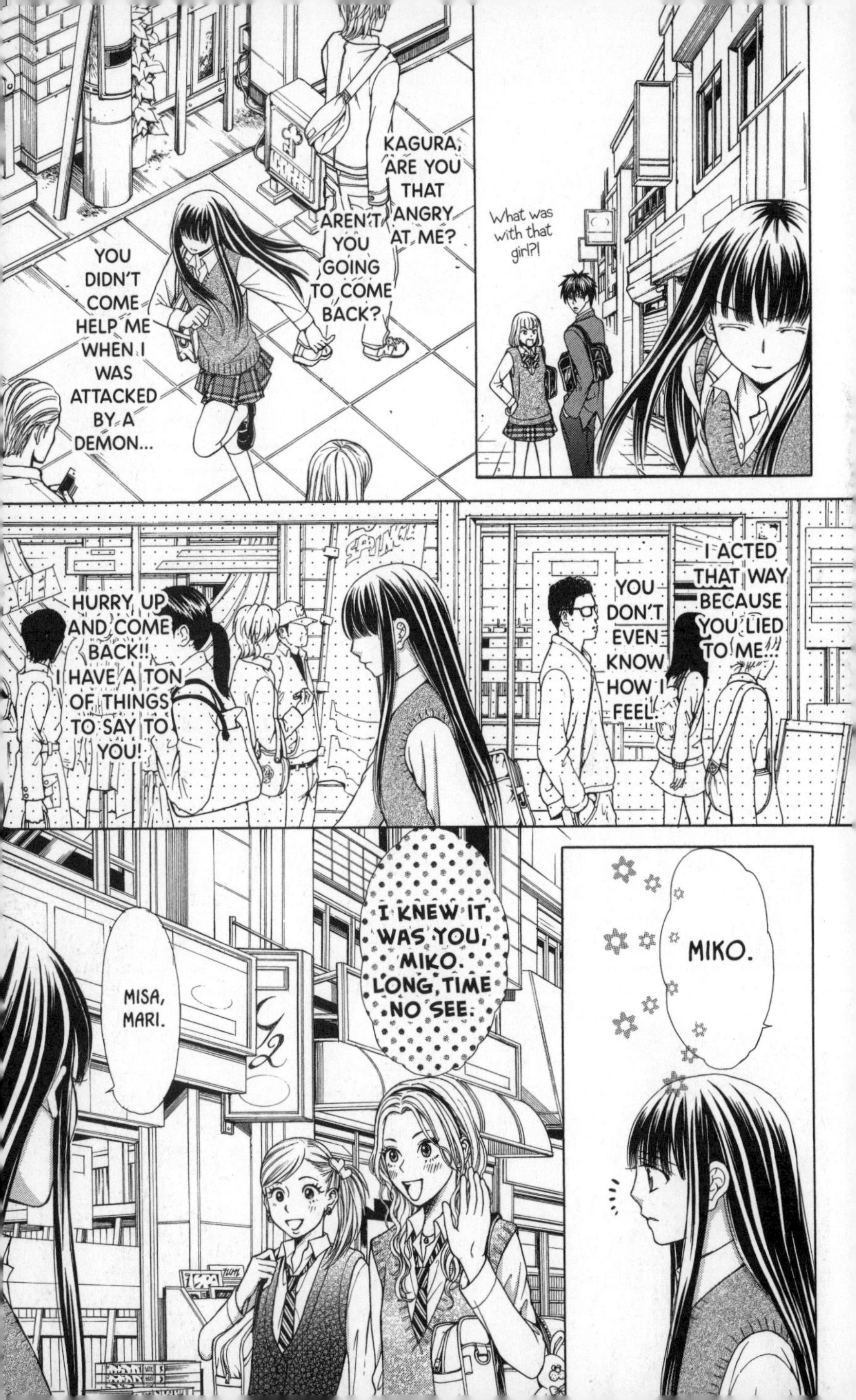

What was with that girl?!
KAGURA, ARE YOU THAT ANGRY AT ME?
AREN'T YOU GOING TO COME BACK?
YOU DIDN'T COME HELP ME WHEN I WAS ATTACKED BY A DEMON...
I ACTED THAT WAY BECAUSE YOU LIED TO ME...
YOU DON'T EVEN KNOW HOW I FEEL.
HURRY UP AND COME BACK!! I HAVE A TON OF THINGS TO SAY TO YOU!
MIKO.
I KNEW IT WAS YOU, MIKO. LONG TIME NO SEE.
MISA, MARI.

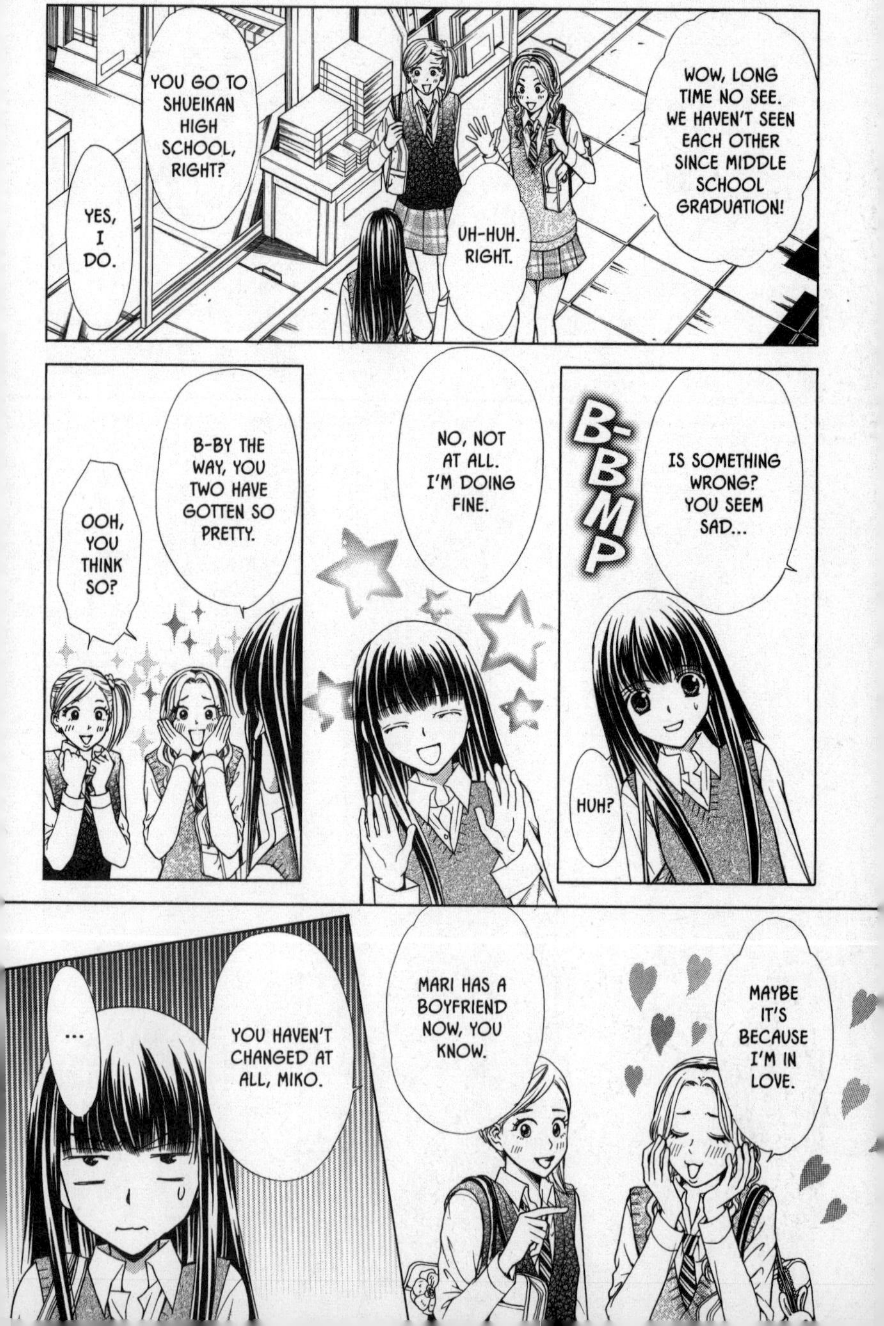
WOW, LONG TIME NO SEE. WE HAVEN'T SEEN EACH OTHER SINCE MIDDLE SCHOOL GRADUATION!
UH-HUH. RIGHT.
YOU GO TO SHUEIKAN HIGH SCHOOL, RIGHT?
YES, I DO.
B-BMP
IS SOMETHING WRONG? YOU SEEM SAD...
HUH?
NO, NOT AT ALL. I'M DOING FINE.
B-BY THE WAY, YOU TWO HAVE GOTTEN SO PRETTY.
OOH, YOU THINK SO?
MAYBE IT'S BECAUSE I'M IN LOVE.
MARI HAS A BOYFRIEND NOW, YOU KNOW.
YOU HAVEN'T CHANGED AT ALL, MIKO.
...

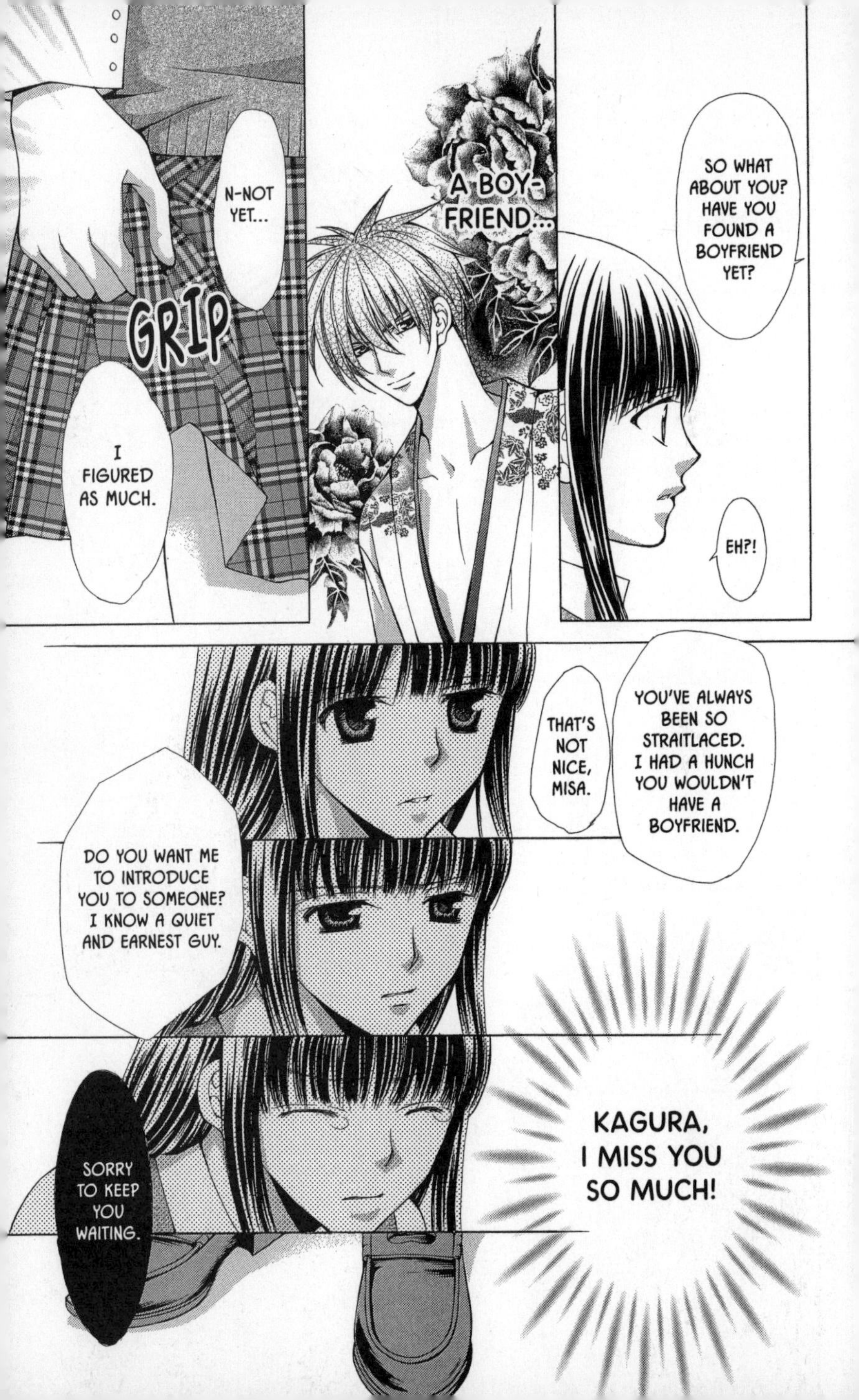
SO WHAT ABOUT YOU? HAVE YOU FOUND A BOYFRIEND YET?
EH?!
A BOY-FRIEND...
N-NOT YET...
GRIP
I FIGURED AS MUCH.
YOU'VE ALWAYS BEEN SO STRAITLACED. I HAD A HUNCH YOU WOULDN'T HAVE A BOYFRIEND.
THAT'S NOT NICE, MISA.
DO YOU WANT ME TO INTRODUCE YOU TO SOMEONE? I KNOW A QUIET AND EARNEST GUY.
KAGURA, I MISS YOU SO MUCH!
SORRY TO KEEP YOU WAITING.

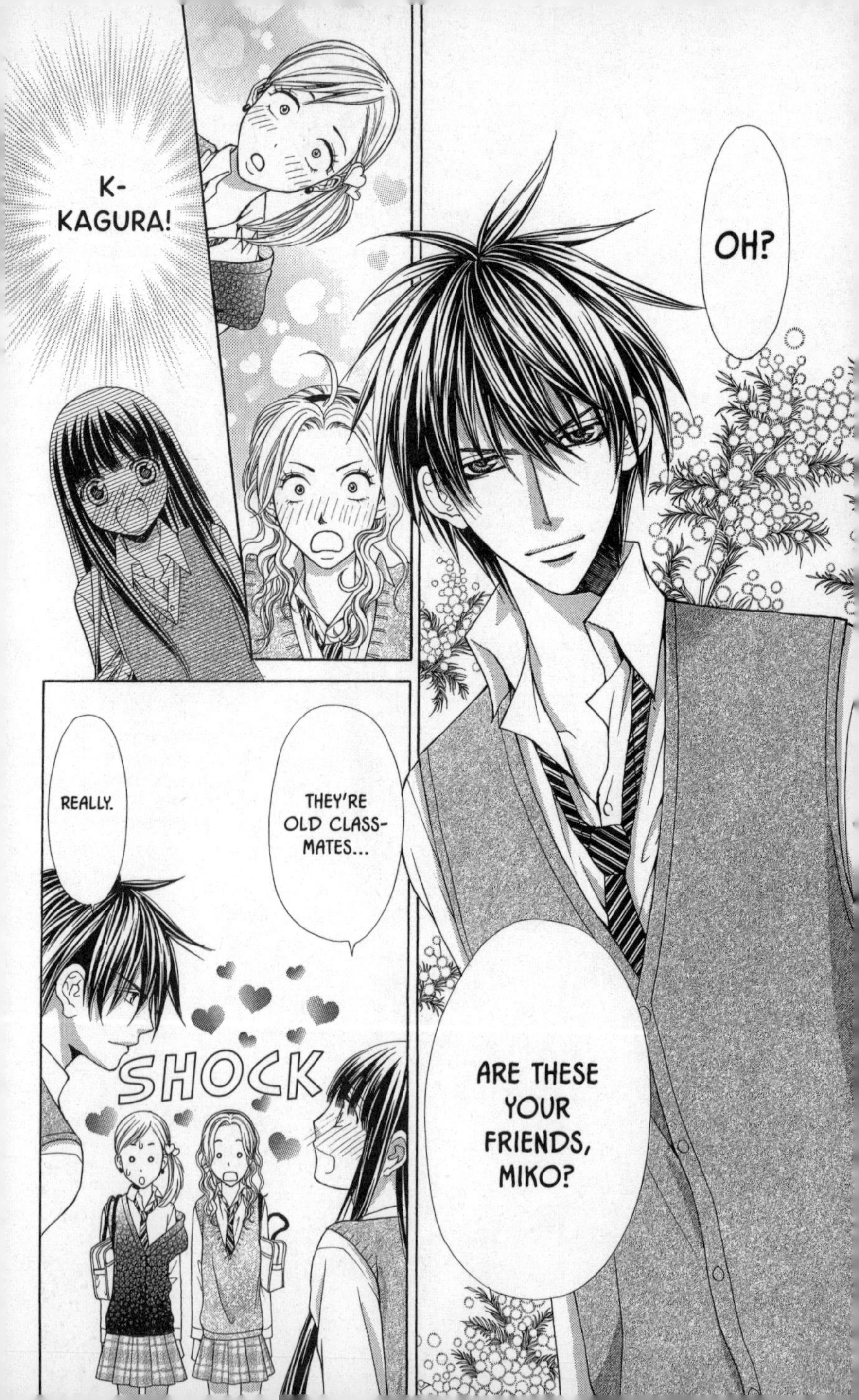
OH?
ARE THESE YOUR FRIENDS, MIKO?
K-KAGURA!
THEY'RE OLD CLASS-MATES...
REALLY.
SHOCK

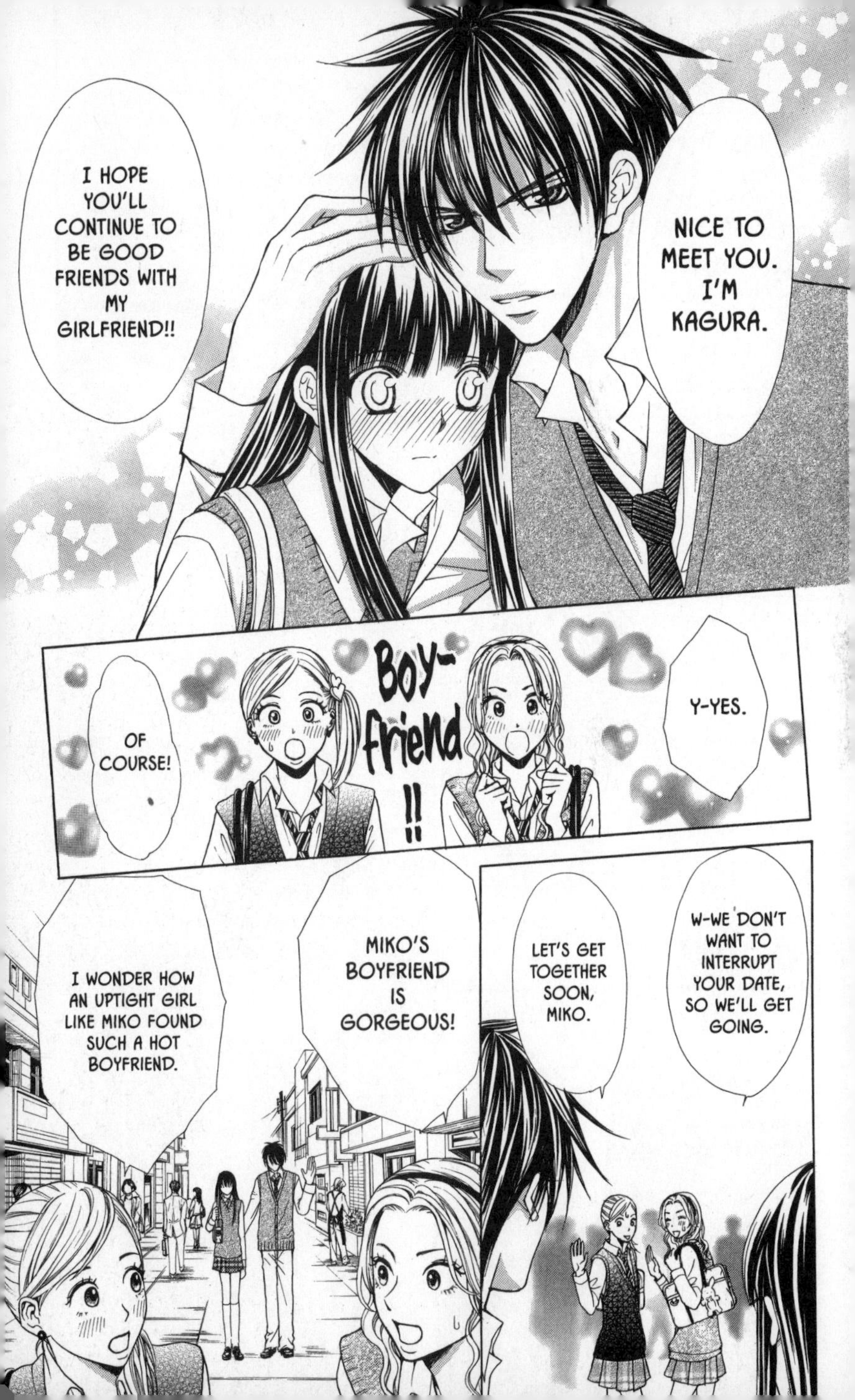
NICE TO MEET YOU. I'M KAGURA.
I HOPE YOU'LL CONTINUE TO BE GOOD FRIENDS WITH MY GIRLFRIEND!!
Y-YES.
Boy-friend!!
OF COURSE!
W-WE DON'T WANT TO INTERRUPT YOUR DATE, SO WE'LL GET GOING.
LET'S GET TOGETHER SOON, MIKO.
MIKO'S BOYFRIEND IS GORGEOUS!
I WONDER HOW AN UPTIGHT GIRL LIKE MIKO FOUND SUCH A HOT BOYFRIEND.

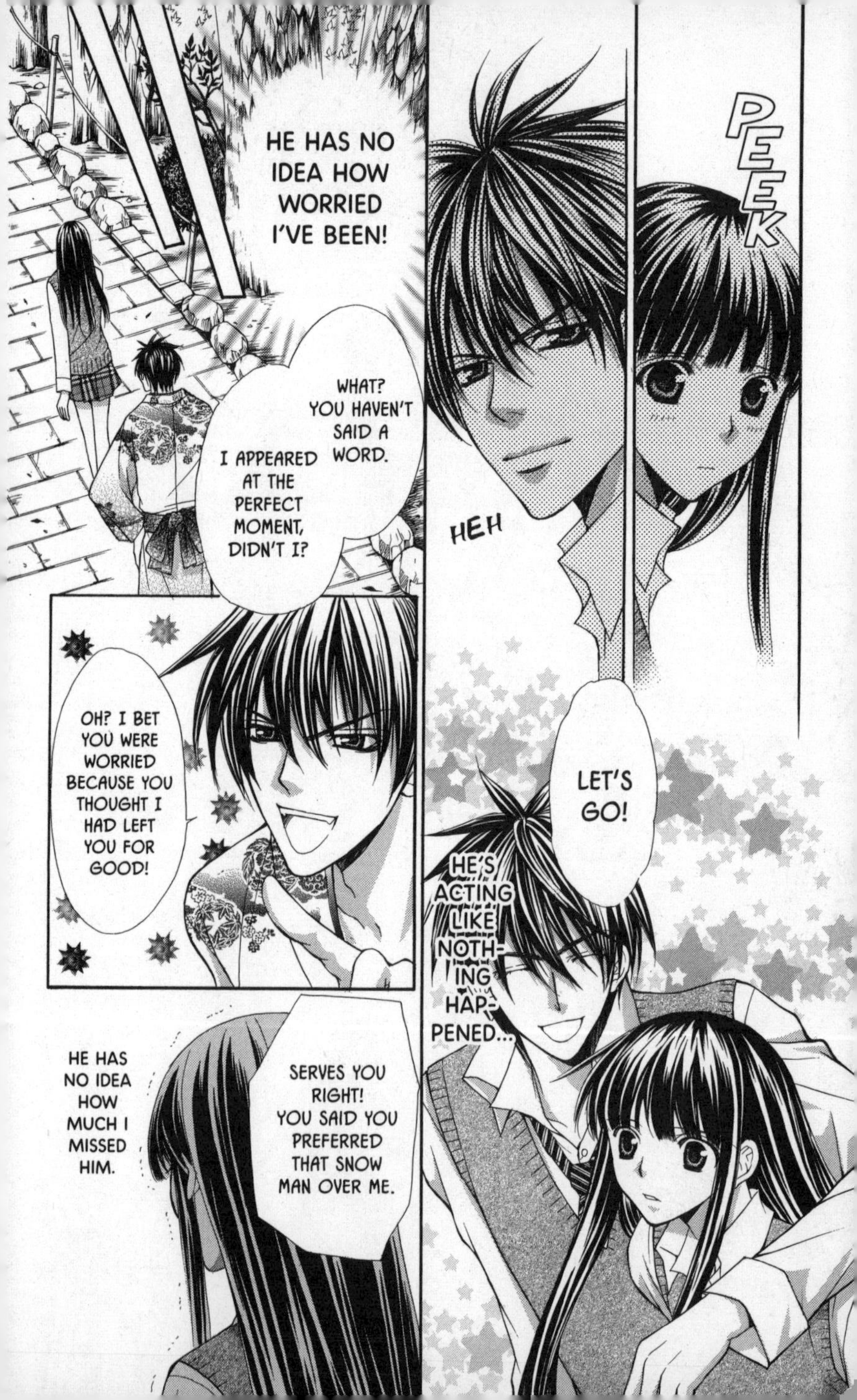
PEEK
HEH
HE HAS NO IDEA HOW WORRIED I'VE BEEN!
WHAT? YOU HAVEN'T SAID A WORD.
I APPEARED AT THE PERFECT MOMENT, DIDN'T I?
OH? I BET YOU WERE WORRIED BECAUSE YOU THOUGHT I HAD LEFT YOU FOR GOOD!
SERVES YOU RIGHT! YOU SAID YOU PREFERRED THAT SNOW MAN OVER ME.
HE HAS NO IDEA HOW MUCH I MISSED HIM.
LET'S GO!
HE'S ACTING LIKE NOTHING HAPPENED...

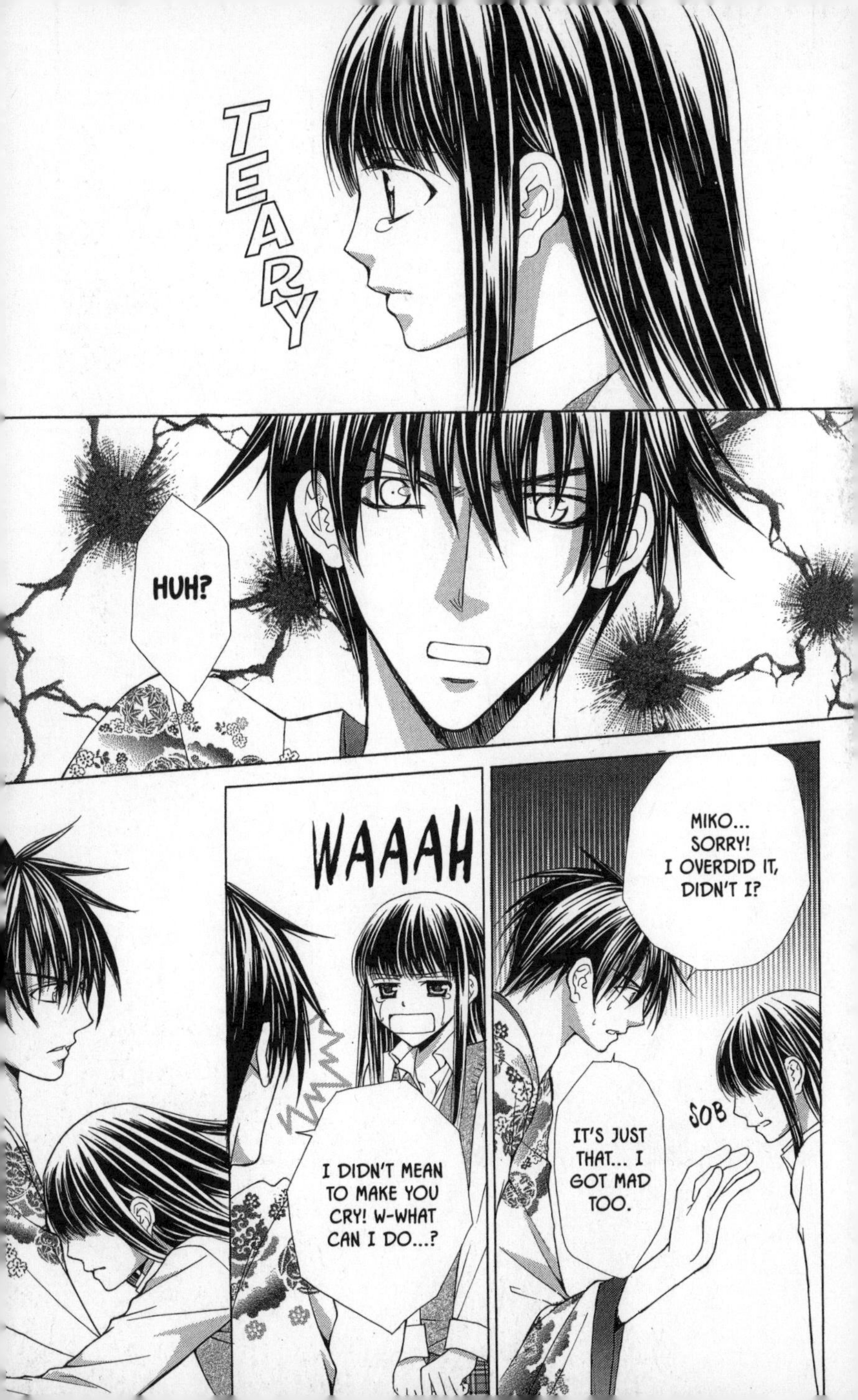
TEARY
HUH?
MIKO... SORRY! I OVERDID IT, DIDN'T I?
SOB
IT'S JUST THAT... I GOT MAD TOO.
WAAAH
I DIDN'T MEAN TO MAKE YOU CRY! W-WHAT CAN I DO...?

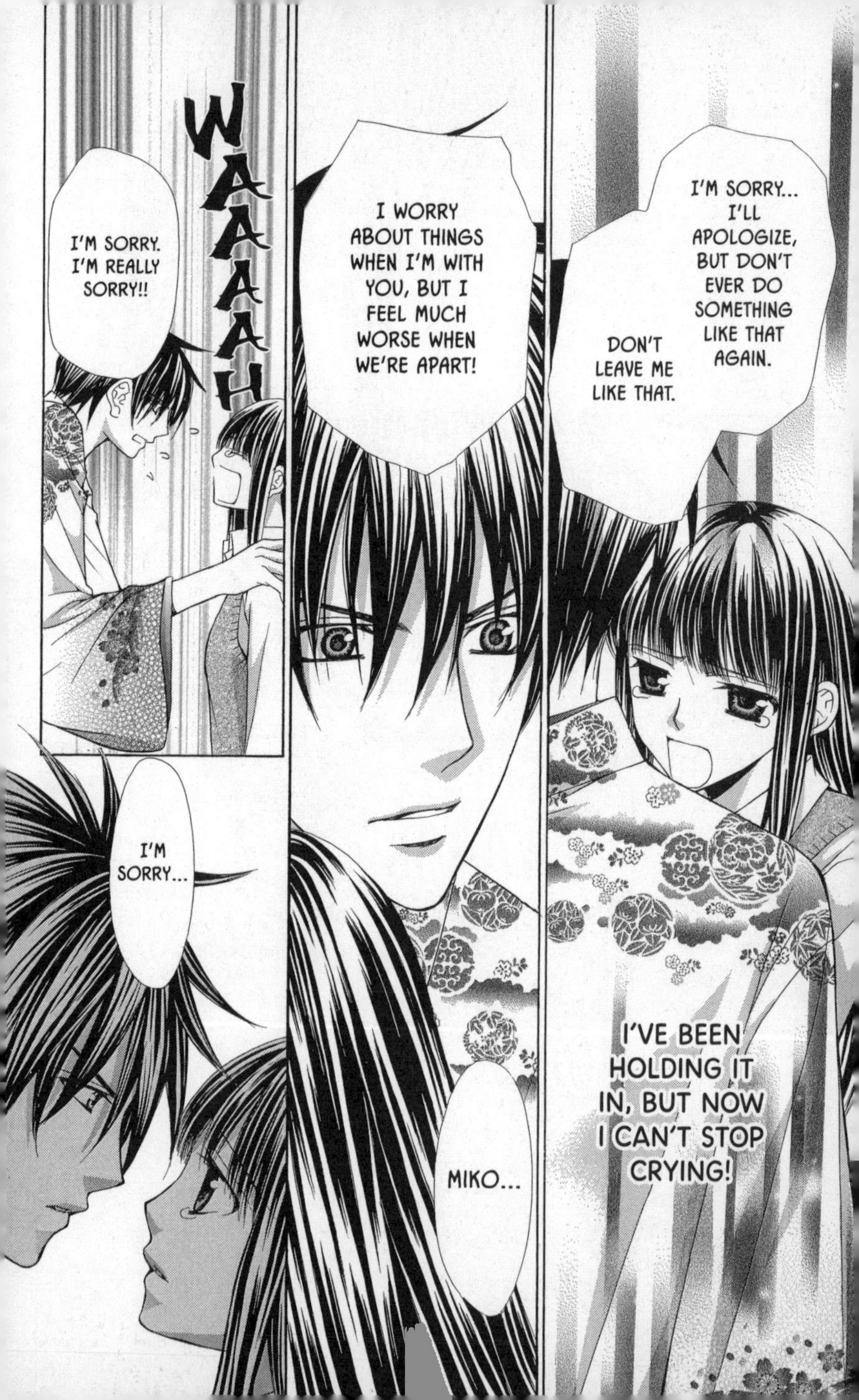
I'M SORRY... I'LL APOLOGIZE, BUT DON'T EVER DO SOMETHING LIKE THAT AGAIN.
DON'T LEAVE ME LIKE THAT.
I'VE BEEN HOLDING IT IN, BUT NOW I CAN'T STOP CRYING!
I WORRY ABOUT THINGS WHEN I'M WITH YOU, BUT I FEEL MUCH WORSE WHEN WE'RE APART!
MIKO...
WAAAAH
I'M SORRY. I'M REALLY SORRY!!
I'M SORRY...

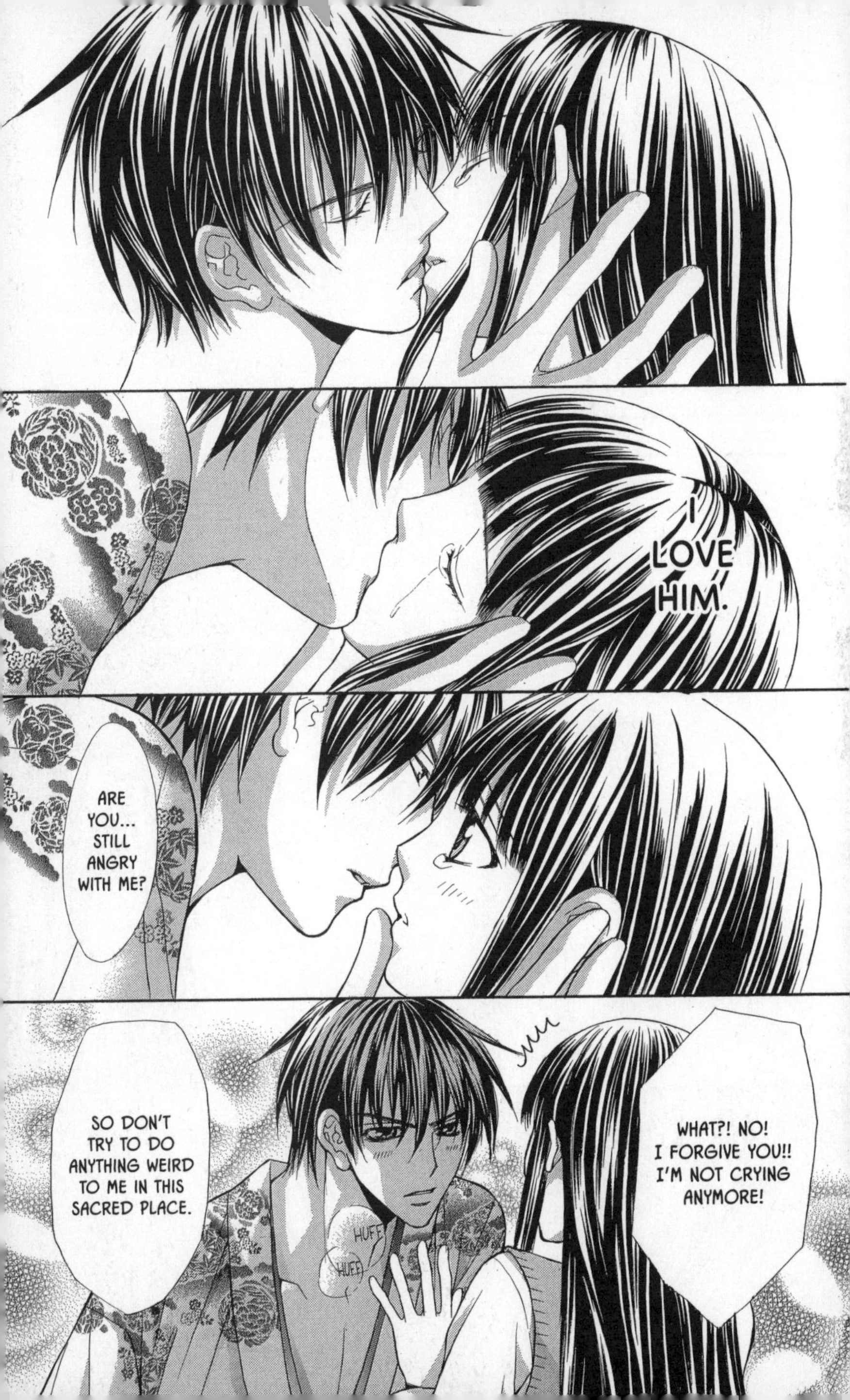
I LOVE HIM.
ARE YOU... STILL ANGRY WITH ME?
WHAT?! NO! I FORGIVE YOU!! I'M NOT CRYING ANYMORE!
SO DON'T TRY TO DO ANYTHING WEIRD TO ME IN THIS SACRED PLACE.
HUFF
HUFF

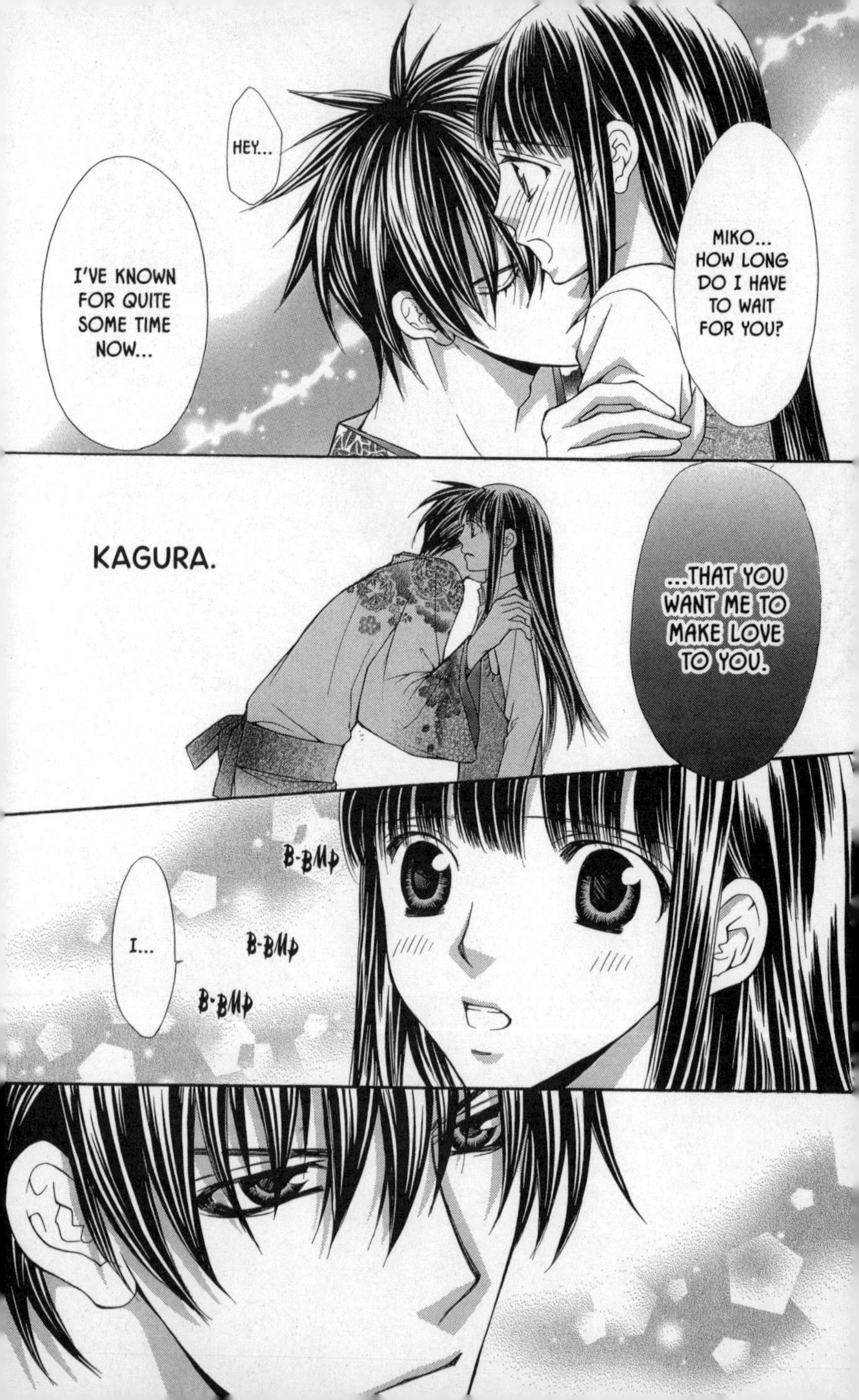
MIKO... HOW LONG DO I HAVE TO WAIT FOR YOU?
HEY...
I'VE KNOWN FOR QUITE SOME TIME NOW...
...THAT YOU WANT ME TO MAKE LOVE TO YOU.
KAGURA.
B-BMP
B-BMP
I...
B-BMP

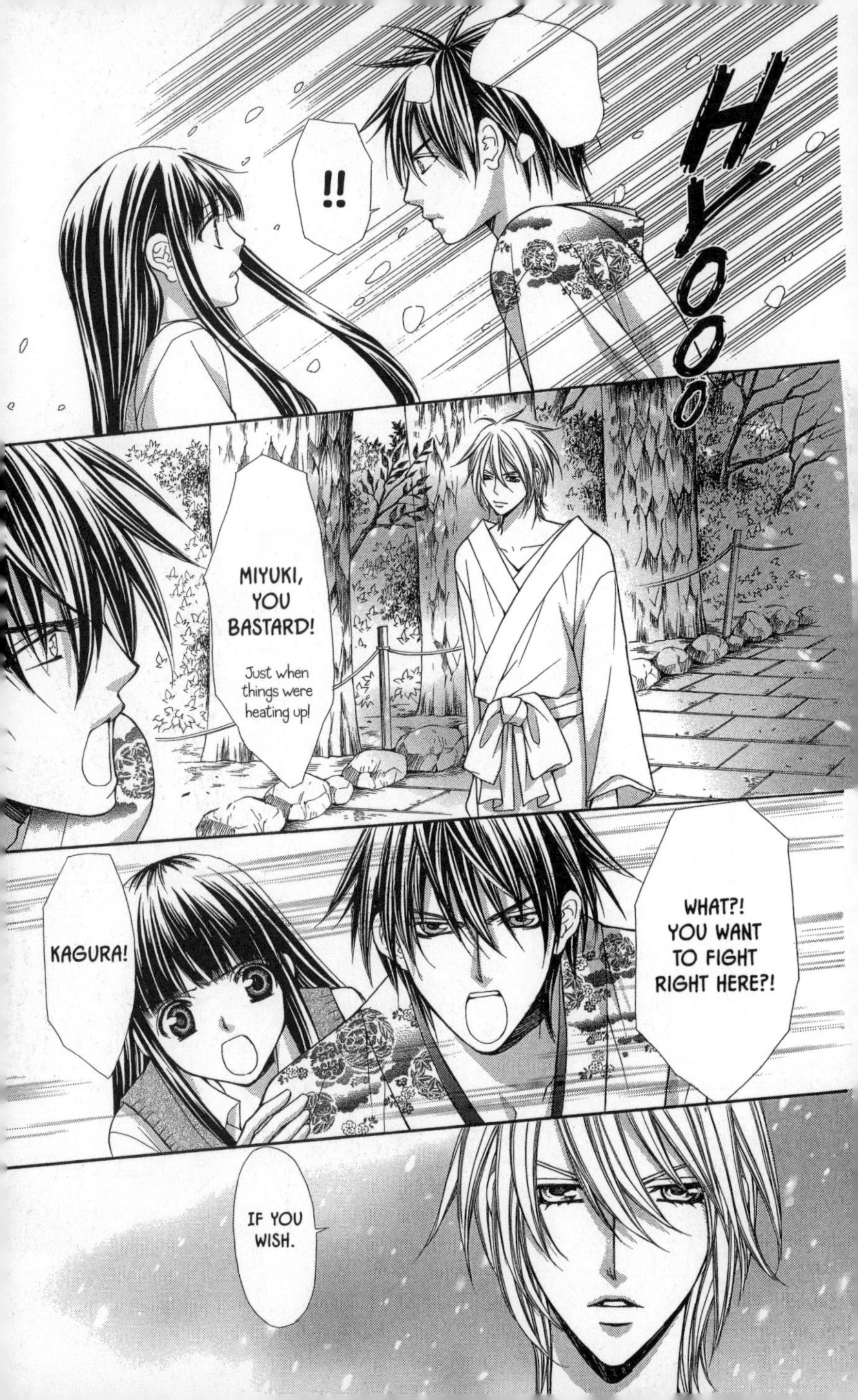
HYOOOO
!!
MIYUKI, YOU BASTARD!
Just when things were heating up!
WHAT?! YOU WANT TO FIGHT RIGHT HERE?!
KAGURA!
IF YOU WISH.

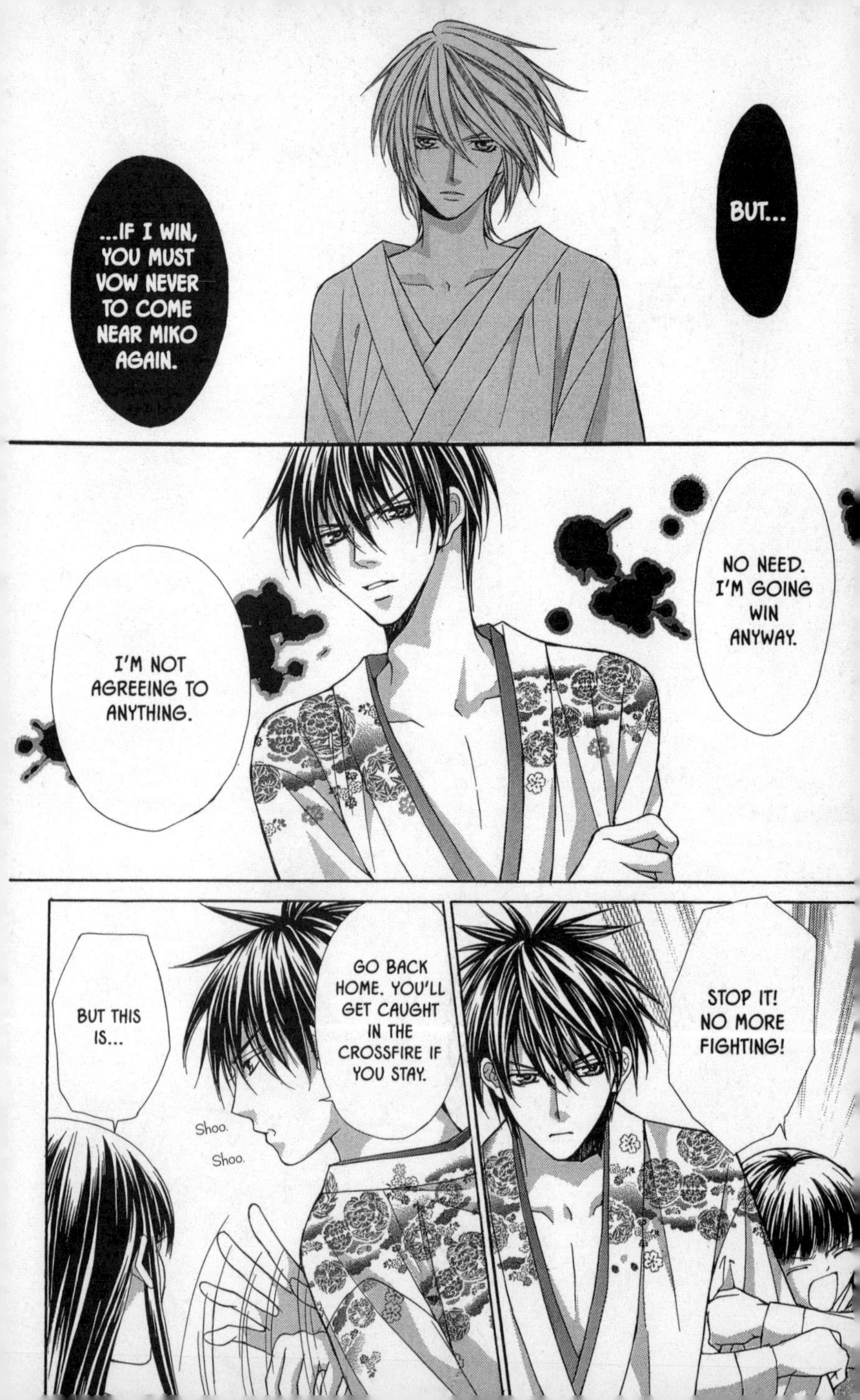
BUT...
...IF I WIN, YOU MUST VOW NEVER TO COME NEAR MIKO AGAIN.
NO NEED. I'M GOING WIN ANYWAY.
I'M NOT AGREEING TO ANYTHING.
STOP IT! NO MORE FIGHTING!
GO BACK HOME. YOU'LL GET CAUGHT IN THE CROSSFIRE IF YOU STAY.
Shoo.
Shoo.
BUT THIS IS...

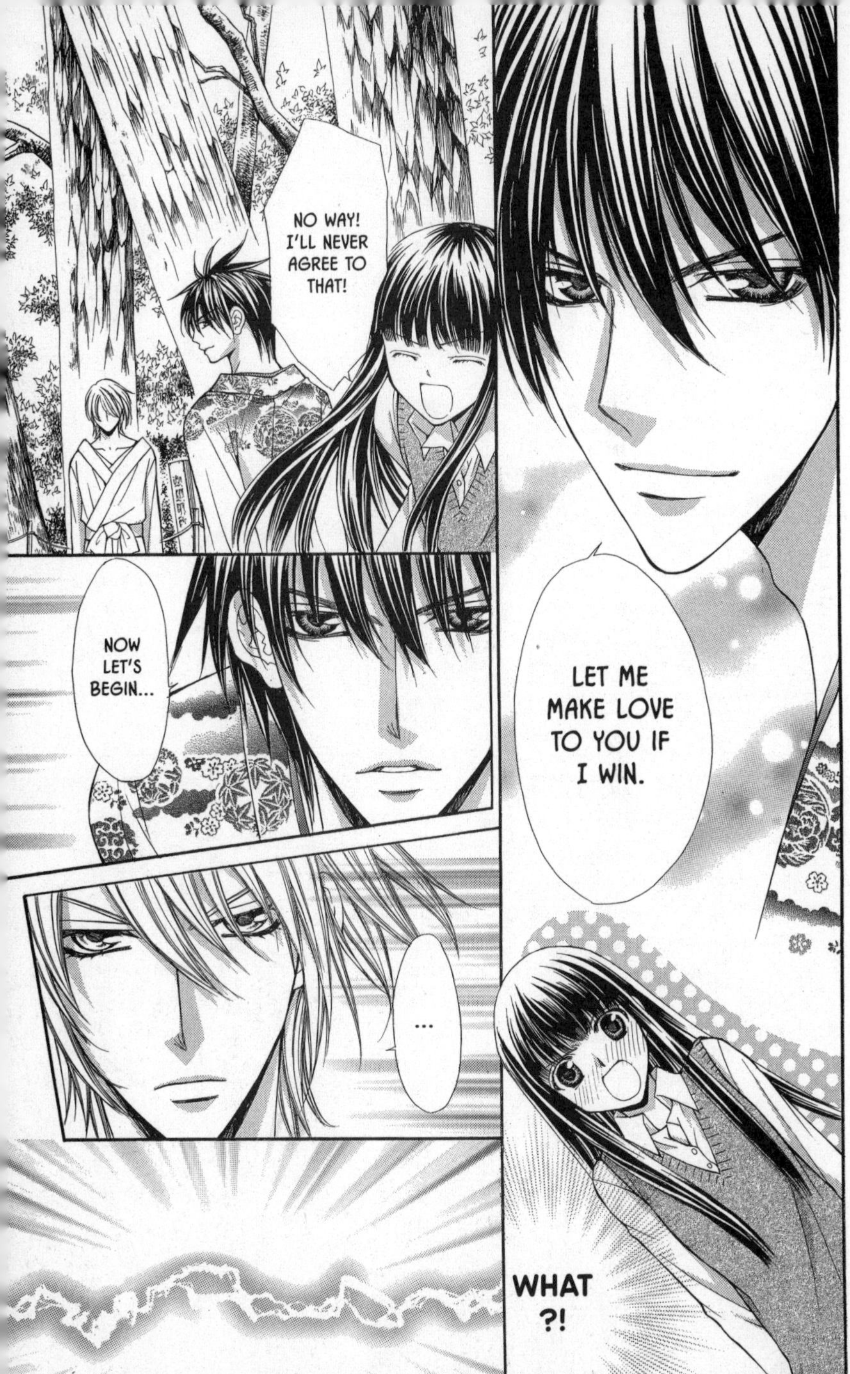
LET ME MAKE LOVE TO YOU IF I WIN.
WHAT?!
NO WAY! I'LL NEVER AGREE TO THAT!
NOW LET'S BEGIN...
...

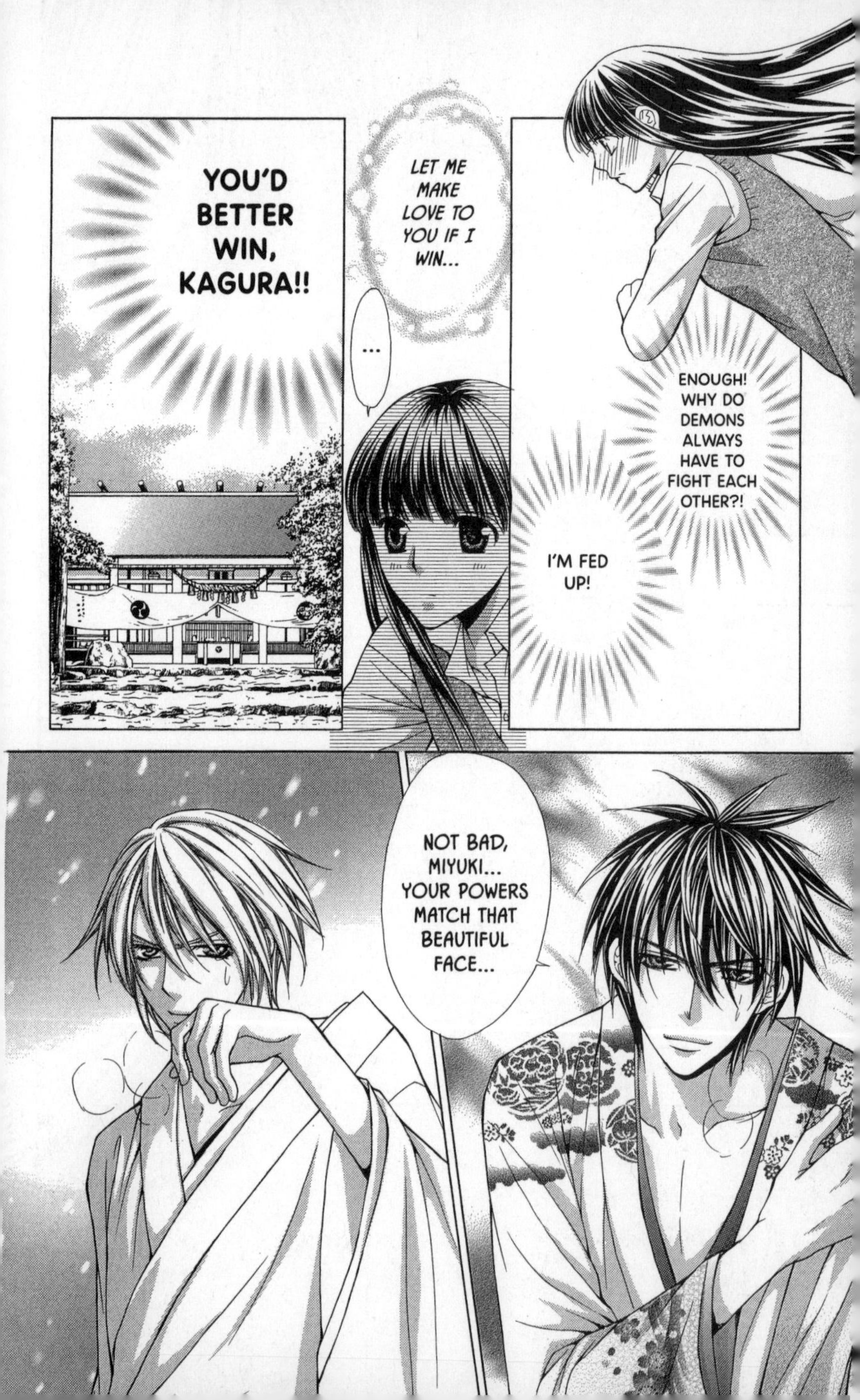
ENOUGH! WHY DO DEMONS ALWAYS HAVE TO FIGHT EACH OTHER?!
I'M FED UP!
LET ME MAKE LOVE TO YOU IF I WIN...
...
YOU'D BETTER WIN, KAGURA!!
NOT BAD, MIYUKI... YOUR POWERS MATCH THAT BEAUTIFUL FACE...

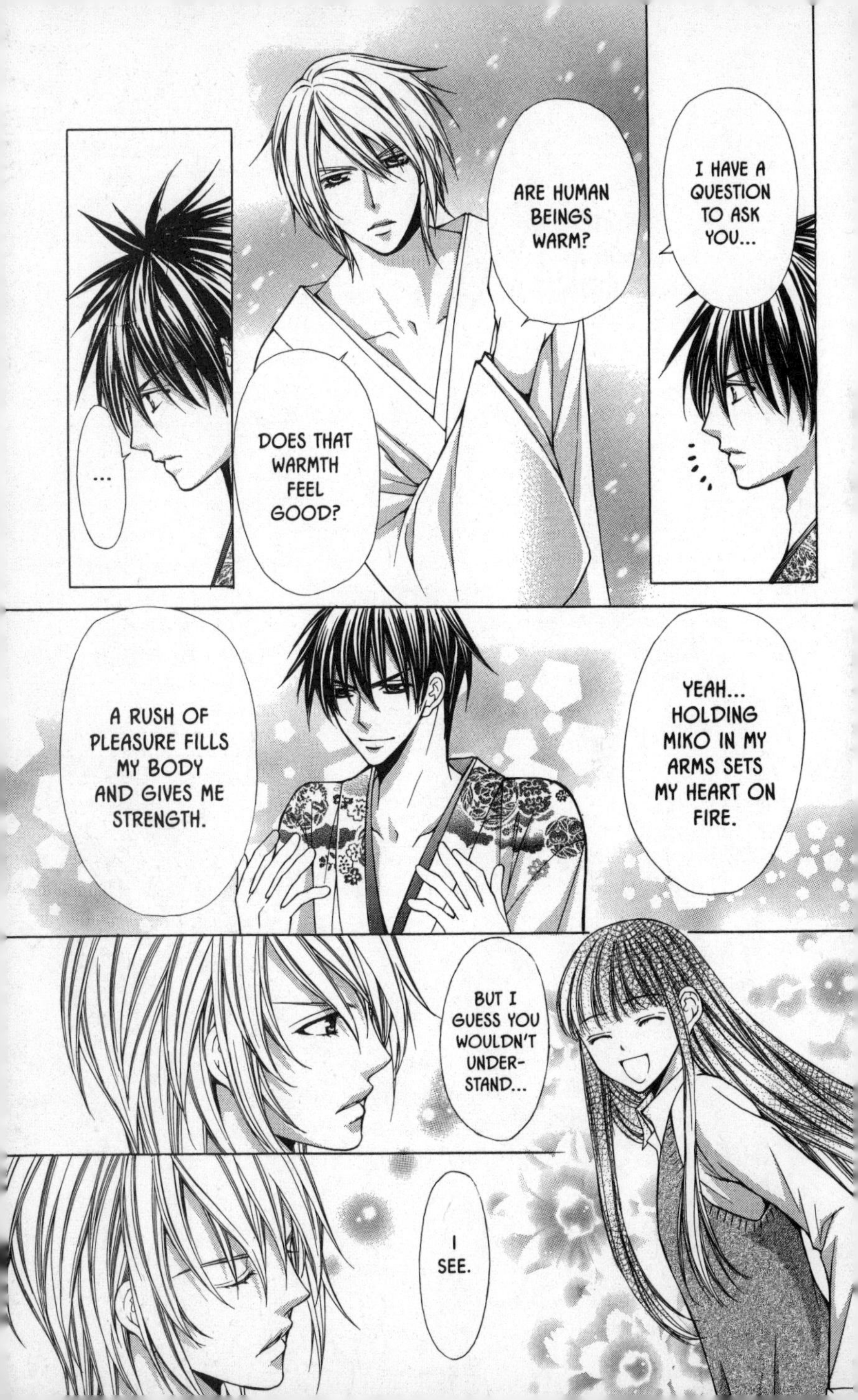
I HAVE A QUESTION TO ASK YOU...
......
ARE HUMAN BEINGS WARM?
DOES THAT WARMTH FEEL GOOD?
...
YEAH... HOLDING MIKO IN MY ARMS SETS MY HEART ON FIRE.
A RUSH OF PLEASURE FILLS MY BODY AND GIVES ME STRENGTH.
BUT I GUESS YOU WOULDN'T UNDER-STAND...
I SEE.

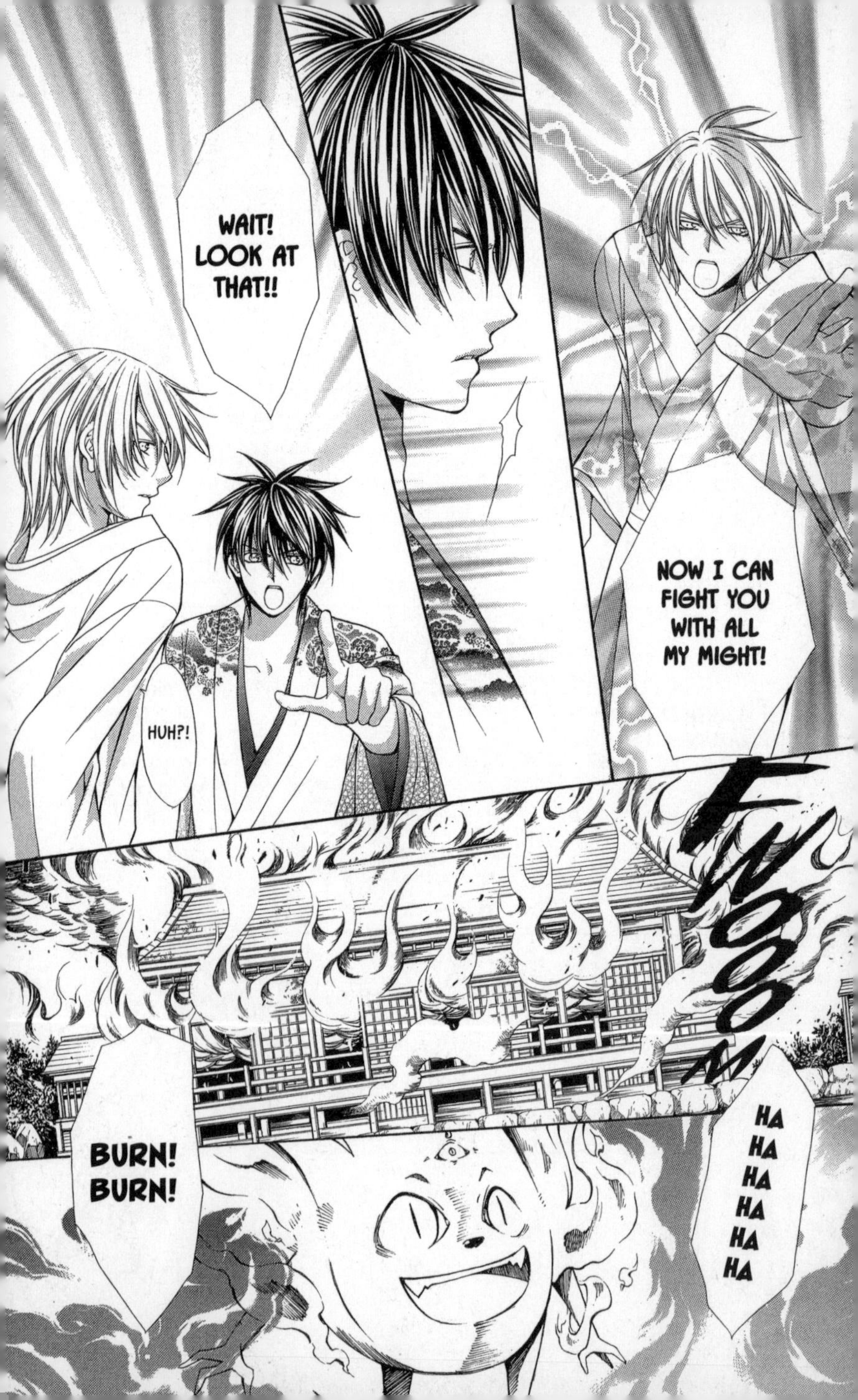
NOW I CAN FIGHT YOU WITH ALL MY MIGHT!
WAIT! LOOK AT THAT!!
HUH?!
FWOOOM
HA HA HA HA HA HA HA
BURN! BURN!

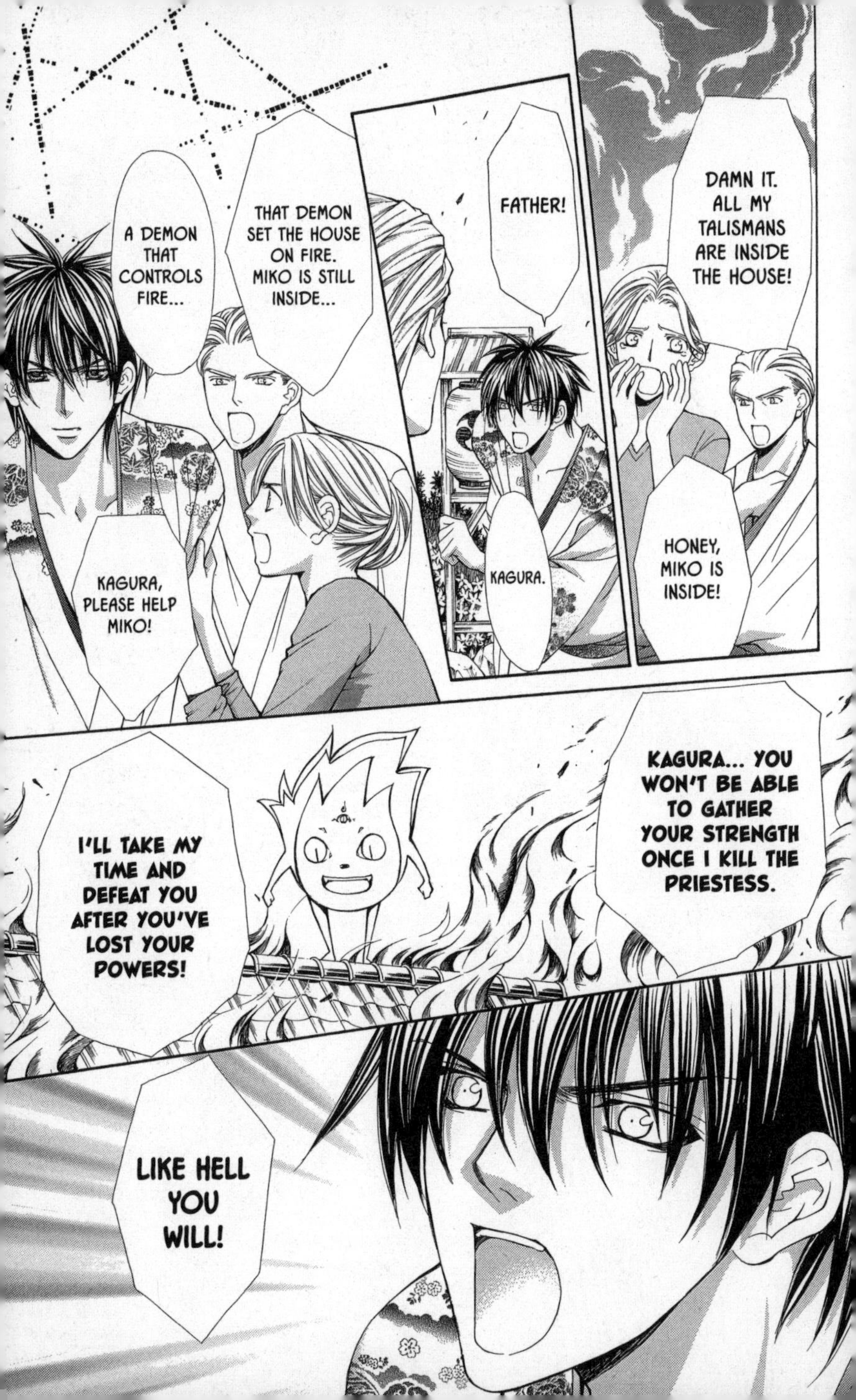
DAMN IT. ALL MY TALISMANS ARE INSIDE THE HOUSE!
HONEY, MIKO IS INSIDE!
FATHER!
KAGURA.
THAT DEMON SET THE HOUSE ON FIRE. MIKO IS STILL INSIDE...
A DEMON THAT CONTROLS FIRE...
KAGURA, PLEASE HELP MIKO!
KAGURA... YOU WON'T BE ABLE TO GATHER YOUR STRENGTH ONCE I KILL THE PRIESTESS.
I'LL TAKE MY TIME AND DEFEAT YOU AFTER YOU'VE LOST YOUR POWERS!
LIKE HELL YOU WILL!

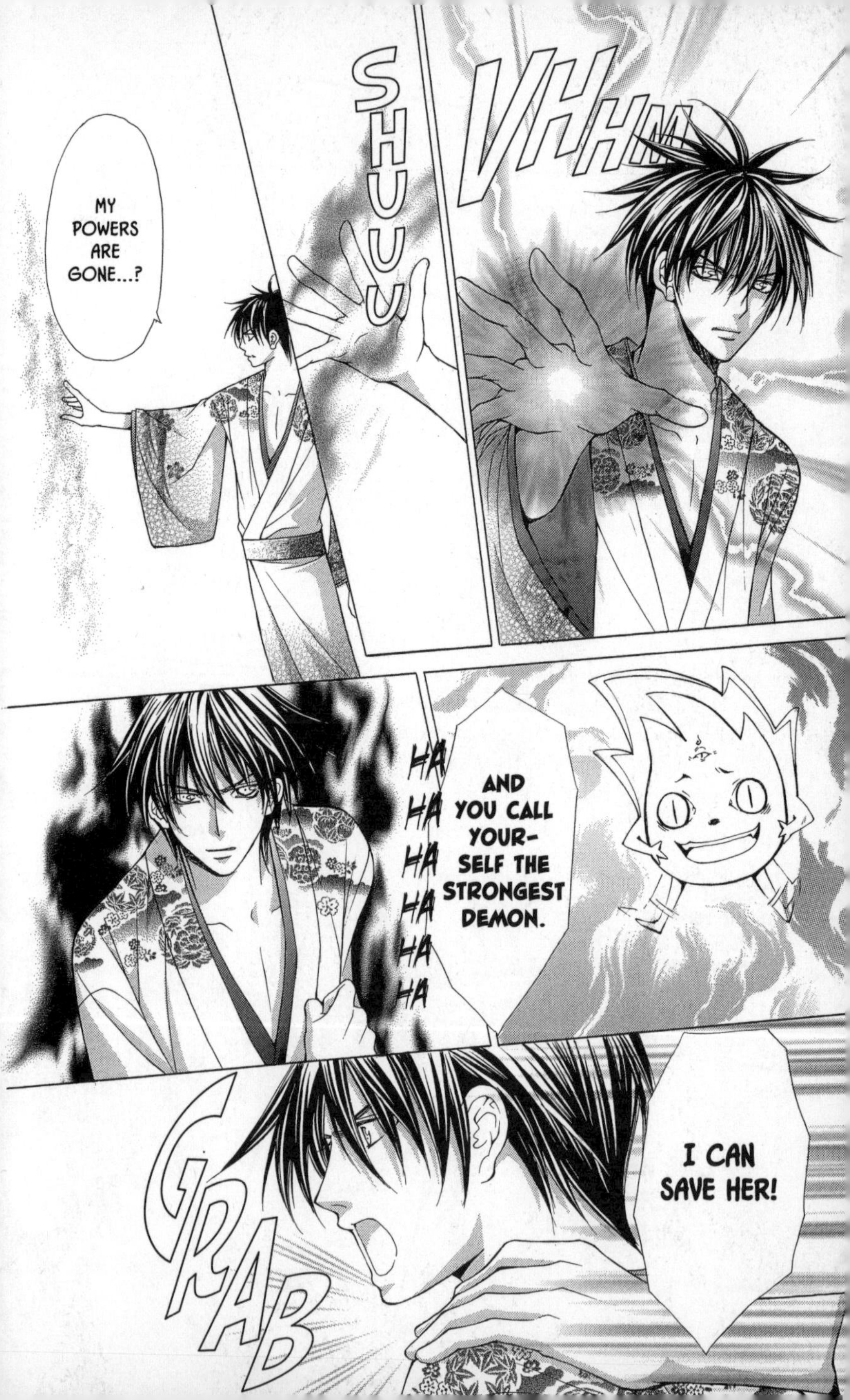
VHHM
SHUUU
MY POWERS ARE GONE...?
AND YOU CALL YOUR-SELF THE STRONGEST DEMON.
HA HA HA HA HA HA HA
GRAB
I CAN SAVE HER!

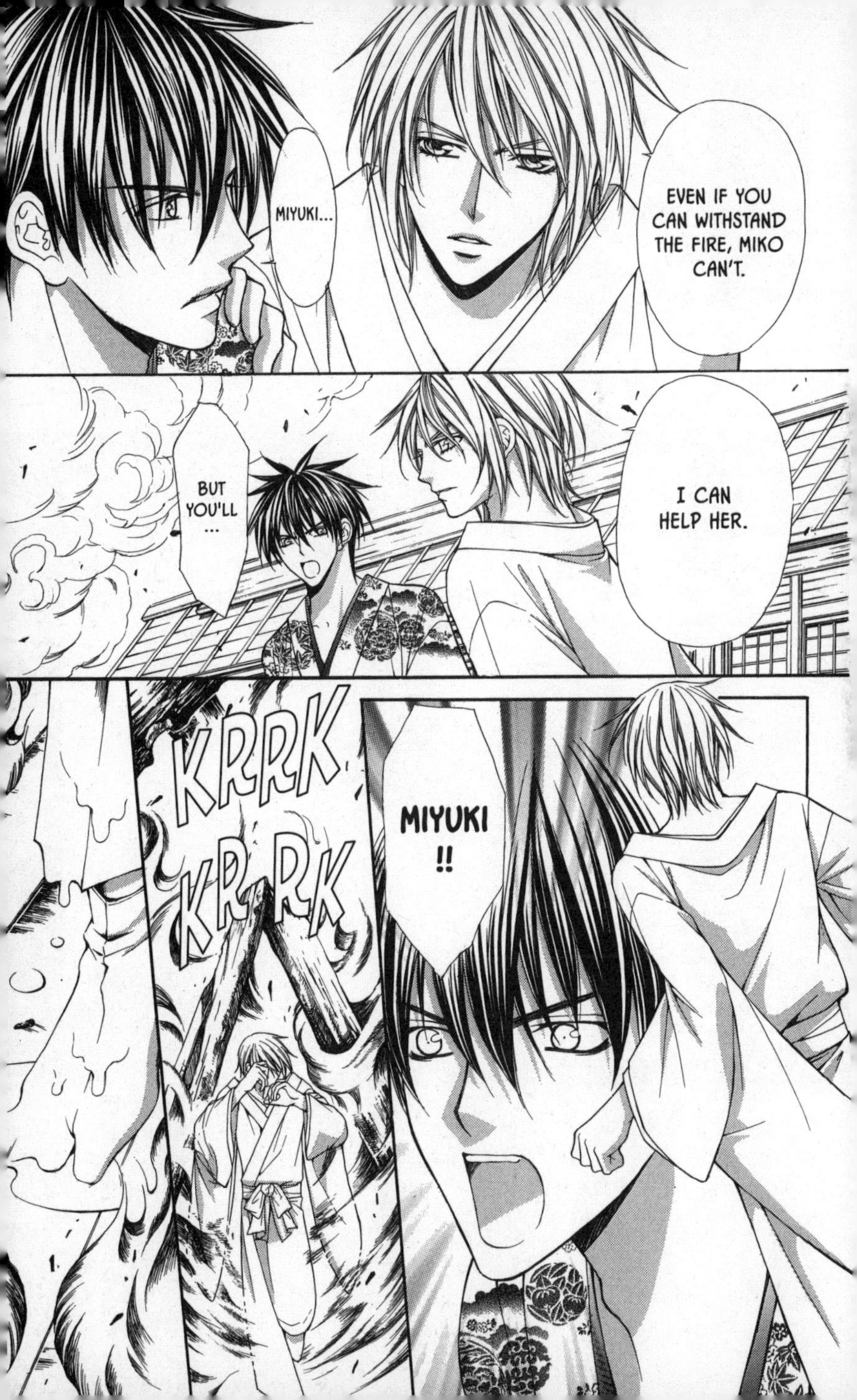
EVEN IF YOU CAN WITHSTAND THE FIRE, MIKO CAN'T.
MIYUKI...
I CAN HELP HER.
BUT YOU'LL ...
MIYUKI !!
KRRK KRRK

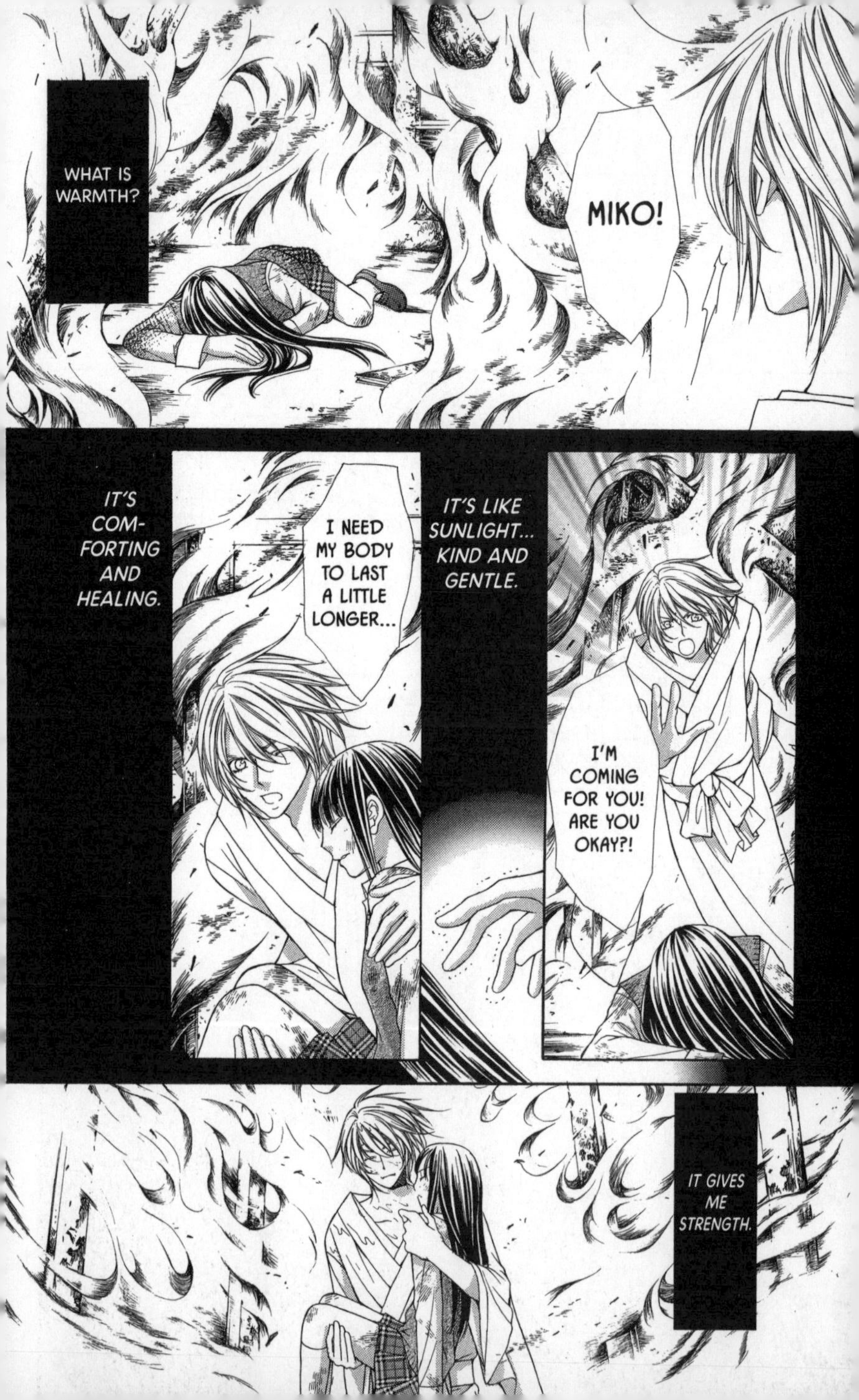
MIKO!
WHAT IS WARMTH?
I'M COMING FOR YOU! ARE YOU OKAY?!
IT'S LIKE SUNLIGHT... KIND AND GENTLE.
I NEED MY BODY TO LAST A LITTLE LONGER...
IT'S COM-FORTING AND HEALING.
IT GIVES ME STRENGTH.

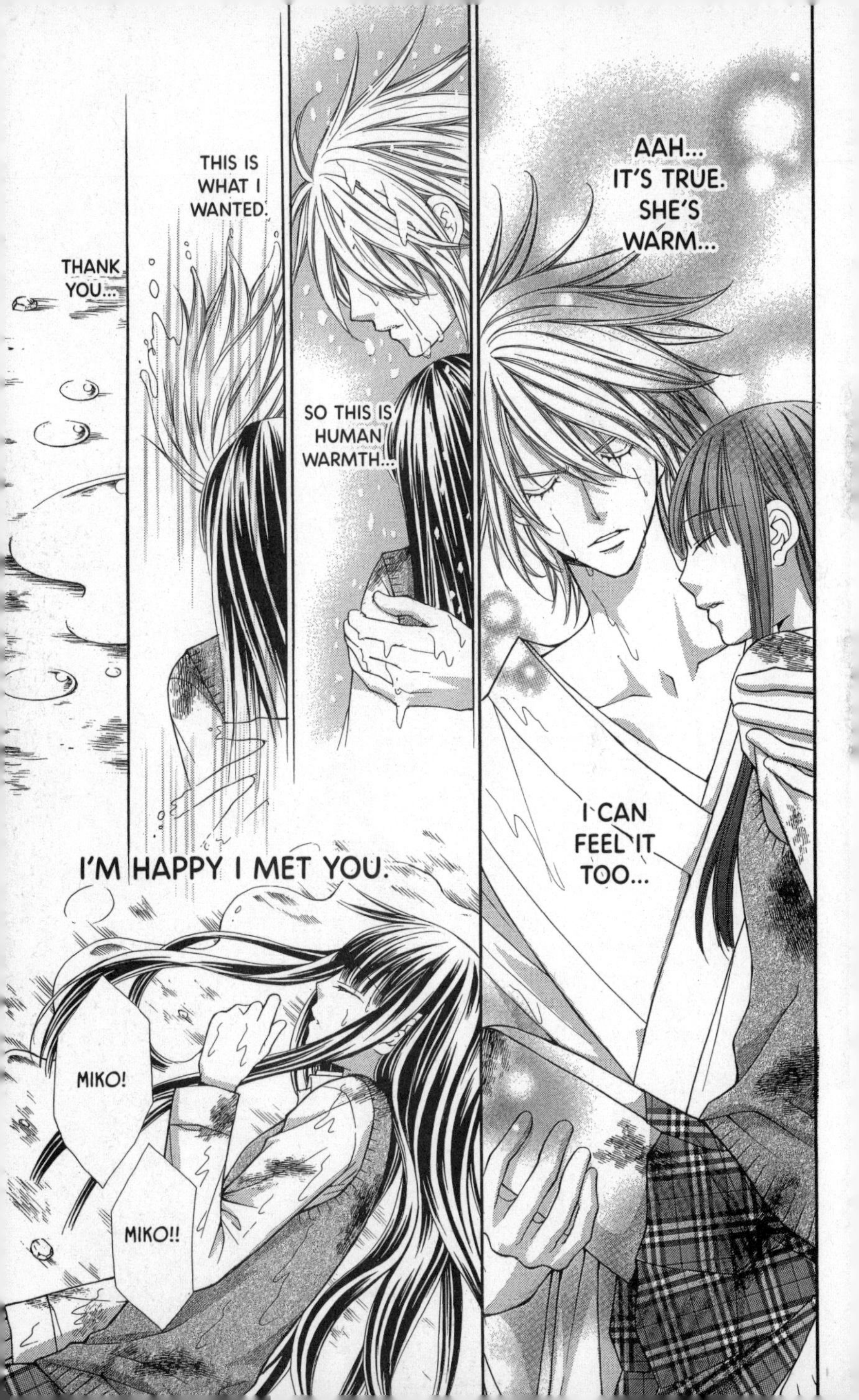
AAH... IT'S TRUE. SHE'S WARM...
I CAN FEEL IT TOO...
SO THIS IS HUMAN WARMTH...
THIS IS WHAT I WANTED.
THANK YOU...
I'M HAPPY I MET YOU.
MIKO!
MIKO!!

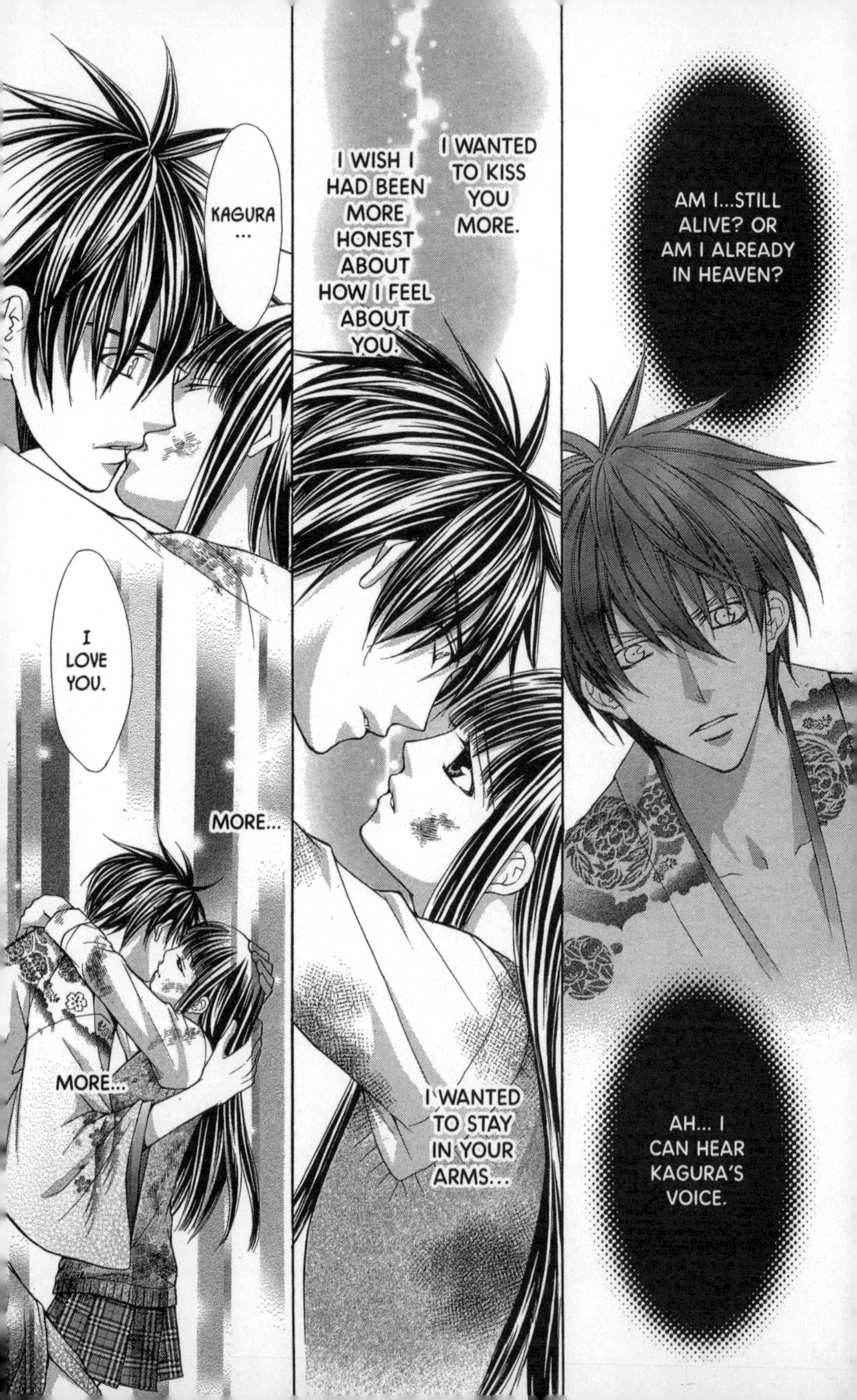
AM I...STILL ALIVE? OR AM I ALREADY IN HEAVEN?
AH... I CAN HEAR KAGURA'S VOICE.
I WANTED TO KISS YOU MORE.
I WISH I HAD BEEN MORE HONEST ABOUT HOW I FEEL ABOUT YOU.
I WANTED TO STAY IN YOUR ARMS...
KAGURA ...
I LOVE YOU.
MORE...
MORE...

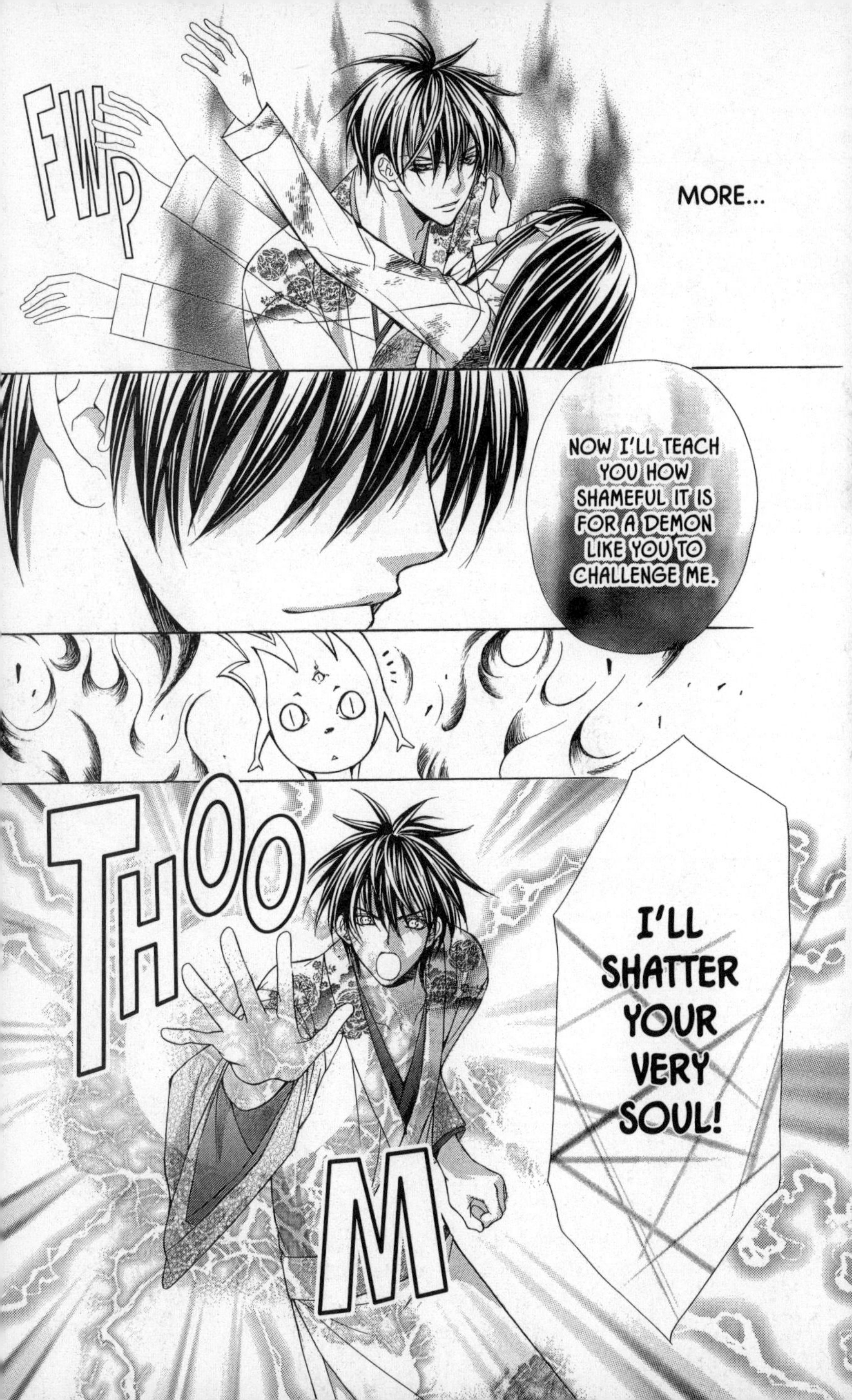
MORE...
FWP
NOW I'LL TEACH YOU HOW SHAMEFUL IT IS FOR A DEMON LIKE YOU TO CHALLENGE ME.
I'LL SHATTER YOUR VERY SOUL!
THOOOM

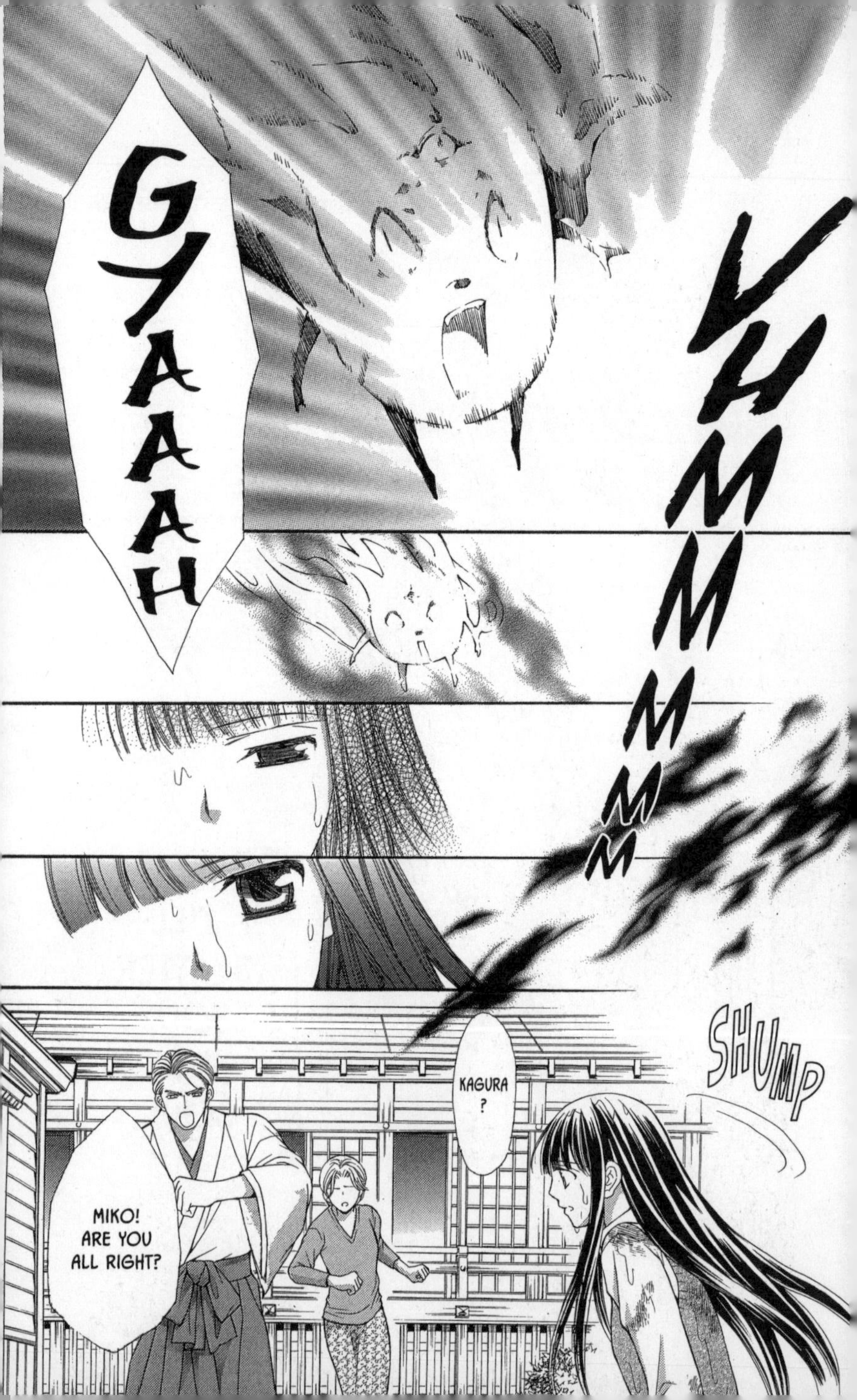
GYAAAH
VUHMMMMMM
SHUMP
KAGURA ?
MIKO! ARE YOU ALL RIGHT?

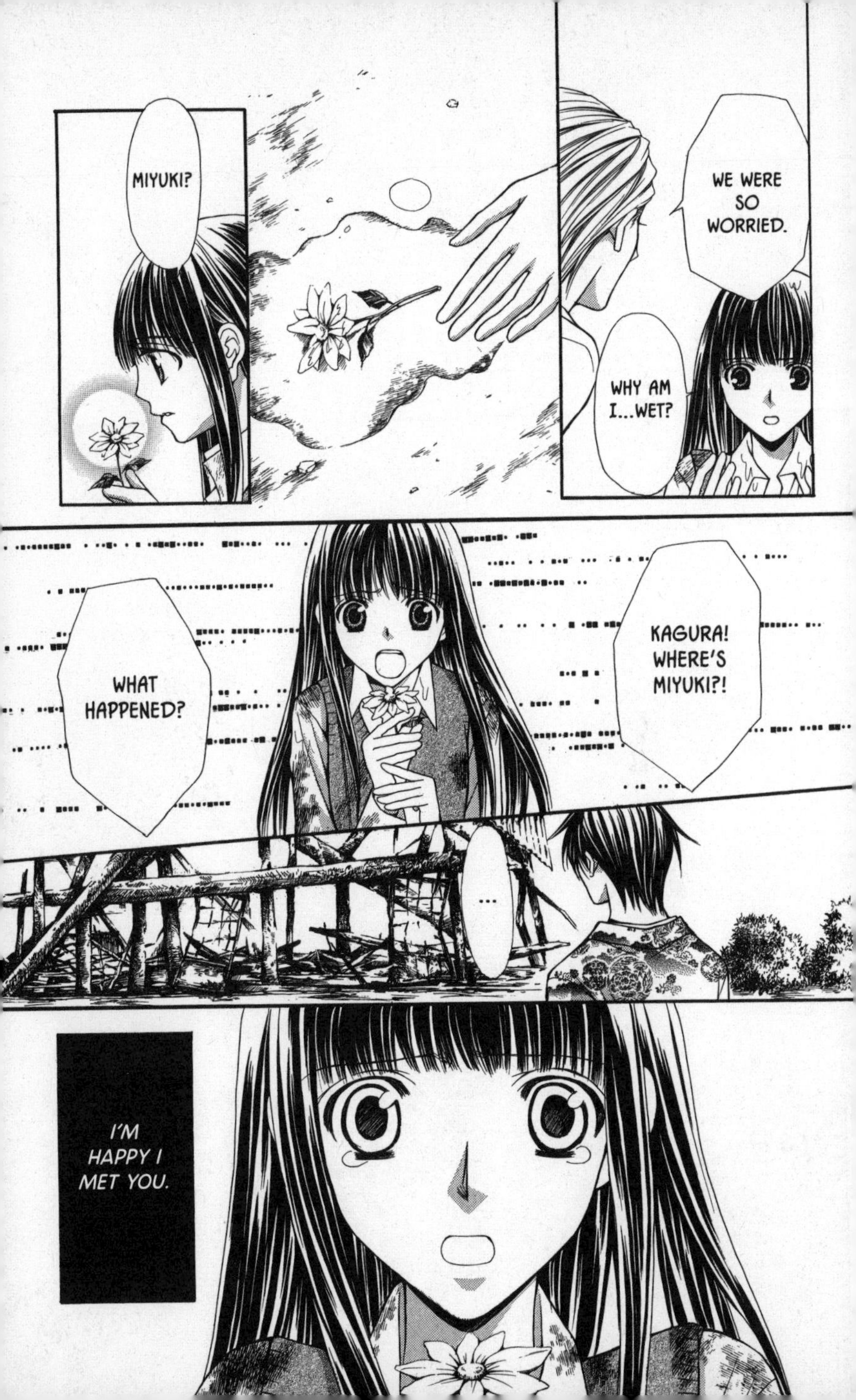
WE WERE SO WORRIED.
WHY AM I...WET?
MIYUKI?
KAGURA! WHERE'S MIYUKI?!
WHAT HAPPENED?
...
I'M HAPPY I MET YOU.

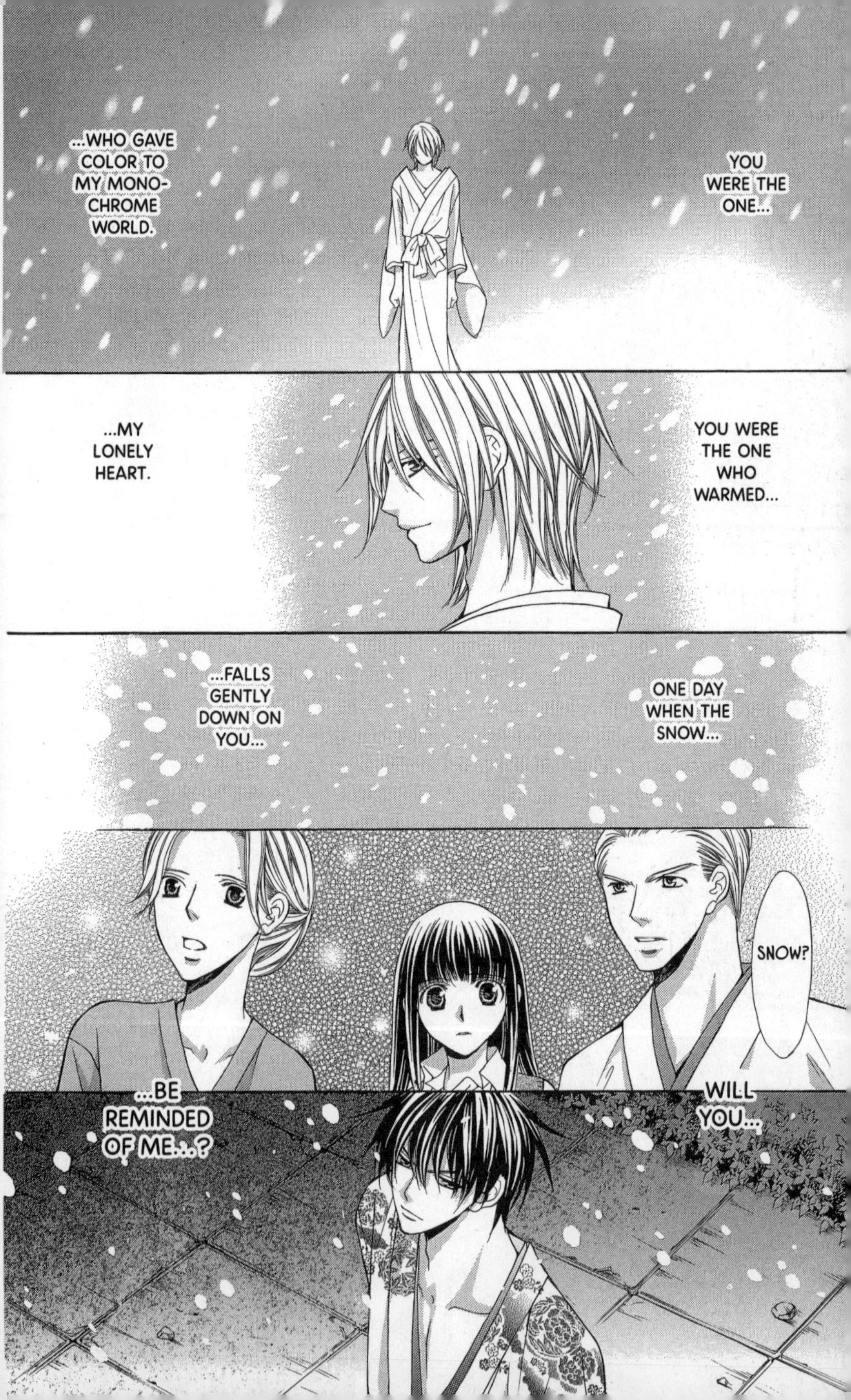
YOU WERE THE ONE...
...WHO GAVE COLOR TO MY MONO-CHROME WORLD.
YOU WERE THE ONE WHO WARMED...
...MY LONELY HEART.
ONE DAY WHEN THE SNOW...
...FALLS GENTLY DOWN ON YOU...
SNOW?
WILL YOU...
...BE REMINDED OF ME...?

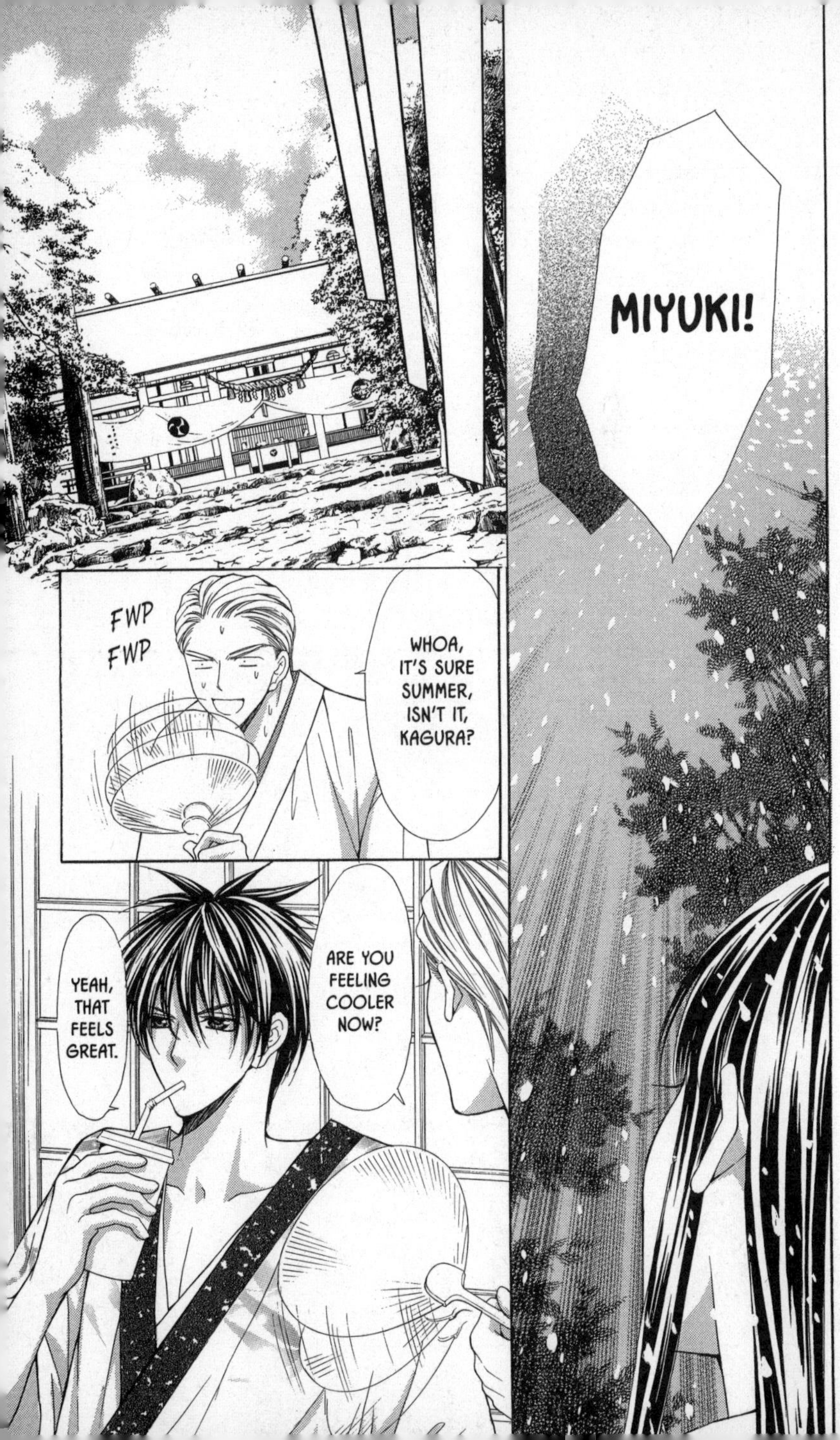
MIYUKI!
WHOA, IT'S SURE SUMMER, ISN'T IT, KAGURA?
FWP FWP
ARE YOU FEELING COOLER NOW?
YEAH, THAT FEELS GREAT.

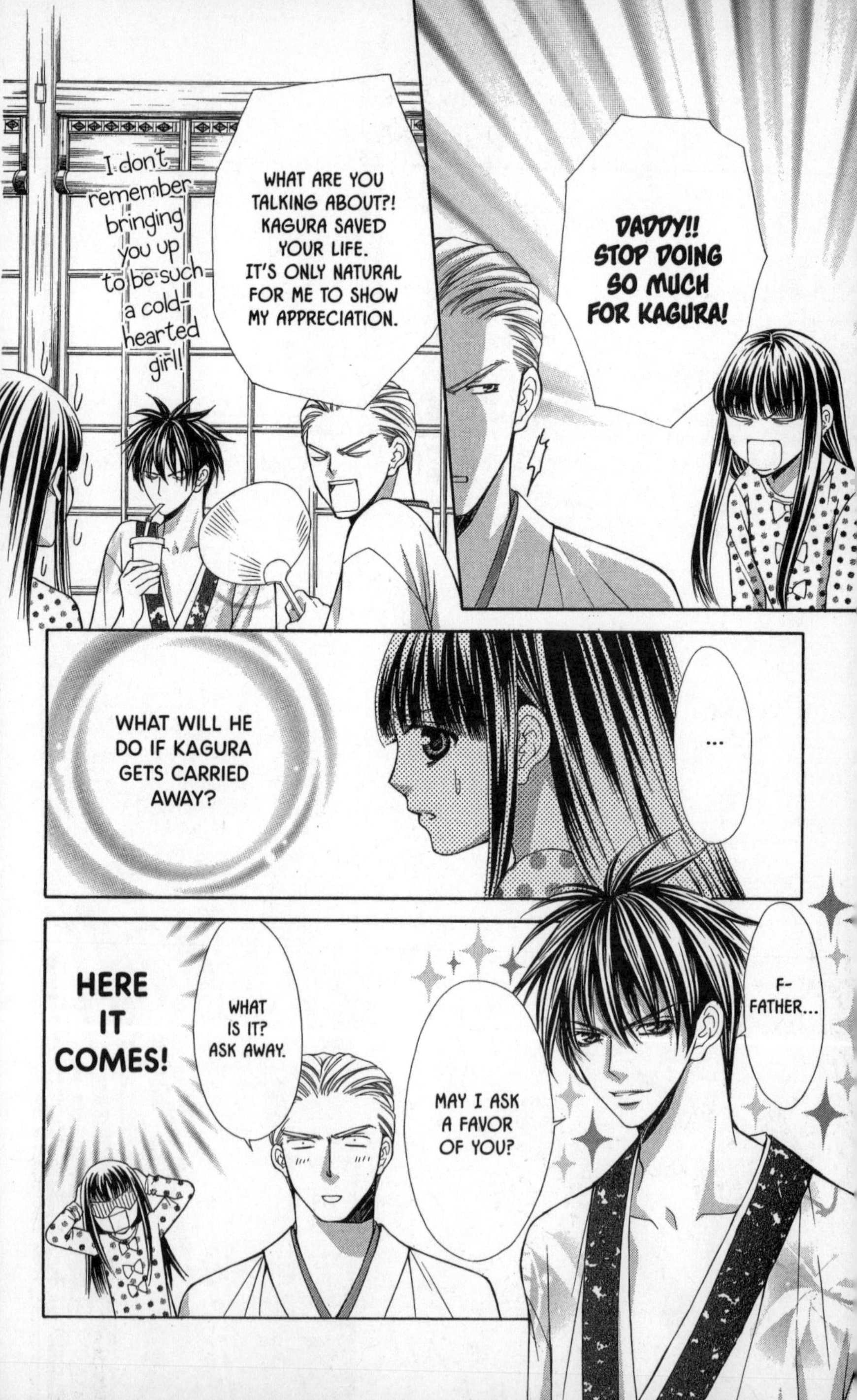
DADDY!! STOP DOING SO MUCH FOR KAGURA!
WHAT ARE YOU TALKING ABOUT?! KAGURA SAVED YOUR LIFE. IT'S ONLY NATURAL FOR ME TO SHOW MY APPRECIATION.
I don't remember bringing you up to be such a cold-hearted girl!
...
WHAT WILL HE DO IF KAGURA GETS CARRIED AWAY?
F-FATHER...
MAY I ASK A FAVOR OF YOU?
WHAT IS IT? ASK AWAY.
HERE IT COMES!

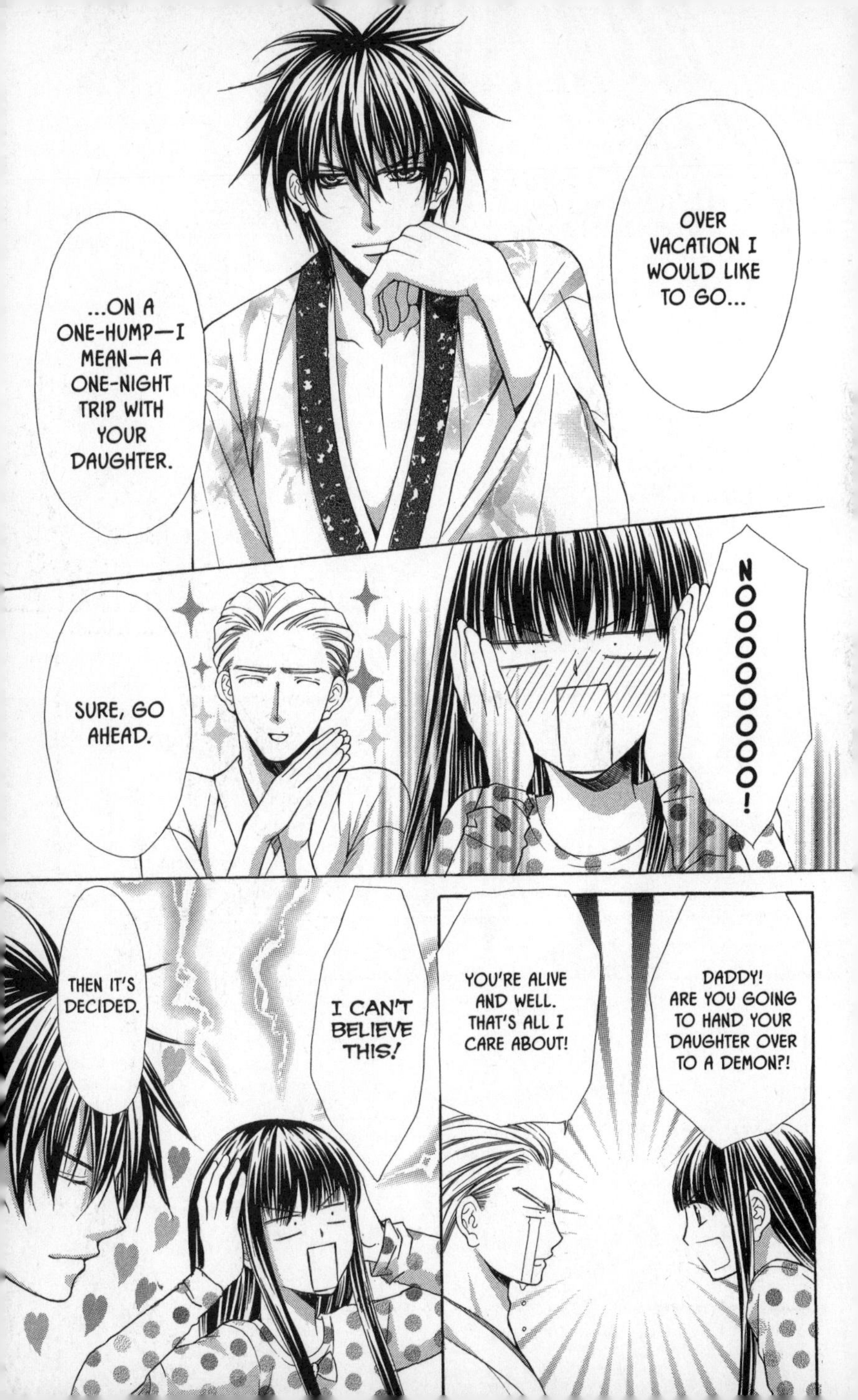
OVER VACATION I WOULD LIKE TO GO...
...ON A ONE-HUMP—I MEAN—A ONE-NIGHT TRIP WITH YOUR DAUGHTER.
NOOOOOOOO!
SURE, GO AHEAD.
DADDY! ARE YOU GOING TO HAND YOUR DAUGHTER OVER TO A DEMON?!
YOU'RE ALIVE AND WELL. THAT'S ALL I CARE ABOUT!
I CAN'T BELIEVE THIS!
THEN IT'S DECIDED.

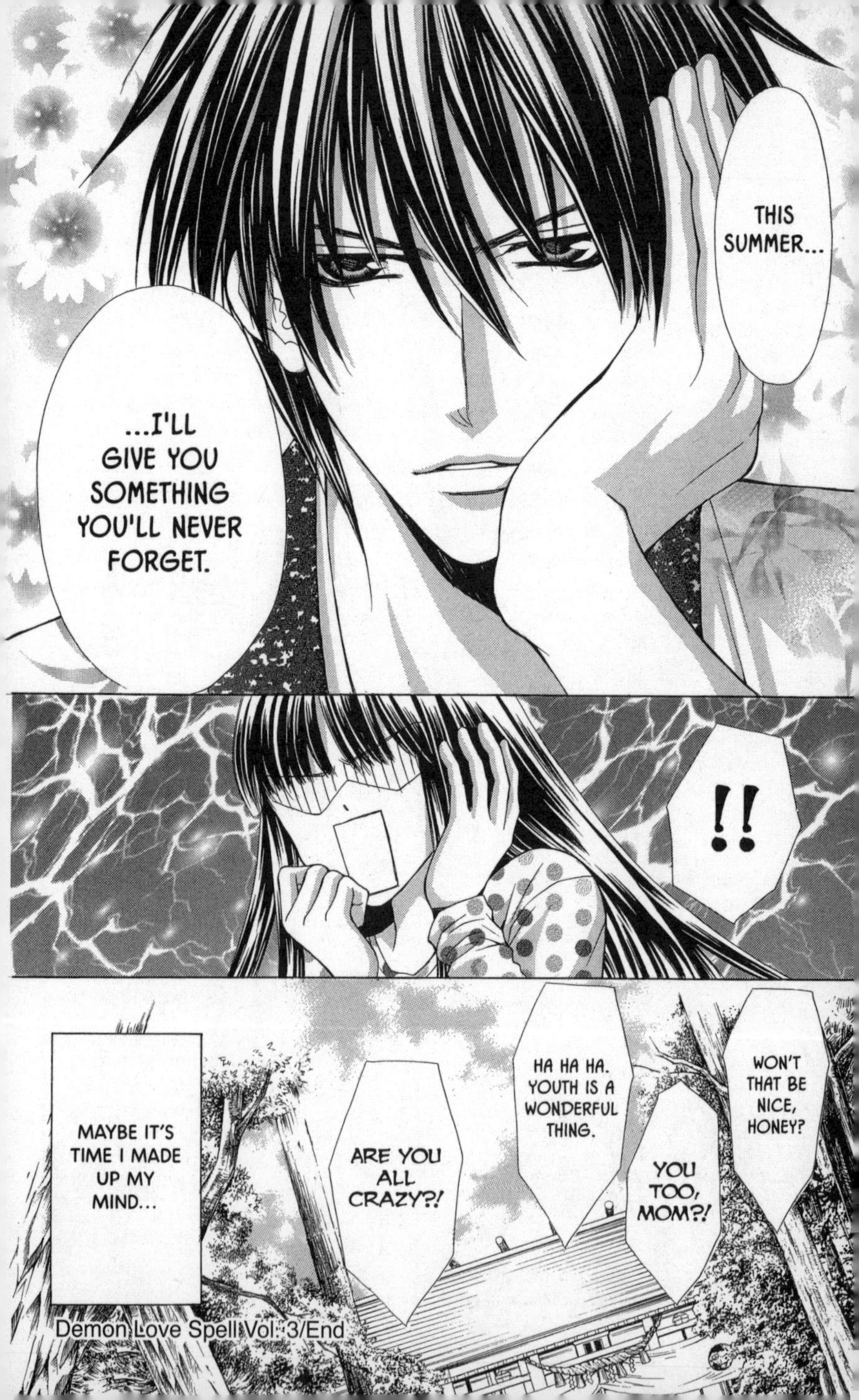
THIS SUMMER...
...I'LL GIVE YOU SOMETHING YOU'LL NEVER FORGET.
!!
WON'T THAT BE NICE, HONEY?
HA HA HA. YOUTH IS A WONDERFUL THING.
YOU TOO, MOM?!
ARE YOU ALL CRAZY?!
MAYBE IT'S TIME I MADE UP MY MIND...
Demon Love Spell Vol. 3/End

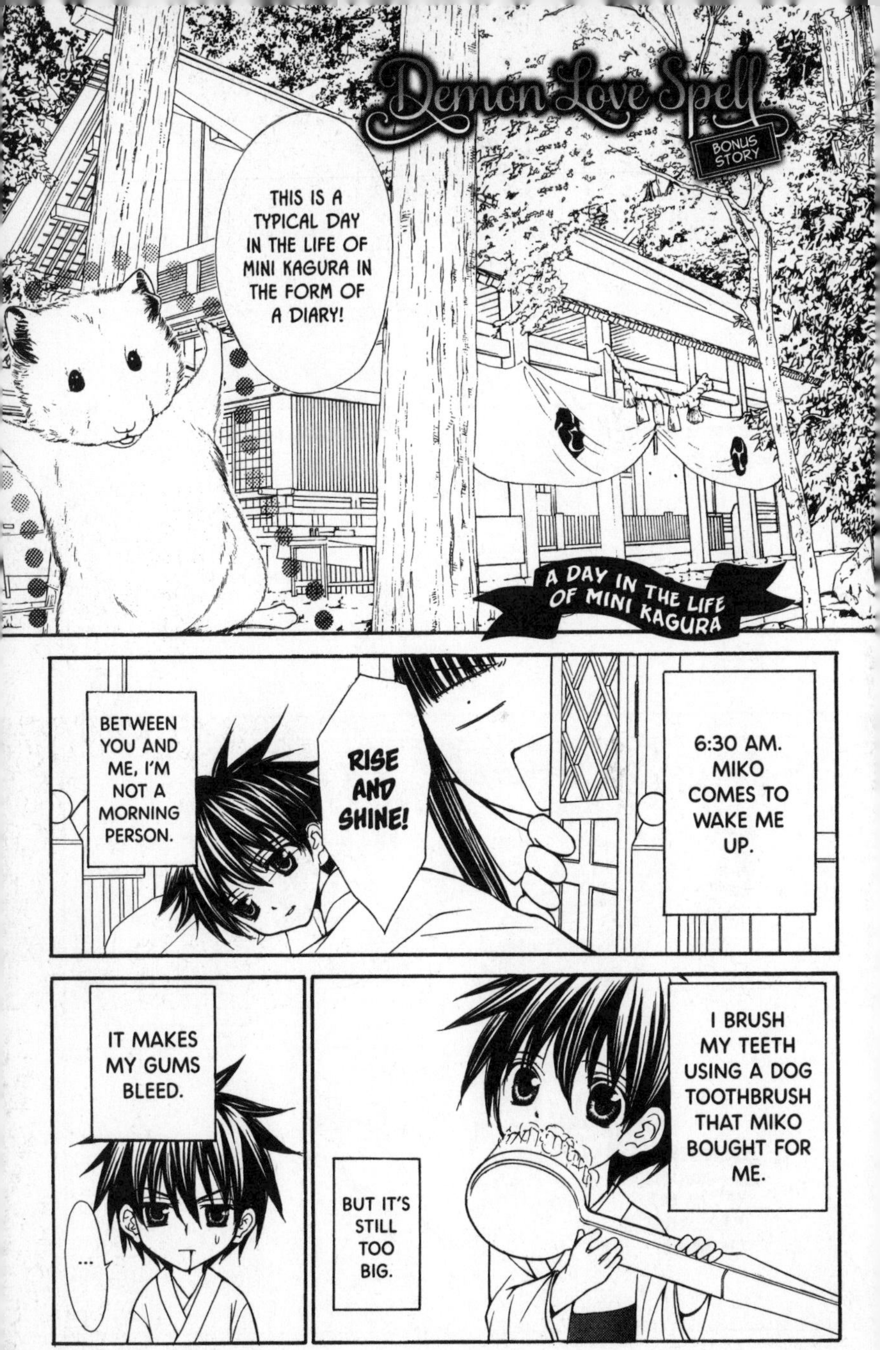
Demon Love Spell
BONUS STORY
THIS IS A TYPICAL DAY IN THE LIFE OF MINI KAGURA IN THE FORM OF A DIARY!
A DAY IN THE LIFE OF MINI KAGURA
6:30 AM. MIKO COMES TO WAKE ME UP.
RISE AND SHINE!
BETWEEN YOU AND ME, I'M NOT A MORNING PERSON.
I BRUSH MY TEETH USING A DOG TOOTHBRUSH THAT MIKO BOUGHT FOR ME.
BUT IT'S STILL TOO BIG.
IT MAKES MY GUMS BLEED.
...

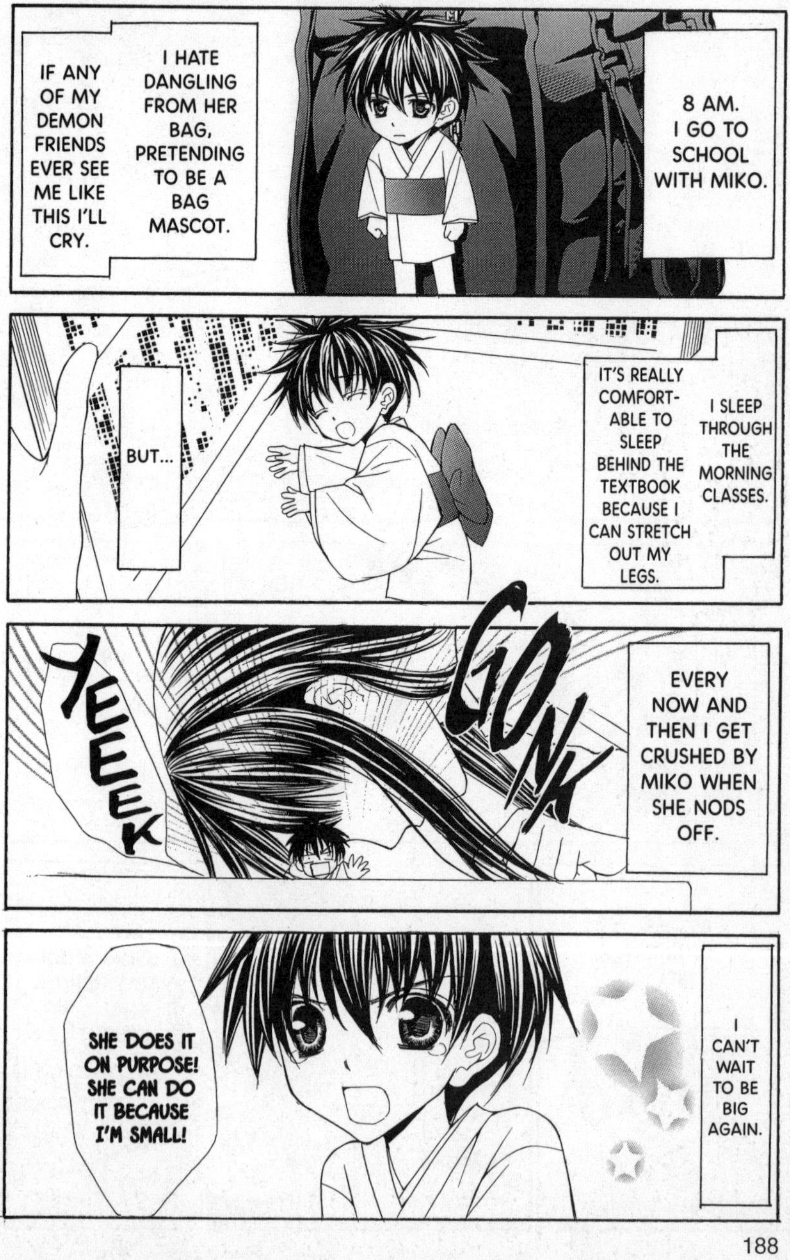
8 AM. I GO TO SCHOOL WITH MIKO.
I HATE DANGLING FROM HER BAG, PRETENDING TO BE A BAG MASCOT.
IF ANY OF MY DEMON FRIENDS EVER SEE ME LIKE THIS I'LL CRY.
I SLEEP THROUGH THE MORNING CLASSES.
IT'S REALLY COMFORT-ABLE TO SLEEP BEHIND THE TEXTBOOK BECAUSE I CAN STRETCH OUT MY LEGS.
BUT...
EVERY NOW AND THEN I GET CRUSHED BY MIKO WHEN SHE NODS OFF.
GONK
YEEEK
I CAN'T WAIT TO BE BIG AGAIN.
SHE DOES IT ON PURPOSE! SHE CAN DO IT BECAUSE I'M SMALL!

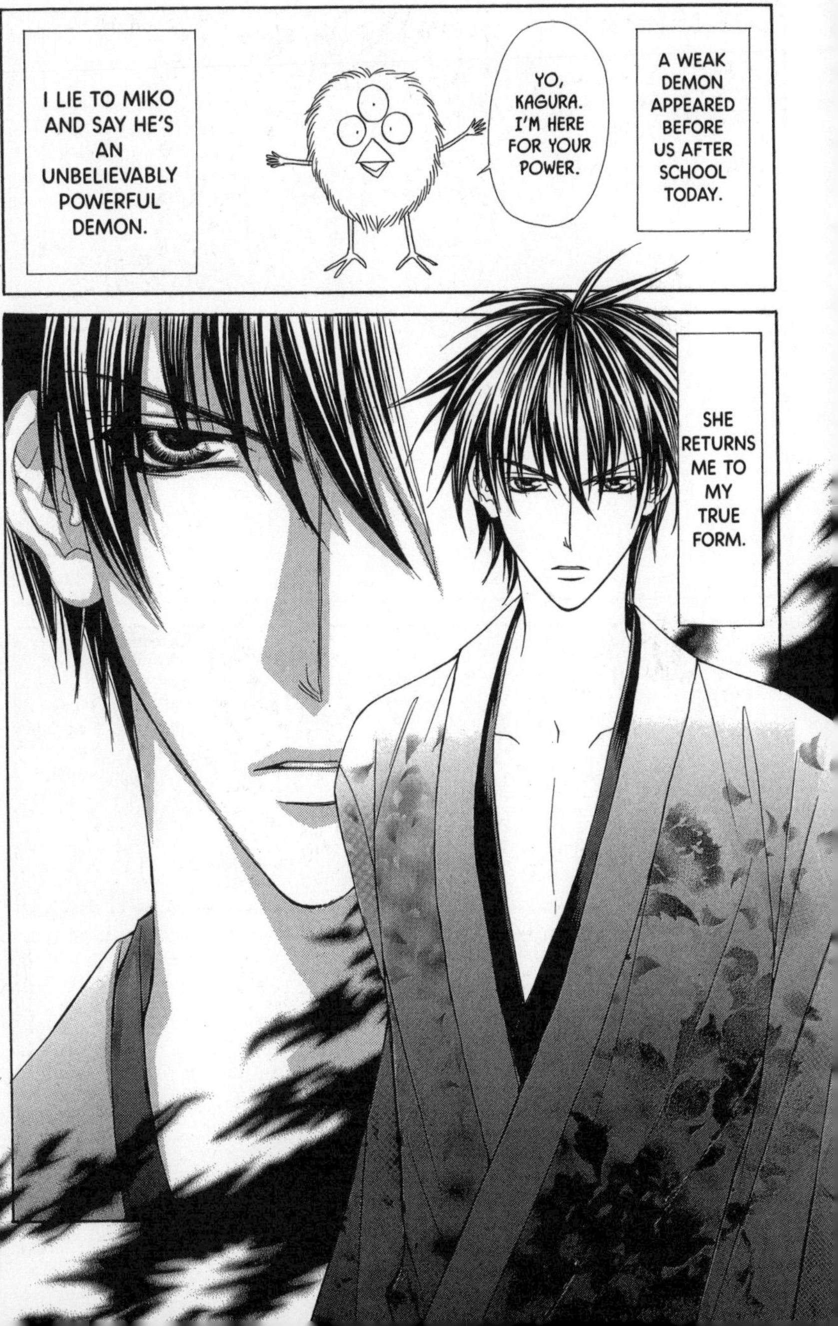
A WEAK DEMON APPEARED BEFORE US AFTER SCHOOL TODAY.
YO, KAGURA. I'M HERE FOR YOUR POWER.
I LIE TO MIKO AND SAY HE'S AN UNBELIEVABLY POWERFUL DEMON.
SHE RETURNS ME TO MY TRUE FORM.

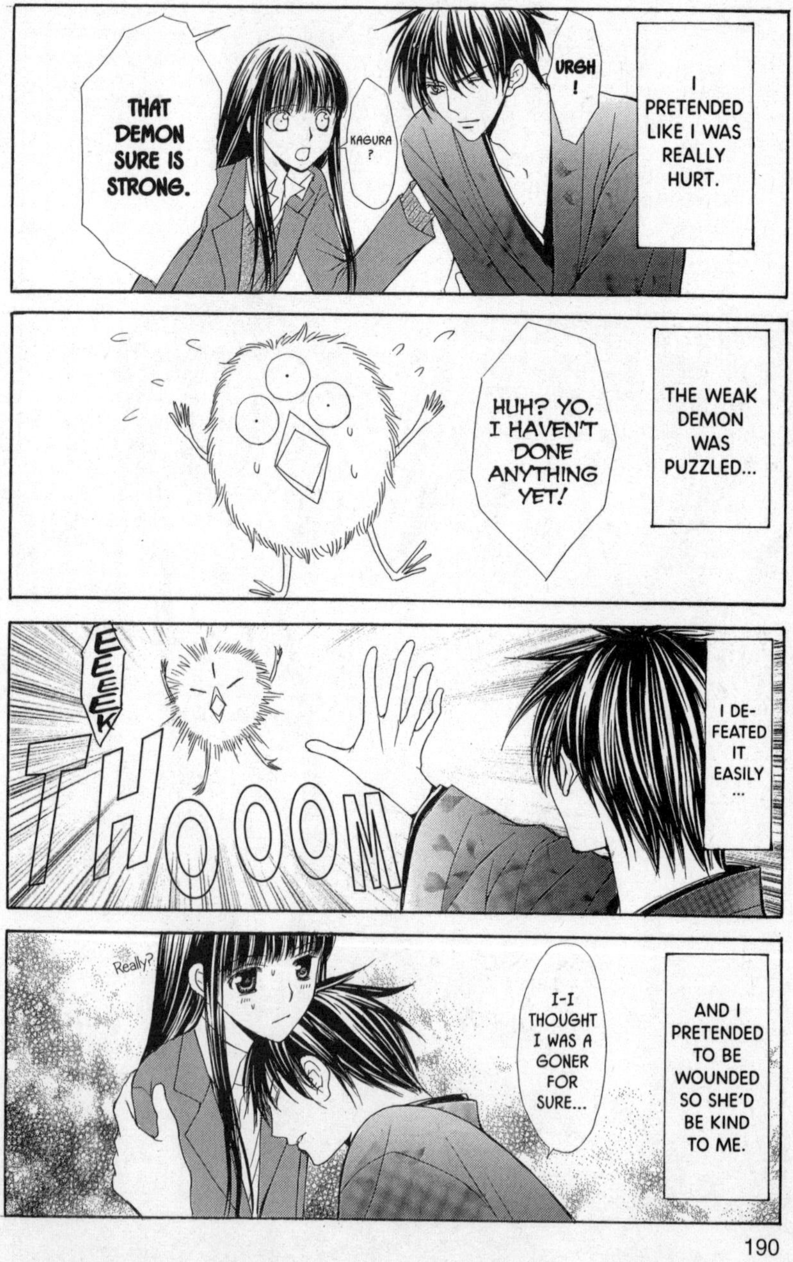
I PRETENDED LIKE I WAS REALLY HURT.
URGH!
KAGURA?
THAT DEMON SURE IS STRONG.
THE WEAK DEMON WAS PUZZLED...
HUH? YO, I HAVEN'T DONE ANYTHING YET!
I DEFEATED IT EASILY...
THOOOM
EEEEK
AND I PRETENDED TO BE WOUNDED SO SHE'D BE KIND TO ME.
I-I THOUGHT I WAS A GONER FOR SURE...
Really?

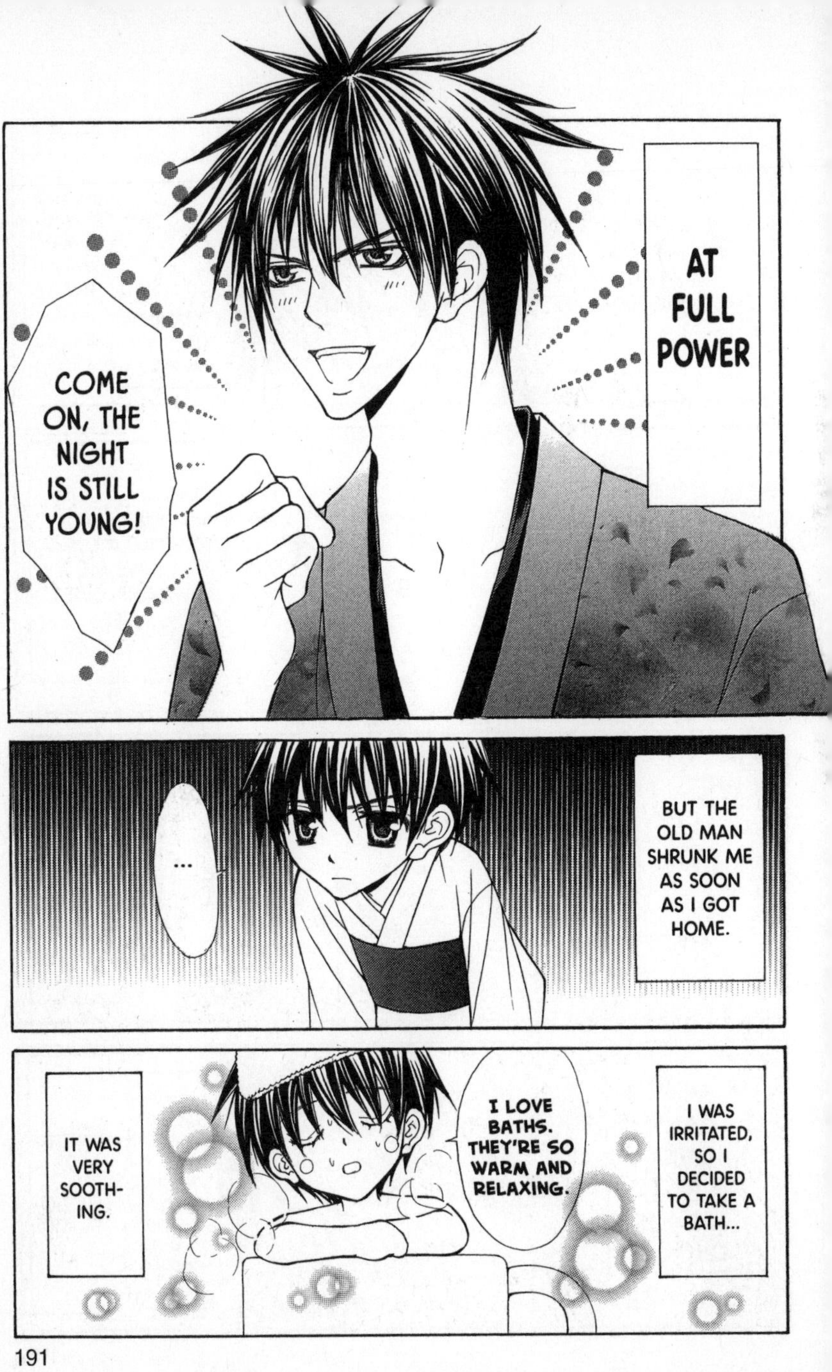
AT FULL POWER
COME ON, THE NIGHT IS STILL YOUNG!
BUT THE OLD MAN SHRUNK ME AS SOON AS I GOT HOME.
...
I WAS IRRITATED, SO I DECIDED TO TAKE A BATH...
I LOVE BATHS. THEY'RE SO WARM AND RELAXING.
IT WAS VERY SOOTH-ING.

THE HAMSTER ASKED ME TO PLAY WITH HIM...
...BUT I DON'T WANT A HAMSTER FOR A FRIEND SO I IGNORED HIM AS USUAL.
Meh.
Hey, hey. Let's play.
BUT... HE TOLD ME HE'D GIVE ME A SUNFLOWER SEED.
You can have this. It's yummy!
Try it.
HE GETS ON MY NERVES.
I don't want it!
SO I DECIDED TO PLAY WITH HIM FOR A WHILE ANYWAY.
KRK
KRK
KRK
I WAITED FOR MIKO TO FALL ASLEEP...
...BUT SHE TALKED TO A FRIEND OVER THE PHONE FOR HOURS. AND SHE DIDN'T DO HER HOMEWORK.
Yeah, do you want to?
WHY CAN'T THEY JUST TALK AT SCHOOL?!

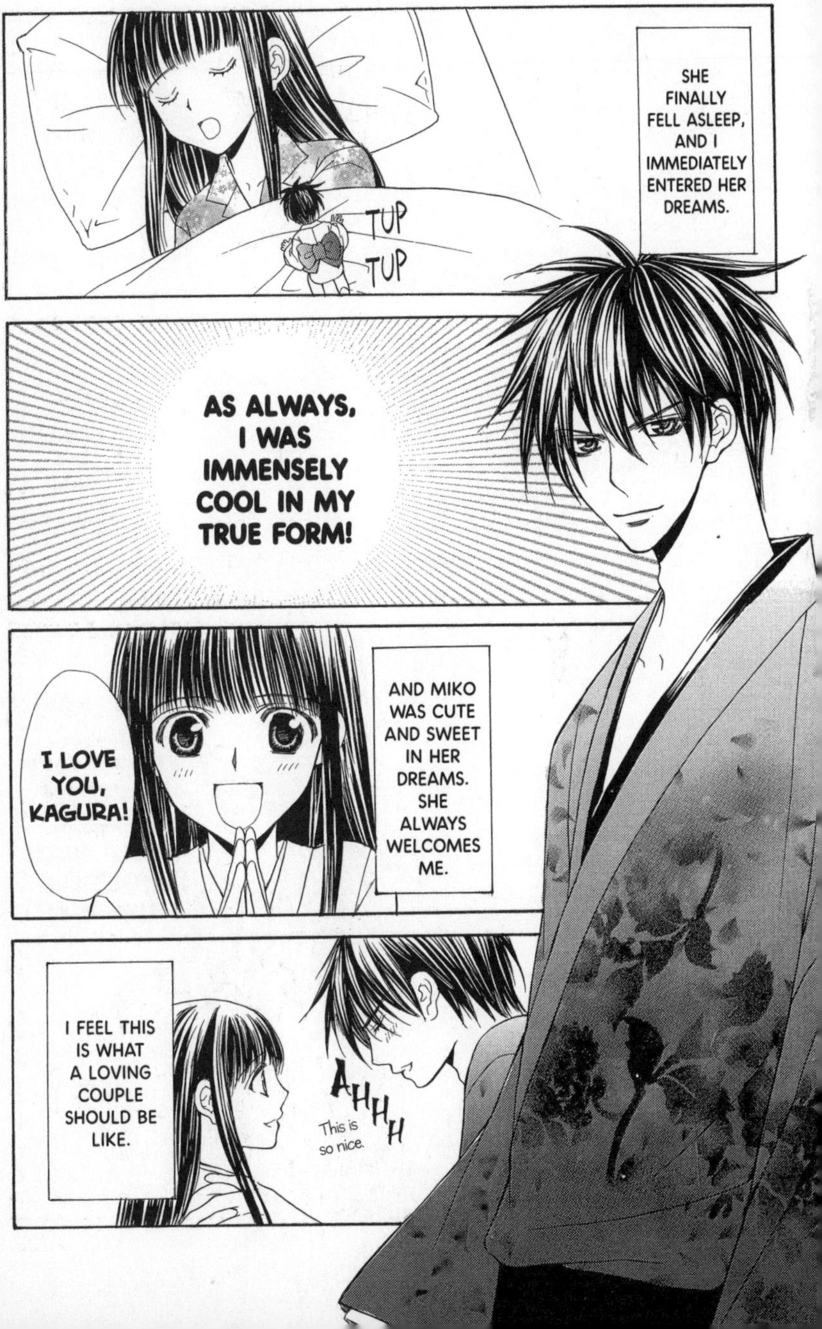
SHE FINALLY FELL ASLEEP, AND I IMMEDIATELY ENTERED HER DREAMS.
TUP TUP
AS ALWAYS, I WAS IMMENSELY COOL IN MY TRUE FORM!
AND MIKO WAS CUTE AND SWEET IN HER DREAMS. SHE ALWAYS WELCOMES ME.
I LOVE YOU, KAGURA!
AHHHH
This is so nice.
I FEEL THIS IS WHAT A LOVING COUPLE SHOULD BE LIKE.

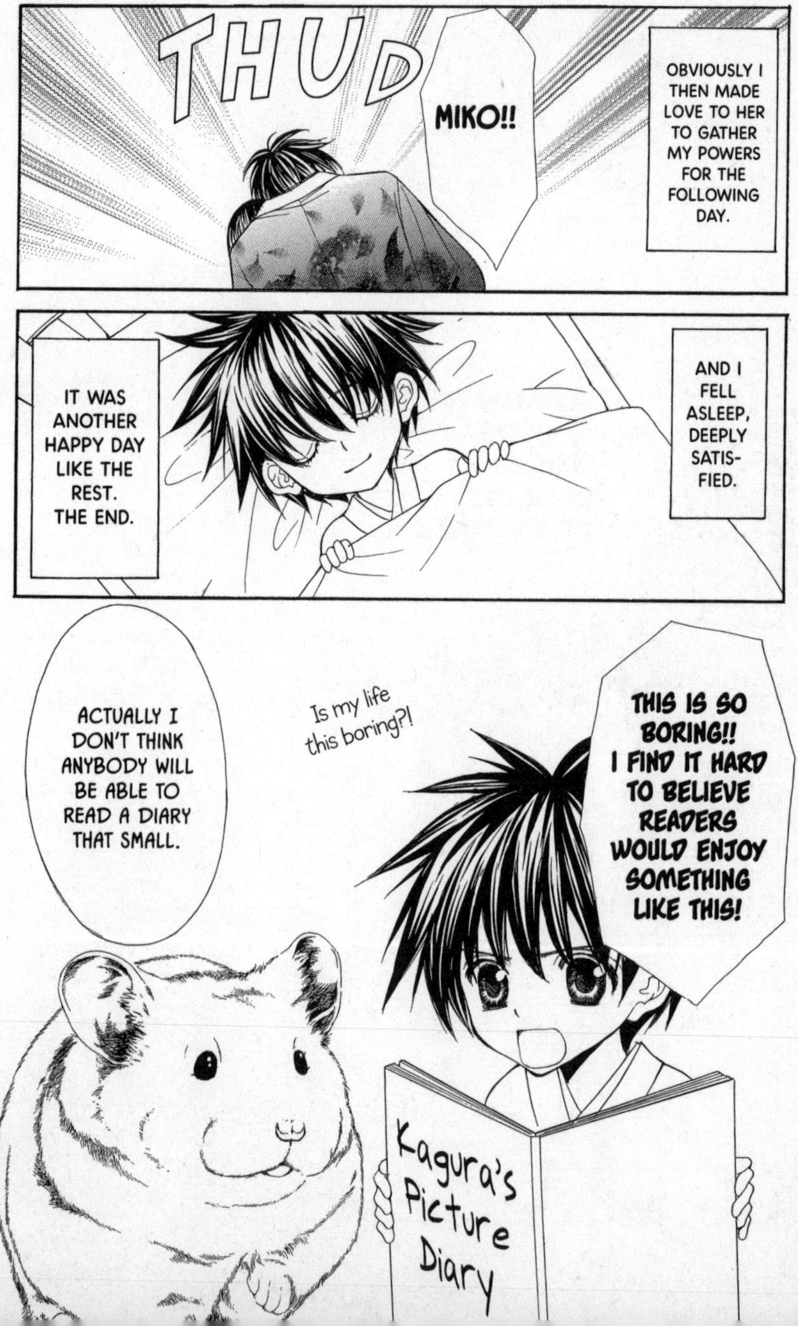
OBVIOUSLY I THEN MADE LOVE TO HER TO GATHER MY POWERS FOR THE FOLLOWING DAY.
MIKO!!
THUD
AND I FELL ASLEEP, DEEPLY SATIS-FIED.
IT WAS ANOTHER HAPPY DAY LIKE THE REST. THE END.
THIS IS SO BORING!! I FIND IT HARD TO BELIEVE READERS WOULD ENJOY SOMETHING LIKE THIS!
Is my life this boring?!
ACTUALLY I DON'T THINK ANYBODY WILL BE ABLE TO READ A DIARY THAT SMALL.
Kagura's Picture Diary

Time flies! This is already volume 3 of
Demon Love Spell. This series runs in
the magazine in big chapters, but it isn't
monthly, so I think both "I'm still on
volume 3?!" as well as "I'm already on
volume 3?!" Volume 4 will probably come
out in Japan within a year, and I hope this
manga will become a long, beloved series.

—Mayu Shinjo

MAYU SHINJO was born on January 26.
She is a prolific writer of shojo manga,
including the series *Sensual Phrase*
and *Ai Ore!* Her hobbies are cars,
shopping and taking baths. Shinjo
likes The Prodigy, Nirvana, U2 and
Masaharu Fukuyama.

Demon Love Spell

Vol. 3
Shojo Beat Edition

STORY AND ART BY *Mayu Shinjo*

Translation & Adaptation
Tetsuichiro Miyaki

Touch-up Art & Lettering
Inori Fukuda Trant

Design
Fawn Lau

Editor
Nancy Thistlethwaite

AYAKASHI KOI EMAKI © 2008 by Mayu Shinjo
All rights reserved.
First published in Japan in 2008 by SHUEISHA Inc., Tokyo.
English translation rights arranged by SHUEISHA Inc.

The stories, characters and incidents mentioned in
this publication are entirely fictional.

No portion of this book may be reproduced or
transmitted in any form or by any means without written
permission from the copyright holders.

Printed in the U.S.A.

Published by VIZ Media, LLC
P.O. Box 77010
San Francisco, CA 94107

10 9 8 7 6 5 4 3
First printing, June 2013
Third printing, July 2015

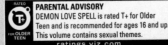

RATED T+ **PARENTAL ADVISORY**
DEMON LOVE SPELL is rated T+ for Older
Teen and is recommended for ages 16 and up.
This volume contains sexual themes.
ratings.viz.com

www.viz.com

www.shojobeat.com

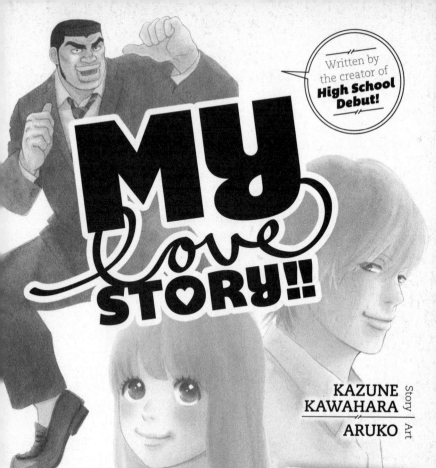

Written by the creator of **High School Debut!**

MY love STORY!!

KAZUNE KAWAHARA *Story*

ARUKO *Art*

Takeo Goda is a **GIANT** guy with a **GIANT** *heart*

Too bad the girls don't want him!
(They want his good-looking best friend, Sunakawa.)

Used to being on the sidelines, Takeo simply stands tall and accepts his fate. But one day when he saves a girl named Yamato from a harasser on the train, his (love!) life suddenly takes an incredible turn!

www.viz.com

www.shojobeat.c

RATED T

ORE MONOGATARI!! © 2011 by Kazune Kawahara, Aruko/SHUEISHA Inc.

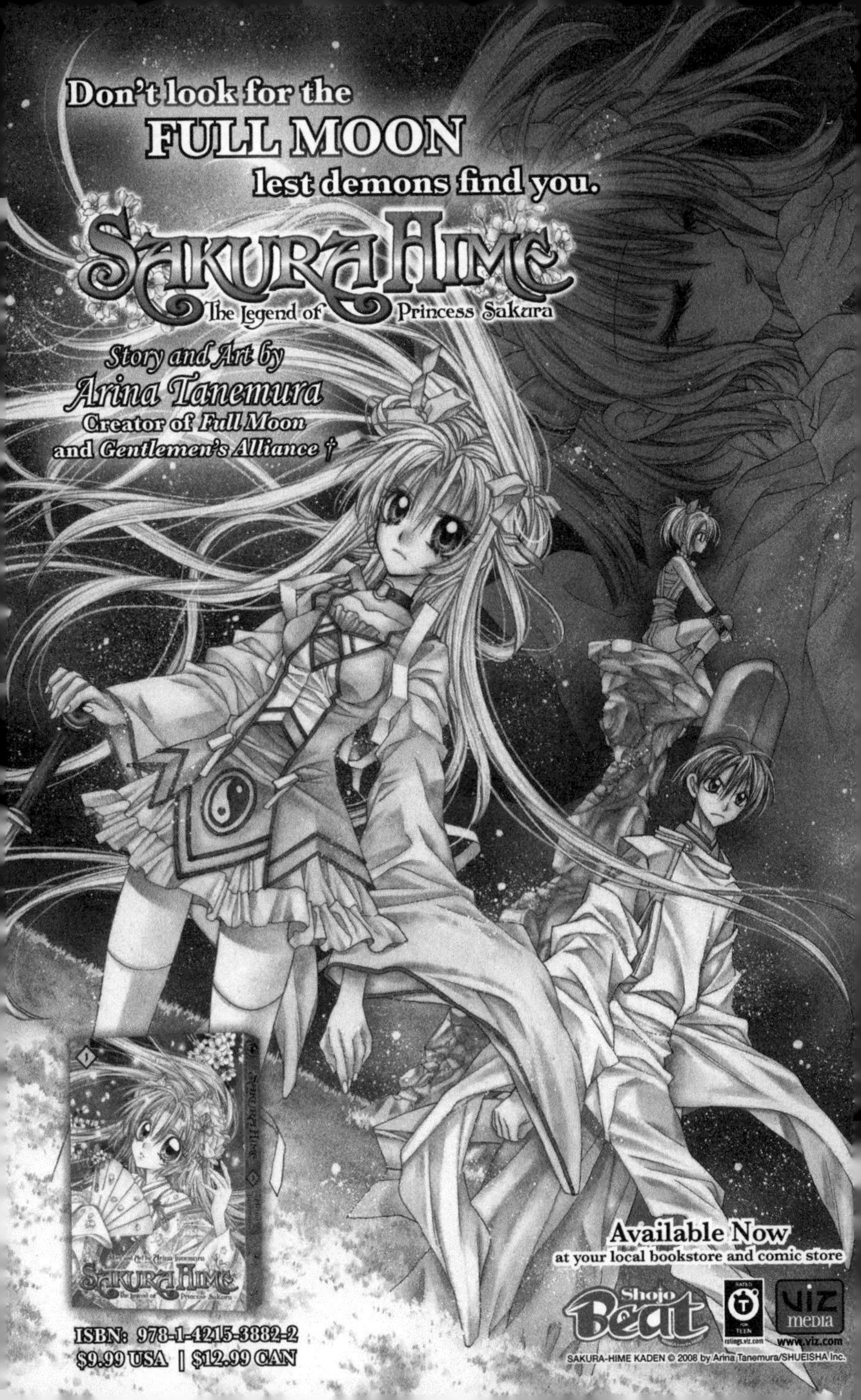
Don't look for the
FULL MOON
lest demons find you.
SAKURA HIME
The Legend of Princess Sakura
Story and Art by
Arina Tanemura
Creator of Full Moon
and Gentlemen's Alliance †
Available Now
at your local bookstore and comic store
Shojo Beat
T
VIZ media
www.viz.com
SAKURA-HIME KADEN © 2008 by Arina Tanemura/SHUEISHA Inc.
ISBN: 978-1-4215-3882-2
$9.99 USA | $12.99 CAN

You may be reading the wrong way!

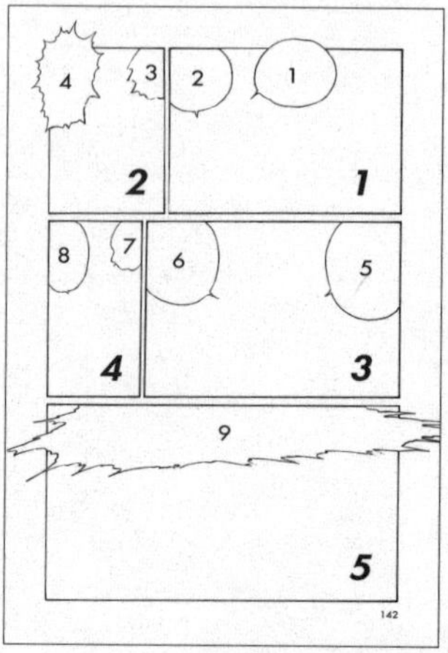
1
2
1
3
4
2
5
6
3
7
8
4
9
5
142

IT'S TRUE: In keeping with the original Japanese comic format, this book reads from right to left—so action, sound effects, and word balloons are completely reversed. This preserves the orientation of the original artwork—plus, it's fun! Check out the diagram shown here to get the hang of things, and then turn to the other side of the book to get started!

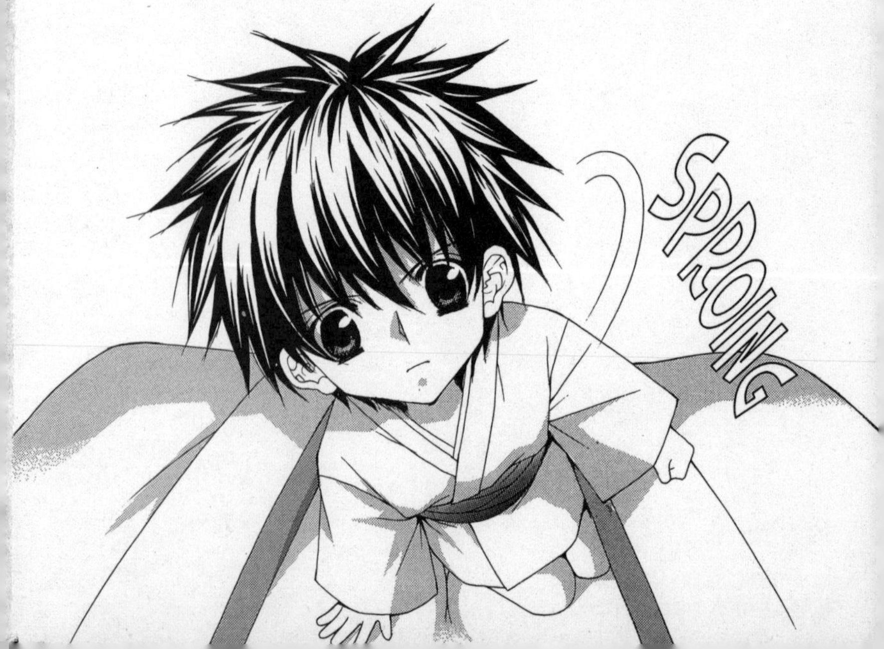
SPROING